Cases and Materials on Contract Law

Authors

Kate Hutchings
Lucy Kuzmicki
Gavin Gray
Daniel Newbound
Caroline Barrow
Betty Mwamuye

Ninth edition July 2019

Published ISBN 9781509730735

British Library Cataloguing-in-Publication Data
A catalogue record for this book is available from the British Library

Published by BPP Law School

Printed by
Ashford Colour Press Ltd
Unit 600, Fareham Reach
Fareham Road
Gosport, Hampshire
PO13 0FW

Your learning materials, published by BPP Law School, are printed on paper obtained from traceable sustainable sources.

Extracts from the Law Reports, the Weekly Law Reports and the Industrial Cases Reports are reproduced by permission of:

The Incorporated Council of Law Reporting for England and Wales, Megarry House,
119 Chancery Lane, London WC2A 1PP

Extracts from the All England Reports, and other LexisNexis titles are reproduced by permission of LexisNexis which is a trading name of, Reed Elsevier (UK) Limited, Registered office, 1-3 Strand, London WC2N 5JR

Extracts from Westlaw publications (including journal articles) are reproduced with permission of Thomson Reuters (Legal) Limited, Registered Office, 100 Avenue Road, London NW3 3PF

Contents

A note about copyright

Index of Cases

A

B

C

D

E

1

Agreement I (Offer)

Topic List

Introduction

According to the academic, Treitel, 'an offer is an expression of willingness to contract on specified terms, made with the intention that it is to become binding as soon as it is accepted by the person to whom it is addressed'. By necessity, therefore, an offer must be clear and certain so that it can be accepted by the offeree. An offer must also demonstrate intention to be legally bound. An offer can be accepted at any point until it is terminated.

A valid offer can be contrasted with an invitation to treat which is the name for any preliminary stage of negotiation before an offer is made.

Before the requirements of a valid offer can be considered, there are two preliminary issues which need to be understood: first, the objective approach to agreement, and second the distinction between bilateral and unilateral contracts. Next, this chapter focuses on the requirements for a valid offer and how to distinguish between an offer and an invitation to treat. Finally, the chapter deals with the revocation of a valid offer.

1.1 The Objective Approach to Agreement

It is clear from Treitel's definition that, for there to be a valid offer, the offeror must have an intention to be bound. However, it is necessary to determine whether this is a subjective or an objective test of intention. If it is a subjective test, then the question is: what was the actual intention of the offeror? If, on the other hand, it is an objective test, the question is: what would the reasonable person understand the offeror to mean?

If it was a subjective test, then it would be open to abuse. It would always be open to a contracting party, at a later date, to deny that he had the requisite subjective intention to be bound by his offer. Accordingly, the general principle of English law is that the test for assessing the intention of contracting parties is an objective one. The rationale for having an objective test is the need for contractual certainty. This principle was established in *Smith v Hughes* (1870-1871) LR 6 QB 597 in which Blackburn J set out the approach as follows:

...If, whatever a man's real intention may be, he so conducts himself that a reasonable man would believe that he was assenting to the terms proposed by the other party, and that other party upon that belief enters into the contract with him, the man thus conducting himself would be equally bound as if he had intended to agree to that party's terms.

However, there are situations when the subjective intention of the parties will be considered, for instance, when the offeror has made a mistake as to the terms of the offer and the offeree knows or ought to have known of the mistake.

Hartog v Colin & Shields [1939] 3 All ER 566

Panel: Singleton J

Facts: The defendants mistakenly offered to sell a large quantity of Argentine hare skins at a stipulated price per pound (not per piece) to the plaintiff and the plaintiff accepted this offer. The court found that, in all previous correspondence and negotiations, prices had been quoted per piece, and furthermore it was trade practice to sell at a price per piece. There were roughly three skins to a pound, so the error in pricing would mean that the plaintiff was buying three hare skins for the price of one.

MR JUSTICE SINGLETON

In this case, the plaintiff, a Belgian subject, claims damages against the defendants because he says they broke a contract into which they entered with him for the sale of Argentine hare skins. The defendants' answer to that claim is: 'There really was no contract, because you knew that the document which went forward to you, in the form of an offer, contained a material mistake. You realised that, and you sought to take advantage of it.'

Counsel for the defendants took upon himself the onus of satisfying me that the plaintiff knew that there was a mistake and sought to take advantage of that mistake. In other words, realising that there was a mistake, the plaintiff did that which James LJ, in *Tamplin v James*, at p 221, described as 'snapping up the offer.'...

...I am satisfied, however, from the evidence given to me, that the plaintiff must have realised, and did in fact know, that a mistake had occurred. ...

I am satisfied that it was a mistake on the part of the defendants or their servants which caused the offer to go forward in that way, and I am satisfied that anyone with any knowledge of the trade must have realised that there was a mistake. ...I have seen the witnesses and heard them, and in this case can form no other view than that there was an accident. The offer was wrongly expressed, and the defendants by their evidence, and by the correspondence, have satisfied me that the plaintiff could not reasonably have supposed that that offer contained the offerers' real intention. Indeed, I am satisfied to the contrary. That means that there must be judgment for the defendants.

Since the plaintiff could not reasonably have supposed that the stated price was correct, he could not accept this offer made by mistake. An offeree cannot 'snap up' an offer which he knows or ought to have known was made in error.

1.2 Bilateral and Unilateral Contracts Defined

There are two types of contract: bilateral and unilateral. Bilateral contracts are far more common and are created by the exchange of mutually binding promises. On the other hand, in a unilateral contract, the offer prescribes an act which, when performed, will constitute acceptance.

1.2.1 Bilateral Contracts

The essential feature of a bilateral contract is the reciprocal nature of promises between the parties. One party promises to undertake to do something, or refrain from doing something, in exchange for a promise from the other party, to do, or to refrain from doing something. For example, in a contract for the sale of goods, the seller promises to sell goods to the buyer for a stated price and, in exchange for the seller agreeing to sell the goods to him, the buyer of the goods promises to pay the stated price to the seller.

1.2.2 Unilateral Contracts

Carlill v Carbolic Smoke Ball Co [1893] 1 QB 256

Panel: Lindley, Bowen and AL Smith LJJ

Facts: The Carbolic Smoke Ball Co placed an advertisement in a newspaper offering to pay £100 to anyone who bought their carbolic smoke ball, used it in the prescribed way and still contracted influenza. Carlill bought the smoke ball, used it as prescribed and nonetheless contracted influenza. She then sued the Carbolic Smoke Ball Co for payment of the £100 'reward'.

LORD JUSTICE BOWEN

...[The advertisement] is written in colloquial and popular language, and I think that it is equivalent to this: '100l. will be paid to any person who shall contract the increasing epidemic after having used the carbolic smoke ball three times daily for two weeks.' And it seems to me that the way in which the public would read it would be this, that if anybody, after the advertisement was published, used three times daily for two weeks the carbolic smoke ball, and then caught cold, he would be entitled to the reward. ...

Decipher
£100

Was it intended that the 100l. should, if the conditions were fulfilled, be paid? The advertisement says that 1000l. is lodged at the bank for the purpose. Therefore, it cannot be said that the statement that 100l. would be paid was intended to be a mere puff. I think it was intended to be understood by the public as an offer which was to be acted upon.

But it was said there was no check on the part of the persons who issued the advertisement, and that it would be an insensate thing to promise 100l. to a person who used the smoke ball unless you could check or superintend his manner of using it. The answer to that argument seems to me to be that if a

Decipher
A statement which has no contractual effect because it is too hyperbolic.

person chooses to make extravagant promises of this kind he probably does so because it pays him to make them, and, if he has made them, the extravagance of the promises is no reason in law why he should not be bound by them.

It was also said that the contract is made with all the world - that is, with everybody; and that you cannot contract with everybody. It is not a contract made with all the world. There is the fallacy of the argument. It is an offer made to all the world; and why should not an offer be made to all the world which is to ripen into a contract with anybody who comes forward and performs the condition? It is an offer to become liable to any one who, before it is retracted, performs the condition, and, although the offer is made to the world, the contract is made with that limited portion of the public who come forward and perform the condition on the faith of the advertisement. ...

The advertisement was sufficiently clear and certain and demonstrated the requisite intention to be bound to be an offer. It was a unilateral offer since it prescribed acts which, when performed, would constitute acceptance. The prescribed acts were (i) that the individual should use the smoke ball in the prescribed manner, three times daily for two weeks, and (ii) catch influenza.

Students are often confused by *Carlill* as to the definition of a unilateral offer. A unilateral offer is an offer which prescribes an act which, when performed, constitutes acceptance. It just so happens that the unilateral offer in *Carlill* was made to all the world. However, a unilateral offer can just as easily be made to one individual e.g. 'I will pay you £100 if you walk to York'. This is a unilateral offer since it prescribes an act, the performance of which will constitute acceptance.

It is interesting to note that the court distinguished the offer in this case from a mere puff since the deposit of £1,000 showed that the Carbolic Smoke Ball Co intended to be bound by its offer to pay the stated reward.

1.3 Requirements of a Valid Offer

1.3.1 An Offer Must be Clear and Certain and show Intention to be Bound

An offer must be clear and certain so that it is capable of acceptance. This means that the essential terms of that offer must be made known to the offeree. For example, the offer must be clear in relation to the object of the offer (what is to be sold), the price and any other key terms. An offer must also demonstrate the requisite intention to be legally bound.

Gibson v Manchester City Council [1979] 1 WLR 294

Panel: Lord Diplock, Lord Edmund-Davies, Lord Fraser of Tullybelton, Lord Russell of Killowen and Lord Keith of Kinkel

Facts: Manchester City Council had a policy of selling council houses to tenants. Mr Gibson requested details from the council of the price, and mortgage available to him, for him to buy his council house. On 10 February 1971, the council replied stating: 'The corporation may be prepared to sell the house to you at the purchase price of £2,725 less 20 per cent. = £2,180 (freehold)'. The letter also included details of the maximum mortgage that may be made available to Mr Gibson. The letter concluded with the words: 'If you would like to make formal application to buy your council house, please complete the enclosed application form and return it to me as soon as possible.' Mr Gibson returned the formal application form on 5 March 1971.

Following a change of control of the council in the summer of 1971, the new council decided to discontinue the right to buy scheme. On 27 July, the council wrote to Mr Gibson to tell him that they would not proceed with the sale of his council property to him. Mr Gibson brought an action for specific performance to compel the council to sell him his council house. He argued that the council's letter of 10 February 1971 was an offer to sell him the council property, which he accepted, by submitting the formal application on 5 March 1971.

LORD DIPLOCK

My Lords, the words ['The corporation may be prepared to sell the house to you at the purchase price of £2,725 less 20 per cent. = £2,180 (freehold)'] seem to me ... to make it quite impossible to construe this letter as a contractual offer capable of being converted into a legally enforceable open contract for the sale of land by Mr. Gibson's written acceptance of it. The words 'may be prepared to sell' are fatal to this; so is the invitation, not, be it noted, to accept the offer, but 'to make formal application to buy' upon the enclosed application form. It is ... a letter setting out the financial terms on which it may be the council will be prepared to consider a sale and purchase in due course.

Lord Diplock made it clear that the court considers the language used as well as the context of the statement in determining whether it evidences intention to be bound and it is sufficiently clear and certain to amount to an offer. *Storer v Manchester City Council* [1974] 1 WLR 1403 was another case brought as a result of Manchester City Council withdrawing the same right to buy scheme. On the facts of *Storer*, the court held that the offer was sufficiently clear and certain, demonstrated intention to be bound and was capable of acceptance by Mr Storer.

Storer v Manchester City Council [1974] 1 WLR 1403

Panel: Lord Denning MR, Stephenson and Lawton LJJ

Facts: Manchester City Council wrote to Mr Storer stating that they 'may' be prepared to sell his council house to him. On 11 February 1971, Mr Storer completed the requisite application form and he confirmed that he wanted a loan from the council. The Treasurer wrote two letters to Mr Storer on 9 March 1971, the first contained details of the mortgage offer, and the second letter enclosed an agreement for sale. Mr Storer signed and returned the agreement. The agreement contained only two blanks, being the date that his tenancy would cease and the date the mortgage would start.

Subsequently, the council changed their policy on 'right to buy' council houses and the town clerk wrote to Mr Storer stating that they would not proceed with the sale to him. Mr Storer brought an action for specific performance of the contract.

LORD DENNING MR

[Mr. Storer] had done everything which he had to do to bind himself to the purchase of the property. The only thing left blank was the date when the tenancy ceased.

…

…The contract was concluded by offer and acceptance. The offer was contained in the letter of 9 March in which the town clerk said:

'I enclose the agreement for sale. If you will sign the agreement and return it to me I will send you the agreement signed on behalf of the corporation in exchange.'

The acceptance was made when Mr. Storer did sign it, as he did on March 20. It was then that a contract was concluded. The town clerk was then bound to send back the agreement signed on behalf of the corporation. The agreement was concluded on Mr. Storer's acceptance. It was not dependent on the subsequent exchange.

I appreciate that there was one space in the form which was left blank. It was No 7 for 'the date when your tenancy ceases'. That blank did not mean there was no concluded contract. It was left blank simply for administrative convenience. …

So here the filling in of the date was just a matter of administrative tidying up, to be filled in by the town clerk with a suitable date for the changeover—the date on which Mr. Storer ceased to be a tenant and became a purchaser.

…

The final point was this: [counsel for the council] said that the town clerk did not intend to be bound by the letter of March 9, 1971. He intended that the corporation should not be bound except on exchange. There is nothing in this point. In contracts you do not look into the actual intent in a man's mind. You look at what he said and did. A contract is formed when there is, to all outward appearances, a contract. A man cannot get out of a contract by saying: 'I did not intend to contract' if by his words he has done so. His intention is to be found only in the outward expression which his letters convey. If they show a concluded contract, that is enough.

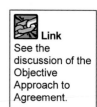

Link
See the discussion of the Objective Approach to Agreement.

The council had made an offer to Mr Storer and the terms of that offer were clear and certain. The price was stated and the council made it clear that they intended to be bound by their offer as soon as it was accepted. This case can be distinguished from the case of *Gibson* by means of the language used since in *Gibson* the council had said that they '*may*' be prepared to sell which was insufficiently certain and lacked the requisite intention to be bound. In *Storer*, the council said: 'If you will sign the agreement and return it to me I *will* send you the agreement signed on behalf of the corporation in exchange.' (Emphasis added).

1.4   An Invitation to Treat is not an Offer

An offer must be clear and certain and evidence an intention to be legally bound upon acceptance. Where a purported offer is not sufficiently clear and certain, or it does not evidence an intention to be bound, it will be an invitation to treat only and have no legal effect. An invitation to treat is the first step in negotiations. In the case of *Gibson* (above), the letter from the council stating that they 'may' be prepared to sell was not sufficiently clear and certain to constitute an offer; instead it was an invitation to treat. It was merely a preliminary step in negotiations in relation to the purchase of Mr Gibson's council property.

There are a number of specific situations in which the courts have developed rules as to when a certain communication will constitute an invitation to treat as opposed to an offer. The situations considered below relate to the display of goods, advertisements, tenders and auction sales.

1.4.1   Advertisements

The general rule is that an advertisement is an invitation to treat.

***Partridge v Crittenden* [1968] 1 WLR 1204**

Panel: Lord Parker CJ, Ashworth and Blain JJ

Statute: Protection of Birds Act 1954

Facts: Mr Partridge placed an advertisement in a periodical called 'Cage and Aviary Birds' dated 13 April 1967, containing the words '...Advertisement of Bramblefinch cocks and hens, at 25s each'. Mr Partridge was convicted of the offence of offering the birds for sale contrary to the provisions of the Protection of Birds Act 1954 which prohibited the sale of certain birds. Mr Partridge appealed.

MR JUSTICE ASHWORTH

[After referring to Lord Parker CJ's judgment in *Fisher v Bell*, Ashworth J continued:]

The words [of the Protection of Birds Act 1954] are the same here 'offer for sale' [as they were in the relevant Act in *Fisher v Bell*], and in my judgment the law of the country is equally plain as it was in regard to articles in a shop window, namely that the insertion of an advertisement in the form adopted here under the title 'Classified Advertisements' is simply an invitation to treat.

That is really sufficient to dispose of this case. …

The advertisement did not constitute an offer to sell the birds; it was merely an invitation to treat. Mr Partridge's appeal was allowed.

1.4.1.1   Exceptions to the general rule

Seller is the manufacturer

In *Partridge v Crittenden*, Lord Parker CJ agreed with Ashworth J's judgment as follows:

LORD PARKER CJ

I agree and with less reluctance than in *Fisher v Bell* … I say 'with less reluctance' because I think that when one is dealing with advertisements and circulars, unless they indeed come from manufacturers, there is business sense in their being construed as invitations to treat and not offers for sale.

Lord Parker CJ then referred to Lord Herschell's *obiter* comments in *Grainger & Son v Gough (Surveyor of Taxes)* [1896] AC 325. In *Grainger v Gough*, it was held that a price list for wine was simply an invitation to treat, not an offer to sell.

Lord Herschell made the following *obiter* comments:

…The transmission of such a price-list does not amount to an offer to supply an unlimited quantity of the wine described at the price named, so that as soon as an order is given there is a binding contract to supply that quantity. If it were so, the merchant might find himself involved in any number of contractual obligations to supply wine of a particular description which he would be quite unable to carry out, his stock of wine of that description being necessarily limited.

Lord Herschell adopted a pragmatic view and illustrated that, if a price list were an offer to sell, then the seller would be bound to satisfy all orders, even when stock is limited. He would otherwise be in breach of contract for all the orders he could not fulfil. Lord Parker CJ, in *Partridge v Crittenden* expands on this comment and suggests that, if the seller is the manufacturer, then perhaps this justification for the rule does not apply. Consequently, if the seller is the manufacturer, it is arguable that the advertisement may constitute an offer.

Unilateral offers

An advertisement may constitute an offer where it prescribes an act which, when performed, would constitute acceptance; in other words, it is a unilateral offer.

Note that, as well as prescribing an act, in order for the advertisement to constitute a unilateral offer, it must also evidence a sufficient intention to be bound. In *Carlill*, such an intention was evidenced by the deposit of £1,000 into a bank account.

 Link
See the discussion of *Carlill v Carbolic Smoke Ball*.

1.4.2   Display of Goods

The general rule is that the display of goods is an invitation to treat.

Fisher v Bell [1960] 1 QB 394

Panel: Lord Parker CJ, Ashworth and Elwes JJ

Statute: Restriction of Offensive Weapons Act 1959 s 1(1)

Facts: Bell was charged with the offence of offering for sale an offensive weapon as prohibited by the Restriction of Offensive Weapons Act 1959 s 1(1), and convicted at trial. He had displayed knives in a shop window and in front of them was a sign which stated 'Ejector knife - 4s.'

LORD PARKER CJ

In ordinary language [the knife] is there inviting people to buy it, and it is for sale; but any statute must of course be looked at in the light of the general law of the country. Parliament in its wisdom in passing an Act must be taken to know the general law. It is perfectly clear that according to the ordinary law of contract the display of an article with a price on it in a shop window is merely an invitation to treat. It is in no sense an offer for sale the acceptance of which constitutes a contract. That is clearly the general law of the country. Not only is that so, but it is to be observed that in many statutes and orders which prohibit selling and offering for sale of goods it is very common when it is so desired to insert the words 'offering or exposing for sale', 'exposing for sale'

 Alert

being clearly words which would cover the display of goods in a shop window. Not only that, but it appears that under several statutes ... Parliament, when it desires to enlarge the ordinary meaning of those words, includes a definition section enlarging the ordinary meaning of 'offer for sale' to cover other matters including, be it observed, exposure of goods for sale with the price attached.

In those circumstances I am driven to the conclusion, though I confess reluctantly, that no offence was here committed. ...

Bell won his appeal on the basis that a display of goods is an invitation to treat; it is not an offer. Consequently, he was not guilty of offering the knives for sale.

The case of *Pharmaceutical Society of Great Britain v Boots Cash Chemists (Southern) Ltd* [1953] 1 QB 401 considered the position in relation to goods in a self-service shop. The issue in this case was whether such a display constituted an offer to sell those goods and accordingly was capable of acceptance by the customer merely picking up the goods and placing them in their basket.

Pharmaceutical Society of Great Britain v Boots Cash Chemists (Southern) Ltd [1952] 2 QB 795

Panel: Lord Goddard CJ

Statute: Pharmacy and Poisons Act 1933 s 18(1)(a)(iii)

Facts: On 13 April 1951, two customers bought medicines from Boots Cash Chemist that fell within the restrictions of the Pharmacy and Poisons Act 1933. It was an offence under s 18(1)(a)(iii) to sell prohibited medicines (referred to as poisons) unless the sale was under the supervision of a registered pharmacist. This shop was a self-service shop. Customers took items off the shelf (as opposed to assistants waiting on them, as was the custom in that era) and then proceeded to the till. The pharmacist supervised the sale of items at the till. Accordingly, the issue for the court to decide was when a sale is concluded in a self-service shop. Lord Goddard CJ considered the matter in the lower court, but, since his judgment was approved in the Court of Appeal, it is extracted below.

LORD GODDARD CJ

...I think that it is a well-established principle that the mere exposure of goods for sale by a shopkeeper indicates to the public that he is willing to treat but does not amount to an offer to sell. I do not think I ought to hold that that principle is completely reversed merely because there is a self-service scheme, such as this, in operation. In my opinion it comes to no more than that the customer is informed that he may himself pick up an article and bring it to the shopkeeper with a view to buying it, and if, but only if, the shopkeeper then expresses his willingness to sell, the contract for sale is completed. …

Ordinary principles of common sense and of commerce must be applied in this matter, and to hold that in the case of self-service shops the exposure of an article is an offer to sell, and that a person can accept the offer by picking up the article, would be contrary to those principles and might entail serious results. On the customer picking up the article the property would forthwith pass to him and he would be able to insist upon the shopkeeper allowing him to take it away, though in some particular cases the shopkeeper might think that very undesirable. On the other hand, if a customer had picked up an article, he would never be able to change his mind and to put it back; the shopkeeper could say, 'Oh no, the property has passed and you must pay the price.'

It seems to me, therefore, that the transaction is in no way different from the normal transaction in a shop in which there is no self-service scheme. I am quite satisfied it would be wrong to say that the shopkeeper is making an offer to sell every article in the shop to any person who might come in and that that person can insist on buying any article by saying 'I accept your offer.' I agree with the illustration put forward during the case of a person who might go into a shop where books are displayed. In most book-shops customers are invited to go in and pick up books and look at them even if they do not actually buy them. There is no contract by the shopkeeper to sell until the customer has taken the book to the shopkeeper or his assistant and said 'I want to buy this book' and the shopkeeper says 'Yes.' That would not prevent the shopkeeper, seeing the book picked up, Saying: 'I am sorry I cannot let you have that book; it is the only copy I have got and I have already promised it to another customer.' Therefore, in my opinion, the mere fact that a customer picks up a bottle of medicine from the shelves in this case does not amount to an acceptance of an offer to sell. It is an offer by the customer to buy and there is no sale effected until the buyer's offer to buy is accepted by the acceptance of the price. The offer, the acceptance of the price, and therefore the sale, take place under the supervision of the pharmacist. …

 Alert

The display of goods is simply an invitation to treat, not an offer to sell. The offer is made by the purchaser and this is accepted by the seller at the till. Consequently, the sale, in this case, took place under the supervision of the pharmacist at the till and no offence was committed.

Although Lord Goddard CJ was very clear that the actual display of the goods is merely an invitation to treat, what is slightly less clear is when the offer and acceptance themselves occur. Lord Goddard CJ seems to have suggested (although he is not clear) that the offer takes place when the customer takes the item off the shelf. Although his judgment was approved by the Court of Appeal, this particular suggestion is at odds with the position as set out by Somervell LJ in the Court of Appeal ([1953] 1 QB 401).

LORD JUSTICE SOMERVELL

...I agree with what the Lord Chief Justice [Lord Goddard CJ] has said, and with the reasons which he has given for his conclusion, that in the case of an ordinary [non-self-service] shop, although goods are displayed and it is intended that customers should go and choose what they want, the contract is not completed until, the customer having indicated the articles which he needs, the shopkeeper, or someone on his behalf, accepts that offer. Then the contract is completed. I can see no reason at all, that being clearly the normal position, for drawing any different implication as a result of this [self-service] layout.

The Lord Chief Justice, I think, expressed one of the most formidable difficulties in the way of the plaintiffs' contention when he pointed out that, if the plaintiffs are right, once an article has been placed in the receptacle the customer himself is bound and would have no right, without paying for the first article, to substitute an article which he saw later of a similar kind and which he perhaps preferred. I can see no reason for implying from this self-service arrangement any implication other than that which the Lord Chief Justice found in it, namely, that it is a convenient method of enabling customers to see what there is and choose, and possibly put back and substitute, articles which they wish to have, and then to go up to the cashier and offer to buy what they have so far chosen. On that conclusion the case fails, because it is admitted that there was supervision in the sense required by the Act and at the appropriate moment of time. ...

 Alert

In his judgment, Somervell LJ is of the view that the customer makes the offer on presenting the goods at the cash desk and this offer is then accepted by the seller.

1.4.3 Invitations to Tender

The general rule is that an invitation to tender is an invitation to treat. A submission of a tender is an offer to carry out work for the price stated, and on the other terms contained within that tender document. The party who has requested the tenders is free to accept or reject any tender he wishes, even if it is the most competitive tender.

Spencer and others v Harding and others (1869- 70) LR 5 CP 561

Panel: Willes, Keating and Montague Smith JJ

Facts: The defendants issued a circular stating that the stock of a certain trader was to be sold, in one lot, for payment in cash. This circular further stated a deadline by which any tenders for the stock had to be submitted. The plaintiffs submitted the highest tender but the defendants did not sell the stock to them.

MR JUSTICE WILLES

...The action is brought against persons who issued a circular offering a stock for sale by tender, to be sold at a discount in one lot. The plaintiffs sent in a tender which turned out to be the highest, but which was not accepted. They now insist that the circular amounts to a contract or promise to sell the goods to the highest bidder, that is, in this case, to the person who should tender for them at the smallest rate of discount; and reliance is placed on the cases as to rewards offered for the discovery of an offender. In those cases, however, there never was any doubt that the advertisement amounted to a promise to pay the money to the person who first gave information. The difficulty suggested was that it was a contract with all the world. But that, of course, was soon overruled. It was an offer to become liable to any person who before the offer should be retracted should happen to be the person to fulfil the contract of which the advertisement was an offer or tender. That is not the sort of difficulty which presents itself here. If the circular had gone on, 'and we undertake to sell to the highest bidder,' the reward cases would have applied, and there would have been a good contract in respect of the persons. But the question is, whether there is here any offer to enter into a contract at all, or whether the circular amounts to anything more than a mere proclamation that the defendants are ready to chaffer for the sale of the goods, and to receive offers for the purchase of them. In advertisements for tenders for buildings it is not usual to say that the contract will be given to the lowest bidder, and it is not always that the contract is made with the lowest bidder. Here there is a total absence of any words to intimate that the highest bidder is to be the purchaser. It is a mere attempt to ascertain whether an offer can be obtained within such a margin as the sellers are willing to adopt.

The defendants were not obliged to sell to the plaintiffs since the defendants' invitation to submit tenders was simply an invitation to treat. The plaintiffs made an offer when they submitted the highest tender, but, since this was not accepted, there could be no binding contract.

Mr Justice Willes introduced an exception to the general rule that the party inviting tenders (the invitor) can accept or reject any bid. If the invitor had stated that they would accept the highest bid, then the invitor would be bound to sell to the highest bidder. This exception was confirmed in the case of *Harvela Investments Ltd v Royal Trust Company of Canada (C.I.) Ltd and others* [1986] AC 207 below.

1.4.3.1 Exceptions to the general rule

An undertaking to sell to the highest (or lowest) bidder

Harvela Investments Ltd v Royal Trust Company of Canada (C.I.) Ltd and others **[1986] AC 207**

Panel: Lord Fraser of Tullybelton, Lord Diplock, Lord Edmund-Davies, Lord Bridge of Harwich and Lord Templeman

Facts: The first defendant, the Royal Trust Co, by telex invited sealed bids from two parties for shares and stated that they would accept the highest bid. The plaintiff company, Harvela, submitted a bid of C$2,175,000 for the shares. The second defendant, Sir Leonard, submitted a bid of 'C$2,100,000, or C$101,000 in excess of any other offer … expressed as a fixed monetary amount, whichever is the higher'. The Royal Trust Co sold the shares to Sir Leonard and Harvela brought a claim for specific performance for the sale of the shares to itself. The House of Lords found that, in these circumstances, referential bids were not valid. Since Sir Leonard's referential bid was not valid, Harvela's bid was the highest. The question remained as to whether the Royal Trust Co was bound to accept Harvela's bid since they had stated that they would accept the highest bid.

 Decipher
A bid that can only be understood by reference to another's bid (ie I will pay £x more than any other bid).

LORD DIPLOCK

…[The meaning of the invitation to tender] turns upon the wording of the telex of 15 September 1981 referred to by Lord Templeman as 'the invitation' and addressed to both Harvela and Sir Leonard. It was not a mere invitation to negotiate for the sale of the shares... . Its legal nature was that of a unilateral or 'if' contract, or rather of two unilateral contracts in identical terms to one of which the vendors and Harvela were the parties as promisor and promisee respectively, while to the other the vendors were promisor and Sir Leonard was promisee. Such unilateral contracts were made at the time when the invitation was received by the promisee to whom it was addressed by the vendors; under neither of them did the promisee, Harvela and Sir Leonard respectively, assume any legal obligation to anyone to do or refrain from doing anything.

 Decipher
Lord Diplock refers to there being two unilateral contracts. See the slightly clearer explanation below as to how the contracts in this case can be analysed.

The vendors, on the other hand, did assume a legal obligation to the promisee under each contract. That obligation was conditional upon the happening, after the unilateral contract had been made, of an event which was specified in the invitation; the obligation was to enter into a synallagmatic contract to sell the shares to the promisee, the terms of such synallagmatic contract being also set out in the invitation. The event upon the happening of which the vendor's obligation to sell the shares to the promisee arose was the doing by the promisee of an act which was of such a nature that it might be done by either promisee or neither promisee but could not be done by both. The vendors thus did not by entering into the two unilateral contracts run any

 Decipher
A synallagmatic contract equates to a bilateral contract.

risk of assuming legal obligations to enter into conflicting synallagmatic contracts to sell the shares to each promisee.

The two unilateral contracts were of short duration; for the condition subsequent to which each was subject was the receipt by the vendors' solicitors on or before 3 p.m. on the following day, 16 September 1981, of a sealed tender or confidential telex containing an offer by the promisee to buy the shares for a single sum of money in Canadian dollars. If such an offer was received from each of the promisees under their respective contracts, the obligation of the promisor, the vendors, was to sell the shares to the promisee whose offer was the higher; and any obligation which the promisor had assumed to the promisee under the other unilateral contract came to an end, because the event the happening of which was the condition subsequent to which the vendors' obligation to sell the shares to that promisee was subject had not happened before the unilateral contract with that promisee expired.

 Alert

Since the invitation in addition to containing the terms of the unilateral contract also embodied the terms of the synallagmatic contract into which the vendors undertook to enter upon the happening of the specified event, the consequence of the happening of that event would be to convert the invitation into a synallagmatic contract between the vendors and whichever promisee had offered, by sealed tender or confidential telex, the higher sum. ...

Lord Diplock's explanation involves the formation of two unilateral contracts and is rather complicated. A better explanation has been put forward in Smith and Thomas, *A Casebook on Contract* (12th Edn, Sweet & Maxwell, 2009):

...The Royal Trust's telex to Harvela and Sir Leonard was an offer to each of them which could be accepted only by one – the one who made the higher valid bid. The telex was an offer of a unilateral contract, like an offer to give a prize to the one of two entrants for a race who comes first. The 'prize' was a contract for the sale of the shares – the Trust was bound to accept the higher bidder's offer to buy them.

Until that bid was made, no one was under any obligation. The Trust could have withdrawn its offer and the two offerees were under no obligation to bid. While the offer stood, the Trust was, of course, liable to become bound to one of the offerees through the acceptance of its offer, but that is the position of all offerors, so long as their offer remains open to acceptance. When the higher bid was ascertained, the Trust was bound to accept it. At that moment there was just one contract – a contract by the Trust to accept the higher bidder's offer – a unilateral contract. The bidder was free to withdraw his bid until the Trust accepted it, but when they did he became bound to buy the shares. ...

Undertaking to consider tenders submitted

In certain circumstances, there will be a contractual obligation on the person inviting tenders to consider such tenders that are submitted in accordance with the prescribed method.

Blackpool & Fylde Aero Club Ltd v Blackpool Borough Council [1990] 1 WLR 1195

Panel: Stocker, Bingham and Farquharson LJJ

Facts: The defendant council invited tenders from seven parties with respect to operating pleasure flights from the airport. The tenders were to be submitted by 12 noon on 17 March 1983 and would not be considered if they were submitted after this time. The plaintiffs placed their tender in the letter box at the Town Hall at 11am on the stated day. The letter box was usually emptied at noon. However, the council failed to empty the letter box and, consequently, the plaintiffs' tender was not considered. The question for the court was whether the council was under an obligation to consider the plaintiffs' tender.

LORD JUSTICE BINGHAM

A tendering procedure of this kind is, in many respects, heavily weighted in favour of the invitor. He can invite tenders from as many or as few parties as he chooses. He need not tell any of them who else, or how many others, he has invited. The invitee may often, although not here, be put to considerable labour and expense in preparing a tender, ordinarily without recompense if he is unsuccessful. The invitation to tender may itself, in a complex case, although again not here, involve time and expense to prepare, but the invitor does not commit himself to proceed with the project, whatever it is; he need not accept the highest tender; he need not accept any tender; he need not give reasons to justify his acceptance or rejection of any tender received. The risk to which the tenderer is exposed does not end with the risk that his tender may not be the highest (or, as the case may be, lowest). But where, as here, tenders are solicited from selected parties all of them known to the invitor, and where a local authority's invitation prescribes a clear, orderly and familiar procedure - draft contract conditions available for inspection and plainly not open to negotiation, a prescribed common form of tender, the supply of envelopes designed to preserve the absolute anonymity of tenderers and clearly to identify the tender in question and an absolute deadline - the invitee is in my judgment protected at least to this extent: if he submits a conforming tender before the deadline he is entitled, not as a matter of mere expectation but of contractual right, to be sure that his tender will after the deadline be opened and considered in conjunction with all other conforming tenders or at least that his tender will be considered if others are. Had the club, before tendering, inquired of the council whether it could rely on any timely and conforming tender being considered along with others,

Alert

I feel quite sure that the answer would have been 'of course'. The law would, I think, be defective if it did not give effect to that.

It is of course true that the invitation to tender does not explicitly state that the council will consider timely and conforming tenders. That is why one is concerned with implication. But the council do not either say that they do not bind themselves to do so, and in the context a reasonable invitee would understand the invitation to be saying, quite clearly, that if he submitted a timely and conforming tender it would be considered, at least if any other such tender were considered.

I readily accept that contracts are not to be lightly implied. Having examined what the parties said and did, the court must be able to conclude with confidence both that the parties intended to create contractual relations and that the agreement was to the effect contended for. ...

In the particular circumstances, it was held that the council had made an offer to consider all conforming tenders. The particular facts in this case which appear to have influenced the court in finding such an offer were: (i) the invitation was made to a specified number of parties, and (ii) there are specific and absolute conditions governing the manner of, and timing for, the submission of tenders.

1.4.4   Auctions

The general rule in relation to an auction sale is that, when the auctioneer requests bids, that request is a mere invitation to treat. A bid made by a bidder is an offer to buy the lot being sold, and this offer is accepted by the fall of the auctioneer's hammer. In *Payne v Cave* 100 ER 50, the defendant made a bid of £40 for the lot in question but, when the auctioneer delayed in accepting his bid, he declared that he would not buy it and refused to pay. It was held that the defendant was entitled to withdraw his bid since his bid was simply an offer which he was entitled to withdraw any time before acceptance.

1.4.4.1   Exceptions to the general rule

Auctions without reserve

When an auction is held 'without reserve', meaning without a reserve price, the auctioneer is in effect undertaking to sell the lot in question to the highest bidder. This proposition was originally considered in the case of *Warlow v Harrison* (1859) 1 E & E 309 and was confirmed in *Barry v Davies (trading as Heathcote Ball & Co)* [2000] 1 WLR 1962.

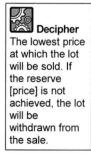

Decipher
The lowest price at which the lot will be sold. If the reserve [price] is not achieved, the lot will be withdrawn from the sale.

Barry v Davies (trading as Heathcote Ball & Co) [2000] 1 WLR 1962

Panel: Pill LJ and Sir Murray Stuart-Smith

Statute: Sale of Goods Act 1979 s 57

Facts: The claimant made a bid of £200 each for two new engine analysers at an auction without reserve. The list price for these items was £14,000 each. The auctioneer withdrew the lot from the sale on the basis that the bid was too low and accordingly refused to sell the lot to the claimant. The claimant sought damages to the sum of £27,600 (£28,000, being their combined list price, - £400, being the bid made).

SIR MURRAY STUART-SMITH

The [original trial] judge held that it would be the general and reasonable expectation of persons attending at an auction sale without reserve that the highest bidder would and should be entitled to the lot for which he bids. Such an outcome was in his view fair and logical. As a matter of law he held that there was a collateral contract between the auctioneer and the highest bidder constituted by an offer by the auctioneer to sell to the highest bidder which was accepted when the bid was made. In so doing he followed the views of the majority of the Court of Exchequer Chamber in *Warlow v. Harrison* (1859) 1 E. & E. 309.

…

First, [counsel for the defendant] submitted that the holding of an auction without reserve does not amount to a promise on the part of the auctioneer to sell the lots to the highest bidder. There are no express words to the effect, merely a statement of fact that the vendor has not placed a reserve on the lot. Such an intention, he submitted, is inconsistent with two principles of law, namely that the auctioneer's request for bids is not an offer which can be accepted by the highest bidder (*Payne v. Cave* (1789) 3 Durn. & E. 148) and that there is no completed contract of sale until the auctioneer's hammer falls and the bidder may withdraw his bid up until that time... .

Secondly, [counsel for the defendant] submitted that there is no consideration for the auctioneer's promise. He submitted that the bid itself cannot amount to consideration because the bidder has not promised to do anything, he can withdraw the bid until it is accepted and the sale completed by the fall of the hammer. At most the bid represents a discretionary promise, which amounts to illusory consideration, for example promising to do something 'if I feel like it.' The bid only had real benefit to the auctioneer at the moment the sale is completed by the fall of the hammer. Furthermore, the suggestion that consideration is provided because the auctioneer has the opportunity to accept the bid or to obtain a higher bid as the bidding is driven up depends upon the bid not being withdrawn.

> **Link**
> See Chapter 8 on Privity which deals with collateral contracts. For your current purposes, think of a collateral contract as one which co-exists alongside another contract.

...The authorities, such as they were, do not speak with one voice. The starting point is section 57 of the Sale of Goods Act 1979, which re-enacted the Sale of Goods Act 1893 (56 & 57 Vict. c. 71), itself in this section a codification of the common law. I have already referred to the effect of subsection (2). Subsections (3) and (4) are also important. They provide:

'3.   A sale by auction may be notified to be subject to a reserve or upset price, and a right to bid may also be reserved expressly by or on behalf of the seller.

4.   Where a sale by auction is not notified to be subject to the right to bid by or on behalf of the seller, it is not lawful for the seller to bid himself or to employ any person to bid at the sale, or for the auctioneer knowingly to take any bid from the seller or any such person.'

Although the Act does not expressly deal with sales by auction without reserve, the auctioneer is the agent of the vendor and, unless subsection (4) has been complied with, it is not lawful for him to make a bid. Yet withdrawing the lot from the sale because it has not reached the level which the auctioneer considers appropriate is tantamount to bidding on behalf of the seller. The highest bid cannot be rejected simply because it is not high enough.

The [original trial] judge based his decision on the reasoning of the majority of the Court of Exchequer Chamber in *Warlow v. Harrison*, 1 E. & E. 309. ... Martin B. gave the judgment of the majority... . He said, at pp. 316–317:

'...It seems to us that the highest bona fide bidder at an auction may sue the auctioneer as upon a contract that the sale shall be without reserve. We think the auctioneer who puts the property up for sale upon such a condition pledges himself that the sale shall be without reserve; or, in other words, contracts that it shall be so; and that this contract is made with the highest bona fide bidder; and, in case of breach of it, that he has a right of action against the auctioneer...'

 Alert

...In my judgment there is [in an auction without reserve] consideration both in the form of detriment to the bidder, since his bid can be accepted unless and until it is withdrawn, and benefit to the auctioneer as the bidding is driven up. Moreover, attendance at the sale is likely to be increased if it is known that there is no reserve.

The rationale for auction without reserve cases is that there are two potential contracts. There is a bilateral contract that can be formed in the usual way at an auction, by a bidder making a bid (which is the offer) and the auctioneer accepting that bid by the fall of the hammer (which is the acceptance). On these facts, no such bilateral contract was formed as the lot was withdrawn from sale and the auctioneer did not accept the claimant's offer.

There is a second, unilateral contract. The auctioneer makes a unilateral offer to sell the goods to the person who makes the highest bid; this offer is accepted by the act of making the highest bid. The claimant had made the highest bid and therefore the unilateral contract between the claimant and the auctioneer had been formed and the auctioneer was in breach of that (collateral) unilateral contract. Accordingly, the claimant was entitled to damages amounting to the difference between the bid price of £400 and the actual value of the goods, taken as their list price of £28,000. Note that, since the claimant's contract was with the auctioneer, he would not be entitled to the goods themselves, which were owned by the seller, not the auctioneer.

1.5 Termination of an Offer

An offer can be terminated in the following three ways: first by rejection, so the offeree rejects the offer; second, by revocation, meaning the offeror revokes (or withdraws) his offer; and finally, by lapse. Once an offer has been terminated in one of these three ways, it can no longer be accepted. Another way of expressing this is that an offer can be accepted at any time prior to its termination.

1.5.1 Rejection

An offeree is free to reject an offer addressed to him. A rejection is a negative response indicating that you do not accept the offer; in its simplest form, it is a straightforward 'no'. A rejection has the effect of 'killing off' the original offer, meaning that, once an offer has been rejected, it can no longer be accepted.

1.5.1.1 Counter-offers

A rejection may not be easy to identify. A counter-offer operates as a rejection of the original offer (*Hyde v Wrench* (1840) 3 Beav 334).

Hyde v Wrench (1840) 3 Beav 334

Panel: Lord Langdale MR

Facts: On 6 June, the defendant, Mr Wrench, offered to sell his farm to Mr Hyde for £1,000 and Mr Hyde replied with a counter-offer to buy it for £950. On 27 June, Mr Wrench rejected Mr Hyde's counter-offer. On 29 June, Mr Hyde purported to accept the original offer to sell for £1,000. Mr Hyde sought an order for specific performance of the contract.

LORD LANGDALE MR

...I think there exists no valid binding contract between the parties for the purchase of the property. The Defendant offered to sell it for £1000, and if that had been at once unconditionally accepted, there would undoubtedly have been a perfect binding contract; instead of that, the Plaintiff made an offer of his own, to purchase the property for £950, and he thereby rejected the offer previously made by the Defendant. I think that it was not afterwards competent for him to revive the proposal of the Defendant, by tendering an acceptance of it; and that, therefore, there exists no obligation of any sort between the parties... .

Having made a counter-offer of £950, Mr Hyde could not subsequently resurrect the original offer and accept it; the original offer had been 'killed off' by the counter-offer. Mr Hyde's purported acceptance of the original offer to sell for £1,000 on 29 June could have operated as a new offer capable of acceptance by Mr Wrench, however, Mr Wrench did not accept this new offer. This meant that there was no contract between the parties.

The effect of a counter-offer is therefore two fold: first, it rejects the original offer and extinguishes it and, second, it is itself a new offer which will be capable of acceptance.

1.5.1.2 A request for further information

A request for further information does not affect the original offer. The original offer remains valid and capable of acceptance.

Stevenson, Jacques & Co v McLean (1880) 5 QBD 346

Panel: Lush J

Facts: The parties were in negotiations for the sale of iron. The defendant wrote to the plaintiff and stated that he would accept 40s net cash per ton of iron. The plaintiff responded by saying: 'Please wire whether you would accept forty for delivery over two months, or, if not, the longest limit you would give.' Later, the plaintiff, having had no response to his inquiry, accepted the original offer. In the meantime, the defendant had sold the iron to someone else. The question for the court was whether the inquiry was a counter-offer which had the effect of 'killing off' the original offer.

MR JUSTICE LUSH

...[T]he form of the telegram is one of inquiry. It is not 'I offer forty for delivery over two months,' which would have likened the case to *Hyde v. Wrench* (1), where one party offered his estate for 1000l., and the other answered by offering 950l. Lord Langdale, in that case, held that after the 950l. had been refused, the party offering it could not, by then agreeing to the original proposal, claim the estate, for the negotiation was at an end by the refusal of his counter proposal. Here there is no counter proposal. The words are, 'Please wire whether you would accept forty for delivery over two months, or, if not, the longest limit you would give.' There is nothing specific by way of

> offer or rejection, but a mere inquiry, which should have been answered and not treated as a rejection of the offer. ...

On the facts of this case, this was an inquiry seeking clarification as to modes and timing of payment. The court referred to the language used in the plaintiff's telegram in reaching this conclusion since the language was that of an inquiry. There was nothing sufficiently specific to either act as a counter-offer or a rejection. Consequently, the words were simply a request for information and the original offer remained open to be accepted by the plaintiff. On the facts, the original offer was accepted; consequently, there was a binding contract.

1.5.2 Lapse

Offers can lapse through (i) the passage of time (*Ramsgate Victoria Hotel Co Ltd v Montefiore* (1866) LR 1 Ex 109), (ii) the death of a party (*Bradbury v Morgan, Executors of Joseph Manuel Leigh, deceased* 158 ER 877, *Kennedy v Thomassen* [1929] 1 Ch 426) or (iii) as a result of non-fulfilment of a condition precedent (*Financings v Stimson* [1962] 1 WLR 1184).

1.5.3 Revocation

An offeror can revoke his offer at any time prior to it being accepted. As referred to above, in the case of *Payne v Cave*, the defendant made a bid at auction which he subsequently withdrew before the fall of the auctioneer's hammer. Since the bid constituted the offer, he was free to revoke this offer any time before it was accepted by the fall of the auctioneer's hammer.

Once an offer has been accepted, a contract has been formed and revocation is not possible.

1.5.3.1 Options

When a party makes an offer, he may agree to keep it open for a specified period of time. That promise by the offeror to keep the offer open can be a separate contract that is itself enforceable by the offeree; this is referred to as an 'option' or an 'option contract'. An option contract will only arise when the offeree has given consideration to the offeror for the promise to keep the offer open. Consideration will be covered in detail in Chapter 5, however, for our current purposes think of 'consideration' as being something of value – the price of the promise. If an option contract has been created, the offeror will still be able to revoke his offer in relation to the main contract, but he will be in breach of the option contract if he does so. If no consideration is provided for the promise to keep the offer open, no option contract is created and any promise that the offeror makes about keeping the offer open will not be binding.

In *Dickinson v Dodds* (1876) 2 Ch D 463, since no consideration had been provided to keep the offer open, no option contract had been created and the offeror could withdraw his offer as he wished without any consequences.

Dickinson v Dodds (1876) 2 Ch D 463

Panel: James and Mellish LJJ and Baggallay JA

Facts: On Wednesday 10 June 1874, Mr Dodds made an offer to sell his property to Mr Dickinson and the notice which contained the offer also contained the following words: 'This offer [is] to be left over until Friday, 9 o'clock A.M., 12th June, 1874.' On Thursday afternoon, Mr Dickinson was told by a third party, Mr Berry, that Mr Dodds had been offering or agreeing to sell the property to Mr Allan. Mr Dickinson then delivered an acceptance to Mr Dodds. Mr Dodds had sold the property to Mr Allan on Thursday.

LORD JUSTICE JAMES

...There was no consideration given for the undertaking or promise, to whatever extent it may be considered binding, to keep the property unsold until 9 o'clock on Friday morning; but apparently Dickinson was of opinion, and probably Dodds was of the same opinion, that he (Dodds) was bound by that promise, and could not in any way withdraw from it, or retract it, until 9 o'clock on Friday morning, and this probably explains a good deal of what afterwards took place. But it is clear settled law, on one of the clearest principles of law, that this promise, being a mere nudum pactum, was not binding, and that at any moment before a complete acceptance by Dickinson of the offer, Dodds was as free as Dickinson himself.

 Decipher A promise which is unsupported by consideration.

In the absence of any consideration for the promise to keep the offer open, that promise was unenforceable. If consideration had been given by Mr Dickinson in return for Mr Dodds's promise to keep the offer open, then that would have been binding; an 'option contract' would have been created.

1.5.3.2 Revocation must be communicated

Revocation is only effective when it is communicated.

Byrne & Co v Leon Van Tienhoven & Co (1880) 5 CPD 344

Panel: Lindley J

Facts: The case concerns the sale of 1,000 boxes of tinplates. The defendants, based in Cardiff, wrote to the plaintiff, who was located in New York, on 1 October 1879 offering boxes of tinplates for sale at a specified price. The plaintiff received the offer on 11 October and accepted it by telegram that day and by letter on 15 October. Unbeknown to the plaintiff, on 8 October, the defendants posted a letter to the plaintiff, withdrawing their offer of 1 October. This purported revocation reached the plaintiff on the 20 October, which was after the plaintiff had accepted the offer.

MR JUSTICE LINDLEY

…I pass, therefore, to the next question, viz., whether posting the letter of revocation was a sufficient communication of it to the plaintiff. The offer was posted on the 1st of October, the withdrawal was posted on the 8th, and did not reach the plaintiff until after he had posted his letter of the 11th, accepting the offer. It may be taken as now settled that where an offer is made and accepted by letters sent through the post, the contract is completed the moment the letter accepting the offer is posted ... even although it never reaches its destination. When, however, these authorities are looked at, it will be seen that they are based upon the principle that the writer of the offer has expressly or impliedly assented to treat an answer to him by a letter duly posted as a sufficient acceptance and notification to himself, or, in other words, he has made the post office his agent to receive the acceptance and notification of it. But this principle appears to me to be inapplicable to the case of the withdrawal of an offer. In this particular case I can find no evidence of any authority in fact given by the plaintiffs to the defendants to notify a withdrawal of their offer by merely posting a letter; and there is no legal principle or decision which compels me to hold, contrary to the fact, that the letter of the 8th of October is to be treated as communicated to the plaintiff on that day or on any day before the 20th, when the letter reached them. But before that letter had reached the plaintiffs they had accepted the offer, both by telegram and by post; and they had themselves resold the tin plates at a profit. In my opinion the withdrawal by the defendants on the 8th of October of their offer of the 1st was inoperative; and a complete contract binding on both parties was entered into on the 11th of October, when the plaintiffs accepted the offer of the 1st, which they had no reason to suppose had been withdrawn. Before leaving this part of the case it may be as well to point out the extreme injustice and inconvenience which any other conclusion would produce. If the defendants' contention were to prevail no person who had received an offer by post and had accepted it would know his position until he had waited such a time as to be quite sure that a letter withdrawing the offer had not been posted before his acceptance of it. It appears to me that both legal principles, and practical convenience require that a person who has accepted an offer not known to him to have been revoked, shall be in a position safely to act upon the footing that the offer and acceptance constitute a contract binding on both parties.

Link
See the discussion of the Postal Rule in the next chapter.

Since a revocation is only effective on communication, the revocation in this case came too late because the offer had already been accepted on 11 October. It should be noted that the postal rule (*Adams v Lindsell* 106 ER 250), which will be dealt with in the next chapter, applies only to acceptance.

The position in relation to the revocation of an offer made to all the world, may be different. We do not have an English authority on this point of law, but the case of *Shuey v US* (1875) 92 US, is an American reward case in which the court felt that it was a requirement that the same notoriety must be given to the revocation as to the original offer.

1.5.3.3   Indirect communication of revocation

Dickinson v Dodds (1876) 2 Ch D 463 is authority for the principle that an offer can be revoked by a third party communicating that information to the offeree.

Link
See the facts above.

LORD JUSTICE MELLISH

Then Dickinson is informed by Berry that the property has been sold by Dodds to Allan. Berry does not tell us from whom he heard it, but he says that he did hear it, that he knew it, and that he informed Dickinson of it. Now, stopping there, the question which arises is this—If an offer has been made for the sale of property, and before that offer is accepted, the person who has made the offer enters into a binding agreement to sell the property to somebody else, and the person to whom the offer was first made receives notice in some way that the property has been sold to another person, can he after that make a binding contract by the acceptance of the offer? I am of opinion that he cannot. The law may be right or wrong in saying that a person who has given to another a certain time within which to accept an offer is not bound by his promise to give that time; but, if he is not bound by that promise, and may still sell the property to some one else, and if it be the law that, in order to make a contract, the two minds must be in agreement at some one time, that is, at the time of the acceptance, how is it possible that when the person to whom the offer has been made knows that the person who has made the offer has sold the property to someone else, and that, in fact, he has not remained in the same mind to sell it to him, he can be at liberty to accept the offer and thereby make a binding contract? It seems to me that would be simply absurd. ...

Treitel (Peel, *'The Law of Contract'* 12th Edition) has criticised the rule that communication of revocation need not come from the offeror as follows:

The rule that communication of withdrawal need not come from the offeror can be a regrettable source of uncertainty. It puts on the offeree the possibly difficult task of deciding whether his source of information is reliable... . Certainty would be promoted if the rule were that withdrawal must be communicated by the offeror, as well as to the offeree.

1.5.3.4   Revocation of a unilateral offer

The rule that an offeror can revoke his offer any time before acceptance, is modified in relation to unilateral offers. For a unilateral offer, once the offeree has started to perform the prescribed act, the offeror cannot revoke his offer partway through the offeree's performance (which is, after all, the offeree's acceptance of a unilateral offer). The offeror can, however, revoke his offer any time before performance of the prescribed act has commenced.

Errington v Errington and Woods [1952] 1 KB 290

Panel: Somervell, Denning and Hodson LJJ

Facts: A father purchased a house with the aid of a mortgage. He paid a lump sum upfront and told his son and daughter-in-law that if they continued to pay all the mortgage repayments, he would transfer the house to them on payment of the last instalment. The father then died and his estate was left to his widow in his will. The son and daughter-in-law separated, but the daughter-in-law remained in the house and she continued to make the mortgage payments. The widow brought an action for recovery of the property.

The court held that the daughter-in-law could not be prevented from continuing to perform her acceptance of the father's original unilateral offer and accordingly judgment was entered in her favour.

LORD JUSTICE DENNING

…The parties did not discuss what was to happen if the couple failed to pay the instalments to the building society, but I should have thought it clear that, if they did fail to pay the instalments, the father would not be bound to transfer the house to them. The father's promise was a unilateral contract - a promise of the house in return for their act of paying the instalments. It could not be revoked by him once the couple entered on performance of the act, but it would cease to bind him if they left it incomplete and unperformed, which they have not done. If that was the position during the father's lifetime, so it must be after his death. If the daughter-in-law continues to pay all the building society instalments, the couple will be entitled to have the property transferred to them as soon as the mortgage is paid off; but if she does not do so, then the building society will claim the instalments from the father's estate and the estate will have to pay them. I cannot think that in those circumstances the estate would be bound to transfer the house to them, any more than the father himself would have been.

…

In the present case it is clear that the father expressly promised the couple that the property should belong to them as soon as the mortgage was paid, and impliedly promised that so long as they paid the instalments to the building society they should be allowed to remain in possession. They were not purchasers because they never bound themselves to pay the instalments, but nevertheless they were in a position analogous to purchasers. They have acted on the promise, and neither the father nor his widow, his successor in title, can eject them in disregard of it. ...

Although the unilateral offer would only be accepted on complete performance of the prescribed act i.e. completion of payment of all the mortgage instalments, once the couple had started to pay those instalments, the unilateral offer could not be withdrawn.

Further Reading

Cheshire, Fifoot & Furmston's Law of Contract. Furmston. Oxford University Press. Ch.3

Chitty on Contracts (2008) Sweet & Maxwell. Ch.2

McKendrick, E., *Contract Law* (2017) 12th ed. Palgrave MacMillan. Ch.2 & 3

Peel, E., *The Law of Contract*. Sweet & Maxwell. Treitel. Ch.1 & 2

2

Agreement II (Acceptance)

Topic List

Introduction

In the previous chapter, the essential elements of an offer were examined. In this chapter, the key elements of a valid acceptance will be considered.

2.1 Acceptance Must be in Response to an offer

2.1.1 Acceptance Must be Made by the Offeree

An offer can only be accepted by the offeree, being the person to whom the offer is made.

Boulton v Jones (1857) 2 H & N 564

Panel: Pollock CB, Martin, Bramwell and Channell BB

Facts: The defendant, Jones, had been in the habit of dealing with Brocklehurst, who owned a shop. Brocklehurst sold the shop to the plaintiff, Boulton. On the day of the sale, Boulton received an order for goods from Jones addressed to Brocklehurst. Boulton fulfilled the order and did not give Jones notice that it was he, Boulton, not Brocklehurst who fulfilled the order. Whether Jones was dealing with Brocklehurst was relevant since Jones had a right of set-off against Brocklehurst which he did not have against Boulton.

BRAMWELL B

...If plaintiff were now at liberty to sue defendants, they would be deprived of their right of set-off as against Brocklehurst. When a contract is made, in which the personality of the contracting party is or may be of importance, as a contract with a man to write a book, or the like, or where there might be a set-off, no other person can interpose and adopt the contract. As to the difficulty that defendants need not pay anybody, I do not see why they should, unless they have made a contract either express or implied. I decide the case on the ground that defendants did not know that plaintiff was the person who supplied the goods, and that allowing plaintiff to treat the contract as made with him would be a prejudice to the defendants.

The court held that Boulton could not succeed in a claim for the price of the goods. The offer from Jones was made to Brocklehurst and it was not open to Boulton to accept it.

2.1.2 Acceptance in Ignorance of an Offer

An acceptance cannot be made in ignorance of the offer, but the motive for the acceptance is not important.

Williams v Carwardine (1833) 5 C & P 566

Panel: Parke J

Facts: The defendant had published a handbill which offered a reward of £20 for information which led to the conviction of the person responsible for the robbery and murder of a William Carwardine. The plaintiff knew about the reward but, since she feared that she was going to die, she gave the information in the hope of forgiveness. Her statement under oath explained 'that, in consequence of her miserable and unhappy situation, and believing that she has not long to live, she makes this voluntary statement to ease her conscience, and in hopes of forgiveness hereafter'. Following her statement, the murderers were convicted. Counsel for the defendant argued her motive was not the reward and therefore she could not claim it.

> **MR JUSTICE PARKE**
>
> If the plaintiff comes within the conditions of the handbill, I think she is entitled to the reward. The jury will probably find that the £20 was not the motive. We may, I think, assume that it was not. The motive was the state of her own feelings. My opinion is, that the motive is not material; and that, if she comes within the terms of the handbill, that is sufficient.

Mr Justice Parke was clear that the motive for acceptance is not relevant. In this case, it was not disputed that the plaintiff knew of the offer; the issue was whether that was her motivation. The court held that motivation is not relevant when accepting an offer and accordingly the plaintiff was entitled to the reward.

The operation of this rule can have undesirable consequences. A person who is acting as a good citizen by providing information, but is not aware of the offer of a reward, will not be able to claim it. Conversely, someone who is motivated solely by financial gain because they know of the reward, will be entitled to claim it.

2.2   Acceptance Must be Unqualified

A valid acceptance must be an unqualified acceptance of all the terms of the offer (*Hyde v Wrench* (1840) 3 Beav 334). As you will see an acceptance must be a 'mirror image' of the offer. If any of the terms of the offer are changed in the purported acceptance, this will not constitute a valid acceptance. Mr Wrench offered to sell for £1,000 and in response, Mr Hyde said that he would pay £950. This was not a valid acceptance since it did not mirror the terms of the offer.

Link
For a fuller discussion of this case, please see the section relating to counter-offers in the previous chapter.

2.3   Prescribed Mode of Acceptance

The next issue to be considered is whether it is possible to prescribe a mode of acceptance.

Manchester Diocesan Council for Education v Commercial and General Investments [1970] 1 WLR 241

Panel: Buckley J

Facts: The plaintiff owned a freehold property and invited tenders from potential purchasers. Condition 4 of the request for tenders stated 'The person whose tender is accepted shall be the purchaser and shall be informed of the acceptance of his tender by letter sent to him by post addressed to the address given in the tender...'. The defendant completed and submitted the tender form (which constituted an offer by the defendant) on 25 August 1964 and provided 15 Berkeley Street as the address. On 15 September, the plaintiff's surveyor wrote to the defendant's surveyor (not using the Berkeley Street address of the defendant) stating that the defendant's offer had been accepted. On 7 January 1965, the plaintiff's solicitor wrote to the defendant at the appropriate address (in accordance with Condition 4) giving the defendant formal notice that its tender had been accepted. The defendant argued that its offer had lapsed by the time the letter was sent to the Berkeley Street address on 7 January. The issue for the court was whether the letter to the defendant's surveyor on 15 September constituted an effective acceptance, or whether it was only the later letter (which conformed to Condition 4) which would constitute such acceptance.

MR JUSTICE BUCKLEY

...There can be no doubt that in the present case, if the plaintiff or its authorised agent had posted a letter addressed to the defendant at 15 Berkeley Street on or about 15 September informing the defendant of the acceptance of its tender, the contract would have been complete at the moment when such letter was posted, but that of course was not taken. Condition 4, however, does not say that that shall be the sole permitted method of communicating an acceptance. It may be that an offeror, who by the terms of his offer insists on acceptance in a particular manner, is entitled to insist that he is not bound unless acceptance is effected or communicated in that precise way, although it seems probable that, even so, if the other party communicates his acceptance in some other way, the offeror may by conduct or otherwise waive his right to insist on the prescribed method of acceptance. Where, however, the offeror has prescribed a particular method of acceptance, but not in terms insisting that only acceptance in that mode shall be binding, I am of opinion that acceptance communicated to the offeror by any other mode which is no less advantageous to him will conclude the contract. Thus in *Tinn v Hoffman & Co* ((1873), 29 LT 271), where acceptance was requested by return of post, Honeyman J said at p 274:

'That does not mean exclusively a reply by letter by return of post, but you may reply by telegram or by verbal message, or by any means not later than a letter written and sent by return of post ...'

If an offeror intends that he shall be bound only if his offer is accepted in some particular manner, it must be for him to make this clear. Condition 4 in the present case had not, in my judgment, this effect.

...[Condition 4] should not, I think, be regarded as a condition or stipulation imposed by the defendant as offeror on the plaintiff as offeree, but as a term introduced into the bargain by the plaintiff and presumably considered by the plaintiff as being in some way for the protection or benefit of the plaintiff. It would consequently be a term strict compliance with which the plaintiff could waive, provided the defendant was not adversely affected. The plaintiff did not take advantage of the condition which would have resulted in a contract being formed as soon as a letter of acceptance complying with the condition was posted, but adopted another course, which could only result in a contract when the plaintiff's acceptance was actually communicated to the defendant.

For these reasons, I have reached the conclusion that in accordance with the terms of the tender it was open to the plaintiff to conclude a contract by acceptance actually communicated to the defendant in any way; and, in my judgment, the letter of 15 September constituted such an acceptance.

It is possible for an offeror to prescribe a mode of acceptance, but, Buckley J makes it clear that if he wants this mode to be mandatory (ie the only permitted mode of accepting his offer), he must explicitly rule out all other methods. If the offeror does not expressly exclude the use of other modes of acceptance, any method of acceptance which is no less advantageous to the offeror will be a permitted mode of acceptance.

If the prescribed mode of acceptance has been introduced by the offeree, it is open to the offeree to waive the prescribed mode provided this does not prejudice the offeror. In this case, since Condition 4 had been introduced by the plaintiff (offeree) it was open to the plaintiff to comply with that condition, or to waive it, provided there was no prejudice to the defendant (offeror). Consequently, the plaintiff had accepted the offer on 15 September, but by a means other than that specified in Condition 4.

2.4   Acceptance Must be Communicated

2.4.1   Silence Cannot Constitute Acceptance

The general rule is that acceptance must be communicated. Silence cannot amount to acceptance as the case of *Paul Felthouse v Bindley* (1862) 11 CBR (NS) 869 demonstrates.

Paul Felthouse v Bindley (1862) 11 CBR (NS) 869

Panel: Byles, Willes and Keating JJ

Facts: An uncle and his nephew had discussed the sale of the nephew's horse to the uncle. The uncle wrote to his nephew stating: 'If I hear no more about him, I consider the horse is mine at 30l. 15s.' The nephew did not reply. Six weeks later, there was a sale of some farming stock from the nephew's farm and the auctioneer running the sale sold the horse in question. The nephew had instructed the auctioneer not to sell it as it was already sold. The uncle brought an action for conversion against the auctioneer.

Decipher
Conversion is an action in tort.

Alert

MR JUSTICE WILLES

...The uncle had no right to impose upon the nephew a sale of his horse for 30l. 15s. Unless he chose to comply with the condition of writing to repudiate the offer. The nephew might, no doubt, have bound his uncle to the bargain by writing to him: the uncle might also have retracted his offer at any time before acceptance. It stood an open offer: and so things remained until [the day of the auction], when the nephew was about to sell his farming stock by auction. The horse in question being catalogued with the rest of the stock, the auctioneer (the defendant) was told that it was already sold. It is clear, therefore, that the nephew in his own mind intended his uncle to have the horse at the price which he (the uncle) had named,—30l. 15s.: but he had not communicated such his intention to his uncle, or done anything to bind himself. Nothing, therefore, had been done to vest the property in the horse in the plaintiff down to the [the day of the auction], when the horse was sold by the defendant. It appears to me that ... there had been no bargain to pass the property in the horse to the plaintiff, and therefore that he had no right to complain of the sale. ...

Mr Justice Willes is very clear that, as a matter of law, the offeror cannot make an offer and within that offer impose a positive obligation on the offeree to reject that offer. Consequently, since the nephew had not communicated an acceptance of his uncle's offer, there could be no valid acceptance.

2.4.2   Third Party Communication of Acceptance

A third party can validly accept an offer on behalf of the offeree, provided that he is authorised by the offeree to do so, and the acceptance indicates an intention to be irrevocably bound.

In the case of *Powell v Lee* (1908) 99 LT 284, the third party did not have the offeree's authority to accept. The plaintiff, Powell, offered to take up the position of headmaster in a school. The managers of the school considered his offer and they resolved to appoint him as headmaster. The committee of managers did not communicate this to the plaintiff. One of the committee, however, did tell the plaintiff that he was to be appointed. The managers later reversed their decision and the plaintiff brought an action for breach of contract.

It was held that no contract had been formed. The committee member who communicated acceptance of the plaintiff's offer (to take up the post of headmaster) was not authorised by the offeree (the committee of managers); consequently, his communication could not constitute acceptance by a third party.

2.5 Exceptions to the General Rule that Acceptance Must be Communicated

There are three key exceptions to the general rule that acceptance must be communicated. The first is acceptance of a unilateral offer and the second is the postal rule. The third exception relates specifically to acceptances sent by instantaneous methods of communication. If an acceptance, sent via an instantaneous method, is not received due to the offeror's fault, he will be estopped from denying receipt (*Entores v Miles Far East Corporation* [1955] 2 QB 327). This third exception is considered later in the chapter.

2.6 Unilateral Contracts

You will remember from the previous chapter that a unilateral offer is an offer which prescribes an act which, when performed, will constitute acceptance. Since acceptance of a unilateral offer is the performance of the act itself, the offeree does not have to communicate that he is going to perform the act. In *Carlill v Carbolic Smoke Ball Co* [1893] 1 QB 256, the defendant raised the argument that the offeree must communicate his intention to perform the prescribed act (ie the intention to accept the offer). It was held that the offeree does not need to communicate this intention. Simply using the smoke ball as prescribed and catching influenza was sufficient to accept the offer.

 **Link**
See Chapter 1 for a fuller discussion of *Carlill v Carbolic Smoke Ball Co.*

LORD JUSTICE BOWEN

...If the person making the offer, expressly or impliedly intimates in his offer that it will be sufficient to act on the proposal without communicating acceptance of it to himself, performance of the condition is a sufficient acceptance without notification.

...

Now, if that is the law, how are we to find out whether the person who makes the offer does intimate that notification of acceptance will not be necessary in order to constitute a binding bargain? In many cases you look to the offer itself. In many cases you extract from the character of the transaction that notification is not required, and in the advertisement cases it seems to me to follow as an inference to be drawn from the transaction itself that a person is not to notify his acceptance of the offer before he performs the condition, but that if he performs the condition notification is dispensed with. It seems to me that from the point of view of common sense no other idea could be entertained. If I advertise to the world that my dog is lost, and that anybody

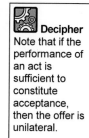 **Decipher**
Note that if the performance of an act is sufficient to constitute acceptance, then the offer is unilateral.

who brings the dog to a particular place will be paid some money, are all the police or other persons whose business it is to find lost dogs to be expected to sit down and write me a note saying that they have accepted my proposal? Why, of course, they at once look after the dog, and as soon as they find the dog they have performed the condition. The essence of the transaction is that the dog should be found, and it is not necessary under such circumstances, as it seems to me, that in order to make the contract binding there should be any notification of acceptance. It follows from the nature of the thing that the performance of the condition is sufficient acceptance without the notification of it, and a person who makes an offer in an advertisement of that kind makes an offer which must be read by the light of that common sense reflection. He does, therefore, in his offer impliedly indicate that he does not require notification of the acceptance of the offer.

2.7 The Postal Rule

The rule established in *Adams and Others v Lindsell and Another* (1818) 106 ER 250 is known as the postal rule. This is an exception to the rule that acceptance must be communicated. The rule provides that, where post is deemed to be the proper method of acceptance, acceptance is deemed to take effect from the moment of proper posting.

Adams and Others v Lindsell and Another (1818) 106 ER 250

Facts: On 2 September 1817, the defendants wrote to the plaintiffs offering to sell them a quantity of 'good fair quality … country wool' at a stated price. The letter was only received by the plaintiffs on 5 September since the defendants had misaddressed it. The plaintiffs posted their acceptance that evening. The acceptance was received by the defendants on 9 September. However, on 8 September, the defendants had sold the wool to a third party. The court held that the acceptance of 5 September was effective from the time of proper posting; consequently, there was a binding contract between the plaintiffs and the defendants.

The court reasoned that, if a posted acceptance needs to be received before it is effective, how would the offeree know when their acceptance had been received? Would it then be necessary for the offeror to confirm receipt of the acceptance? There is a risk that confirmations would be required ad infinitum. Such a state of affairs would make the conclusion of a contract by post impossible. The court felt that the postal rule for acceptance, addressed this difficulty.

It should be noted that the postal rule applies to acceptance only; it does not apply to the revocation of an offer (*Byrne & Co v Leon Van Tienhoven & Co* (1880) 5 CPD 344). A revocation is only effective when it is actually communicated.

Link
See Chapter 1 for a fuller discussion of this case.

2.7.1 The Postal Rule Operates even when the Acceptance is Lost or Destroyed

The postal rule will still operate when letters are delayed or, indeed, never arrive at their destination, as was the case in *Household Fire and Carriage Accident Insurance Company (Limited) v Grant* (1879) 4 Ex D 216.

Household Fire and Carriage Accident Insurance Company (Limited) v Grant (1879) 4 Ex D 216

Panel: Thesiger, Baggallay and Bramwell LJJ

Facts: The defendant applied for 100 shares to be allotted to him in the plaintiffs' company on 30 September 1874. On 25 October 1874, the plaintiffs allotted 100 shares to the defendant and wrote to him, enclosing a letter of allotment. The letter never reached the defendant. The company went into liquidation, and the official liquidator applied to the defendant for the sum owing on the shares. The defendant argued that there was no contract since the plaintiffs' acceptance letter had never reached him.

LORD JUSTICE THESIGER

[Lord Justice Thesiger referred to Lord Cottenham's judgment in the case of *Dunlop v Higgins* 1 HLC 381 and then continued:] …In short, Lord Cottenham appears to have held that, as a rule, a contract formed by correspondence through the post is complete as soon as the letter accepting an offer is put into the post, and is not put an end to in the event of the letter never being delivered. …I see no better mode [of explaining the postal rule] than that of treating the post office as the agent of both parties … . Alderson, B. … in *Stocken v. Collin* 7 M. & W. at p. 516 … Lord Cottenham says: 'If the doctrine that the post office is only the agent for the delivery of the notice were correct no one could safely avail himself of that mode of transmission.' But if the post office be such common agent, then it seems to me to follow that, as soon as the letter of acceptance is delivered to the post office, the contract is made as complete and final and absolutely binding as if the acceptor had put his letter into the hands of a messenger sent by the offerer himself as his agent to deliver the offer and receive the acceptance.

The acceptance of the defendant's offer to purchase shares was valid from the time of proper posting, despite never reaching the defendant. This rule can, therefore, have harsh consequences. The offeror does not know that the offeree has accepted but is nevertheless bound by that acceptance even though it is lost or destroyed. Lord Justice Bramwell delivered a strong dissenting judgment.

LORD JUSTICE BRAMWELL (dissenting)

…That because a man, who may send a communication by post or otherwise, sends it by post, he should bind the person addressed, though the communication never reaches him, while he would not so bind him if he had sent it by hand, is impossible. There is no reason in it; it is simply arbitrary. I ask whether any one who thinks so is prepared to follow that opinion to its consequence; suppose the offer is to sell a particular chattel, and the letter accepting it never arrives, is the property in the chattel transferred? Suppose it is to sell an estate or grant a lease, is the bargain completed? The lease might be such as not to require a deed, could a subsequent lessee be ejected by the would-be acceptor of the offer because he had posted a letter? Suppose an article is advertised at so much, and that it would be sent on receipt of a post office order. Is it enough to post the letter? If the word 'receipt' is relied on, is it really meant that that makes a difference? If it should be said let the offerer wait, the answer is, may be he may lose his market meanwhile. Besides, his offer may be by advertisement to all mankind. Suppose a reward for information, information posted does not reach, some one else gives it and is paid, is the offerer liable to the first man?

It is said that a contrary rule would be hard on the would-be acceptor, who may have made his arrangements on the footing that the bargain was concluded. But to hold as contended would be equally hard on the offerer, who may have made his arrangements on the footing that his offer was not accepted; his non-receipt of any communication may be attributable to the person to whom it was made being absent. What is he to do but to act on the negative, that no communication has been made to him? Further, the use of the post office is no more authorized by the offerer than the sending an answer by hand, and all these hardships would befall the person posting the letter if he sent it by hand. Doubtless in that case he would be the person to suffer if the letter did not reach its destination. Why should his sending it by post relieve him of the loss and cast it on the other party. It was said, if he sends it by hand it is revocable, but not if he sends it by post, which makes the difference. But it is revocable when sent by post, not that the letter can be got back, but its arrival might be anticipated by a letter by hand or telegram, and there is no case to shew that such anticipation would not prevent the letter from binding. It would be a most alarming thing to say that it would. That a letter honestly but mistakenly written and posted must bind the writer if hours before its arrival he informed the person addressed that it was coming, but was wrong and recalled; suppose a false but honest character given, and the mistake found out after the letter posted, and notice that it was wrong given to the person addressed. ...

Mischief may arise if my opinion prevails. It probably will not, as so much has been said on the matter that principle is lost sight of. I believe equal if not greater, will, if it does not prevail. I believe the latter will be obviated only by the rule being made nugatory by every prudent man saying, 'your answer by post is only to bind if it reaches me.' ...

Link
See the discussion of ousting the Postal Rule below.

Notwithstanding the potential for injustice for the offeror in the operation of the postal rule, as outlined by Bramwell LJ in his dissent, the postal rule was approved and applied by the majority in this case.

2.7.2 The Postal Rule Only Operates when it is Reasonable to Accept by Post

The postal rule will only apply when it is reasonable to use the post, having regard to all the circumstances of the case. In *Henthorn v Fraser* [1892] 2 Ch 27, Lord Herschell held that, where the use of the post to accept the offer is within the contemplation of the parties, the postal rule will operate.

Henthorn v Fraser **[1892] 2 Ch 27**

Panel: Lord Herschell, Lindley and Kay LJJ

Facts: On 7 July 1891, the plaintiff, who lived in Birkenhead, attended an office of the Land Society in Liverpool in order to negotiate house purchases. The secretary of the society signed a note which constituted an option to buy properties. The following day, the secretary posted a revocation of the option between 12pm and 1pm, which reached Birkenhead at 5pm. At 3.50pm, the plaintiff had posted an acceptance which was delivered that evening, and received at the offices of the Land Society when they opened the following morning. The issue in the case was whether the postal rule applied on the facts.

LORD HERSCHELL

…The question therefore arises in what circumstances the acceptance of an offer is to be regarded as complete as soon as it is posted. In the case of the *Household Fire and Carriage Accident Insurance Company v. Grant* 4 Ex. D. 216., Lord Justice Baggallay said at page 227: 'I think that the principle established in *Dunlop v Higgins* [ie the postal rule] is limited in its application to cases in which by reason of general usage, or of the relations between the parties to any particular transactions, or of the terms in which the offer is made, the acceptance of such offer by a letter through the post is expressly or impliedly authorized.' …Applying the law thus laid down by the Court of Appeal, I think in the present case an authority to accept by post must be implied. Although the Plaintiff received the offer at the Defendants' office in Liverpool, he resided in another town, and it must have been in contemplation that he would take the offer, which by its terms was to remain open for some days, with him to his place of residence, and those who made the offer must have known that it would be according to the ordinary usages of mankind that if he accepted it he should communicate his acceptance by means of the post. I am not sure that I should myself have regarded the doctrine that an acceptance is complete as soon as the letter containing it is posted as resting upon an implied authority by the person making the offer to the person receiving it to accept by those means. It strikes me as somewhat artificial to speak of the person to whom the offer is made as having the implied authority of the other party to send his acceptance by post. He needs no authority to transmit the acceptance through any particular channel; he may select what means he pleases, the Post Office no less than any other. The only effect of the supposed authority is to make the acceptance complete so soon as it is posted, and authority will obviously be implied only when the tribunal considers that it is a case in which this result ought to be reached. I should prefer to state the rule thus: Where the circumstances are such that it must have been within the contemplation of the parties that, according to the ordinary usages of mankind, the post might be used as a means of communicating the acceptance of an offer, the acceptance is complete as soon as it is posted. It matters not in which way the proposition be stated, the present case is in either view within it.

Since the plaintiff resided in a different town from the defendants, it would have been in the contemplation of the parties that the post would be used. Consequently, the postal rule applied and the plaintiff's acceptance was valid from the moment of posting. By contrast, in *Quenerduaine v Cole* (1883) 32 WR 185, the fact that the counter-offer was sent by telegraph implied a condition that prompt acceptance was required and accordingly the postal rule did not apply.

The postal rule will not operate where it will result in 'manifest inconvenience and absurdity' as the judgment of Lawton LJ demonstrated in *Holwell Securities Ltd v Hughes* [1974] 1 WLR 155.

Holwell Securities Ltd v Hughes [1974] 1 WLR 155

Panel: Russell, Buckley and Lawton LJJ

Facts: The defendant granted the plaintiff an option to buy a property. The terms for exercising the option were that it was '…exercisable by notice in writing to the [defendant] at any time within six months from the date hereof…'. The plaintiff wrote to the defendant exercising the option but the letter never reached the defendant.

Lord Justice Lawton referred to examples of cases where the application of the postal rule would lead to manifest inconvenience and absurdity, which were originally cited by Bramwell B in *British & American Telegraph C v Colson* (1871) LR 6 Exch 108:

LORD JUSTICE LAWTON

…Is a stockbroker who is holding shares to the orders of his client liable in damages because he did not sell in a falling market in accordance with the instructions in a letter which was posted but never received? Before the passing of the Law Reform (Miscellaneous Provisions) Act 1970 (which abolished actions for breach of promise of marriage), would a young soldier ordered overseas have been bound in contract to marry a girl to whom he had proposed by letter, asking her to let him have an answer before he left and she had replied affirmatively in good time but the letter had never reached him? In my judgment, the factors of inconvenience and absurdity are but illustrations of a wider principle, namely, that the rule does not apply if, having regard to all the circumstances, including the nature of the subject-matter under consideration, the negotiating parties cannot have intended that there should be a binding agreement until the party accepting an offer or exercising an option had in fact communicated the acceptance or exercise to the other. ...

2.7.3 Ousting the Postal Rule

The harsh effects of the postal rule may be avoided where the offeror ousts the postal rule. In other words, the postal rule will not apply if the offeror specifies that the acceptance will only be binding when it reaches him. In *Holwell Securities Ltd v Hughes* [1974] 1 WLR 155 the question for the court was whether the words 'by notice in writing' would oust the postal rule.

 **Link**
For the facts of this case, please see the discussion in the previous section.

LORD JUSTICE LAWTON

Does the rule apply in all cases where one party makes an offer which both he and the person with whom he was dealing must have expected the post to be used as a means of accepting it? In my judgment, it does not. First, [the postal rule] does not apply when the express terms of the offer specify that the acceptance must reach the offeror. ...

LORD JUSTICE RUSSELL

...In any case, before one can find that the basic principle of the need for communication of acceptance to the offeror is displaced by this artificial concept of communication by the act of posting, it is necessary that the offer is in its terms consistent with such displacement and not one which by its terms points rather in the direction of actual communication. ...

The relevant language here is, 'The said option shall be exercised by notice in writing to the intending vendor ...,' a very common phrase in an option agreement. There is, of course, nothing in that phrase to suggest that the notification to the defendant could not be made by post. But the requirement of 'notice ... to,' in my judgment, is language which should be taken expressly to assert the ordinary situation in law that acceptance requires to be communicated or notified to the offeror, and is inconsistent with the theory that acceptance can be constituted by the act of posting... .

The language used in each case must be considered to establish whether it expressly or impliedly requires that acceptance is actually communicated to the offeror, thereby ousting the postal rule, and accordingly avoiding its application. 'By notice in writing' was held to be sufficient to oust the postal rule. Since the letter of acceptance never reached the defendant, no contract was formed.

In, *Household Fire and Carriage Accident Insurance v Grant* (1879) 4 Ex D 216, Bramwell LJ suggested that the postal rule could be ousted by the words: 'your answer by post is only to bind if it reaches me'.

2.8 Instantaneous Communications

2.8.1 Acceptance by Instantaneous Communication

The rules that apply to acceptance by instantaneous methods of communication can be seen as a development of the rule that acceptance must be communicated (*Felthouse v Bindley*). The general rule for communication of acceptance by an instantaneous method is that actual communication is required.

Entores v Miles Far East Corporation [1955] 2 QB 327

Panel: Denning, Birkett and Parker LJJ

Facts: The plaintiff was based in London. During a series of negotiations by telex, the plaintiff made a counter-offer which was accepted by telex by the defendant's agents, based in Holland. The plaintiff alleged breach of contract and brought an action for leave to serve a writ outside the jurisdiction. The English courts only had authority to grant such leave if the contract was formed in England thereby giving the English courts jurisdiction. The crucial issue in the case was where the contract was formed: was it formed in Holland, from where the acceptance telex was sent, or was it formed in London, where the acceptance telex was received? The latter was held to be correct.

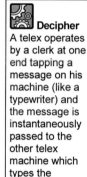

Decipher
A telex operates by a clerk at one end tapping a message on his machine (like a typewriter) and the message is instantaneously passed to the other telex machine which types the message onto paper at the receiving end.

LORD JUSTICE DENNING

...The offer was sent by Telex from England offering to pay £239 10s. a ton for 100 tons, and accepted by Telex from Holland. The question for our determination is where was the contract made?

When a contract is made by post it is clear law throughout the common law countries that the acceptance is complete as soon as the letter is put into the post box, and that is the place where the contract is made. But there is no clear rule about contracts made by telephone or by Telex. Communications by these means are virtually instantaneous and stand on a different footing. ...The problem can only be solved by going in stages. Let me first consider a case where two people make a contract by word of mouth in the presence of one another. Suppose, for instance, that I shout an offer to a man across a river or a courtyard but I do not hear his reply because it is drowned by an aircraft flying overhead. There is no contract at that moment. If he wishes to make a contract, he must wait till the aircraft is gone and then shout back his acceptance so that I can hear what he says. Not until I have his answer am I bound. ...Now take a case where two people make a contract by telephone. Suppose, for instance, that I make an offer to a man by telephone and, in the middle of his reply, the line goes 'dead' so that I do not hear his words of acceptance. There is no contract at that moment. The other man may not know the precise moment when the line failed. But he will know that the telephone conversation was abruptly broken off: because people usually say something to signify the end of the conversation. If he wishes to make a contract, he must therefore get through again so as to make sure that I heard. Suppose next, that the line does not go dead, but it is nevertheless so indistinct that I do not catch what he says and I ask him to repeat it. He then repeats it and I hear his acceptance. The contract is made, not on the first time when I do not hear, but only the second time when I do hear. If he does not repeat it, there is no contract. The contract is only complete when I have his answer accepting the offer.

Lastly, take the Telex. Suppose a clerk in a London office taps out on the teleprinter an offer which is immediately recorded on a teleprinter in a Manchester office, and a clerk at that end taps out an acceptance. If the line goes dead in the middle of the sentence of acceptance, the teleprinter motor will stop. There is then obviously no contract. The clerk at Manchester must get through again and send his complete sentence. But it may happen that the line does not go dead, yet the message does not get through to London. Thus the clerk at Manchester may tap out his message of acceptance and it will not be recorded in London because the ink at the London end fails, or something of that kind. In that case, the Manchester clerk will not know of the failure but the London clerk will know of it and will immediately send back a message 'not receiving.' Then, when the fault is rectified, the Manchester clerk will repeat his message. Only then is there a contract. If he does not repeat it, there is no contract. It is not until his message is received that the contract is complete.

In all the instances I have taken so far, the man who sends the message of acceptance knows that it has not been received or he has reason to know it. So he must repeat it. But, suppose that he does not know that his message did not get home. He thinks it has. This may happen if the listener on the telephone does not catch the words of acceptance, but nevertheless does not trouble to ask for them to be repeated: or the ink on the teleprinter fails at the receiving end, but the clerk does not ask for the message to be repeated: so that the man who sends an acceptance reasonably believes that his message has been received. The offeror in such circumstances is clearly bound, because he will be estopped from saying that he did not receive the message of acceptance. It is his own fault that he did not get it. But if there should be a case where the offeror without any fault on his part does not receive the message of acceptance - yet the sender of it reasonably believes it has got home when it has not - then I think there is no contract.

My conclusion is, that the rule about instantaneous communications between the parties is different from the rule about the post. The contract is only complete when the acceptance is received by the offeror: and the contract is made at the place where the acceptance is received.

…

 Decipher Estoppel is a principle in English law which operates to stop (or 'estop') a party from reneging on a statement they have made, or an action they have performed, where to do so would be unjust or inequitable.

Applying the principles which I have stated, I think that the contract in this case was made in London where the acceptance was received. It was, therefore, a proper case for service out of the jurisdiction.

In *Entores*, Denning LJ established that for instantaneous communications:

1.   The general rule is that acceptance must be communicated in order to be effective.

2.   If the acceptance is not communicated through the fault of the offeree, there will be no contract.

3.   If the acceptance is not communicated through the fault of the offeror, he will be estopped from denying that the acceptance was received and there will be a contract.

4.   If the acceptance is not communicated and there is no fault on the part of either party, there will be no contract.

In *Brinkibon Ltd v Stahag Stahl und Stahlwarenhandels-Gesellschaft m.b.H* [1983] 2 AC 34, the House of Lords considered whether there is one rule to fit all instantaneous acceptances in all circumstances. Like *Entores*, the issue in this case was as to whether the English courts had jurisdiction; this depended on whether the contract was made in England.

Brinkibon Ltd v Stahag Stahl und Stahlwarenhandels-Gesellschaft m.b.H [1983] 2 AC 34

Panel: Lord Russell of Killowen, Lord Bridge of Harwich, Lord Brandon of Oakbrook, Lord Wilberforce and Lord Fraser of Tullybelton

Facts: The plaintiff was an English company and the defendant was Austrian. The acceptance was sent by telex from London to Vienna. The question for the court was whether this contract was made in London or Vienna.

LORD WILBERFORCE

...In Entores Ltd. v. Miles Far East Corporation [1955] 2 Q.B. 327 the Court of Appeal classified [telexes] with instantaneous communications. Their ruling, which has passed into the textbooks, including Williston on Contracts, 3rd ed. (1957), appears not to have caused either adverse comment, or any difficulty to business men. I would accept it as a general rule. Where the condition of simultaneity is met, and where it appears to be within the mutual intention of the parties that contractual exchanges should take place in this way, I think it a sound rule, but not necessarily a universal rule.

Since 1955 the use of telex communication has been greatly expanded, and there are many variants on it. The senders and recipients may not be the principals to the contemplated contract. They may be servants or agents with limited authority. The message may not reach, or be intended to reach, the designated recipient immediately: messages may be sent out of office hours, or at night, with the intention, or upon the assumption, that they will be read at a later time. There may be some error or default at the recipient's end which prevents receipt at the time contemplated and believed in by the sender. The message may have been sent and/or received through machines operated by third persons. And many other variations may occur. No universal rule can cover all such cases: they must be resolved by reference to the intentions of the parties, by sound business practice and in some cases by a judgment where the risks should lie… .

The present case is, as Entores Ltd. v. Miles Far East Corporation [1955] 2 QB 327 itself, the simple case of instantaneous communication between principals, and, in accordance with the general rule, involves that the contract (if any) was made when and where the acceptance was received.

LORD FRASER OF TULLYBELTON

…The posting rule is based on considerations of practical convenience, arising from the delay that is inevitable in delivering a letter. But it has been extended to apply to telegrams sent through the post office, and in strict logic there is much to be said for applying it also to telex messages sent by one business firm directly to another. There is very little, if any, difference in the mechanics of transmission between a private telex from one business office to another, and a telegram sent through the post office - especially one sent from one large city to another. Even the element of delay will not be greatly different in the typical case where the operator of the recipient's telex is a clerk with no authority to conclude contracts, who has to hand it to his principal. In such a case a telex message is not in fact received instantaneously by the responsible principal. I assume that the present case is a case of that sort.

Nevertheless I have reached the opinion that, on balance, an acceptance sent by telex directly from the acceptor's office to the offeror's office should be treated as if it were an instantaneous communication between principals, like a telephone conversation. One reason is that the decision to that effect in Entores v. Miles Far East Corporation [1955] 2 Q.B. 327 seems to have worked without leading to serious difficulty or complaint from the business community. Secondly, once the message has been received on the offeror's telex machine, it is not unreasonable to treat it as delivered to the principal offeror, because it is his responsibility to arrange for prompt handling of messages within his own office. Thirdly, a party (the acceptor) who tries to send a message by telex can generally tell if his message has not been received on the other party's (the offeror's) machine, whereas the offeror, of course, will not know if an unsuccessful attempt has been made to send an acceptance to him. It is therefore convenient that the acceptor, being in the better position, should have the responsibility of ensuring that his message is received. For these reasons I think it is right that in the ordinary simple case, such as I take this to be, the general rule and not the postal rule should apply. But I agree with both my noble and learned friends that the general rule will not cover all the many variations that may occur with telex messages.

Lord Wilberforce reiterated the rule in *Entores* to explain that telexes can be treated as instantaneous communications, and the acceptance accordingly took place at the time and in the place of receipt of the telex ie Vienna. However, he was careful to state that there is not a universal rule which can be applied in all circumstances.

One difficulty in relation to instantaneous communications, is that they are not always read immediately upon receipt. The courts have, therefore, developed rules which apply to communications sent within office hours and those which are sent outside of office hours.

2.8.2   Instantanous Communications sent within Office Hours

Tenax Steamship Co. Ltd. v The Brimnes (Owners) (The Brimnes) [1975] QB 929 involved a telex sent inside office hours. The case, in fact, involved a withdrawal notice sent within office hours, but the principle it establishes would be equally applicable to acceptances sent within office hours.

Tenax Steamship Co. Ltd. v The Brimnes (Owners) (The Brimnes) [1975] QB 929

Panel: Edmund Davies, Megaw and Cairns LJJ

Facts: The charterers hired a ship from the owners. The owners of the ship sent a withdrawal notice to the charterers by telex. It was found by the court that the notice arrived at the charterers' office at 17.45 B.S.T. The evidence from the charterers was that their offices were staffed until 18.30. The court had to consider when the withdrawal notice was actually effective. Timing of the withdrawal notice was important because it affected whether the owners had successfully withdrawn from the charterparty or whether they were too late.

Decipher
A notice sent on behalf of the ship owner to indicate that they want to withdraw the use of their ship from the charterers (ie the hirers).

LORD JUSTICE EDMUND DAVIES

Brandon J. [at first instance] held here that the notice of withdrawal was sent during ordinary business hours, and that he was driven to the conclusion either that the charterers' staff had left the office on April 2 'well before the end of ordinary business hours' or that, if they were indeed there, they 'neglected to pay attention to the Telex machine in the way which they claimed it was their ordinary practice to do' [1973] 1 W.L.R. 386, 406. He therefore concluded that the withdrawal Telex must be regarded as having been 'received,' as required by *Empresa Cubana de Fletes v. Lagonisi Shipping Co. Ltd.* [1971] 1 Q.B. 488, at 17.45 hours B.S.T. on April 2 and that the withdrawal was effected at that time. I propose to say no more than that I respectfully agree with that conclusion... .

LORD JUSTICE MEGAW

...I think that the principle which is relevant is this: if a notice arrives at the address of the person to be notified, at such a time and by such a means of communication that it would in the normal course of business come to the attention of that person on its arrival, that person cannot rely on some failure of himself or his servants to act in a normal businesslike manner in respect of taking cognisance of the communication so as to postpone the effective time of the notice until some later time when it in fact came to his attention.

Since the withdrawal notice was sent within office hours, it was effective at 17:45. It would be reasonable to expect a business to check their telex machines during their office hours. It was the recipients who were at fault for not checking messages during working hours and, consequently, they were estopped from denying receipt. In this case, the recipients accepted that their offices were staffed until 18:30. What constitutes 'office hours' will need to be considered on the facts of each case.

2.8.3   Instantaneous Communications Sent Outside of Office Hours

The case of *Mondial Shipping and Chartering BV v Astarte Shipping Ltd* [1995] 2 Lloyd's Rep 249 addressed the issue of when an instantaneous communication will be deemed received when it is sent outside of office hours.

Mondial Shipping and Chartering BV v Astarte Shipping Ltd [1995] 2 Lloyd's Rep 249

Panel: Gatehouse J

Facts: A withdrawal notice was sent by telex from the ship owners to the charterers. The telex arrived instantaneously on transmission at 23.41 on Friday night. The question for the court was when it would be deemed received. For reasons which are not relevant for our purposes, the charterers argued that the acceptance should be deemed received at 23.41 on Friday night and the owners argued that it should be deemed received first thing the next working day.

MR JUSTICE GATEHOUSE

What matters is not when the notice is given/sent/despatched/issued by the owners but when its content reaches the mind of the charterer. If the telex is sent in ordinary business hours, the time of receipt is the same as the time of despatch because it is not open to the charterer to contend that it did not in fact then come to his attention (see *The Brimnes* per Mr. Justice Brandon [1972] 2 Lloyd's Rep. 465 at p. 480; [1973] 1 W.L.R. 386 at p. 406, and per the Court of Appeal [1974] 2 Lloyd's Rep. 241; [1975] Q.B. 929).

The problem has, of course, been referred to. See the well-known passage in the speech of Lord Wilberforce in *Brinkibon Ltd. v. Stahag und Stahlwarenhandelsgesellschaft m.b.H.*, [1982] 1 Lloyd's Rep. 217 at p. 220; [1983] 2 A.C. 34 at p. 42, a case concerned, inter alia, with where a contract was made by telex. After referring to *Entores v. Miles Far East Corporation*,

[1955] 1 Lloyd's Rep. 511; [1955] 2 Q.B. 327, where the Court of Appeal classified telex communications with instantaneous communications, e.g. by telephone, Lord Wilberforce said:

I would accept [the *Entores* rule] as a general rule. Where the condition of simultaneity is met, and where it appears to be within the mutual intention of the parties that contractual exchanges should take place in this way, I think it a sound rule, but not necessarily a universal rule.

Since 1955 the use of telex communication has been greatly expanded and there are many variants on it. The senders and recipients may not be the principals to the contemplated contract. They may be servants or agents with limited authority. The message may not reach or be intended to reach the designated recipient immediately: messages may be sent out of office hours, or at night, with the intention, or upon the assumption, that they will be read at a later time. . .and many other variations may occur. No universal rule can cover all such cases: they must be resolved by reference to the intentions of the parties, by sound business practice and in some cases by a judgment where the risks should lie. . .

Mr. Justice Brandon also referred, in passing, to an out-of hours telex in *The Brimnes*, loc. cit. at p. 479, col. 2; p. 405F.

The charterers in order to found their contention that the telex message was premature, are in fact contending for a universal rule for telex communications which, they say, has the commercial advantage of certainty. But I propose to follow Lord Wilberforce's words and resolve this issue by reference to the particular circumstances. His Lordship's words, quoted above, were spoken with reference to where a contract is to be regarded as having been concluded: hence, as I think, his reference to the intentions of the parties and in some cases, where the risks should lie (both the cases cited were concerned with the risks which arise from a postal acceptance). A notice such as the one with which I am concerned is clearly of a quite different type and does not involve any consideration of the mutual intentions of contracting parties or of where the risks should lie. But I think the tribunal were entitled to find (par. 25 of their reasons) that a notice which arrives at 23 41 on a Friday night is not to be expected to be read before opening hours on the following Monday, and that was a conclusion of fact arrived at by the arbitrators as a matter of commercial commonsense. ...

In this case, since the message was sent outside of office hours, it would be effective at the start of business on the next working day. The issue again seems to be which party was at fault. In accordance with commercial commonsense, since the recipient in this case could not be said to be at fault for not reading the message at 23:41 on Friday night, the telex would be deemed received first thing the next working day.

Further Reading

Cheshire, Fifoot & Furmston's Law of Contract (2007) 15th ed. Furmston. Oxford University Press. Ch.3

Chitty on Contracts (2008) 30th ed. Sweet & Maxwell. Ch.2

McKendrick, E., *Contract Law* (2017) 12th ed. Palgrave MacMillan. Ch.2 & 3

Peel, E., *The Law of Contract*. Sweet & Maxwell. Treitel. Ch.1 & 2

3

Intention to Create Legal Relations

Topic List

1. Commercial or Business Agreements
2. Social and Domestic Agreements

Introduction

An essential element for an agreement to be binding is that the parties must have had an intention to create legal relations. The test for intention to create legal relations is objective. In the Court of Appeal case of *Rose & Frank Co v JR Crompton & Bros Ltd* [1925] AC 445, Atkin LJ said: 'To create a contract there must be a common intention of the parties to enter into legal obligations, mutually communicated expressly or impliedly.' In the same case, Scrutton LJ said:

'Now it is quite possible for parties to come to an agreement by accepting a proposal with the result that the agreement does not give rise to legal relations. The reason for this is that the parties do not intend that their agreement shall give rise to legal relations. This intention may be implied from the subject matter of the agreement, but it may also be expressed by the parties. In social and family relations such an intention is readily implied, while in business matters, the opposite result would ordinarily follow.'

As a general rule then, there is a presumption that, where an agreement is made in a commercial context, the parties intend it to be legally binding. In the case of social, family or domestic agreements, the presumption is that the parties do not intend the agreement to be legally binding. Both of these presumptions may be rebutted.

In the cases below, the courts have considered both the intentions of the parties and policy issues in order to reach their conclusions.

3.1 Commercial or Business Agreements

Generally, in a commercial or business context, there is a presumption that the parties intend to create legal relations. However, this presumption may be rebutted if the parties make clear their intention that they do not wish to be legally bound.

Edwards v Skyways [1964] 1 WLR 349

Panel: Megaw J

Facts: The defendant company agreed to make an *ex gratia* payment to a pilot who was being made redundant. They later reneged on the agreement, claiming that they were not legally obliged to make the payment.

MR JUSTICE MEGAW

...In the present case, the subject-matter of the agreement is business relations, not social or domestic matters. There was a meeting of minds — an intention to agree. There was, admittedly, consideration for the company's promise. I accept the propositions of counsel for the plaintiff that in a case of this nature the onus is on the party who asserts that no legal effect was intended, and the onus is a heavy one. …

[T]he company says, first, as I understand it, that the mere use of the phrase 'ex gratia' by itself, as a part of the promise to pay, shows that the parties contemplated that the promise, when accepted, should have no binding force in law. It says, secondly, that even if the first proposition is not correct as a general proposition, nevertheless here there was certain background knowledge, present in the minds of everyone, which gave unambiguous significance to 'ex gratia' as excluding legal relationship.

As to the first proposition, the words 'ex gratia,' in my judgment, do not carry a necessary, or even a probable, implication that the agreement is to be without legal effect. It is, I think, common experience amongst practitioners of the law that litigation or threatened litigation is frequently compromised on the terms that one party shall make to the other a payment described in express terms as 'ex gratia' or 'without admission of liability.' The two phrases are, I think, synonymous. No one would imagine that a settlement, so made, is unenforceable at law. The words 'ex gratia' or 'without admission of liability' are used simply to indicate — it may be as a matter of amour propre, or it may be to avoid a precedent in subsequent cases — that the party agreeing to pay does not admit any pre-existing liability on his part; but he is certainly not seeking to preclude the legal enforceability of the settlement itself by describing the contemplated payment as 'ex gratia.' So here. There are obvious reasons why the phrase might have been used by the company in just such a way. It might have desired to avoid conceding that any such payment was due under the employers' contract of service. It might have wished — perhaps ironically in the event — to show, by using the phrase, its generosity in making a payment beyond what was required by the contract of service. I see nothing in the mere use of the words 'ex gratia,' unless in the circumstances some very special meaning has to be given to them, to warrant the conclusion that this promise, duly made and accepted, for valid consideration, was not intended by the parties to be enforceable in law.

The company's second proposition seeks to show that in the circumstances here the words 'ex gratia' had a special meaning. What is said is this: when a payment such as this is made by an employer to a dismissed employee the question whether it is subject to income tax in the hands of the recipient is important. It was understood by the company and by the association, and by all their respective representatives at the meeting, that if the company's payment were made as the result of a legally binding obligation, it would be taxable in the hands of the recipient; whereas, if it were to be made without legal obligation on the part of the company, it would not be taxable. It was not argued before me whether this assertion is right or wrong in law. It was said by the company that that is quite immaterial; what is material is that the parties so believed. Thus, it is said, the phrase 'ex gratia' was used, and was understood by all present to be used, deliberately and advisedly as a formula to achieve that there would be no binding legal obligation on the company to pay, and hence to save the recipient from a tax liability. It is said that the offer was accepted by the association with full knowledge and understanding of these matters. Hence, it is said, the agreement by tacit consent, a consent evidenced by the use of the words 'ex gratia' against this background of common understanding, was an agreement from which legal sanction and consequences were excluded.

In my judgment, that submission also fails because the evidence falls far short of showing that this supposed background of avoidance of tax liability was present as an important element in the minds of all, or indeed any, of the persons who attended the meeting of February 8; or, if this be something different, in the minds of the company or of the association; or that they all, or any of them, directed their minds to the significance of the words 'ex gratia' which is now suggested on behalf of the company. The question of the liability, and the possible influence thereon of the use of the words 'ex gratia,' may indeed have been present in some degree, and as one element, in the minds of some of the persons present at the meeting. That, however, is far from sufficient to establish that the parties — both of them — affirmatively intended not to enter into legal relations in respect of the company's promise to pay. ...

Thus, it is clear from this case that the presumption in the commercial context that there is an intention to create legal relations is a heavy one to rebut. The parties must make such intention very clear.

Regarding the sale of land, by including the words 'subject to contract', the parties will not be presumed to have intended the agreement to be legally binding since they have made their intention clear.

One further manner in which the parties may successfully avoid being legally bound by an agreement is to include what is know as an 'honour clause'. This has the effect of making the agreement binding in honour only. *Rose and Frank v Crompton Bros* illustrates the way in which an 'honour clause' can be used.

Rose & Frank Co v JR Crompton & Bros Ltd [1925] AC 445

Panel: Earl of Birkenhead, Lord Atkinson, Lord Sumner, Lord Buckmaster and Lord Phillimore

Facts: This case involved an agreement between the plaintiffs, an American firm, and the defendants, an English firm. The parties drew up a document setting out their business arrangements. This document contained an honour clause which stated 'This arrangement is not entered into, nor is this memorandum written, as a formal or legal agreement, and shall not be subject to legal jurisdiction in the law courts either in the United States or England, but is only a definite expression and record of the purpose and intention of the three parties concerned to which they each honourably pledge themselves with the fullest confidence, based on past business with each other, that it will be carried through by each of the three parties with mutual loyalty and friendly co-operation.' The defendants sought to terminate the agreement without giving the notice period specified, and refused to complete on orders already placed. The plaintiffs brought an action for breach of contract.

The Court of Appeal found that the document was not a legally binding contract by reason of the honour clause. They also held (Atkin LJ dissenting) that the orders already placed could not constitute legally binding contracts. The plaintiffs appealed to the House of Lords.

LORD PHILLIMORE

...There is no explanation upon the record, and no suggestion was made by counsel at the Bar of any reason for the introduction of this remarkable clause [i.e. the honour clause]. During the progress of the hearing it occurred to some of your Lordships that it might have been inserted in order to avoid the operation of some American law discouraging monopolies. But this was a mere surmise. For whatever reason it was introduced the clause is there, and it remains for the Courts to give the proper effect to it. ...

Here, I think, the overriding clause in the document is that which provides that it is to be a contract of honour only and unenforceable at law.

With regard to the next point - namely, the right of the plaintiffs to recover damages for non-delivery of the goods specified in the particular orders for the year 1919... .

According to the course of business between the parties which is narrated in the unenforceable agreement, goods were ordered from time to time, shipped, received, and paid for, under an established system; but the agreement being unenforceable, there was no obligation on the American company to order goods or upon the English companies to accept an order. Any actual transaction between the parties, however, gave rise to the ordinary legal rights; for the fact that it was not of obligation to do the transaction did not divest the transaction when done of its ordinary legal significance. This, my Lords, will, I think, be plain if we begin at the latter end of each transaction.

Goods were ordered, shipped, and received. Was there no legal liability to pay for them? One stage further back. Goods were ordered, shipped, and invoiced. Was there no legal liability to take delivery? I apprehend that in each of these cases the American company would be bound. If the goods were short-shipped or inferior in quality, or if the nature of them was such as to be deleterious to other cargo on board or illegal for the American company to bring into their country, the American company would have its usual legal remedies against the English companies or one of them. Business usually begins in some mutual understanding without a previous bargain. ...

In the above case, the House of Lords was willing to give effect to an honour clause and held that the main agreement was not a legally binding contract.

However, individual orders executed did constitute legally binding contracts. Note, however, that when drafting an honour clause, clear words need to be used in order for the courts to give effect to it.

3.2 Social and Domestic Agreements

As stated above, in relation to social and domestic agreements, there is a rebuttable presumption against an intention to create legal relations.

Balfour v Balfour [1919] 2 KB 571

Panel: Warrington, Duke and Atkin LJJ

Facts: This case concerned an alleged verbal agreement between a husband and wife made in August 1916. The husband and wife returned to England from Ceylon, where the husband held a government appointment. When the time came for him to return to Ceylon, the wife remained in England on medical advice. The wife alleged that the husband had promised to send her £30 per month for maintenance until such time as he was able to return. A few months later, he wrote to suggest that they remain apart and the marriage subsequently broke down.

The wife sued the husband on the basis of the alleged agreement. Mr Justice Sargant, sitting as an additional judge of the King's Bench Division, gave judgment for the wife; the husband appealed.

LORD JUSTICE WARRINGTON

...We have to say whether there is a legal contract between the parties, in other words, whether what took place between them was in the domain of a contract or whether it was merely a domestic arrangement such as may be made every day between a husband and wife who are living together in friendly intercourse. It may be, and I do not for a moment say that it is not, possible for such a contract as is alleged in the present case to be made between husband and wife. The question is whether such a contract was made. That can only be determined either by proving that it was made in express terms, or that there is a necessary implication from the circumstances of the parties, and the transaction generally, that such a contract was made. It is quite plain that no such contract was made in express terms, and there was no bargain on the part of the wife at all. All that took place was this: The husband and wife met in a friendly way and discussed what would be necessary for her support while she was detained in England, the husband being in Ceylon, and they came to the conclusion that 30l. a month would be about right, but there is no evidence of any express bargain by the wife that she would in all the circumstances treat that as in satisfaction of the obligation of the husband to maintain her. Can we find a contract from the position of the parties? It seems to me it is quite impossible. If we were to imply such a contract in this case we should be implying on the part of the wife that whatever happened and whatever might be the change of circumstances

 Alert

while the husband was away she should be content with this 30l. a month, and bind herself by an obligation in law not to require him to pay anything more; and on the other hand we should be implying on the part of the husband a bargain to pay 30l. a month for some indefinite period whatever might be his circumstances. ...

LORD JUSTICE ATKIN

The defense [sic] to this action on the alleged contract is that the defendant, the husband, entered into no contract with his wife, and for the determination of that It is necessary to remember that there are agreements between parties which do not result in contracts within the meaning of that term in our law. The ordinary example is where two parties agree to take a walk together, or where there is an offer and an acceptance of hospitality. Nobody would suggest in ordinary circumstances that those agreements result in what we know as a contract, and one of the most usual forms of agreement which does not constitute a contract appears to me to be the arrangements which are made between husband and wife. It is quite common, and it is the natural and inevitable result of the relationship of husband and wife, that the two spouses should make arrangements between themselves – agreements such as are in dispute in this action – agreements for allowances, by which the husband agrees that he will pay to his wife a certain sum of money, per week, or per month, or per year, to cover either her own expenses or the necessary expenses of the household and of the children of the marriage, and in which the wife promises either expressly or impliedly to apply the allowance for the purpose for which it is given. To my mind those agreements, or many of them, do not result in contracts at all, and they do not result in contracts even though there may be what as between other parties would constitute consideration for the agreement. ...They are not contracts, and they are not contracts because the parties did not intend that they should be attended by legal consequences. To my mind it would be of the worst possible example to hold that agreements such as this resulted in legal obligations which could be enforced in the Courts. It would mean this, that when the husband makes his wife a promise to give her an allowance of 30s. or 2l. a week, whatever he can afford to give her, for the maintenance of the household and children, and she promises so to apply it, not only could she sue him for his failure in any week to supply the allowance, but he could sue her for non-performance of the obligation, express or implied, which she had undertaken upon her part. All I can say is that the small Courts of this country would have to be multiplied one hundredfold if these arrangements were held to result in legal obligations. They are not sued upon, not because the parties are reluctant to enforce their legal rights when the agreement is broken, but because the parties, in the inception of the arrangement, never intended that they should be sued upon. Agreements such as these are outside the realm of contracts altogether. The common law does not regulate the form of agreements between spouses. Their promises are not sealed with seals and sealing wax. The consideration that really obtains for them is that natural love and affection which counts for so little in these cold Courts. ...In respect of these promises

Alert

each house is a domain into which the King's writ does not seek to run, and to which his officers do not seek to be admitted. The only question in this case is whether or not this promise was of such a class or not. For the reasons given by my brethren it appears to me to be plainly established that the promise here was not intended by either party to be attended by legal consequences. I think the onus was upon the plaintiff, and the plaintiff has not established any contract. The parties were living together, the wife intending to return. The suggestion is that the husband bound himself to pay 30l. a month under all circumstances, and she bound herself to be satisfied with that sum under all circumstances, and, although she was in ill-health and alone in this country, that out of that sum she undertook to defray the whole of the medical expenses that might fall upon her, whatever might be the development of her illness, and in whatever expenses it might involve her. To my mind neither party contemplated such a result. I think that the parol evidence upon which the case turns does not establish a contract. I think that the letters do not evidence such a contract, or amplify the oral evidence which was given by the wife, which is not in dispute. For these reasons I think the judgment of the Court below was wrong and that this appeal should be allowed.

Although there is a presumption against an intention to create legal relations where the agreement is between spouses, Warrington LJ makes it clear that this may be rebuttable in appropriate circumstances.

Note the clear emphasis placed on policy in Atkin LJ's judgment. He places crucial importance on the floodgates argument and is of the view that it is not appropriate for the courts to regulate the realm of agreements made between spouses.

Another key factor in this case was that the parties were living in amity at the time the alleged agreement was made. If that is not the case, the courts may be more willing to recognise that the parties intended the agreement to give rise to legal relations. *Merritt v Merritt* [1970] 1 WLR 1211 clearly illustrates this distinction.

Merritt v Merritt [1970] 1 WLR 1211

Panel: Lord Denning MR, Widgery and Karminski LJJ

Facts: In this case, the husband left the matrimonial home to live with another woman after 25 years of marriage to the plaintiff. The matrimonial home had an outstanding mortgage of £180 and was in joint names. After the husband had moved out, the wife arranged a meeting in the car to discuss financial arrangements. They agreed that the wife would stay in the marital home and the husband agreed to pay her £40 every month, out of which she should make the mortgage payments. She made him sign a written statement which read: 'In consideration of the fact that you [the wife] will pay all charges in connection with the house … until such time as the mortgage repayment has been completed, when the mortgage has been completed I [the husband] will agree to transfer the property in to your sole ownership.'

The wife paid off the outstanding mortgage, but the husband refused to transfer the house to her sole name. Mr Justice Stamp ordered that the house be transferred to the wife's sole name; the husband appealed.

LORD DENNING MR

…The first point taken on his behalf by [counsel for the husband] was that the agreement was not intended to have legal relations. It was, he says, a family arrangement such as was considered by the court in Balfour v Balfour [1919] 2 K.B. 571 and in Jones v Padavatton [1969] 1 W.L.R. 328. So the wife could not sue on it.

 Alert

I do not think that those cases have any application here. The parties there were living together in amity. In such cases their domestic arrangements are ordinarily not intended to create legal relations. It is altogether different when the parties are not living in amity but are separated, or about to separate. They then bargain keenly. They do not rely on honourable understandings. They want everything cut and dried. It may safely be presumed that they intend to create legal relations.

[Counsel for the husband] then relied on the recent case of *Gould v Gould* [1970] 1 Q.B. 275, when the parties had separated, and the husband agreed to pay the wife £12 a week 'so long as he could manage it'. The majority of the court thought that those words introduced such an element of uncertainty that the agreement was not intended to create legal relations. But for that element of uncertainty, I am sure that the majority would have held the agreement to be binding. They did not differ from the general proposition which I stated at p. 280 that:

'when husband and wife, at arm's length, decide to separate, and the husband promises to pay a sum as maintenance to the wife during the separation, the court does, as a rule, impute to them an intention to create legal relations."

In all these cases the court does not try to discover the intention by looking into the minds of the parties. I[t] looks at the situation in which they were placed and asks itself: would reasonable people regard the agreements as intended to be binding?

[Counsel for the husband] sought to say that this agreement was uncertain because of the arrangement for £40 a month maintenance. That is obviously untenable. Next he said that there was no consideration for the agreement. That point is no good. The wife paid the outstanding amount to the building society. That was ample consideration. It is true that the husband paid her £40 a month which she may have used to pay the building society. But still her act in paying was good consideration. …

I find myself in entire agreement with the judgment of Stamp J. This appeal should be dismissed.

LORD JUSTICE WIDGERY

When a husband and wife are living together in amity it is natural enough to presume that their discussions about money matters are not intended to create legally binding contracts. ...

But, of course, once that natural love and affection has gone, as it normally has when the marriage has broken up, there is no room at all for the application of such a presumption. ...

It is clear that in circumstances where husband and wife are no longer living in amity, the presumption against an intention to create legal relations in a social, family or domestic context, does not apply. In fact, whenever family members are bargaining in a commercial sense, the presumption does not apply. See the case of *Snelling v John G Snelling Ltd*. [1973] 1 QB 87 for an example of this point.

Jones v Padavatton [1969] 1 WLR 328 illustrates the principle that, in general, there is a presumption against an intention to create legal relations in agreements between other family members too. The case involved an agreement between a mother and daughter.

Jones v Padavatton [1969] 1 WLR 328

Panel: Danckwerts, Salmon and Fenton Atkinson LJJ

Facts: In this case, the daughter agreed to give up her job in Washington to study for the Bar examinations in London at the mother's request. The mother agreed to pay the daughter $200 per month as an allowance until she finished the examinations. In 1962, the daughter went to London and commenced her studies and the mother made the monthly payments.

In 1964, the mother agreed to buy a house in London for the daughter to live in. The daughter would rent out rooms in the house for an income, and the mother would no longer make the monthly maintenance payments.

In 1967, when the daughter had still not completed the examinations, the mother brought an action for possession of the house. The daughter counterclaimed for the expenses she had incurred in the purchase and furnishing of the property.

The lower court gave judgment for the daughter; the mother appealed.

LORD JUSTICE DANCKWERTS

There is no doubt that this case is a most difficult one, but I have reached a conclusion that the present case is one of those family arrangements which depend on the good faith of the promises which are made and are not intended to be rigid, binding agreements. Balfour v Balfour was a case of husband and wife, but there is no doubt that the same principles apply to dealings between other relations, such as father and son and daughter and mother. This, indeed, seems to me a compelling case. Mrs. Jones and her

Alert

daughter seem to have been on very good terms before 1967. The mother was arranging for a career for her daughter which she hoped would lead to success. This involved a visit to England in conditions which could not be wholly foreseen. What was required was an arrangement which was to be financed by the mother, and was such as would be adaptable to circumstances, as it in fact was. The operation about the house was, in my view, not a completely fresh arrangement, but an adaptation of the mother's financial assistance to her daughter due to the situation which was found to exist in England. It was not a stiff contractual operation any more than the original arrangement.

In the result, of course, on this view, the daughter cannot resist her mother's rights as the owner of the house to the possession of which the mother is entitled.

What the position is as regards the counterclaim is another matter. It may be that, at least in honesty, the daughter should be reimbursed for the expenditure which she had incurred.

In my opinion, therefore, the appeal should be allowed.

LORD JUSTICE SALMON

I agree with the conclusion at which Danckwerts LJ has arrived, but I have reached it by a different route. ...

[Counsel for the mother] has said, quite rightly, that as a rule when arrangements are made between close relations, for example, between husband and wife, parent and child or uncle and nephew in relation to an allowance, there is a presumption against an intention of creating any legal relationship. This is not a presumption of law, but of fact. It derives from experience of life and human nature which shows that in such circumstances men and women usually do not intend to create legal rights and obligations, but intend to rely solely on family ties of mutual trust and affection. ...There may, however, be circumstances in which this presumption, like all other presumptions of fact, can be rebutted. ...

 Alert

...In the present case the county court judge, having had the advantage of seeing the mother and daughter in the witness-box, entirely accepted the daughter's version of the facts. He came to the conclusion that on these very special facts the true inference must be that the arrangement between the parties prior to the daughter's leaving Washington were intended by both to have contractual force.

On the facts as found by the county court judge this was entirely different from the ordinary case of a mother promising her daughter an allowance whilst the daughter read for the Bar, or a father promising his son an allowance at university if the son passed the necessary examinations to gain admission. The daughter here was thirty-four years of age in 1962. She had left Trinidad and settled in Washington as long ago as 1949. In Washington she had a comfortable flat and was employed as an assistant accountant in the Indian

Embassy at a salary of $500 a month (over £2,000 a year). This employment carried a pension. She had a son of seven years of age who was an American citizen, and had, of course, already begun his education. There were obviously solid reasons for her staying where she was. For some years prior to 1962, however, her mother, who lived in Trinidad, had been trying hard to persuade her to throw up all that she had achieved in Washington and go to London to read for the Bar. The mother would have been very proud to have a barrister for a daughter. She also thought that her plan was in the interest of her grandson, to whom she was much attached. She envisaged that, after her daughter had been called to the Bar, she would practice in Trinidad and thereafter presumably she (the mother) would be able to see much more of her daughter than formerly. The daughter was naturally loth to leave Washington, and did not regard her mother's suggestion as feasible. The mother, however, eventually persuaded the daughter to do as she wished by promising her that, if she threw up her excellent position in Washington and came to study for the Bar in England, she would pay her daughter an allowance of $200 a month until she had completed her studies. The mother's attorney in Trinidad wrote to the daughter to confirm this. I cannot think that either intended that if, after the daughter had been in London, say, for six months, the mother dishonoured her promise and left her daughter destitute, the daughter would have no legal redress.

In the very special circumstances of this case, I consider that the true inference must be that neither the mother nor the daughter could have intended that the daughter should have no legal right to receive, and the mother no legal obligation to pay, the allowance of $200 a month. ...

Then again it is said that the duration of the agreement was not specified. No doubt, but I see no difficulty in implying the usual term that it was to last for a reasonable time. The parties cannot have contemplated that the daughter should go on studying for the Bar and draw the allowance until she was seventy, nor on the other hand that the mother could have discontinued the allowance if the daughter did not pass her examinations within, say, 18 months. The promise was to pay the allowance until the daughter's studies were completed, and to my mind there was a clear implication that they were to be completed within a reasonable time. Studies are completed either by the student being called to the Bar or giving up the unequal struggle against the examiners.

 Alert

It may not be easy to decide, especially when there is such a paucity of evidence, what is a reasonable time. The daughter, however, was a well-educated intelligent woman capable of earning the equivalent of over £2,000 a year in Washington. It is true that she had a young son to look after, and may well (as the learned judge thought) have been hampered to some extent by the worry of this litigation. But, making all allowance for these factors and any other distraction, I cannot think that a reasonable time could possibly exceed five years from November 1962, the date when she began her studies. ...

LORD JUSTICE FENTON ATKINSON

...In my judgment it is the subsequent history which gives the best guide to the parties' intention at the material time. ...The mother promised ... £42 a month, and that was what she in fact paid from November 1962 to December 1964. ...When the arrangements for the purchase of no 181, Highbury Quadrant were being discussed, and the new arrangement was made for maintenance to come out of the rents, many material matters were left open: How much accommodation was the daughter to occupy; how much money was she to have out of the rents; if the rents fell below expectation, was the mother to make up the difference below £42, or £42 less the sum saved by the daughter in rent; for how long was the arrangement to continue, and so on. The whole arrangement was, in my view, far too vague and uncertain to be itself enforceable as a contract; but at no stage did the daughter bring into the discussions her alleged legal right of £42 per month until her studies were completed, and how that right was to be affected by the new arrangement. ...It is perhaps not without relevance to look at the daughter's evidence in cross-examination. She was asked about the occasion when the mother visited the house, and she, knowing perfectly well that the mother was there, refused for some hours to open the door. She said: 'I didn't open the door because a normal mother doesn't sue her daughter in court. Anybody with normal feelings would feel upset by what was happening.' Those answers and the daughter's conduct on that occasion provide a strong indication that she had never for a moment contemplated the possibility of the mother or herself going to court to enforce legal obligations, and that she felt it quite intolerable that a purely family arrangement should become the subject of proceedings in a court of law.

At the time when the first arrangement was made, the mother and the daughter were, and always had been, to use the daughter's own words, 'very close'. I am satisfied that neither party at that time intended to enter into a legally binding contract, either then or later when the house was bought. The daughter was prepared to trust the mother to honour her promise of support, just as the mother no doubt trusted the daughter to study for the Bar with diligence, and to get through her examinations as early as she could.

It follows that in my view the mother's claim for possession succeeds, and her appeal should be allowed.

There remains the counterclaim. As to that I fully endorse what Salmon LJ has said as to the manner in which that should be disposed of.

Note the differences in the reasoning of the judges. Lords Justices Danckwerts and Fenton Atkinson allowed the appeal as they held there was no intention to create legal relations between the parties. Lord Justice Salmon, on the other hand, held that there was an intention to create legal relations but found that there was an implied term that the agreement was to last for a reasonable time. In his opinion, the agreement had lapsed by the time the mother brought the action for an order for possession; he also allowed the appeal, but on this different basis.

Further Reading

Hedley, (1985), Keeping Contract in its Place: Balfour v Balfour and the Enforceability of Informal Agreements, 5 OJLS 391

Hepple (1970), Intention to Create Legal Relations, CLJ 122

McKendrick, E., *Contract Law* (2017) 12th ed. Ch.6

4

Capacity

Topic List

Introduction

As a general rule, all adults of sound mind have the capacity to contract. The statutory and common law rules on capacity exist to ensure that more vulnerable members of society are protected if they purportedly enter into a contract. The types of vulnerable people protected are minors, the mentally ill and those who might temporarily lack the mental capacity to contract.

4.1 Minors

A minor is anyone below the age of legal majority (that is, below the age of 18). To avoid confusion when looking at older case law, it is important to understand that the age of majority was only reduced from 21 to 18 in 1969 (by the Family Law Reform Act 1969). Since a minor cannot be classified as an adult of sound mind, their capacity to contract is called into question, and the relevant law must be applied to determine the validity of the contract.

As a general rule (with a number of important exceptions), a minor will lack the capacity to contract and will not be bound by a contract they have entered into. However, the contract will not be void and the other party will still be bound by it. The exceptions to the general rule are contracts for necessaries; beneficial contracts; and contracts with continuing obligations, which the minor ratifies on reaching the age of majority. These exceptions are explored in more detail below.

4.1.1 Necessaries

A minor is bound by a contract to supply 'necessaries' to him where that contract is for the minor's benefit. Under the Sale of Goods Act 1979 s 3(3), 'necessaries' are defined as 'goods suitable to the condition in life of the minor or other person concerned and to his actual requirements at the time of the sale and delivery'. The Act provides that a minor must pay a 'reasonable price' for such goods rather than the actual cost of the 'necessaries' supplied.

***Nash v Inman* [1908] 2 KB 1**

Panel: Cozens-Hardy MR, Fletcher Moulton and Buckley LJJ

Statute: The Sale of Goods Act 1893

Facts: This case involved a minor, who had just commenced his undergraduate studies at Cambridge University. He purchased various items of clothing including 11 fancy waistcoats from a tailor. The minor pleaded incapacity in a claim by the tailor for non-payment for the goods. The court ruled that, under the provisions of the Sale of Goods Act 1893 (as it then was), the defence succeeded because the goods were not 'necessaries'. The court ruled that the Act stipulated a two-fold test. Not only did the claimant have the burden of showing that the goods supplied were suitable to the condition in life of the infant, but he had to prove that they were also suitable to his actual requirements at the time of sale and delivery. In other words, the claimant had to show that the defendant did not already have an adequate supply of the goods in question from other sources.

COZENS-HARDY MR

...[Section]. 2 of the Sale of Goods Act, 1893, provides as follows: 'Capacity to buy and sell is regulated by the general law concerning capacity to contract, and to transfer and acquire property'. ...Then follows this proviso: 'Provided that where necessaries are sold and delivered to an infant, or minor, or to a person who by reason of mental incapacity or drunkenness is incompetent to contract, he must pay a reasonable price therefor.' The section then defines necessaries as follows: 'Necessaries in this section mean goods suitable to the condition in life of such infant or minor or other person, and to his actual requirements at the time of the sale and delivery.' What is the effect of that? The plaintiff sues for goods sold and delivered. The defendant pleads infancy. The plaintiff must then reply, 'The goods sold were necessaries within the meaning of the definition in s. 2 of the Sale of Goods Act, 1893.' It is not sufficient, in my view, for him to say, 'I have discharged the onus which rests upon me if I simply shew that the goods supplied were suitable to the condition in life of the infant at the time.' There is another branch of the definition which cannot be disregarded. Having shewn that the goods were suitable to the condition in life of the infant, he must then go on to shew that they were suitable to his actual requirements at the time of the sale and delivery. Unless he establishes that fact, either by evidence adduced by himself or by cross-examination of the defendant's witnesses, as the case may be, in my opinion he has not discharged the burden which the law imposes upon him. ...[T]he infancy of the defendant was not admitted, and the father was called to prove the date of his son's birth. There was no cross-examination as to that, and the infancy is not disputed. Then he went on to give evidence, which was quite clear and explicit and was not shaken in cross-examination, that the infant, who was an undergraduate at Cambridge, and had just gone up to the university when these goods were supplied, was in fact supplied with clothes suitable and necessary and proper for his condition in life, and for his position as an undergraduate of Trinity College, Cambridge. The learned judge ruled as a matter of law that there was no evidence fit to be submitted to the jury that these articles, or any of them, were necessaries within the meaning of the statutory definition, and, thinking as I do that there was no evidence in support of that which was a necessary issue, I cannot say that the learned judge was wrong in the view which he took.

The tailor had failed in his action since he was unable to prove that the minor was not already supplied with sufficient clothing. Consequently, the clothing purchased could not be classed as 'necessaries'.

4.1.2   Beneficial Contracts

In addition to contracts for necessaries, a minor can also be bound by a contract of employment, or a contract which is closely analogous to a contract of employment. A minor will only be bound by such a contract if, taken as a whole, it is for the minor's benefit. Without this exception, minors would be unable to obtain gainful employment.

Doyle v White City Stadium Limited **[1935] 1 KB 110**

Panel: Lord Hanworth MR, Slesser and Romer LJJ

Facts: While still a minor, the claimant, Mr Doyle, applied for a licence to be a boxer; this licence was subsequently granted. In applying for the licence, the claimant had agreed to be bound by the rules made and amended from time to time by the Boxing Board of Control. One of the rules gave the Board of Control the power to withhold money which was otherwise due to Doyle following a fight at White City Stadium, because Doyle had been disqualified from the boxing match for breaching the rules. Doyle claimed that the contract with the Board of Control was not binding on him because of his infancy, and that the Board therefore had no right to withhold the money from him. The court decided against Doyle because the contract was akin to an employment contract which is binding on the infant if it is for his benefit.

LORD JUSTICE SLESSER

...Subject to the particular matters which have been argued before us and considered in the Court below and in this Court, it would appear that this plaintiff had agreed, first, by his application, which was accepted, and secondly, by the actual provisions of the rules themselves, to be a member of this society and to be bound by its rules and regulations. It would follow that the rules and regulations would authorise the society dealing with the money which was to be his prize or reward for taking part in this contest in the way in which they have dealt with it. But in substance two arguments have been used in this case to support the view that they are not so entitled to deal with this money and that the plaintiff is entitled himself to have it paid over to him by the promoters. The first of those arguments rests upon the fact that he is an infant. It is said that whatever contract or alleged contract he has entered into under these rules is not binding on him on account of his infancy. If that contention is right, it is an answer to the defendant's claim to keep this money. It is an argument which has not found favour with MacKinnon J., and it does not find favour with me either. It depends really on two separate considerations - first, whether this agreement is of the order of agreement under which an infant can properly bind himself; and secondly, if it does come within that order, whether this particular agreement can be stated to be so for the benefit of the infant as to be binding upon him. On the first point [Counsel for Doyle] has relied very strongly on the argument that for many, many years the types of agreement which are binding upon infants have been narrowly prescribed and defined, and that as this particular agreement is not within that narrow definition and prescription, it is not one which can properly be said to be binding upon the infant. ...

I am not prepared here to say that there is any general principle that all agreements for the benefit of an infant will necessarily bind him. In my view that question does not arise in the present case, because the contract with which we have here to deal is so analogous, so similar in character, to the classes of agreement which have been held to be binding upon infants, if for their benefit, that it can properly be brought within the old category of decisions without having to rely on any more general principle. ... If the realities of the present case be looked to and the dicta which are to be found scattered in the authorities that the opportunity of an infant to earn his living is one of the matters which may properly be said to be binding when that opportunity has been given to him by a contract, it becomes clear, I think, that as the licence which this infant obtained was the means whereby he was able to enter into a contract of service or performance, whichever it may be, as a boxer, and thereby to earn his living, it was ancillary and incidental to the contract which he made with the promoter of the fight.

 Alert

LORD JUSTICE ROMER

...In considering whether any particular contract is detrimental to the interests of the infant the Court has to look at the contract as a whole, and if it comes to the conclusion looking at the contract as a whole that it is for the benefit of the infant, it disregards the fact that it contains some clauses which, standing by themselves, might not appear to be so. I agree entirely with the Master of the Rolls in thinking that the clauses which in the present case impose restrictions upon the liberty of action of the boxer are in the interests of clean boxing in this country and therefore are in the interests of the boxers themselves of whom the plaintiff is one. The particular clause, reg. 20, para. 16, is merely one of the sanctions, and, I think, necessary sanctions, available for securing the fulfilment of the rules imposed upon boxers and others subjected to them.

I therefore come to the conclusion that this contract is binding upon the plaintiff. I am very glad to be able to come to that conclusion, because if this Court came to any other it would follow that at no time during the last three or four years during which, as I understand, the plaintiff has been boxing has he been eligible to take any part in a contest held under the sanction of the British Boxing Board of Control, a conclusion, I should have thought, from which the plaintiff would shrink. However that may be, I agree that the contract is in fact binding on him and that he is a member of this association. If the contract were not binding upon him, he would not be a member of this association, with the consequences I have just indicated.

Although some of the rules may have acted to Doyle's detriment, taken as a whole, the licensing agreement was for Doyle's benefit. Consequently, the licensing agreement was enforceable.

Proform Sports Management Ltd v Proactive Sports Management Ltd [2006] EWHC 2903 (Ch); [2007] 1 All ER 542

Panel: Judge Hodge QC

Facts: In 2000, the professional footballer, Wayne Rooney, purportedly entered into a player representation agreement with the claimant company, Proform Sports Management Ltd., when he was 15 years old. Proform was to act as his executive agent and to carry out all the functions in respect of personal representation on behalf of his work as a professional football player. In 2002, Wayne Rooney terminated the agreement and entered into a new contract with the defendant company, Proactive Sports Management Ltd. The claim against the defendant was for unlawful interference with the original contract and/or procuring a breach of that contract.

Judge Hodge QC gave judgment for the defendant on the basis that the original contract was a voidable contract with a minor which had been avoided. The court ruled that it was not possible to interfere unlawfully with a contract which had been validly avoided. For our purposes, it is important to consider the reasons why the judge decided that the contract was voidable as set out in his judgment below.

JUDGE HODGE QC

21. The defence, amongst other things, challenges the validity and/or enforceability of the Proform agreement. In particular it asserts: (1) that the Proform agreement was an unreasonable restraint of trade, contrary to public policy and therefore void; (2) further, or alternatively, that it was voidable as a contract with a minor; (3) in so far as Proform seeks to contend that its agreement was analogous to a contract for necessaries or of apprenticeship, that the agreement was not necessary for Mr Rooney when he entered into it and did not contain any obligation on Proform to provide Mr Rooney with training; (4) alternatively, if the Proform agreement was analogous to a contract for necessaries or of apprenticeship, it was not for Mr Rooney's benefit...

34. It then becomes necessary to consider the next stage in [Counsel for the defendant's] argument. He submits that the law as to minors' contracts is correctly stated in *Chitty on Contracts*, 29th ed (2004), paras 8–004 to 8–005. Para 8–004 identifies the only contracts which are binding on the minor as contracts for necessaries. However, a diversity of meanings has been given to the word 'necessaries'. In one sense the term is confined to necessary goods and services supplied to the minor, but in another it extends to contracts for the minor's benefit and in particular to contracts of apprenticeship, education and service. Para 8–005 provides that, apart from contracts for necessaries and contracts of apprenticeship education and service, the general rule at common law is that a minor's contract is voidable at his option; i.e. not binding on the minor, but binding on the other party.

35. As to other beneficial contracts, [Counsel for the defendants] relies on para 8–028: 'The principle that contracts beneficial to a minor are binding on him is not confined to contracts for necessaries and contracts of employment, apprenticeship or education in a strict sense. It extends also to other contracts which in a broad sense may be treated as analogous to contracts of service, apprenticeship or education. ...'

36. Thus, two questions arise. First, whether the contract between Wayne Rooney and Proform falls within the class of contracts analogous to contracts for necessaries and contracts of employment, apprenticeship or education. Secondly, and only if the first question is answered in a positive sense, whether this particular contract was one which was beneficial to Wayne Rooney. ...

39. Clearly Wayne Rooney's agreement with Everton Football Club would fall squarely within the class of contracts identified at para 8–028 of *Chitty*. However, it does seem to me that the same cannot be said of the Proform agreement. On the evidence, Mr Rooney was already engaged with Everton. Under the terms of the Football Association Rules, he could not enter into any contract of employment until he was 17, if then not in full-time education. Even if he entered into a contract with Everton when he was 17, that contract, if not for his benefit, would of course be voidable at his election. It does not seem to me that a contract in the terms of the Proform agreement, whereby Proform was to act as his executive agent and to carry out all the functions in respect of personal representation on behalf of his work as a professional football player, falls to be considered as analogous to the class of contracts considered at para 8–028 of *Chitty*. As I say, Mr Rooney was already with Everton on Mr McIntosh's own evidence. At this time, and indeed in 2002, Wayne Rooney only wanted to play for Everton; he did not wish to play for any other club. He was already doing so. ...

40. Players' representatives do not undertake matters that are essential to the player's training or his livelihood. They do not enable the minor to earn a living or to advance his skills as a professional footballer. In my judgment, cases such as *Chaplin v Leslie Frewin (Publishers) Ltd* [1966] Ch 71 and *Doyle v White City Stadium Ltd* [1935] 1 KB 110 make it clear that the basis of the class of analogous contracts is that the minor is entitled to earn his living or to start to do so. It does not seem to me that the Proform agreement is analogous to such a contract. I say that particularly bearing in mind the fact that, under the Football Association Rules, no contract can be entered into by a player as young as Wayne Rooney then was. No contract could properly be entered into by him until a time less than two months before this representation agreement was due to expire; and even if entered into by Wayne Rooney at that time, it would have been voidable at his instance if not genuinely for his benefit. That would have continued to be so throughout the remaining short duration of the management and agency

agreement. It seems to me that the Proform agreement is at one remove from the class of contract that has been treated in the authorities as being subject to the exception to the general voidability of minors' contracts, applicable where such a contract is for the minor's benefit. As para 8–028 of *Chitty* makes clear: 'A minor's trading contracts are not binding on him, even if beneficial.' It seems to me that this case falls within the general principle that merely because a contract is beneficial to a minor, if such is the case, it is not binding on him unless it falls within a particular category.

41.   So for those reasons, it seems to me that [Counsel for the defendants] is correct in saying that the Proform agreement does not fall within the class of minors' contracts which are analogous to contracts of apprenticeship, education and service. On that footing, it is unnecessary for me to consider the point that was addressed at length in [Counsel for the defendant's] skeleton argument, whether the Proform agreement was for Mr Rooney's benefit. Given that this is a summary judgment application, it seems to me that it would be undesirable for me to venture any expression of judicial opinion on that issue; and I do not propose to do so. ...

The Judge decided that Wayne Rooney's contract with his football club, Everton, was analogous to a contract of employment, apprenticeship or education. It follows that if the Everton contract was also beneficial to Wayne Rooney (which it clearly was), he would be bound by it. On the other hand, the Judge determined that Wayne Rooney's contract with his agent, Proform, was not analogous to a contract of employment. This is because a football player's agent does not provide services that are essential to a player's training and livelihood, in the same way as a football club does. In other words, Wayne Rooney could be employed to play football for Everton football club irrespective of whether or not he had an agent. The case is interesting because it demonstrates the fine distinctions which can be drawn between contracts falling within the class of contracts analogous to contracts for necessaries, of employment, apprenticeship or education by which a minor may be bound, and those which do not. In this case, because the contract with Proform was not analogous to a contract of employment, Wayne Rooney was not bound by it and it was not necessary for the judge to consider the other element which needs to be satisfied, i.e. whether or not the contract was for Wayne Rooney's benefit.

4.1.3   Continuing Obligations

In relation to contracts involving continuing obligations, a minor can avoid the contract prior to reaching the age of majority or within a reasonable time thereafter. Unless the contract has been repudiated by the minor, it will become binding on him when he reaches this age. The other party is given no option to avoid the contract. A minor who repudiates the contract will not be liable to perform any future obligations under it, but they will only be able to recover any money paid under the contract if there has been a total failure of consideration.

Steinberg v Scala (Leeds), Limited [1923] 2 Ch 452

Panel: Lord Sterndale MR, Warrington and Younger LJJ

Facts: In this case, a minor entered into a contract to purchase shares in a company. She repudiated the contract while still an infant. It was held that, while she was released of any further obligations under the contract, she was unable to recover the money she had paid for the shares because there had not been a total failure of consideration.

LORD STERNDALE MR

There is no doubt that she was entitled ... to have the register rectified by the removal of her name therefrom. But then there came another question. She also wanted the 250l. back, and, to a certain extent, I think the argument for the respondent has rather proceeded upon the assumption that the question whether she can rescind and the question whether she can recover her money back are the same. They are two quite different questions, as is pointed out by Turner L.J. in his judgment in *Ex parte Taylor.* He there says: 'It is clear that an infant cannot be absolutely bound by a contract entered into during his minority. He must have a right upon his attaining his majority to elect whether he will adopt the contract or not.' Then he proceeds: 'It is, however, a different question whether, if an infant pays money on the footing of a contract, he can afterwards recover it back. If an infant buys an article which is not a necessary, he cannot be compelled to pay for it, but if he does pay for it during his minority he cannot on attaining his majority recover the money back.' That seems to me to be only stating in other words the principle which is laid down in a number of other cases that, although the contract may be rescinded the money paid cannot be recovered back unless there has been an entire failure of the consideration for which the money has been paid. Therefore it seems to me that the question to which we have to address ourselves is: Has there here been a total failure of the consideration for which the money was paid?

Now the plaintiff has had the shares ... and there is evidence that they were of some value, that they had been dealt in at from 9s. to 10s. a share. ...

In those circumstances is it possible to say that there was a total failure of consideration? If the plaintiff were a person of full age suing to recover the money back on the ground, and the sole ground, that there had been a failure of consideration it seems to me it would have been impossible for her to succeed, because she would have got the very thing for which the money was paid and would have got a thing of tangible value. ...

I cannot see any difference when you come to consider whether there has been consideration or not between the position of a person of full age and an infant. The question whether there has been consideration or not must, I think, be the same in the two cases.

4.2   Mental Incapacity

The first requirement is to ascertain what is meant by a person of unsound mind. According to The Mental Capacity Act 2005 s 2, a person lacks capacity if he is 'unable to make a decision for himself in relation to the matter' at the time the contract is made, whether the impairment is permanent or temporary. Sections 3(1) and 3(4) of the Act describe (for the purposes of the Act) what is meant by an inability to make decisions. The Act also gives a new Court of Protection the power to make declarations as to a person's capacity and ability to contract in specified situations (s 15).

If a person of unsound mind has purported to enter into a contract, to what extent is that person bound by the contract? Under the 2005 Act, the position is similar to the position with minors under the Sale of Goods Act 1979. Under the 2005 Act s 7, the mentally impaired person still remains liable to pay a reasonable price for goods and services which are 'necessaries'. These are defined, in s 7(2), as goods or services 'suitable to a person's condition of life and to his actual requirements at the time when the goods or services are supplied'.

Not all cases will be covered by the 2005 Act, in that not all contracts will be contracts for the supply of necessary goods or services covered by s 7. In such cases, the contract will be binding unless the person claiming incapacity can establish that (1) he did not understand what he was doing; and (2) the other party knew that to be the case. In such circumstances, the contract will be voidable (but not automatically void).

The Imperial Loan Company, Limited v Stone [1892] 1 QB 599

Panel: Lord Esher MR, Fry and Lopes LJJ

Facts: This case concerns a promissory note signed by the defendant who was later found to be insane.

LORD ESHER MR

...What I am about to state appears to me to be the result of all the cases. When a person enters into a contract, and afterwards alleges that he was so insane at the time that he did not know what he was doing, and proves the allegation, the contract is as binding on him in every respect, whether it is executory or executed, as if he had been sane when he made it, unless he can prove further that the person with whom he contracted knew him to be so insane as not to be capable of understanding what he was about. ...

LORD JUSTICE LOPES

It seems to me that the principle to be deduced from the cases may be summarised thus: A contract made by a person of unsound mind is not voidable at that person's option if the other party to the contract believed at the time he made the contract that the person with whom he was dealing was of sound mind. In order to avoid a fair contract on the ground of insanity, the mental incapacity of the one must be known to the other of the contracting parties. A defendant who seeks to avoid a contract on the ground of his insanity, must plead and prove, not merely his incapacity, but also the plaintiff's knowledge of that fact, and unless he proves these two things he cannot succeed.

4.3 Intoxication

The rules applying to contracts entered into by those heavily under the influence of alcohol (and presumably, other drugs which might affect that person's capacity to enter into a contract) are similar to those for mental incapacity generally. If someone becomes so intoxicated that he does not know or understand what he is doing, then a contract which he enters into will not be binding on him (save where it is a contract for necessaries, in which case he will have to pay a reasonable price).

Matthews v Baxter (1872-73) LR 8 Ex 132

Panel: Kelly CB, Martin, Pigott and Pollock BB

Facts: This case relates to a defendant who was too drunk to know what he was doing when he entered into a contract. The case confirms that such a contract is voidable rather than void because in this instance, after becoming sober, the defendant ratified and confirmed the contract.

KELLY CB

I am of opinion that our judgment must be for the plaintiff. It has been argued that a contract made by a person who was in the position of the defendant, is absolutely void. But it is difficult to understand this contention. For, surely, the defendant, upon coming to his senses, might have said to the plaintiff, 'True, I was drunk when I made this contract, but still I mean, now that I am sober, to hold you to it.' And if the defendant could say this, there must be a reciprocal right in the other party. The contract cannot be voidable only as regards one party, but void as regards the other; and if the drunken man, upon coming to his senses, ratifies the contract, I think he is bound by it.

Further Reading

Peel, E., 2008. Chitty on Contracts Part 3. Sweet & Maxwell. Ch.8. Vol.1

McKendrick, E., *Contract Law* (2017) 12th ed. Ch.16

5

Consideration

Topic List

Introduction

The doctrine of consideration is fundamental to classical contract law theory. At its simplest, it recognises the necessity of a bargaining element in making an agreement enforceable in that each party to a contract must provide something to the other. What that something is has been subject to much scrutiny over the years and it seems there is no single rule that can encompass all the different aspects of consideration. Additionally, although consideration has to comprise 'something of value', recently the courts have become more relaxed in their definition of 'value' in favour of finding consideration in situations where, in accordance with the traditional doctrine, this would not have been possible.

The cases reviewed in this chapter fall roughly into two categories: those which set out the requirements of consideration in relation to when something will constitute 'good' consideration; and, those which help determine when performance of an obligation which is already owed by a party will constitute 'good' consideration.

5.1 Definition

Dunlop Pneumatic Tyre Company Limited v Selfridge and Company Limited [1915] AC 847

Panel: Viscount Haldane LC, Lord Dunedin, Lord Atkinson, Lord Parker of Waddington, Lord Sumner and Lord Parmoor

Facts: The Dunlop Pneumatic Tyre Company, the appellants, had a trade agreement in place with a wholesale customer, A J Dew & Co, for the sale of tyres; under the agreement, Dunlop would allow Dew a discount on its wholesale prices. In return, Dew agreed to limit any discount it passed onto its customers and to ensure that it secured an undertaking from its customers that they would only sell at list prices to private customers. A model undertaking was provided to Dew by Dunlop which was to be signed by each of Dew's customers. This undertaking provided, among other things, that Dew's customers were to pay Dunlop an amount for every tyre which they sold below list price to a private buyer.

One of Dew's customers was Selfridge & Co, the respondents, who provided Dew with the relevant undertaking and signed the document. However, Selfridge subsequently broke the agreement and Dunlop claimed damages against them. The issue for the House of Lords was whether an enforceable contract had been concluded between Dunlop and Selfridge. One of the key issues in the case was whether Dunlop had provided Selfridge with any consideration

VISCOUNT HALDANE LC

...If a person with whom a contract not under seal has been made is to be able to enforce it consideration must have been given by him to the promisor or to some other person at the promisor's request. ...

LORD DUNEDIN

My Lords, I confess that this case is to my mind apt to nip any budding affection which one might have had for the doctrine of consideration. For the effect of that doctrine in the present case is to make it possible for a person to snap his fingers at a bargain deliberately made, a bargain not in itself unfair, and which the person seeking to enforce it has a legitimate interest to enforce. Notwithstanding these considerations I cannot say that I have ever had any doubt that the judgment of the Court of Appeal was right.

My Lords, I am content to adopt from a work of Sir Frederick Pollock, to which I have often been under obligation, the following words as to consideration: 'An act or forbearance of one party, or the promise thereof, is the price for which the promise of the other is bought, and the promise thus given for value is enforceable.' (Pollock on Contracts, 8th ed., p. 175.)

LORD SUMNER

...The appellants, as alleged promisees, neither did nor suffered nor forbore anything, nor promised to do any of these things or anything at all, in exchange for the undertaking purporting to be given by the respondents. ...

Alert

It is clear, particularly from Lord Dunedin's speech, that despite apparent unfairness, consideration is a core requirement for making an agreement enforceable. What is less clear, however, is a definition of what comprises consideration. Lord Dunedin adopts Pollock's definition of consideration, which can be seen as requiring an exchange of things of value between the contracting parties. In the case, since Dunlop had provided nothing of value to Selfridge, no consideration was found to have been exchanged for Selfridge's undertaking and so Dunlop's claim failed; the lack of consideration meant that there was no contract between them. (Please note that Dunlop's claim also failed on the basis that they were not privy to the agreement between Dew and Selfridge which contained the undertaking. This will be considered in detail in the chapter on privity.)

Link
Please see chapter 8

A slightly different definition of consideration is found in Lush J's judgment in *Currie v Misa* (1874-75) LR 10 Ex 153 where he states that: 'A valuable consideration, in the sense of the law, may consist either in some right, interest, profit, or benefit accruing to the one party, or some forbearance, detriment, loss, or responsibility, given, suffered, or undertaken by the other... [.]'

Mr Justice Lush's explanation of what constitutes consideration takes a slightly different tack to that in *Dunlop v Selfridge*. Instead of the concept of mutual exchange of something of value, this wider definition allows for a party to act to their own detriment in some way without the necessity for the other party to gain anything.

5.2 Requirements for 'Good' Consideration

5.2.1 Consideration must not be Past

Since consideration is required in order that a party may 'buy into' a contract, it follows that, if a party has already done whatever it brings to the table *before* a promise of payment is made and asks that their deed be counted as consideration, this will not be good consideration. This is known as 'past consideration'. The point is illustrated in *Roscorla v Thomas* (1842) 3 QB 234, where the plaintiff had bought a horse from the defendant for £30. After the sale had been agreed, the defendant promised that the horse was 'free of vice' which, it later turned out, was not the case. Lord Denman CJ held that, since the consideration for the horse was past, i.e. the promise to pay the money and take the horse had already been made, it would not support such a promise that the horse was free of vice.

However, the courts have found that, exceptionally, when certain criteria are met, past consideration may be good consideration. These criteria were considered and set out in full in *Pao On v Lau Yiu Long* [1980] AC 614.

Pao On v Lau Yiu Long **[1980] AC 614**

Panel: Lord Wilberforce, Viscount Dilhorne, Lord Simon of Glaisdale, Lord Salmon and Lord Scarman

Facts: The plaintiffs were owners of a company, Shing On, whose main asset was a building under construction; the defendant's were majority shareholders in a company called Fu Chip. The defendants wished to acquire the building owned by Shing On. It was decided that this purchase would be accommodated by the exchange of shares instead of cash. The defendants would provide the plaintiffs with shares in Fu Chip in exchange for the plaintiffs providing the defendants with shares in Shing On (i.e. the company that owned the building).

So as not to depress the market by flooding it with Fu Chip shares, the plaintiffs undertook, at the defendant's request, to retain 60 per cent of their newly acquired shares in Fu Chip until after 30 April 1974. Subsequently, the defendants agreed to indemnify the plaintiffs against any loss from a possible fall in the value of those Fu Chip shares between the date of the acquisition and 30 April 1974. Subsequent to the agreement, the price of Fu Chip shares fell and the plaintiffs sought to enforce the indemnity.

The defendants refused to honour the agreement to indemnify the plaintiffs, stating that any consideration which had been provided by the plaintiffs, i.e. the promise not to sell 60 per cent of the shares in Fu Chip, was past consideration and therefore not valid. The plaintiffs succeeded in their action in the High Court of Hong Kong but the Court of Appeal of Hong Kong reversed the decision. The plaintiffs then appealed to the Privy Council.

LORD SCARMAN

The Board agrees with [counsel for the plaintiffs'] submission that the consideration expressly stated in the written guarantee is sufficient in law to support the defendants' promise of indemnity. An act done before the giving of a promise to make a payment or to confer some other benefit can sometimes be consideration for the promise. The act must have been done at the promisors' request: the parties must have understood that the act was to be remunerated either by a payment or the conferment of some other benefit: and payment, or the conferment of a benefit, must have been legally enforceable had it been promised in advance. All three features are present in this case. The promise given to Fu Chip under the main agreement not to sell the shares for a year was at the first defendant's request. The parties understood at the time of the main agreement that the restriction on selling must be compensated for by the benefit of a guarantee against a drop in price: and such a guarantee would be legally enforceable. The agreed cancellation of the subsidiary agreement left, as the parties knew, the plaintiffs unprotected in a respect in which at the time of the main agreement all were agreed they should be protected.

Alert

[Counsel for the plaintiffs'] submission is based on *Lampleigh v. Brathwait* (1615) Hobart 105. In that case the judges said, at p. 106:

'First.... a meer voluntary courtesie will not have a consideration to uphold an assumpsit. But if that courtesie were moved by a suit or request of the party that gives the assumpsit, it will bind, for the promise, though it follows, yet it is not naked, but couples it self with the suit before, and the merits of the party procured by that suit. which is the difference.'

The modern statement of the law is in the judgment of Bowen L.J. in In *re Casey's Patents* [1892] 1 Ch. 104, 115-116; Bowen L.J. said:

'Even if it were true, as some scientific students of law believe, that a past service cannot support a future promise, you must look at the document and see if the promise cannot receive a proper effect in some other way. Now, the fact of a past service raises an implication that at the time it was rendered it was to be paid for, and, if it was a service which was to be paid for, when you get in the subsequent document a promise to pay, that promise may be treated either as an admission which evidences or as a positive bargain which fixes the amount of that reasonable remuneration on the faith of which the service was originally rendered. So that here for past services there is ample justification for the promise to give the third share.'

It can be seen, therefore, that even where consideration is past, it may still be good consideration if three criteria are met:

(i)   The act constituting the consideration must be done at the request of the promisor.

(ii)   There must have been an understanding that the act would be remunerated.

(iii)   The promise must have been legally enforceable had it been promised in advance of the act.

In order for the exception to apply, each of these three criteria must be met.

5.2.2   Consideration Must Move from the Promisee

There is a requirement that consideration must move from the promisee. It should be noted that this does not mean that it is required to move *to* the promisor so if the consideration consists of a promise to benefit a third party then this rule will be satisfied. The case of *Tweddle v Atkinson* (1861) 1 B & S 393; 121 ER 762, while comprising a fairly complex factual matrix, demonstrates the rule that consideration must move from the promisee.

Tweddle v Atkinson (1861) 1 B & S 393; 121 ER 762

Panel: Wightman, Crompton, Blackburn JJ

Facts: The fathers of a young, engaged couple promised each other that, on the marriage of the couple, each would pay a sum of money to the groom; £200 was to be paid by the groom's father, John Tweddle, and £100 was to be paid by the bride's father, William Guy. By their written agreement, the plaintiff was to have full power to sue them for the same.

However, following the marriage, Guy failed to pay the amount promised and, following his death, the executor of his estate was sued by the claimant groom for the amount. The court held that, since the claimant had not himself provided any consideration for the promise, he was a stranger to the contract and, therefore, unable to enforce the promise.

MR JUSTICE WIGHTMAN

Some of the old decisions appear to support the proposition that a stranger to the consideration of a contract may maintain an action upon it, if he stands in such a near relationship to the party from whom the consideration proceeds, that he may be considered a party to the consideration. The strongest of those cases is that cited in *Bourne v Mason* (1 Ventr. 6), in which it was held that the daughter of a physician might maintain assumpsit upon a promise to her father to give her a sum of money if he performed a certain cure. But there is no modern case in which the proposition has been supported. On the contrary, it is now established that no stranger to the consideration can take advantage of a contract, although made for his benefit.

MR JUSTICE CROMPTON

It is admitted that the plaintiff cannot succeed unless this case is an exception to the modern and well established doctrine of the action of assumpsit. At the time when the cases which have been cited were decided the action of assumpsit was treated as an action of trespass upon the case, and therefore in the nature of a tort; and the law was not settled, as it now is, that natural love and affection is not a sufficient consideration for a promise upon which an action may be maintained; nor was it settled that the promisee cannot bring an action unless the consideration for the promise moved from him. The modern cases have, in effect, overruled the old decisions; they shew that the consideration must move from the party entitled to sue upon the contract. It would be a monstrous proposition to say that a person was a party to the contract for the purpose of suing upon it for his own advantage, and not a party to it for the purpose of being sued. It is said that the father in the present case was agent for the son in making the contract, but that argument ought also to make the son liable upon it. I am prepared to overrule the old decisions, and to hold that, by reason of the principles which now govern the action of assumpsit, the present action is not maintainable.

5.2.3 Consideration Must be Sufficient but need not be Adequate

This rule recognises that it is not for the courts to decide whether a bargain or an agreement is fairly balanced insofar as each party giving and receiving something of equal value; in other words, the court will not enquire into the 'adequacy' of the consideration. For many reasons, this would not be possible, not the least of which is that to do otherwise would require the courts to place a value on everything that passed between parties to a contract and effectively to intervene if a bargain seemed one-sided.

However, consideration does require that each side provide something that has *some* value; it is said that consideration must be 'sufficient'. Provided it has some value in the eyes of the law, the court will look no further to ascertain whether the consideration is adequate such that the bargain is fair.

Chappell & Co Limited and Another v Nestlé Co Limited and Another [1960] AC 87

Panel: Viscount Simonds, Lord Reid, Lord Tucker, Lord Keith of Avonholm and Lord Somervell of Harrow

Facts: The appellants, Chappell, owned the copyright to a number of gramophone records, including a musical piece called 'Rockin' Shoes'. The respondents, Nestlé, were the manufacturers of chocolate bars. Nestlé had run a promotion whereby customers could collect a number of chocolate bar wrappers and send them back to Nestlé, along with 1s 6d; in return, Nestlé would send the customer a gramophone record of 'Rockin' Shoes'. However, by the Copyright Act 1956 s 8 the appellants were entitled to royalties of 6¼% of the 'ordinary retail selling price' of each record that was sold. They contended that, in calculating the amount of royalty payable, the 1s 6d should be taken into account as well as a value to be placed on the wrappers, which were also part of the selling price. Nestlé contended that the wrappers were not a part of the selling price since they were worthless and would be thrown away once received, and were therefore not part of the consideration. The

House of Lords found (Lord Keith and Viscount Simonds dissenting) that the wrappers did form part of the contract price.

LORD REID

I can now turn to what appears to me to be the crucial question in this case: was the 1s. 6d. an 'ordinary retail selling price' within the meaning of section 8? That involves two questions, what was the nature of the contract between the Nestlé Co. and a person who sent 1s. 6d. plus 3 wrappers in acceptance of their offer, and what is meant by 'ordinary retail selling price' in this context.

To determine the nature of the contract one must find the intention of the parties as shown by what they said and did. The Nestlé Co.'s intention can hardly be in doubt. They were not setting out to trade in gramophone records. They were using these records to increase their sales of chocolate. Their offer was addressed to everyone. It might be accepted by a person who was already a regular buyer of their chocolate; but, much more important to them, it might be accepted by people who might become regular buyers of their chocolate if they could be induced to try it and found they liked it. The inducement was something calculated to look like a bargain, a record at a very cheap price. It is in evidence that the ordinary price for a dance record is 6s. 6d. It is true that the ordinary record gives much longer playing time than the Nestlé records and it may have other advantages. But the reader of the Nestlé offer was not in a position to know that.

It seems to me clear that the main intention of the offer was to induce people interested in this kind of music to buy (or perhaps get others to buy) chocolate which otherwise would not have been bought. It is, of course, true that some wrappers might come from the chocolate which had already been bought or from chocolate which would have been bought without the offer, but that does not seem to me to alter the case. Where there is a large number of transactions - the notice mentions 30,000 records – I do not think we should simply consider an isolated case where it would be impossible to say whether there had been a direct benefit from the acquisition of the wrappers or not. The requirement that wrappers should be sent was of great importance to the Nestlé Co.; there would have been no point in their simply offering records for 1s. 6d. each. It seems to me quite unrealistic to divorce the buying of the chocolate from the supplying of the records. It is a perfectly good contract if a person accepts an offer to supply goods if he (a) does something of value to the supplier and (b) pays money: the consideration is both (a) and (b). There may have been cases where the acquisition of the wrappers conferred no direct benefit on the Nestlé Co., but there must have been many cases where it did. I do not see why the possibility that in some cases the acquisition of the wrappers did not directly benefit the Nestlé Co. should require us to exclude from consideration the cases where it did and even where there was no direct benefit from the acquisition of the wrappers there may have been an indirect benefit by way of advertisement.

I do not think that it matters greatly whether this kind of contract is called a sale or not. The appellants did not take the point that this transaction was not a sale.

But I am bound to say that I have some doubts. If a contract under which a person is bound to do something as well as to pay money is a sale, then either the price includes the obligation as well as the money, or the consideration is the price plus the obligation. And I do not see why it should be different if he has to show that he has done something of value to the seller. It is to my mind illegitimate to argue – this is a sale, the consideration for a sale is the price, price can only include money or something which can be readily converted into an ascertainable sum of money, therefore anything like wrappers which have no money value when delivered cannot be part of the consideration.

The respondents avoid this difficulty by submitting that acquiring and delivering the wrappers was merely a condition which gave a qualification to buy and was not part of the consideration for sale. Of course, a person may limit his offer to persons qualified in a particular way, e.g., members of a club. But where the qualification is the doing of something of value to the seller, and where the qualification only suffices for one sale and must be re-acquired before another sale, I find it hard to regard the repeated acquisitions of the qualification as anything other than parts of the consideration for the sales. The purchaser of records had to send 3 wrappers for each record, so he had first to acquire them. The acquisition of wrappers by him was, at least in many cases, of direct benefit to the Nestlé Co., and required expenditure by the acquirer which he might not otherwise have incurred. To my mind the acquiring and delivering of the wrappers was certainly part of the consideration in these cases, and I see no good reason for drawing a distinction between these and other cases. ...

In its context I cannot interpret the phrase 'ordinary retail selling price' as applying to all sales however extraordinary in character and as meaning whatever money price may be charged irrespective of the type of transaction or of conditions attached to the sale or of collateral advantages accruing to the seller or of whether the money price is really the whole consideration for the sale. I am of opinion that the ... notice that the ordinary retail selling price was 1s. 6d. was invalid, that there was no ordinary retail selling price in this case and that the respondents' operations were not within the ambit of section 8. They were therefore infringements of the appellants' copyright and in my judgment this appeal should be allowed.

LORD SOMERVELL

The question, then, is whether the three wrappers were part of the consideration or, as Jenkins L.J. held, a condition of making the purchase, like a ticket entitling a member to buy at a co-operative store.

I think they are part of the consideration. They are so described in the offer. 'They,' the wrappers, 'will help you to get smash hit recordings.' They are so described in the record itself - 'all you have to do to get such new record is to send three wrappers from Nestlé's 6d. milk chocolate bars, together with postal order for 1s. 6d.' This is not conclusive but, however described, they are, in my view, in law part of the consideration. It is said that when received the wrappers are of no value to Nestlé's. This I would have thought irrelevant. A contracting party can stipulate for what consideration he chooses. A peppercorn does not cease to be good consideration if it is established that the promisee does not like pepper and will throw away the corn. As the whole object of selling the record, if it was a sale, was to increase the sales of chocolate, it seems to me wrong not to treat the stipulated evidence of such sales as part of the consideration. For these reasons I would allow the appeal.

The wrappers counted as consideration. Lord Somervell made it plain that the court will not enquire as to whether the bargain is fair. Something as insignificant as a peppercorn will constitute good consideration (hence the phrase 'peppercorn rent'). In their Lordships' view, the wrappers had some value to Nestlé in that they increased the sale of chocolate bars and as *per* Lord Reid, in those instances where the bars would have been purchased anyway, the scheme provided advertising exposure.

5.3 Performance of an Existing Obligation

One area in which the courts have developed particular rules in relation to consideration is regarding the performance of existing obligations. If a person is already obliged to do something, is it possible for them to provide good consideration by merely doing that which they are already obliged to do? This area can be split into three distinct situations: performance of existing contractual obligations; performance of existing obligations under a public duty; and, performance of existing obligations owed to a third party.

5.3.1 Existing Contractual Obligations Owed to the Promisor

Performance of an existing contractual obligation owed to the promisor is not good consideration to enforce a new promise from that promisor to pay more. Compare *Stilk v Myrick* (1809) 2 Campbell 317; 170 ER 1168 and *Hartley v Ponsonby* (1857) 7 Ellis and Blackburn 872; 119 ER 1471 and consider why, in *Stilk v Myrick*, the court gave judgment in favour of the captain, and in *Hartley v Ponsonby* the court gave judgment in favour of the sailor.

Stilk v Myrick (1809) 2 Campbell 317; 170 ER 1168

Panel: Lord Ellenborough

Facts: Ten sailors had contracted to serve on a ship. In the course of a sea voyage to the Baltic, two of the ten sailors deserted. The captain, who was unable to find replacements for them, promised the remaining eight sailors that, if they sailed the ship back to England, he would divide the wages of the deserting sailors between those who remained. On their arrival in England, however, the Captain refused to honour his promise and the sailors brought an action for the payment.

LORD ELLENBOROUGH

...Here, I say, the agreement is void for want of consideration. There was no consideration for the ulterior pay promised to the mariners who remained with the ship. Before they sailed from London they had undertaken to do all that they could under all the emergencies of the voyage. They had sold all their services till the voyage should be completed. If they had been at liberty to quit the vessel at Cronstadt, the case would have been quite different; or if the captain had capriciously discharged the two men who were wanting, the others might not have been compellable to take the whole duty upon themselves, and their agreeing to do so might have been a sufficient consideration for the promise of an advance of wages. But the desertion of a part of the crew is to be considered an emergency of the voyage as much as their death; and those who remain are bound by the terms of their original contract to exert themselves to the utmost to bring the ship in safety to her destined port. Therefore, without looking to the policy of this agreement, I think it is void for want of consideration, and that the plaintiff can only recover at the rate of £5 a month.

Hartley v Ponsonby (1857) 7 Ellis and Blackburn 872; 119 ER 1471

Panel: Lord Campbell CJ, Coleridge, Erle and Crompton JJ

Facts: The plaintiff was the ship's captain and the defendant was a sailor on the ship. The crew had an agreement to sail the ship from Liverpool to Port Philip in Australia, then to Bombay. The proper complement of crew members for a ship of this type was 36. However, when the vessel reached Port Philip, 17 of the crew refused to continue and were imprisoned. Of the 19 remaining crew, only four or five were able seamen and the captain was unable to obtain replacements at reasonable cost. He therefore promised the remaining crew that if they sailed the ship to Bombay, he would pay them extra, to which they agreed. During the voyage, the weather was so severe and the crew members so few that 'extraordinary labour fell upon' them. The jury found in favour of the defendant sailor.

LORD CAMPBELL CJ

I think that this verdict should stand. The answer given by the jury to the third question imports to my mind that for the ship to go to sea with so few hands was dangerous to life. If so, it was not incumbent on the plaintiff to perform the work; and he was in the condition of a free man. There was therefore a consideration for the contract; and the captain made it without coercion. This is therefore a voluntary agreement upon sufficient consideration. This decision will not conflict with any former decisions. In *The Araminta (Feran)* (1 Spinks' Ecc. & Adm. Rep. 229) Dr. Lushington says: 'I do not wish it to be inferred from anything I now say, that mariners, having completed the voyage outwards, are compellable to make the return voyage when the number of the crew is so small that risk of life may be incurred.' ...

MR JUSTICE COLERIDGE

I am of the same opinion, and for the same reasons. I understand the finding of the jury to be, that the ship was unseaworthy; and that, owing to the excessive labour which would be imposed, it was not reasonable to require the mariners to go to sea. If they were not bound to go, they were free to make a new contract: and the master was justified in hiring them on the best terms he could make. It may be that the plaintiff took advantage of his position to make a hard bargain; but there was no duress.

MR JUSTICE ERLE

I am of the same opinion. I was deeply impressed with the consequence of not holding the plaintiff liable to perform his original engagement. But there is a point of danger at which it becomes unreasonable for mariners to be required to go on. That is a question for a jury. The mariners, not being bound to go on, were to all intents and purposes free, and might make the best contract they could.

MR JUSTICE CROMPTON

The jury have found that this was a free bargain. As regards public policy, it would be very dangerous to lay down that, under all circumstances and at any risk of life, seamen are bound to proceed on a voyage. The jury have found in this case (and, I think, upon the evidence, correctly,) that it was not reasonable to require the seamen to go on. Where, from a ship being short-handed, it would be unsafe for the seamen to go to sea, they become free to make any new contract that they like.

It can be seen from these two cases that the general rule is that performance of an existing obligation under a contract will not be sufficient to constitute good consideration for a promise to pay more. However, where the promisee goes beyond the scope of their original obligation, this will be good consideration. In *Stilk v Myrick*, the sailors 'had undertaken to do all that they could under all the emergencies of the voyage' – the desertion of two men was simply an emergency of the voyage. Consequently, they were merely carrying out the obligations they already had and, therefore, this was not good consideration for the captain's promise of additional payment.

By contrast, in *Hartley v Ponsonby*, more of the crew deserted. The court took note of the increased danger which the drastically reduced crew faced and held that the ongoing voyage was so different from that for which they had originally been contracted that performance of it constituted good consideration for the captain's promise. They were doing something over and above what they had originally contracted to do.

Until the case of *Williams v Roffey Bros. & Nichol (Contractors) Ltd* [1991] 1 QB 1, this used to be the end of the matter: if you did not go over and above your existing contractual obligation, then you would not be providing good consideration since there was no legal benefit. However, in *Williams v Roffey* the concept of 'practical' or 'factual' benefit was born. Since *Williams v Roffey*, you can provide good consideration if you provide a practical or factual benefit to the promisor even if you are simply performing your existing obligations under the contract.

Williams v Roffey Bros. & Nichol (Contractors) Ltd. [1991] 1 QB 1

Panel: Purchas, Glidewell and Russell LJJ

Facts: The defendants, Roffey Bros, had been contracted to build a block of flats and they sub-contracted the plaintiff, Lester Williams, to carry out the carpentry work in 27 of the flats for an agreed price of £20,000. Before the work was completed, Williams got into financial difficulty and it was clear that, without additional money, he would be unable to finish and would, therefore, be in breach of contract. Had the work not been finished on time, Roffey Bros would have been liable for substantial penalties to the main contractors under their contract to build the flats. Consequently, they promised Williams an additional £575 per completed flat. Roffey Bros did not stick to their promise and Williams sued for the additional sum.

LORD JUSTICE GLIDEWELL

Was there consideration for the defendants' promise made on 9 April 1986 to pay an additional price at the rate of £575 per completed flat?

The judge made the following findings of fact which are relevant on this issue. (i) The subcontract price agreed was too low to enable the plaintiff to operate satisfactorily and at a profit. Mr. Cottrell, the defendants' surveyor, agreed that this was so.

(ii) Mr. Roffey (managing director of the defendants) was persuaded by Mr. Cottrell that the defendants should pay a bonus to the plaintiff. The figure agreed at the meeting on 9 April 1986 was £10,300.

The judge quoted and accepted the evidence of Mr. Cottrell to the effect that a main contractor who agrees too low a price with a subcontractor is acting contrary to his own interests. He will never get the job finished without paying more money. The judge therefore concluded:

'In my view where the original subcontract price is too low, and the parties subsequently agree that additional moneys shall be paid to the subcontractor, this agreement is in the interests of both parties. This is what happened in the present case, and in my opinion the agreement of 9 April 1986 does not fail for lack of consideration.'

In his address to us, [counsel for the defendants] outlined the benefits to his clients, the defendants, which arose from their agreement to pay the additional £10,300 as:

(i) seeking to ensure that the plaintiff continued work and did not stop in breach of the subcontract; (ii) avoiding the penalty for delay; and (iii) avoiding

 **Decipher**
Note that, although this is referred to as a penalty clause, it was in fact a valid liquidated damages clause.

the trouble and expense of engaging other people to complete the carpentry work.

However, [counsel for the defendants] submits that, though his clients may have derived, or hoped to derive, practical benefits from their agreement to pay the 'bonus,' they derived no benefit in law, since the plaintiff was promising to do no more than he was already bound to do by his subcontract, i.e., continue with the carpentry work and complete it on time. Thus there was no consideration for the agreement. ...

...The defendants rely on the principle of law which, traditionally, is based on *Stilk v. Myrick* (1809) 2 Camp. 317. In *North Ocean Shipping Co. Ltd. v. Hyundai Construction Co. Ltd.* [1979] Q.B. 705, 712G-713E, Mocatta J. regarded the general principle in *Stilk v. Myrick*, 2 Camp. 317, as still being good law... [.]

Link
See chapter 18 on Remedies

It was suggested to us in argument that, since the development of the doctrine of promissory estoppel, it may well be possible for a person to whom a promise has been made, on which he has relied, to make an additional payment for services which he is in any event bound to render under an existing contract or by operation of law, to show that the promisor is estopped from claiming that there was no consideration for his promise. However, the application of the doctrine of promissory estoppel to facts such as those of the present case has not yet been fully developed: see e.g. the judgment of Lloyd J. in *Syros Shipping Co. S.A v. Elaghill Trading Co.* [1980] 2 Lloyd's Rep. 390, 392. Moreover, this point was not argued in the court below, nor was it more than adumbrated before us. Interesting though it is, no reliance can in my view be placed on this concept in the present case.

There is, however, another legal concept of relatively recent development which is relevant, namely, that of economic duress. Clearly if a subcontractor has agreed to undertake work at a fixed price, and before he has completed the work declines to continue with it unless the contractor agrees to pay an increased price, the subcontractor may be held guilty of securing the contractor's promise by taking unfair advantage of the difficulties he will cause if he does not complete the work. In such a case an agreement to pay an increased price may well be voidable because it was entered into under duress. Thus this concept may provide another answer in law to the question of policy which has troubled the courts since before *Stilk v. Myrick*, 2 Camp. 317, and no doubt led at the date of that decision to a rigid adherence to the doctrine of consideration.

...The present state of the law on this subject can be expressed in the following proposition: (i) if A has entered into a contract with B to do work for, or to supply goods or services to, B in return for payment by B; and (ii) at some stage before A has completely performed his obligations under the contract B has reason to doubt whether A will, or will be able to, complete his side of the bargain; and (iii) B thereupon promises A an additional payment in return for A's promise to perform his contractual obligations on time; and (iv)

Alert

as a result of giving his promise, B obtains in practice a benefit, or obviates a disbenefit; and (v) B's promise is not given as a result of economic duress or fraud on the part of A; then (vi) the benefit to B is capable of being consideration for B's promise, so that the promise will be legally binding.

As I have said, [counsel for the defendants] accepts that in the present case by promising to pay the extra £10,300 his client secured benefits. There is no finding, and no suggestion, that in this case the promise was given as a result of fraud or duress. If it be objected that the propositions above contravene the principle in *Stilk v. Myrick*, 2 Camp. 317, I answer that in my view they do not; they refine, and limit the application of that principle, but they leave the principle unscathed e.g. where B secures no benefit by his promise. It is not in my view surprising that a principle enunciated in relation to the rigours of seafaring life during the Napoleonic wars should be subjected during the succeeding 180 years to a process of refinement and limitation in its application in the present day. It is therefore my opinion that on his findings of fact in the present case, the judge was entitled to hold, as he did, that the defendants' promise to pay the extra £10,300 was supported by valuable consideration, and thus constituted an enforceable agreement.

LORD JUSTICE RUSSELL

There is no hint in that pleading that the defendants were subjected to any duress to make the agreement or that their promise to pay the extra £10,300 lacked consideration. As the judge found, the plaintiff must have continued work in the belief that he would be paid £575 as he finished each of the 18 uncompleted flats (although the arithmetic is not precisely accurate). For their part the defendants recorded the new terms in their ledger. Can the defendants now escape liability on the ground that the plaintiff undertook to do no more than he had originally contracted to do although, quite clearly, the defendants, on 9 April 1986, were prepared to make the payment and only declined to do so at a later stage. It would certainly be unconscionable if this were to be their legal entitlement.

The submissions advanced on both sides before this court ranged over a wide field. They went far beyond the pleadings, and indeed it is worth noticing that the absence of consideration was never pleaded, although argued before the assistant recorder, Mr. Rupert Jackson Q.C. Speaking for myself – and I notice it is touched upon in the judgment of Glidewell L.J. – I would have welcomed the development of argument, if it could have been properly raised in this court, on the basis that there was here an estoppel and that the defendants, in the circumstances prevailing, were precluded from raising the defence that their undertaking to pay the extra £10,300 was not binding. For example, in *Amalgamated Investment & Property Co. Ltd. v. Texas Commerce International Bank Ltd.* [1982] Q.B. 84 Robert Goff J. said, at p. 105:

'it is in my judgment not of itself a bar to an estoppel that its effect may be to enable a party to enforce a cause of action which, without the estoppel, would not exist. It is sometimes said that an estoppel cannot create a cause of action, or that an estoppel can only act as a shield, not as a sword. In a sense this is true – in the sense that estoppel is not, as a contract is, a source of legal obligation. But as Lord Denning M.R. pointed out in *Crabb v. Arun District Council* [1976] Ch. 179, 187, an estoppel may have the effect that a party can enforce a cause of action which, without the estoppel, he would not be able to do.'

When the case came to the Court of Appeal Lord Denning M.R. said, at p. 122:

'The doctrine of estoppel is one of the most flexible and useful in the armoury of the law. But it has become overloaded with cases. That is why I have not gone through them all in this judgment. It has evolved during the last 150 years in a sequence of separate developments: proprietary estoppel, estoppel by representation of fact, estoppel by acquiescence, and promissory estoppel. At the same time it has been sought to be limited by a series of maxims: estoppel is only a rule of evidence, estoppel cannot give rise to a cause of action, estoppel cannot do away with the need for consideration, and so forth. All these can now be seen to merge into one general principle shorn of limitations. When the parties to a transaction proceed on the basis of an underlying assumption – either of fact or of law – whether due to misrepresentation or mistake makes no difference – on which they have conducted the dealings between them – neither of them will be allowed to go back on that assumption when it would be unfair or unjust to allow him to do so. If one of them does seek to go back on it, the courts will give the other such remedy as the equity of the case demands.'

Brandon L.J. said, at pp. 131-132:

'while a party cannot in terms found a cause of action on an estoppel, he may, as a result of being able to rely on an estoppel, succeed on a cause of action on which, without being able to rely on that estoppel, he would necessarily have failed.'

These citations demonstrate that whilst consideration remains a fundamental requirement before a contract not under seal can be enforced, the policy of the law in its search to do justice between the parties has developed considerably since the early 19th century when *Stilk v. Myrick*, 2 Camp. 317 was decided by Lord Ellenborough C.J. In the late 20th century I do not believe that the rigid approach to the concept of consideration to be found in *Stilk v. Myrick* is either necessary or desirable. Consideration there must still be but, in my judgment, the courts nowadays should be more ready to find its existence so as to reflect the intention of the parties to the contract where the bargaining powers are not unequal and where the finding of consideration reflect the true intention of the parties.

What was the true intention of the parties when they arrived at the agreement pleaded by the defendants in paragraph 5 of the amended defence? The plaintiff had got into financial difficulties. The defendants, through their employee Mr. Cottrell, recognised the price that had been agreed originally with the plaintiff was less than what Mr. Cottrell himself regarded as a reasonable price. There was a desire on Mr. Cottrell's part to retain the services of the plaintiff so that the work could be completed without the need to employ another subcontractor. There was further a need to replace what had hitherto been a haphazard method of payment by a more formalised scheme involving the payment of a specified sum on the completion of each flat. These were all advantages accruing to the defendants which can fairly be said to have been in consideration of their undertaking to pay the additional £10,300. True it was that the plaintiff did not undertake to do any work additional to that which he had originally undertaken to do but the terms upon which he was to carry out the work were varied and, in my judgment, that variation was supported by consideration which a pragmatic approach to the true relationship between the parties readily demonstrates.

For my part I wish to make it plain that I do not base my judgment upon any reservation as to the correctness of the law long ago enunciated in *Stilk v. Myrick*. A gratuitous promise, pure and simple, remains unenforceable unless given under seal. But where, as in this case, a party undertakes to make a payment because by so doing it will gain an advantage arising out of the continuing relationship with the promisee the new bargain will not fail for want of consideration. As I read the judgment of the assistant recorder this was his true ratio upon that part of the case wherein the absence of consideration was raised in argument. For the reasons that I have endeavoured to outline, I think that the assistant recorder came to a correct conclusion and I too would dismiss this appeal.

LORD JUSTICE PURCHAS

The point of some difficulty which arises on this appeal is whether the judge was correct in his conclusion that the agreement reached on 9 April did not fail for lack of consideration because the principle established by the old cases of *Stilk v. Myrick*, 2 Camp. 317 approving *Harris v. Watson*, Peake 102 did not apply. [Counsel for the plaintiff] ... was bold enough to submit that ... this court was bound by neither authority. I feel I must say at once that, for my part, I would not be prepared to overrule two cases of such veneration involving judgments of judges of such distinction except on the strongest possible grounds since they form a pillar stone of the law of contract which has been observed over the years and is still recognised in principle in recent authority: see the decision of *Stilk v. Myrick* to be found in *North Ocean Shipping Co. Ltd. v. Hyundai Construction Co. Ltd.* [1979] Q.B. 705, 712 *per* Mocatta J. ... Although this rule has been the subject of some criticism it is still clearly recognised in current textbooks of authority: see *Chitty on Contracts*, 28th ed. (1989) and *Cheshire, Fifoot and Furmston's Law of Contract*, 11th ed. (1986). ...

In my judgment, therefore, the rule in *Stilk v. Myrick*, 2 Camp. 317 remains valid as a matter of principle, namely that a contract not under seal must be supported by consideration. Thus, where the agreement upon which reliance is placed provides that an extra payment is to be made for work to be done by the payee which he is already obliged to perform then unless some other consideration is detected to support the agreement to pay the extra sum that agreement will not be enforceable. The two cases, *Harris v. Watson*, Peake 102 and *Stilk v. Myrick*, 2 Camp. 317 involved circumstances of a very special nature, namely the extraordinary conditions existing at the turn of the 18th century under which seamen had to serve their contracts of employment on the high seas. There were strong public policy grounds at that time to protect the master and owners of a ship from being held to ransom by disaffected crews. Thus, the decision that the promise to pay extra wages even in the circumstances established in those cases, was not supported by consideration is readily understandable. Of course, conditions today on the high seas have changed dramatically and it is at least questionable ... whether these cases might not well have been decided differently if they were tried today. The modern cases tend to depend more upon the defence of duress in a commercial context rather than lack of consideration for the second agreement. In the present case the question of duress does not arise. The initiative in coming to the agreement of 9 April came from Mr. Cottrell and not from the plaintiff. It would not, therefore, lie in the defendants' mouth to assert a defence of duress. Nevertheless, the court is more ready in the presence of this defence being available in the commercial context to look for mutual advantages which would amount to sufficient consideration to support the second agreement under which the extra money is paid. Although the passage cited below from the speech of Lord Hailsham of St. Marylebone L.C. in *Woodhouse A.C. Israel Cocoa Ltd. S.A. v. Nigerian Produce Marketing Co. Ltd.* [1972] A.C. 741 was strictly obiter dicta I respectfully adopt it as an indication of the approach to be made in modern times. ...

'...Business men know their own business best even when they appear to grant an indulgence, and in the present case I do not think that there would have been insuperable difficulty in spelling out consideration from the earlier correspondence.'

...

The question must be posed: what consideration has moved from the plaintiff to support the promise to pay the extra £10,300 added to the lump sum provision? In the particular circumstances which I have outlined above, there was clearly a commercial advantage to both sides from a pragmatic point of view in reaching the agreement of 9 April. The defendants were on risk that as a result of the bargain they had struck the plaintiff would not or indeed possibly could not comply with his existing obligations without further finance. As a result of the agreement the defendants secured their position commercially. There was, however, no obligation added to the contractual duties imposed upon the plaintiff under the original contract. Prima facie this would appear to be a classic *Stilk v. Myrick* case. It was, however, open to the plaintiff to be in deliberate breach of the contract in order to 'cut his losses' commercially. In normal circumstances the suggestion that a contracting party can rely upon his own breach to establish consideration is distinctly unattractive. In many cases it obviously would be and if there was any element of duress brought upon the other contracting party under the modern development of this branch of the law the proposed breaker of the contract would not benefit. With some hesitation and comforted by the passage from the speech of Lord Hailsham of St. Marylebone L.C. in *Woodhouse A.C. Israel Cocoa Ltd. S.A. v. Nigerian Produce Marketing Co. Ltd.* [1972] A.C. 741, 757-758, to which I have referred, I consider that the modern approach to the question of consideration would be that where there were benefits derived by each party to a contract of variation even though one party did not suffer a detriment this would not be fatal to the establishing of sufficient consideration to support the agreement. If both parties benefit from an agreement it is not necessary that each also suffers a detriment. In my judgment, on the facts as found by the judge, he was entitled to reach the conclusion that consideration existed and in those circumstances I would not disturb that finding. This is sufficient to determine the appeal. ...

It is clear from this case that the courts are now prepared to stretch the strict doctrine of consideration in certain circumstances to ensure the fairness of the case. In *Williams v Roffey*, Glidewell LJ has extended the definition of consideration to encompass more than the strict legal benefit that hitherto had been required. Now, in certain circumstances, a *factual* or *practical benefit* may be sufficient to constitute good consideration even if the promisee is simply performing his existing contractual duties. Lord Justice Glidewell has set out a five stage test to be applied:

1.   A enters a contract with B to supply goods or services to B in return for payment;

2.   Before A completes his obligations, B has reason to doubt whether A will, or will be able to complete his obligations;

3.   B thereupon promises A an additional payment in return for a promise to complete on time;

4.   As a result of receiving the promise, B obtains a *practical benefit* or obviates a disbenefit; and

5.   There is no duress.

In the case, Glidewell LJ found that there was good consideration for Roffey Bros' promise to pay additional money for completion of the work despite the fact that Williams was already obliged to complete on time. The consideration took the form of, firstly, Roffey Bros avoiding having to pay the penalty clause under the main contract if they failed to complete on time. Secondly, they avoided having to find new carpenters to do Williams's job. These were, therefore, practical benefits (in the obviation of disbenefits) and sufficient to fulfil the criteria he had set out. Additionally, Russell LJ found that there was a practical benefit to the contractors in that the original agreement was rather 'haphazard' and this was subsequently replaced with a more structured agreement.

The court felt able to extend the doctrine of consideration to the provision of a practical benefit in light of the development of the doctrine of economic duress. When *Stilk v Myrick* was decided, there was no doctrine of economic duress. However, today, economic duress protects against the risk that a party will be able to extort additional payments for no extra work.

Link

See chapter on Economic Duress

Even so, *Williams v Roffey* has been an extremely controversial decision since it gives a contractor the ability to be paid more money simply for performing his original contractual duties. Another problem with the decision is that it gives no definition of 'practical benefit'.

N.B. *Williams v Roffey* consideration only applies to promises to pay more for existing contractual obligations. Provision of a practical benefit does not constitute good consideration for a promise to accept less (*In Re Selectmove* [1995] 1 WLR 474). However this distinction is being tested by the decision in *MWB Business Exchange Centres Ltd v Rock Advertising Ltd* [2016] EWCA Civ 553. Please note that at the time of print, the judgment of the Supreme Court is still pending. Once handed down, the electronic version of this chapter will be updated on the VLE.

Link

See chapter on Part Payment of a Debt and Promissory Estoppel

5.3.2 Existing Public Duty

Performance of an existing public duty will not constitute good consideration.

Collins v Godefroy (1831) 1 Barnwell and Adolphus 950; 109 ER 1040

Panel: Lord Tenderton CJ

Facts: Godefroy was the plaintiff in a case against an attorney. Collins was a witness who had been subpoenaed to attend the trial but afterwards demanded of Godefroy 'six guineas as his regular fee' for trial attendance.

LORD TENDERTON CJ

Assuming that the offer to pay the six guineas without costs was evidence of an express promise by the defendant to pay that sum to the plaintiff as a compensation to him for his loss of time, still, if the defendant was not bound by law to pay that sum, the offer to do so, not having been accepted, will not avail the plaintiff. If it be a duty imposed by law upon a party regularly subpoenaed, to attend from time to time to give his evidence, then a promise to give him any remuneration for loss of time incurred in such attendance is a promise without consideration. We think that such a duty is imposed by law; and on consideration of the Statute of Elizabeth, and of the cases which have been decided on this subject, we are all of opinion that a party cannot maintain an action for compensation for loss of time in attending a trial as a witness. We are aware of the practice which has prevailed in certain cases, of allowing, as costs between party and party, so much per day for the attendance of professional men; but that practice cannot alter the law. What the effect of our decision may be, is not for our consideration. We think, on principle, that an action does not lie for a compensation to a witness for loss of time in attendance under a subpoena. The rule, therefore, must be discharged.

Since Collins was already under an existing public duty to give evidence as he had been subpoenaed, his attendance at court could not constitute consideration for a promise by Godefroy to pay him.

However, where the promisee goes over and above his existing public duty, this will act as good consideration. In *Glasbrook Bros Limited v Glamorgan County Council* [1925] AC 270, a coal miners' strike required policing and the colliery owners requested of the police that 100 officers be billeted on the premises to keep order. The local police superintendant believed that it would be adequate that a stand-by force be put together with the view to moving onto the colliery should it become necessary. However, the requested 100 officers were provided and it was held that, since this was over and above the superintendant's assessment of requirement, it was a 'special force' for which payment was due.

Similarly, in *Harris v Sheffield United Football Club Limited* [1988] QB 77, the Club requested of the police authority that police services be provided to cover football matches. When the police claimed for payment for their services, the Club responded that the police were merely doing what they already had a public duty to do – to enforce the law. It was held, however, that the police were entitled to payment since they had provided a higher level of service than they would otherwise have provided.

5.3.3   Existing Contractual Obligation Owed to a Third Party

In contrast with the previous two categories (performance of an existing contractual duty owed to the promisor and performance of an existing public duty) performance of an existing contractual obligation owed to a third party does constitute good consideration.

Scotson v Pegg (1861) 6 Hurlstone and Norman 295; 158 ER 121

Panel: Martin and Wilde BB

Facts: The plaintiffs, Scotson, had contracted with a third party (X) that they would deliver a consignment of coal to X or to whomever X elected. Before delivery, X had sold on the consignment to Pegg. Consequently, X elected that Scotson should deliver the consignment to Pegg. Scotson then agreed with Pegg that Pegg would accept and unload the coal at a particular rate if Scotson delivered it directly to them. When the coal was delivered, Pegg refused to unload it and claimed that there was no consideration for their promise to unload. They argued that Scotson's promise to deliver directly to them could not constitute good consideration since Scotson was already under a contractual obligation to X (the third party) to deliver to them (Pegg). The court, however, held otherwise.

MARTIN B

I am of opinion that the plea is bad, both on principle and in law. It is bad in law because the ordinary rule is, that any act done whereby the contracting party receives a benefit is a good consideration for a promise by him. Here the benefit is the delivery of the coals to the defendant. It is consistent with the declaration that there may have been some dispute as to the defendant's right to have the coals, or it may be that the plaintiffs detained them for demurrage; in either case there would be good consideration that the plaintiffs, who were in possession of the coals, would allow the defendant to take them out of the ship. Then is it any answer that the plaintiffs had entered into a prior contract with other persons to deliver the coals to their order upon the same terms, and that the defendant was a stranger to that contract? In my opinion it is not. We must deal with this case as if no prior contract had been entered into. Suppose the plaintiffs had no chance of getting their money from the other persons who might perhaps have become bankrupt. The defendant gets a benefit by the delivery of the coals to him, and it is immaterial that the plaintiffs had previously contracted with third parties to deliver to their order.

WILDE B

I am also of opinion that the plaintiffs are entitled to judgment. The plaintiffs say, that in consideration that they would deliver to the defendant a cargo of coals from their ship, the defendant promised to discharge the cargo in a certain way. The defendant, in answer, says, 'You made a previous contract with other persons that they should discharge the cargo in the same way, and therefore there is no consideration for my promise.' But why is there no consideration? It is said, because the plaintiffs, in delivering the coals are only performing that which they were already bound to do. But to say that there is no consideration is to say that it is not possible for one man to have an interest in the performance of a contract made by another. But if a person chooses to promise to pay a sum of money in order to induce another to perform that which he has already contracted with a third person to do, I confess I cannot see why such a promise should not be binding. Here the defendant, who was a stranger to the original contract, induced the plaintiffs to part with the cargo, which they might not otherwise have been willing to do, and the delivery of it to the defendant was a benefit to him. I accede to the proposition that if a person contracts with another to do a certain thing, he cannot make the performance of it a consideration for a new promise to the same individual. But there is no authority for the proposition that where there has been a promise to one person to do a certain thing, it is not possible to make a valid promise to another to do the same thing. Therefore, deciding this matter on principle, it is plain to my mind that the delivery of the coals to the defendant was a good consideration for his promise, although the plaintiffs had made a previous contract to deliver them to the order of other persons.

The reason why it is good consideration to perform an obligation which you are already obliged to perform to a third party, was made clear by Lord Wilberforce in *New Zealand Shipping Co. Ltd. Appellant v A. M. Satterthwaite & Co. Ltd. (The Eurymedon)* [1975] AC 154 when he said: 'An agreement to do an act which the promisor is under an existing obligation to a third party to do, may quite well amount to valid consideration and does so in the present case: the promisee obtains the benefit of a direct obligation which he can enforce.'

Further Reading

Atiyah Consideration in Contracts: A Fundamental Restatement, (1971) reprinted in *Essays on Contract* (1986) 179

Fuller Consideration and Form, (1941) 41 *Columbia L Rev* 799

Treitel Consideration: A Critical Analysis of Professor Atiyah's Fundamental Restatement, (1976) 50 *Aust* LJ 439

McKendrick, E., *Contract Law* (2017) 12th ed. Ch.5

6

Part-payment of a Debt and Promissory Estoppel

Topic List

Introduction

In the previous chapter the position in relation to promises to pay more for existing contractual obligations was considered. If the promisee is simply performing his existing contractual obligations, then this will not constitute consideration for a promise to pay more (*Stilk v Myrick* (1809) 2 Campbell 317, 170 ER 1168). If, on the other hand, the promisee goes over and above his existing contractual obligations, then this will constitute good consideration (*Hartley v Ponsonby* 7 Ellis and Blackburn 872, 119 ER 1471). The case of *Williams v Roffey Bros & Nicholls (Contractors) Ltd* [1991] 1 QB 1 was also examined. That case provided that, if certain criteria are met, performance of existing contractual obligations will constitute good consideration provided the promisor obtains a practical benefit or obviates a disbenefit.

This chapter focuses on promises to accept less money; in other words, promises to accept part-payment of a debt. The first section will consider the general rule relating to promises to accept less, the second section will focus on the common law exceptions, and the final section will focus on the equitable exception of promissory estoppel.

6.1 Promises to Accept Less – the General Rule

In practice, promises to accept part-payment of a debt are often made by creditors and these promises are intended to be binding. For example, a creditor may be owed £1,000 but agree to accept £800 from the debtor in full and final settlement of the debt. However, the general rule is that, since such promises are unsupported by consideration, they are not binding: despite his promise, the creditor can still enforce the whole debt. The general rule (that a promise to accept less is not good consideration) was set out by Sir Edward Coke in his *obiter* comments in *Pinnel's Case* 77 ER 237, (1602) 5 Co Rep 117a and was later confirmed in *Foakes v Beer* (1883-84) LR 9 App Cas 60.

Foakes v Beer (1883-84) LR 9 App Cas 60

Panel: Earl of Selborne LC, Lord Blackburn, Lord Watson and Lord Fitzgerald

Facts: Mrs Beer (the 'judgment creditor') brought a claim against Dr Foakes (the 'judgment debtor') and obtained judgment against him for the sum of £2,090. Afterwards, the parties agreed in writing that Mrs Beer would not take further court proceedings to enforce the judgment, as long as Dr Foakes paid the sum of £500 upon signing the agreement and paid the remainder in instalments.

Dr Foakes paid all the instalments, but Mrs Beer subsequently made a claim for interest on the whole judgment debt of £2,090, backdated to the date of the judgment. Interest was not mentioned in the written agreement but under statute all judgment debts attracted interest until they were paid. Dr Foakes refused to pay interest and the claim ultimately went to the House of Lords.

EARL OF SELBORNE LC

...The question remains, whether the agreement is capable of being legally enforced. Not being under seal, it cannot be legally enforced against the respondent, unless she received consideration for it from the appellant, or unless, though without consideration, it operates by way of accord and satisfaction, so as to extinguish the claim for interest. What is the consideration? On the face of the agreement none is expressed... [P]ayment at those deferred dates, by the forbearance and indulgence of the creditor, of the residue of the principal debt and costs, could not (in my opinion) be a consideration for the relinquishment of interest and discharge of the judgment. ...

The question, therefore, is nakedly raised by this appeal, whether your Lordships are now prepared, not only to overrule, as contrary to law, the doctrine stated by Sir Edward Coke to have been laid down by all the judges of the Common Pleas in *Pinnel's Case* 5 Rep. 117a in 1602 ... but to treat a prospective agreement, not under seal, for satisfaction of a debt, by a series of payments on account to a total amount less than the whole debt, as binding in law, provided those payments are regularly made... .

The doctrine itself, as laid down by Sir Edward Coke, may have been criticised, as questionable in principle, by some persons whose opinions are entitled to respect, but it has never been judicially overruled; on the contrary I think it has always, since the sixteenth century, been accepted as law. If so, I cannot think that your Lordships would do right, if you were now to reverse, as erroneous, a judgment of the Court of Appeal, proceeding upon a doctrine which has been accepted as part of the law of England for 280 years. The doctrine, as stated in Pinnel's Case, is 'that payment of a lesser sum on the day' (it would of course be the same after the day), 'in satisfaction of a greater, cannot be any satisfaction for the whole, because it appears to the Judges, that by no possibility a lesser sum can be a satisfaction to the plaintiff for a greater sum.' ...

 Alert

If the question be (as, in the actual state of the law, I think it is), whether consideration is, or is not, given in a case of this kind, by the debtor who pays down part of the debt presently due from him, for a promise by the creditor to relinquish, after certain further payments on account, the residue of the debt, I cannot say that I think consideration is given, in the sense in which I have always understood that word as used in our law. It might be (and indeed I think it would be) an improvement in our law, if a release or acquittance of the whole debt, on payment of any sum which the creditor might be content to receive by way of accord and satisfaction (though less than the whole), were held to be, generally, binding, though not under seal; nor should I be unwilling to see equal force given to a prospective agreement, like the present, in writing though not under seal; but I think it impossible, without refinements which practically alter the sense of the word, to treat such a release or acquittance as supported by any new consideration proceeding from the debtor. ...

Consequently, Mrs Beer was able to enforce the full amount of the debt and the interest since her promise to accept part-payment was not supported by consideration. It is interesting to note the criticism of the general rule by Lord Blackburn in *Foakes v Beer* itself.

LORD BLACKBURN

[Lord Blackburn referred to Lord Coke's obiter statement in *Pinnel's Case* that part-payment of a debt is not good consideration and stated that this] was certainly not necessary for the decision of the case; but though the resolution of the Court of Common Pleas was only a dictum, it seems to me clear that Lord Coke deliberately adopted the dictum, and the great weight of his authority makes it necessary to be cautious before saying that what he deliberately adopted as law was a mistake, and though I cannot find that in any subsequent case this dictum has been made the ground of the decision ... yet there certainly are cases in which great judges have treated the dictum in *Pinnel's Case* ... as good law.

After such strong expressions of opinion, I doubt much whether any judge sitting in a Court of the first instance would be justified in treating the question as open. But as this has very seldom, if at all, been the ground of the decision even in a Court of the first instance, and certainly never been the ground of a decision in the Court of Exchequer Chamber, still less in this House, I did think it open in your Lordships' House to reconsider this question. And, notwithstanding the very high authority of Lord Coke, I think it is not the fact that to accept prompt payment of a part only of a liquidated demand, can never be more beneficial than to insist on payment of the whole. ...

What principally weighs with me in thinking that Lord Coke made a mistake of fact is my conviction that all men of business, whether merchants or tradesmen, do every day recognise and act on the ground that prompt payment of a part of their demand may be more beneficial to them than it would be to insist on their rights and enforce payment of the whole. Even where the debtor is perfectly solvent, and sure to pay at last, this often is so. Where the credit of the debtor is doubtful it must be more so. I had persuaded myself that there was no such long-continued action on this dictum as to render it improper in this House to reconsider the question. I had written my reasons for so thinking; but as they were not satisfactory to the other noble and learned Lords who heard the case, I do not now repeat them nor persist in them.

I assent to the judgment proposed, though it is not that which I had originally thought proper.

Although Lord Blackburn 'assented to' the majority's judgment in this case, he originally disagreed with it on the basis that all men of business would recognise that there can be a benefit to the creditor in accepting prompt part-payment of the debt, particularly where the debtor's solvency is doubtful.

It is interesting to compare the legal position in relation to promises to pay more with that in relation to promises to accept less. For promises to pay more, you will remember from the last chapter that, although the promisee was only doing what he was contractually obliged to do, there would be good consideration if the promisor received a *practical* benefit (*Williams v Roffey*). In *Re Selectmove Limited* [1995] 1 WLR 474, it was argued that the same principle should apply to promises to accept less. In other words, since the creditor was receiving a practical benefit from the part-payment, this should constitute good consideration. This argument was not accepted.

Re Selectmove Limited [1995] 1 WLR 474

Panel: Balcombe, Stuart-Smith and Peter Gibson LJJ

Facts: In 1991, Selectmove Limited owed the Inland Revenue income tax and national insurance contributions. At a meeting in July 1991, between the managing director of Selectmove Limited (Mr Ffooks) and a tax collector (Mr Polland) it was proposed by Mr Ffooks that the company from then on pay the tax and national insurance as it fell due and that it would repay the arrears by payments of £1,000 a month commencing in February 1992. The tax collector confirmed that he would have to seek the approval of his superiors and that he would revert to the company if it was unacceptable. The company did not hear anything and it proceeded to make payment of one month's tax and national insurance as it fell due. In October 1991, the Revenue demanded payment of the arrears in full. Following this, the company did make some payments but they were late and in September 1992 the Revenue served a statutory demand on the company and subsequently presented a winding-up petition.

The case was decided on the basis that Mr Polland did not have authority to bind the Revenue and therefore the agreement was not binding. However, Peter Gibson LJ, made the following *obiter* comments in relation to the applicability of *Williams v Roffey* to promises to accept less.

LORD JUSTICE PETER GIBSON

The judge held that the case fell within the principle of *Foakes v Beer* (1884) 9 App Cas 605, [1881–5] All ER Rep 106. In that case a judgment debtor and creditor agreed that in consideration of the debtor paying part of the judgment debt and costs immediately and the remainder by instalments the creditor would not take any proceedings on the judgment. The House of Lords held that the agreement was nudum pactum, being without consideration, and did not prevent the creditor, after payment of the whole debt and costs, from proceeding to enforce payment of the interest on the judgment. Although their Lordships were unanimous in the result, that case is notable for the powerful speech of Lord Blackburn, who made plain his disagreement with the course the law had taken in and since *Pinnel's Case* (1602) 5 Co Rep 117a, [1558–

1774] All ER Rep 612 and which the House of Lords in *Foakes v Beer* decided should not be reversed. Lord Blackburn expressed his conviction that –

'all men of business, whether merchants or tradesmen, do every day recognise and act on the ground that prompt payment of a part of their demand may be more beneficial to them than it would be to insist on their rights and enforce payment of the whole.' (See 9 App Cas 605 at 622, [1881–5] All ER Rep 106 at 115.)

Yet it is clear that the House of Lords decided that a practical benefit of that nature is not good consideration in law. ...

[Counsel for Selectmove], however, submitted that an additional benefit to the Crown was conferred by the agreement in that the Crown stood to derive practical benefits therefrom: it was likely to recover more from not enforcing its debt against the company, which was known to be in financial difficulties, than from putting the company into liquidation. He pointed to the fact that the company did in fact pay its further PAYE and NIC liabilities and £7,000 of its arrears. He relied on the decision of this court in *Williams v Roffey Bros & Nicholls (Contractors) Ltd* [1991] 1 QB 1 for the proposition that a promise to perform an existing obligation can amount to good consideration provided that there are practical benefits to the promisee [sic]. ...

[Counsel for Selectmove] submitted that although Glidewell LJ [in Williams v Roffey] in terms confined his remarks to a case where B is to do the work for or supply goods or services to A, the same principle must apply where B's obligation is to pay A, and he referred to an article by Adams and Brownsword 'Contract, Consideration and the Critical Path' (1990) 53 MLR 536 at 539–540 which suggests that Foakes v Beer might need reconsideration. I see the force of the argument, but the difficulty that I feel with it is that if the principle of Williams' case is to be extended to an obligation to make payment, it would in effect leave the principle in Foakes v Beer without any application. When a creditor and a debtor who are at arm's length reach agreement on the payment of the debt by instalments to accommodate the debtor, the creditor will no doubt always see a practical benefit to himself in so doing. In the absence of authority there would be much to be said for the enforceability of such a contract. But that was a matter expressly considered in Foakes v Beer yet held not to constitute good consideration in law. Foakes v Beer was not even referred to in Williams' case, and it is in my judgment impossible, consistently with the doctrine of precedent, for this court to extend the principle of Williams' case to any circumstances governed by the principle of Foakes v Beer. If that extension is to be made, it must be by the House of Lords or, perhaps even more appropriately, by Parliament after consideration by the Law Commission.

 Alert

In my judgment, the judge was right to hold that if there was an agreement between the company and the Crown it was unenforceable for want of consideration. ...

Lord Justice Peter Gibson made it clear that the principle from *Williams v Roffey* (that a practical benefit can constitute consideration) only applies to promises to pay more, it does not apply to promises to accept less.

However, the recent Court of Appeal decision in *MWB Business Exchange Centres Ltd v Rock Advertising Ltd* has reviewed this limitation.

MWB Business Exchange Centres Ltd v Rock Advertising Ltd [2016] EWCA Civ 553, 21

Panel: Arden, Kitchin and McCombe LJJJ

Facts: a landlord agreed orally to re-schedule rental payments under a licence agreement to give a tenant longer to pay, thereby varying the licence..

Held: The court considered whether there had been valid consideration for the variation. The court acknowledged that part payment of a sum already due is not normally good consideration. However, the judges agreed that there was sufficient consideration. Their justification was: the landlord obtained a practical benefit by keeping the tenant in the property (compared to leaving the property vacant). This benefit went beyond the advantage of receiving prompt payment of a part of the arrears and a promise that it would be paid the balance over the coming months. The court also considered the fact that the landlord was not under economic duress from the tenant relevant. In reaching this decision, the court applied the Court of Appeal's reasoning in *Williams v Roffey Brothers & Nicholls (Contractors) Ltd* [1989] EWCA Civ 5.

On 31 January 2017, MWB Business Exchange Centres Limited was granted permission to appeal against the decision of the Court of Appeal. Their ground of appeal of relevance to us was, whether, following the factual findings of the trial judge, there was a practical benefit which could amount to consideration at law, given the principle that a promise to pay an existing liability cannot amount to good consideration per *Re Selectmove Ltd*.

Rock Advertising Ltd v MWB Business Exchange [2018] UKSC 24

Panel: Lady Hale, Lord Wilson, Lord Sumption, Lord Lloyd-Jones and Lord Briggs.

Held: The Court unanimously allowed the appeal holding the oral variation was invalid for reasons unconnected to consideration. Disappointingly, therefore, that made it unnecessary for the court to deal with the issue of consideration. The question of whether providing a practical benefit in the absence of duress is sufficient to make a promise to accept less binding went unanswered. Whilst Lord Sumption considered that *Foakes v Beer* was 'ripe for re-examination', he stated that if were to be overruled:

'It should be before an enlarged panel of the court and in a case where the decision would be more than obiter dictum.'

For the time being at least, *Foakes v Beer* remains good law.

6.2 Common Law Exceptions

There will be good consideration for a promise to accept less where the debtor provides 'fresh' consideration (*Pinnel's Case*).

Such consideration can take a number forms. For example, if a creditor agrees to accept a different chattel in satisfaction of a debt, then this would amount to 'fresh' consideration and prevent the creditor suing for the whole debt. In *Pinnel's Case* itself, it was said that 'a hawk, a horse, or a robe may clear the debt but an offer of 19s 6d in the £1 on the due date at the appointed place will not suffice.' Remember that the law will not look into whether the chattel is of equal monetary value to the sum which was previously owed since consideration must be sufficient but need not be adequate (*Chappell & Co Limited and Another v Nestlé Co Limited and Another* [1960] AC 87).

In the same way, payment of part of the debt before the date on which it is due may be good consideration (*Pinnel's Case*), as may payment at a different place provided this was at the creditor's request (*Vanbergen v St Edmund Properties* [1933] 2 KB 223) or payment by a third party (*Welby v Drake* (1825) 1 C & P 557). As long as there is 'fresh' consideration, the parties will be bound by this agreement.

Although it is said that the provision of 'fresh' consideration represents an 'exception' to the general rule that part-payment of a debt will not constitute good consideration, this is arguably not an exception at all. Rather, a new contract has been entered into; the promise from the creditor not to enforce the whole debt is supported by the 'fresh' consideration. The other elements required for a binding contract, ie agreement and intention to create legal relations, are also present.

6.3 Promissory Estoppel

The strict rule from *Foakes v Beer* may lead to harsh results, particularly if the debtor has relied on the creditor's promise to accept less. Consequently, equity has stepped in to mitigate these harsh consequences and prevents a creditor from enforcing his strict legal rights if certain criteria are met. The equitable doctrine of promissory estoppel was first alluded to in *Thomas Hughes v The Directors, &C., of the Metropolitan Railway Company* (1876-77) LR 2 App Cas 439 and was later developed by Denning J in *Central London Property Trust Limited v High Trees House Limited* [1947] KB 130.

Thomas Hughes v The Directors, & C., of the Metropolitan Railway Company (1876-77) LR 2 App Cas 439

Panel: Lord Cairns LC, Lord O'Hagan, Lord Selborne, Lord Blackburn and Lord Gordon

Facts: Mr Hughes (the appellant landlord) leased premises to the Metropolitan Rail Company (the respondent tenant). Under the terms of the lease, the tenant agreed to make repairs to the property within six months of receiving notice from the landlord to do so. The landlord gave such notice in October 1874.

In November 1874, the parties entered into negotiations for the sale of the tenant's property interest to the landlord. The tenant wrote to the landlord, advising that it would not undertake repairs while the negotiations were proceeding. The negotiations fell through in December 1874. At the end of the six months following the notice to effect repairs, the landlord sought forfeiture of the lease on the basis of the tenant's failure to comply.

LORD CAIRNS LC

...[I]t is the first principle upon which all Courts of Equity proceed, that if parties who have entered into definite and distinct terms involving certain legal results — certain penalties or legal forfeiture — afterwards by their own act or with their own consent enter upon a course of negotiation which has the effect of leading one of the parties to suppose that the strict rights arising under the contract will not be enforced, or will be kept in suspense, or held in abeyance, the person who otherwise might have enforced those rights will not be allowed to enforce them where it would be inequitable having regard to the dealings which have thus taken place between the parties. ...

The court decided that, because the landlord's conduct had led the tenant to believe that he would not enforce the tenant's obligation to repair while negotiations were ongoing, it would be inequitable for the landlord to enforce the strict obligation to repair until a 'reasonable' period had elapsed following the breakdown of negotiations. The landlord was thus estopped from enforcing his strict legal rights and the lease would not be forfeited.

In *High Trees*, Denning J further developed the doctrine of promissory estoppel. Although his remarks were in fact *obiter* they have subsequently been accepted as the building blocks for promissory estoppel.

Central London Property Trust Limited v High Trees House Limited [1947] KB 130

Panel: Denning J

Facts: In 1937, the plaintiff landlord let a block of flats to the defendant tenant on a 99 year lease at a ground rent of £2,500 a year. When war commenced in 1939, only about one third of the flats had been let and the tenant was having difficulty paying the rent. Consequently, in 1940, the landlord agreed in writing to reduce the ground rent to £1,250. The parties did not specify how long the reduced rent would operate for and there was no consideration for the reduction. By 1945, the flats were fully let. In September 1945, the landlord requested that the full ground rent be paid and he requested payment of the arrears for the last two quarters of 1945 ie the quarter ending 29 September 1945, and the quarter ending 25 December 1945. The tenant argued that the reduced rent was payable for the whole 99 year term or alternatively up until September 1945 on the grounds that the landlord was estopped from claiming the additional rent. Although, the landlord was not seeking to obtain the full rent from 1940, Denning J commented *obiter*, on his ability to do so.

MR JUSTICE DENNING

...If I were to consider this matter without regard to recent developments in the law, there is no doubt that had the plaintiffs claimed it, they would have been entitled to recover ground rent at the rate of 2,500l. a year from the beginning of the term, since the lease under which it was payable was a lease under seal which, according to the old common law, could not be varied by an agreement by parol (whether in writing or not), but only by deed. Equity, however stepped in, and said that if there has been a variation of a deed by a simple contract (which in the case of a lease required to be in writing would have to be evidenced by writing), the courts may give effect to it as is shown in *Berry v. Berry* [1929] 2 K.B. 316. That equitable doctrine, however, could hardly apply in the present case because the variation here might be said to have been made without consideration. With regard to estoppel, the representation made in relation to reducing the rent, was not a representation of an existing fact. It was a representation, in effect, as to the future, namely, that payment of the rent would not be enforced at the full rate but only at the reduced rate. Such a representation would not give rise to an estoppel, because, as was said in *Jorden v. Money* (1854) 5 H. L. C. 185, a representation as to the future must be embodied as a contract or be nothing.

But what is the position in view of developments in the law in recent years? The law has not been standing still since *Jorden v. Money*. There has been a series of decisions over the last fifty years which, although they are said to be cases of estoppel are not really such. They are cases in which a promise was made which was intended to create legal relations and which, to the knowledge of the person making the promise, was going to be acted on by the person to whom it was made and which was in fact so acted on. In such cases the courts have said that the promise must be honoured. The cases to which I particularly desire to refer are: *Fenner v. Blake* [1900] 1 Q. B. 426, In *re Wickham* (1917) 34 T. L. R. 158, Re William Porter & Co., Ld. [1937] 2 All E. R. 361 and *Buttery v. Pickard* [1946] W. N. 25. As I have said they are not cases of estoppel in the strict sense. They are really promises - promises intended to be binding, intended to be acted on, and in fact acted on. *Jorden v. Money* (1854) 5 H. L. C. 185 can be distinguished, because there the promisor made it clear that she did not intend to be legally bound, whereas in the cases to which I refer the proper inference was that the promisor did intend to be bound. In each case the court held the promise to be binding on the party making it, even though under the old common law it might be difficult to find any consideration for it.

The courts have not gone so far as to give a cause of action in damages for the breach of such a promise, but they have refused to allow the party making it to act inconsistently with it.

Link
See discussion of 'shield' not a 'sword' below

It is in that sense, and that sense only, that such a promise gives rise to an estoppel. The decisions are a natural result of the fusion of law and equity: for the cases of *Hughes v. Metropolitan Ry. Co.* (1877) 2 App. Cas. 439, 448, *Birmingham and District Land Co. v. London & North Western Ry. Co.* (1888) 40 Ch. D. 268, 286 and *Salisbury (Marquess) v. Gilmore* [1942] 2 K. B. 38, 51, afford a sufficient basis for saying that a party would not be allowed in equity to go back on such a promise. In my opinion, the time has now come for the validity of such a promise to be recognized. The logical consequence, no doubt is that a promise to accept a smaller sum in discharge of a larger sum, if acted upon, is binding notwithstanding the absence of consideration: and if the fusion of law and equity leads to this result, so much the better. That aspect was not considered in *Foakes v. Beer* (1884) 9 App. Cas. 605. At this time of day however, when law and equity have been joined together for over seventy years, principles must be reconsidered in the light of their combined effect. It is to be noticed that in the Sixth Interim Report of the Law Revision Committee, pars. 35, 40, it is recommended that such a promise as that to which I have referred, should be enforceable in law even though no consideration for it has been given by the promisee. It seems to me that, to the extent I have mentioned that result has now been achieved by the decisions of the courts.

I am satisfied that a promise such as that to which I have referred is binding and the only question remaining for my consideration is the scope of the promise in the present case. I am satisfied on all the evidence that the promise here was that the ground rent should be reduced to 1,250l. a year as a temporary expedient while the block of flats was not fully, or substantially fully let, owing to the conditions prevailing. That means that the reduction in the rent applied throughout the years down to the end of 1944, but early in 1945 it is plain that the flats were fully let, and, indeed the rents received from them (many of them not being affected by the Rent Restrictions Acts), were increased beyond the figure at which it was originally contemplated that they would be let. At all events the rent from them must have been very considerable. I find that the conditions prevailing at the time when the reduction in rent was made, had completely passed away by the early months of 1945. I am satisfied that the promise was understood by all parties only to apply under the conditions prevailing at the time when it was made, namely, when the flats were only partially let, and that it did not extend any further than that. When the flats became fully let, early in 1945, the reduction ceased to apply.

In those circumstances, under the law as I hold it, it seems to me that rent is payable at the full rate for the quarters ending September 29 and December 25, 1945.

If the case had been one of estoppel, it might be said that in any event the estoppel would cease when the conditions to which the representation applied came to an end, or it also might be said that it would only come to an end on notice. In either case it is only a way of ascertaining what is the scope of the representation. I prefer to apply the principle that a promise intended to be binding, intended to be acted on and in fact acted on, is binding so far as its terms properly apply. Here it was binding as covering the period down to the early part of 1945, and as from that time full rent is payable.

I therefore give judgment for the plaintiff company for the amount claimed.

> **Link**
> See the discussion relating to the effect of promissory estoppel below.

In circumstances where the landlord had agreed to accept a lesser sum than due to him and intended the tenant to act on that promise and the tenant subsequently did so act, notwithstanding the absence of consideration for the promise, the landlord would be bound. Mr Justice Denning indicated that if the landlord had claimed the full rent prior to 1945 he would have failed because he would have been estopped from doing so. The promise was, however, temporary and only to last as long as the block was not fully or substantially let. When the conditions which prevailed in 1939 ceased to exist, the landlord could claim the full rent from that point onwards.

This case is of vital importance for the development of promissory estoppel and also very controversial since promissory estoppel allows a promise to be enforced despite the lack of consideration. The fact that a party's conduct after entering into a contract might prevent him from fully enforcing that contract, in circumstances where it would be inequitable for him to do so, could be seen as a seismic shift in the law of contract. Consequently, in subsequent cases, the courts have sought to keep the doctrine of promissory estoppel within narrow limits.

There are a number of criteria which need to be met in order for the doctrine of promissory estoppel to be relied upon; these criteria are considered below.

6.3.1 'Shield', not a 'Sword'

Combe v Combe [1951] 2 KB 215

Panel: Asquith, Denning and Birkett LJJ

Facts: After obtaining a divorce from her husband, Mrs Combe asked him to pay her £100 a year in permanent maintenance and Mr Combe agreed. Mrs Combe provided no consideration for his promise. Mr Combe did not in fact make any payments and Mrs Combe did not apply to the court for an order for permanent maintenance. Some years later, Mrs Combe brought a claim against Mr Combe for the missed payments on the basis of his former promise. Mr Justice Byrne gave judgment in favour of the wife on the basis of promissory estoppel; the husband appealed.

LORD JUSTICE DENNING

...Much as I am inclined to favour the principle stated in the High Trees case, it is important that it should not be stretched too far, lest it should be endangered. That principle does not create new causes of action where none existed before. It only prevents a party from insisting upon his strict legal rights, when it would be unjust to allow him to enforce them, having regard to the dealings which have taken place between the parties. That is the way it was put in *Hughes v. Metropolitan Railway*, the case in the House of Lords in which the principle was first stated, and in *Birmingham, etc., Land Company v. London and North-Western Railway Co.*, the case in the Court of Appeal where the principle was enlarged. It is also implicit in all the modern cases in which the principle has been developed. Sometimes it is a plaintiff who is not allowed to insist on his strict legal rights. Thus, a creditor is not allowed to enforce a debt which he has deliberately agreed to waive, if the debtor has carried on business or in some other way changed his position in reliance on the waiver... . On other occasions it is a defendant who is not allowed to insist on his strict legal rights. His conduct may be such as to debar him from relying on some condition, denying some allegation, or taking some other point in answer to the claim. ... [Denning discussed a number of cases in which the doctrine of promissory estoppel had been relied upon.] In none of these cases was the defendant sued on the promise, assurance, or assertion as a cause of action in itself: he was sued for some other cause, for example, a pension or a breach of contract, and the promise, assurance or assertion only played a supplementary role - an important role, no doubt, but still a supplementary role. That is, I think, its true function. It may be part of a cause of action, but not a cause of action in itself.

The principle, as I understand it, is that, where one party has, by his words or conduct, made to the other a promise or assurance which was intended to affect the legal relations between them and to be acted on accordingly, then, once the other party has taken him at his word and acted on it, the one who gave the promise or assurance cannot afterwards be allowed to revert to the previous legal relations as if no such promise or assurance had been made by him, but he must accept their legal relations subject to the qualification which he himself has so introduced, even though it is not supported in point of law by any consideration but only by his word.

Seeing that the principle never stands alone as giving a cause of action in itself, it can never do away with the necessity of consideration when that is an essential part of the cause of action. The doctrine of consideration is too firmly fixed to be overthrown by a side-wind. Its ill-effects have been largely mitigated of late, but it still remains a cardinal necessity of the formation of a contract, though not of its modification or discharge. I fear that it was my failure to make this clear which misled Byrne, J., in the present case. He held that the wife could sue on the husband's promise as a separate and independent cause of action by itself, although, as he held, there was no consideration for it. That is not correct. The wife can only enforce it if there

Alert

Alert

113

was consideration for it. That is, therefore, the real question in the case: was there sufficient consideration to support the promise?

If it were suggested that, in return for the husband's promise, the wife expressly or impliedly promised to forbear from applying to the court for maintenance - that is, a promise in return for a promise - there would clearly be no consideration, because the wife's promise was not binding on her and was therefore worth nothing. Notwithstanding her promise, she could always apply to the Divorce Court for maintenance - maybe only with leave - and no agreement by her could take away that right: *Hyman v. Hyman*, as interpreted by this court in *Gaisberg v. Storr*. There was, however, clearly no promise by the wife, express or implied, to forbear from applying to the court. All that happened was that she did in fact forbear - that is, she did an act in return for a promise. Is that sufficient consideration? Unilateral promises of this kind have long been enforced, so long as the act or forbearance is done on the faith of the promise and at the request of the promisor, express or implied. The act done is then in itself sufficient consideration for the promise, even though it arises ex post facto... . But my difficulty is to accept the finding of Byrne, J., that the promise was 'intended to be acted upon'. I cannot find any evidence of any intention by the husband that the wife should forbear from applying to the court for maintenance, or, in other words, any request by the husband, express or implied, that the wife should so forbear. He left her to apply if she wished to do so. She did not do so, and I am not surprised, because it is very unlikely that the Divorce Court would have then made any order in her favour, seeing that she had a bigger income than her husband. Her forbearance was not intended by him, nor was it done at his request. It was therefore no consideration. ...

LORD JUSTICE BIRKETT

...I think that the description given by [counsel for the husband] of the doctrine enunciated in the two cases to which Denning, L.J., has referred, as one to be used as a shield and not as a sword, is very vivid. Denning, J., in *Central London Property Trust LD. v. High Trees House LD.*, concluded his judgment with these words: 'I prefer to apply the principle that a promise intended to be binding, intended to be acted upon, and in fact acted upon, is binding so far as its terms properly apply'. ...

LORD JUSTICE ASQUITH

It is unnecessary to express any view as to the correctness of [the *High Trees*] decision, though I certainly must not be taken to be questioning it; and I would remark, in passing, that it seems to me a complete misconception to suppose that it struck at the roots of the doctrine of consideration. But assuming, without deciding, that [the principle as set out in *High Trees*] is good law, I do not think, however, that it helps the plaintiff at all. What that case decides is that when a promise is given which (1.) is intended to create legal relations, (2.) is intended to be acted upon by the promisee, and (3.) is in fact so acted upon, the promisor cannot bring an action against the promisee which involves the repudiation of his promise or is inconsistent with it. It does not, as I read it, decide that a promisee can sue on the promise. ...

This case makes it clear that promissory estoppel can only be used as a defence to an action, rather than as a cause of action. Lord Justice Birkett referred to the vivid metaphor that promissory estoppel can only be used as a shield and not a sword. There was no binding contract in relation to Mr Combe's promise to pay maintenance as Mrs Combe had provided no consideration for that promise. Furthermore, since promissory estoppel cannot be used to create a cause of action, Mrs Combe could not herself bring a claim based on promissory estoppel and sue Mr Combe for the maintenance outstanding.

6.3.2 A Clear and Unequivocal Promise

Woodhouse A.C Israel Cocoa Limited S.A and Another v Nigerian Produce Marketing Co Limited [1972] AC 741

Panel: Lord Hailsham of St Marylebone LC, Viscount Dilhorne, Lord Pearson, Lord Cross of Chelsea and Lord Salmon

Facts: Woodhouse (the appellant buyers) purchased cocoa from the respondent sellers (Nigerian Produce) and the price was to be paid in Nigerian pounds in Lagos. The buyers then asked, by letter, if the sellers would agree to accept sterling in Lagos. The sellers agreed, by letter dated 30 September 1967, that payment could be made 'in sterling and in Lagos'. The pound sterling was then devalued so that it was worth less than the Nigerian pound. The buyers claimed that they could pay one pound sterling to one Nigerian pound. The sellers disagreed. One of the arguments raised by the buyers was that the representation contained in the letter dated 30 September 1967 amounted to an estoppel meaning that the sellers could not go back on it and claim the full price for the contracts.

LORD HAILSHAM OF ST MARYLEBONE LC

...Counsel for the appellants was asked whether he knew of any case in which an ambiguous statement had ever formed the basis of a purely promissory estoppel, as contended for here, as distinct from estoppel of a more familiar type based on factual misrepresentation. He candidly replied that he did not. I do not find this surprising, since it would really be an astonishing thing if, in the case of a genuine misunderstanding as to the meaning of an offer, the offeree could obtain by means of the doctrine of promissory estoppel something that he must fail to obtain under the conventional law of contract. I share the feeling of incredulity expressed by Lord Denning M.R. in the course of his judgment in the instant case when he said [1971] 2 Q.B. 23, 59-60:

 Alert

'If the judge be right, it leads to this extraordinary consequence: letter which is not sufficient to vary a contract is, nevertheless, sufficient to work an estoppel- which will have the same effect as a variation.'

There seem to me to be so many and such conclusive reasons for dismissing this appeal that it may be thought a work of supererogation to add yet another. But basically I feel convinced that there was never here any real room for the doctrine or estoppel at all. If the exchange of letters was not variation, I believe it was nothing. The buyers asked for a variation in the mode of discharge of a contract of sale. If the proposal meant what they claimed, and was accepted and acted upon, I venture to think that the vendors would have been bound by their acceptance at least until they gave reasonable notice to terminate, and I imagine that a modern court would have found no difficulty in discovering consideration for such a promise. Business men know their own business best even when they appear to grant an indulgence, and in the present case I do not think that there would have been insuperable difficulty in spelling out consideration from the earlier correspondence. If, however, the two letters were insufficiently unambiguous and precise to form the basis, if accepted, for a variation in the contract I do not think their combined effect is sufficiently unambiguous or precise to form the basis of an estoppel which would produce the result of reducing the purchase price by no less than 14 per cent. against a vendor who had never consciously agreed to the proposition.

VISCOUNT DILHORNE

...In the alternative it was said, and this was the appellants' main contention, that if the contracts were not varied so that payment might be made on the basis of one pound sterling for one Nigerian pound, at least the respondents had represented that it could and, as the appellants had relied on that representation to their detriment, the respondents were estopped from denying that payment could be so made.

While I recognise that a party to a contract, while not agreeing to a variation of it, may nevertheless say that he will waive the performance by the other party of certain of its terms, and that if the other party relies on the waiver performance of the terms waived cannot be insisted on, in this case there was not a representation of the character alleged contained in or to be implied from the letter of September 30. To found an estoppel, the representation must be clear and unequivocal. In my opinion, the letter of September 30 could not reasonably be understood to contain or to imply a clear and unequivocal representation of the nature alleged. ...

 Alert

The letter did not unambiguously state that the price to be paid would be Nigerian pounds for pounds sterling. In order to give rise to an estoppel a promise must be clear and unequivocal. The letter amounted only to a representation that the seller would accept payment in pounds sterling, rather than the Nigerian pound, to the same value as had been agreed. Lord Hailsham LC in particular made it plain that, if a promise would be insufficiently clear to vary the contract, such a promise could not be sufficiently clear to found the defence of promissory estoppel.

6.3.3 Promisee must Change their Position in Reliance on the Promise

Emmanuel Ayodeji Ajayi v R. T. Briscoe (Nigeria) Limited [1964] 1 WLR 1326

Panel: Lord Morris of Borth-y-Gest, Lord Hodson and Lord Guest

Facts: The defendant hired eleven lorries from the plaintiff owner under two hire-purchase agreements. It was agreed that, after deposits were paid, the remainder of the purchase price would be paid in instalments.

In July 1957, the defendant informed the plaintiffs that the lorries were in need of repairs and were out of service. The defendant wrote to the plaintiffs on 12 July stating that he would agree to contribute towards the costs of repair once the lorries were again in service. The plaintiffs wrote back on 22 July confirming that they agreed to the defendant withholding instalments under the hire-purchase agreements until the lorries were back in service. The defendant subsequently sent eight of the eleven lorries for repair.

The plaintiffs later brought a successful claim against the defendant for payment of all the outstanding instalments. On appeal, first to the Federal Court of Nigeria and then to the Privy Council, the defendant argued that the doctrine of equitable estoppel prevented the plaintiffs from claiming payment of the instalments until the lorries were returned to active service, which allegedly never happened.

LORD HODSON

...By the letter of July 22 it is said that the plaintiffs made plain they were not going to enforce their rights and would not insist on payment before the lorries were all back in service. ...It is said the defendant acted on the letter of July 22 by not putting forward proposals alternative to those he had already made in his letter of the 12th. Further, it is said that after the letter of July 22 he did lay up the lorries by delivering eight to the plaintiffs after that date with the result that they were out of service and earned no revenue. Lastly it is said that he organised his business on the basis that the lorries would be put in repair and he would not have to make the payments due on them until they were back in service and accordingly earning revenue.

The defendant's final contention was that having altered his position in the manner indicated the plaintiffs never gave notice that the period of suspension was at an end before issuing their summons and that accordingly the lorries never having been returned or made available for service he was entitled to rely on the equitable defence... .

The principle, which has been described as quasi estoppel and perhaps more aptly as promissory estoppel, is that when one party to a contract in the absence of fresh consideration agrees not to enforce his rights an equity will be raised in favour of the other party. This equity is, however, subject to the qualifications (1) that the other party has altered his position, (2) that the promisor can resile from his promise on giving reasonable notice, which need not be a formal notice, giving the promisee a reasonable opportunity of resuming his position, (3) the promise only becomes final and irrevocable if the promisee cannot resume his position.

The question remains whether the defendant has made good the defence. In their Lordships' opinion he has not succeeded in so doing. The defendant did not alter his position by not putting forward counter-proposals after receipt of the letter of July 22, 1957. There is no evidence to support the contention that he did so by organising his business in a different way having regard to the fact that the lorries were out of service, and it cannot be inferred from the evidence given that such reorganisation was necessary. It can be said that the lorries were laid up and there is evidence to support the view that they were laid up after the receipt of the letter of July 22, 1957. Nevertheless, in view of the evidence given by the plaintiffs' witness, not rejected by the trial judge (although contradicted by the defendant), it cannot be said to have been proved that the lorries were not made available for the defendant after they had been repaired.

The defendant has accordingly failed to establish any defence to the plaintiffs' claim. Their Lordships will therefore humbly advise Her Majesty that the appeal be dismissed. ...

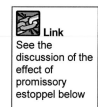 **Link**
See the discussion of the effect of promissory estoppel below

The Privy Council's advice in this case makes it clear that it is not sufficient, in order to found an estoppel, that the promisor led the promisee to believe that they would not enforce their full legal rights. The promisee must also have changed their position in reliance upon that promise, which the defendant had not done here. The defendant had not arranged his business affairs on the basis of the promise nor had he altered his position by not putting forward alternative proposals for payment for the repairs. This case also introduces the principle that estoppel will not be permanent, as the promisor will generally have the opportunity to 'resile' from their promise on the giving of reasonable notice.

6.3.4 Reliance need not be Detrimental

The next case deals with whether reliance must have been 'detrimental' to the promisee, or whether it is enough simply that they changed their position.

WJ Alan & Co Limited v El Nasr Export and Import Co [1972] 2 QB 189

Panel: Lord Denning MR, Megaw and Stephenson LJJ

Facts: The appellant buyers were an Egyptian company and the sellers were coffee producers in Kenya. They entered into two contracts on 12 and 13 July 1967 for the sale of coffee and the price clause in each contract was expressed to be in Kenyan shillings and the method of payment was to be by irrevocable letter of credit. The letter of credit issued by the buyers' bank was for payment in pounds sterling and not Kenyan shillings but the sellers did not question this point and instead drew on the credit in sterling in respect of shipments. Sterling was devalued on 18 November 1967. On the same day, the sellers were paid by the bank in respect of the second contract in sterling, which, because of the devaluation of sterling, was worth less in Kenyan shillings than it would have been. The sellers sought to recover the difference between the amount received in pounds sterling and the amount which they would have received had payment been by Kenyan shillings.

LORD DENNING MR

The principle of waiver is simply this: If one party, by his conduct, leads another to believe that the strict rights arising under the contract will not be insisted upon, intending that the other should act on that belief, and he does act on it, then the first party will not afterwards be allowed to insist on the strict legal rights when it would be inequitable for him to do so: see *Plasticmoda Societa per Azioni v. Davidsons (Manchester) Ltd.* [1952] 1 Lloyd's Rep. 527, 539. There may be no consideration moving from him who benefits by the waiver. There may be no detriment to him by acting on it. There may be nothing in writing. Nevertheless, the one who waives his strict rights cannot afterwards insist on them. His strict rights are at any rate suspended so long as the waiver lasts. He may on occasion be able to revert to his strict legal rights for the future by giving reasonable notice in that behalf, or otherwise making it plain by his conduct that he will thereafter insist upon them: *Tool Metal Manufacturing Co. Ltd. v. Tungsten Electric Co. Ltd.* [1955] 1 W.L.R. 761. But there are cases where no withdrawal is possible. It may be too late to withdraw: or it cannot be done without injustice to the other party. In that event he is bound by his waiver. He will not be allowed to revert to his strict legal rights. He can only enforce them subject to the waiver he has made.

Instances of these principles are ready to hand in contracts for the sale of goods. A seller may, by his conduct, lead the buyer to believe that he is not insisting on the stipulated time for exercising an option: *Bruner v. Moore* [1904] 1 Ch. 305. A buyer may, by requesting delivery, lead the seller to believe that he is not insisting on the contractual time for delivery: *Charles Rickards Ltd. v. Oppenhaim* [1950] 1 K.B. 616, 621. A seller may, by his conduct, lead the buyer to believe that he will not insist on a confirmed letter of credit: *Plasticmoda* [1952] 1 Lloyd's Rep. 527, but will accept an unconfirmed one instead: *Panoustsos v. Raymond Hadley Corporation of New York* [1917] 2 K.B. 473; *Enrico Furst & Co. v. W. E. Fischer* [1960] 2 Lloyd's Rep. 340. A seller may accept a less sum for his goods than the contracted price, thus inducing him to believe that he will not enforce payment of the balance: *Central London Property Trust Ltd. v. High Trees House Ltd.* [1947] K.B. 130 and *D. & C. Builders Ltd. v. Rees* [1966] 2 Q.B. 617, 624. In none of these cases does the party who acts on the belief suffer any detriment. It is not a detriment, but a benefit to him, to have an extension of time or to pay less, or as the case may

Decipher
When Lord Denning MR talks about 'waiver' it seems that he actually means 'promissory estoppel'.

Link
See discussion of the effect of promissory estoppel below

be. Nevertheless, he has conducted his affairs on the basis that he has that benefit and it would not be equitable now to deprive him of it.

The judge rejected this doctrine because, he said, 'there is no evidence of the buyers having acted to their detriment. 'I know that it has been suggested in some quarters that there must be detriment. But I can find no support for it in the authorities cited by the judge. The nearest approach to it is the statement of Viscount Simonds in the Tool Metal case [1955] 1 W.L.R. 761, 764, that the other must have been led 'to alter his position,' which was adopted by Lord Hodson in Ajayi v. R. T. Briscoe (Nigeria) Ltd. [1964] 1 W.L.R. 1326, 1330. But that only means that he must have been led to act differently from what he otherwise would have done and if you study the cases in which the doctrine has been applied, you will see that all that is required is that the one should have 'acted on the belief induced by the other party.' That is how Lord Cohen put it in the Tool Metal case [1955] 1 W.L.R. 761, 799, and that is how I would put it myself. ...

Alert

Conclusion

Applying the principle here, it seems to me that the sellers, by their conduct, waived the right to have payment by means of a letter of credit in Kenyan currency and accepted instead a letter of credit in sterling. It was, when given, conditional payment, with the result that, on being duly honoured (as it was), the payment was no longer conditional. It became absolute, and dated back to the time when the letter of credit was given and acted upon. The sellers have, therefore, received payment of the price and cannot recover more. ...

Lord Denning MR held that, while it must be shown that the promise has been acted on, it is not essential that a detriment is caused by acting on it. Promissory estoppel may however be easier to establish in cases where a detriment is caused, as referred to in the next case.

6.3.5   Inequitable for the Promisor to go Back on their Promise

Societe Italo-Belge pour le Commerce et l'Industrie SA v Palm and Vegetable Oils (Malaysia) Sdn Bhd (The Post Chaser) [1982] 1 All ER 19

Panel: Robert Goff J

Facts: The sellers agreed to sell palm oil to the buyers, who agreed to sell this on to the sub-buyers. A clause in the agreement required that a 'declaration of ship' was to be made to the buyers in writing as soon as possible after the ship sailed. Despite the fact that the sellers did not give the declaration until more than a month after the ship sailed, the buyers raised no objection to this.

The buyers requested that the sellers provide the documents to the sub-buyers. Two days later, the sub-buyers rejected the documents and, that same day, the buyers also rejected the documents. The sellers had to sell the oil to another for less than the price the buyers had agreed to pay. The sellers brought an action against the buyers for the difference in the two prices.

MR JUSTICE ROBERT GOFF

[Mr Justice Robert Goff found that the buyer's request that documents be provided to the sub-buyers constituted a sufficiently unequivocal representation to found a promissory estoppel that they accepted the documents. He then continued:]

However, there next arises the question whether there was any sufficient reliance by the sellers on this representation to give rise to an equitable estoppel. Here there arose a difference between [counsel for the sellers and for the buyers] as to the degree of reliance which is required. It is plain, however, from the speech of Lord Cairns in *Hughes v. Metropolitan Railway Co.*, (1877) 2 App. Cas. 439 at p. 448 that the representor will not be allowed to enforce his rights 'where it would be inequitable having regard to the dealings which have taken place between the parties'; accordingly there must be such action, or inaction, by the representee on the faith of the representation as will render it inequitable to permit the representor to enforce his strict legal rights. ...

The case therefore raises in an acute form the question which was posed by Lord Salmon in the *Vanden Avenne* case (at p. 127), but left unresolved by him, viz. whether it is sufficient for this purpose that the representee should simply have conducted his affairs on the basis of the representation, or whether by so doing he must have suffered some form of prejudice which renders it inequitable for the representor to go back on his representation. ...

In *W. J. Alan & Co. Ltd. v. El Nasr Export and Import Co.*, [1972] 1 Lloyd's Rep. 313; [1972] 2 Q.B. 189, Lord Denning, M.R. (at pp. 323-324 and 213), while stating the principle of equitable estoppel in terms that it must be inequitable for the representor to be allowed to go back on his representation, nevertheless considered that it might be sufficient for that purpose that the representee had conducted his affairs on the basis of the representation, and that it was immaterial whether he has suffered any detriment by doing so.

I approach the matter as follows. The fundamental principle is that stated by Lord Cairns, viz. that the representor will not be allowed to enforce his rights 'where it would be inequitable having regard to the dealings which have thus taken place between the parties'. To establish such inequity, it is not necessary to show detriment; indeed, the representee may have benefited from the representation, and yet it may be inequitable, at least without reasonable notice, for the representor to enforce his legal rights. Take the facts of Central London Property Trust Ltd. v. High Trees House Ltd., [1947] K.B. 130, the case in which Lord Justice Denning, M.R. [sic], breathed new life into the doctrine of equitable estoppel. The representation was by a lessor to the effect that he would be content to accept a reduced rent. In such a case, although the lessee has benefited from the reduction in rent, it may well be inequitable for the lessor to insist upon his legal right to the unpaid rent, because the lessee has conducted his affairs on the basis that he would only have to pay rent at the lower rate; and a Court might well think it right to

Alert

conclude that only after reasonable notice could the lessor return to charging rent at the higher rate specified in the lease. Furthermore it would be open to the Court, in any particular case, to infer from the circumstances of the case that the representee must have conducted his affairs in such a way that it would be inequitable for the representor to enforce his rights, or to do so without reasonable notice. But it does not follow that in every case in which the representee has acted, or failed to act, in reliance on the representation, it will be inequitable for the representor to enforce his rights; for the nature of the action, or inaction may be insufficient to give rise to the equity, in which event a necessary requirement stated by Lord Cairns for the application of the doctrine would not have been fulfilled.

This, in my judgment, is the principle which I have to apply in the present case. Here, all that happened was that the sellers ... presented the documents on the same day as the buyers made their representation; and within two days the documents were rejected. Now on these simple facts, although it is plain that the sellers did actively rely on the buyers' representation, and did conduct their affairs in reliance on it, by presenting the documents, I cannot see anything which would render it inequitable for the buyers thereafter to enforce their legal right to reject the documents. In particular, having regard to the very short time which elapsed between the date of the representation and the date of presentation of the documents on the one hand, and the date of rejection on the other hand, I cannot see that, in the absence of any evidence that the sellers' position had been prejudiced by reason of their action in reliance on the representation, it is possible to infer that they suffered any such prejudice. In these circumstances, a necessary element for the application of the doctrine of equitable estoppel is lacking; and I decide this point in favour of the buyers. ...

It is therefore clear that it is not a requirement that the promisee has been prejudiced by altering his position. However, it is an essential part of the doctrine that it should be inequitable for the promisor to go back on his promise and enforce the strict contractual obligations. In *The Post Chaser*, it was not inequitable for the buyers to go back on their representation since so little time had elapsed since they had made their representation that the sellers were in no way prejudiced.

D & C Builders v Rees [1966] 2 QB 617 provides a further example of when it would not be inequitable to go on the promise.

D & C Builders Limited v Rees [1966] 2 QB 617

Panel: Lord Denning MR, Danckwerts and Winn LJJ

Facts: D & C Builders carried out work for Mr Rees and were owed £482 for that work. They chased Mr Rees for payment and finally Mr Rees's wife, who knew that the builders faced financial difficulties, offered £300 in settlement of the debt stating that if that were not accepted nothing would be paid. The builders accepted and Mrs Rees provided them with a cheque and in return, at her request, the builders provided a receipt containing the words 'received the sum of £300 from Mr Rees in completion of the account. ...' The builders later sued for the balance. The court considered as a preliminary issue whether the claim was barred by reason of a settlement having been reached.

LORD DENNING MR

...This case is of some consequence: for it is a daily occurrence that a merchant or tradesman, who is owed a sum of money, is asked to take less. The debtor says he is in difficulties. He offers a lesser sum in settlement, cash down. He says he cannot pay more. The creditor is considerate. He accepts the proffered sum and forgives him the rest of the debt. The question arises: is the settlement binding on the creditor? The answer is that, in point of law, the creditor is not bound by the settlement. He can the next day sue the debtor for the balance, and get judgment. The law was so stated in 1602 by Lord Coke in *Pinnel's Case*—and accepted in 1884 by the House of Lords in *Foakes v Beer*. ...

This doctrine of the common law has come under heavy fire. ...But a remedy has been found. The harshness of the common law has been relieved. Equity has stretched out a merciful hand to help the debtor [by permitting reliance on the doctrine of promissory estoppel].

 Link
See the discussion of the effect of promissory estoppel below

It is worth noticing that the principle may be applied, not only so as to suspend strict legal rights, but also as to preclude the enforcement of them.

 Alert

In applying this principle, however, we must note the qualification. The creditor is barred from his legal rights only when it would be inequitable for him to insist on them. Where there has been a true accord, under which the creditor voluntarily agrees to accept a lesser sum in satisfaction, and the debtor acts on that accord by paying the lesser sum and the creditor accepts it, then it is inequitable for the creditor afterwards to insist on the balance. But he is not bound unless there has been truly an accord between them.

In the present case, on the facts as found by the judge, it seems to me that there was no true accord. The debtor's wife held the creditor to ransom. The creditor was in need of money to meet his own commitments, and she knew it. When the creditor asked for payment of the £480 due to him, she said to him in effect: 'We cannot pay you the £480. But we will pay you £300 if you will accept it in settlement. If you do not accept it on those terms, you will get nothing. £300 is better than nothing.' She had no right to say any such thing. She could properly have said: 'We cannot pay you more than £300. Please accept it on account.' But she had no right to insist on his taking it in settlement. When she said: 'We will pay you nothing unless you accept £300 in settlement', she was putting undue pressure on the creditor. She was making a threat to break the contract (by paying nothing) and she was doing it so as to compel the creditor to do what he was unwilling to do (to accept £300 in settlement): and she succeeded. He complied with her demand...

In my opinion there is no reason in law or equity why the creditor should not enforce the full amount of the debt due to him. I would, therefore, dismiss this appeal.

Mr Rees could not rely on promissory estoppel because of the pressure his wife placed on the builders to accept the lesser payment. In these circumstances it was not inequitable to allow the builders to go back on the promise to accept less since it had not been freely given. To allow the debtor to rely on the doctrine in such circumstances would be contrary to the equitable maxim that 'he who seeks equity must come with clean hands'.

6.4 The Effect of Promissory Estoppel on Legal Rights

The question as to whether promissory estoppel suspends or extinguishes legal rights is not entirely clear and has been the subject of considerable judicial comment.

Tool Metal Manufacturing Co Ltd v Tungsten Electric Co Ltd [1955] 1 WLR 761

Panel: Viscount Simonds, Lord Oaksey, Lord Tucker and Lord Cohen

Facts: The appellant, Tool Metal, agreed to give the respondent, Tungsten, a non-exclusive licence to import, make, use and sell particular forms of metal (produced via a patented method). Tungsten had to pay 'compensation' to Tool Metal if the quantity of metal made or used by them in a month was higher than a fixed amount. However, from the beginning of the Second World War, Tool Metal agreed not to enforce their right to compensation and consequently, Tungsten stopped paying compensation.

In September 1944, Tungsten proposed a new agreement, which Tool Metal did not accept. Tungsten brought an action against Tool Metal for fraudulent misrepresentation and breach of contract. On 26 March 1946, Tool Metal counterclaimed for compensation for the metal used after 1 June 1945. This counterclaim failed.

In 1950, Tool Metal commenced a new action against Tungsten claiming compensation from 1 January 1947. It was argued that service of the original counterclaim was sufficient to constitute notice to bring the period of estoppel to an end.

LORD TUCKER

...Every case involving the application of this equitable doctrine must depend upon its own particular circumstances. It is, of course, clear, as Pearson J. [the judge at first instance] pointed out, that there are some cases where the period of suspension clearly terminates on the happening of a certain event or the cessation of a previously existing state of affairs or on the lapse of a reasonable period thereafter. In such cases no intimation or notice of any kind may be necessary. But in other cases where there is nothing to fix the end of the period which may be dependent upon the will of the person who has given

Alert

or made the concession, equity will no doubt require some notice or intimation together with a reasonable period for readjustment before the grantor is allowed to enforce his strict rights. No authority has been cited which binds your Lordships to hold that in all such cases the notice must take any particular form or specify a date for the termination of the suspensory period. This is not surprising having regard to the infinite variety of circumstances which may give rise to this principle which was stated in broad terms and must now be regarded as of general application.

My Lords, in the present case I can find nothing which persuades me that equity could require anything further than that which is contained in the counterclaim in the first action. It is true that it does not purport to be putting an end to an existing 'agreement' for a temporary suspension. No such agreement had been pleaded. It does, however, contain a clear intimation of a reversal by [Tool Metal] of their previous attitude with regard to the payment of compensation and of their intention to enforce compliance with clause 5 of the agreement and for an account thereunder.

It does not, I think, lie in the mouth of [Tungsten], who had consistently failed to comply with their obligations to render the returns required by the deed, now to complain that the notice should have specified a named future date upon which the suspensory period was to come to an end. ...

In my view, the counterclaim of March 26, 1946, followed by a period of nine months to January 1, 1947, from which date compensation in the present action is claimed, is sufficient to satisfy the requirements of equity and entitle [Tool Metal] to recover compensation under clause 5 of the deed as from the latter date. In the somewhat peculiar circumstances of the present case any other result would, I think, be highly inequitable. ...

Tool Metal was able to claim the compensation from 1 January 1947 onwards since the counterclaim of 26 March 1946 constituted sufficient notice of Tool Metal's intention to resume their strict legal rights.

It is clearly indicated in this case that, in general, promissory estoppel suspends as opposed to extinguishes legal rights. The period of estoppel may come to an end either on the giving of reasonable notice or, alternatively, on the cessation of the circumstances which made it inequitable to go back on the promise (See *High Trees* above).

On the other hand, there have been some conflicting dicta from Lord Denning MR in *D & C Builders v Rees* where he said: 'It is worth noticing that the principle may be applied, not only so as to suspend strict legal rights, but also as to preclude the enforcement of them'. It is not entirely clear what Lord Denning MR meant by this. It is arguable that he was referring to individual periodic payments. It would seem from both *Tool Metal* and *High Trees* that the right to the individual periodic payments payable during the period of the estoppel is extinguished.

This may be contrasted with the right to lump sum payments, which is merely suspended. If this distinction is correct it is interesting since, in relation to lump sum payments, promissory estoppel simply has the effect of giving the debtor more time to pay. This would mean that the doctrine of promissory estoppel has a far less devastating effect on the general rule relating to part-payment of a debt, as set out in *Foakes v Beer*, than may appear at first glance.

Further Reading

O'Sullivan, J., 1996. *In Defence of Foakes v Beer, Cambridge Law Journal.* 55(2). pp.219–228

Halson, R., 1999. The Offensive Limits of Promissory Estoppel, Lloyd's *Maritime and Commercial Law Quarterly.* pp.256–277

Trukhtanov, A., 2008. Foakes v Beer: Reform of Common Law at the Expense of Equity. *LQR.* 124 (Jul). pp 364–368

McKendrick, E., 2011. *Contract Law.* 9th ed. Palgrave MacMillan. Ch.5

McKendrick, E., *Contract Law* (2017) 12th ed. Ch.5

7

Duress

Topic List

Introduction

Duress means coercion. Whether the coercion suffered by the claimant will be deemed by a court to be legal duress depends on the extent and form of the coercion applied. There are three recognised forms of duress: duress of the person, duress of goods (rare) and economic duress. For each of these three types of duress there are different criteria that must be established by seeking a remedy. A contract which has been entered into under duress is voidable (i.e. capable of being set aside) but not void (i.e. a nullity from its beginning).

This chapter will briefly consider the first two forms of duress mentioned above before focusing on economic duress.

7.1   Duress of the Person

Duress of the person, as the name suggests, is where a contract is entered into unwillingly by one contracting party because they are being physically threatened by the other. The leading case on duress to the person is the Privy Council case *Barton v Armstrong* [1976] AC 104.

Barton v Armstrong **[1976] AC 104**

Panel: Lord Wilberforce, Lord Simon of Glaisdale, Lord Cross of Chelsea, Lord Kilbrandon and Sir Garfield Barwick

Facts: Armstrong was the chairman and largest shareholder of a public company and Barton was the managing director of that company. Barton began to resent Armstrong's interference in the management of the company. With the assistance of two other directors, Barton forced the removal of Armstrong as chairman. In order to achieve the total removal of Armstrong from the company, Barton agreed to pay $140,000 in Australian dollars, cash, to Armstrong. Barton alleged that Armstrong had extorted the sums of money on the basis of duress. He alleged that Armstrong had, *inter alia*, uttered threats to kill Barton, made threatening phone calls, and caused Barton a genuine belief that Armstrong had hired a contract-killer to terminate him. Further to this, Barton also alleged that Armstrong had phoned Barton at his office saying: 'You had better sign this agreement – or else.' The case was appealed to the Judicial Committee of the Privy Council. The Board agreed that on the evidence it was clear that Armstrong had threatened Barton.

LORD CROSS OF CHELSEA

The three judges in the Court of Appeal Division were in substantial agreement on the facts of the case but they reached different conclusions because they differed as to the law applicable to them. Mason J.A. and Taylor A.-J.A. thought that Barton could not succeed unless he could establish that but for the threats he would not have signed the agreement and that he had failed to establish that fact. Jacobs J.A. agreed that if Barton had indeed to show that but for the threats he would not have signed the agreement he had failed to do so. He thought, however, that if the evidence showed that one party to the transaction had put the other in fear of his life during the negotiations leading up to the execution of the deed in question the common law would assume that he was not a free agent and that he could consequently avoid the transaction. Furthermore he thought that in any case equity would allow him to avoid the transaction if the evidence showed that the threats had any appreciable effect in inducing him to execute the agreement even if he would in fact have executed it if there had been no threats and that the evidence did at least establish that.

As can be seen from the above, the Australian Court of Appeal Division differed on the question of causation. Two of the judges thought that the correct test was the 'but for' test ie but for the duress would Barton have entered into the contract; whereas the other judge, Jacobs, thought it sufficient that Armstrong's threats were *one* of the reasons for Barton executing the agreement. The Privy Council went on to consider this issue:

...Had Armstrong made a fraudulent misrepresentation to Barton for the purpose of inducing him to execute the deed of January 17, 1967, the answer to the problem which has arisen would have been clear. ...Armstrong could not have defeated his [Barton's] claim to relief by showing that there were other more weighty causes which contributed to his decision to execute the deed, for in this field the court does not allow an examination into the relative importance of contributory causes.

Once make [*sic*] out that there has been anything like deception, and no contract resting in any degree on that foundation can stand: *per* Lord Cranworth L.J. in *Reynell v. Sprye* (1852) 1 De G.M. & G 660, 708 ...Their Lordships think that the same rule should apply in cases of duress and that if Armstrong's threats were a reason for Barton's executing the deed he is entitled to relief even though he might well have entered into the contract if Armstrong had uttered no threats to induce him to do so.

After concluding that the causation test for duress of the person is that it be 'a' factor in the victim's decision to enter into the contract, the Board then considered which party had the burden of proving that the duress satisfied the test:

...If Barton had to establish that he would not have made the agreement but for Armstrong's threats, then their Lordships would not dissent from the view that he had not made out his case. But no such onus lay on him. On the contrary it was for Armstrong to establish, if he could, that the threats which he was making and the unlawful pressure which he was exerting for the purpose of inducing Barton to sign the agreement and which Barton knew were being made and exerted for this purpose in fact contributed nothing to Barton's decision to sign. The judge has found that during the 10 days or so before the documents were executed Barton was in genuine fear that

Armstrong was planning to have him killed if the agreement was not signed. His state of mind was described by the judge as one of very real mental torment and he believed that his fears would be at end when once the documents were executed. ...

7.2   Duress of Goods

Duress of goods (ie the unlawful detention of property) was not recognised as a valid form of duress for many years, following Lord Denman CJ's judgment in *Skeate v Beale* (1841) 11 Adolphus and Ellis 983.   The position was complicated in that a *promise* to pay money extracted by the unlawful detention of the promisor's goods was not invalid while on the other hand, where money was *paid* to release goods that had been unlawfully detained, the money could be recovered.

Skeate v Beale (1841) 11 Adolphus and Ellis 983

Panel: Lord Denman CJ

Facts: Skeate detained Beale's property, claiming that Beale owed him £19 10s rent. Beale agreed to pay £3 7s immediately if Skeate would release his property and the balance within a month.   Beale then refused to pay the outstanding amount claiming that he had only entered into the agreement to pay to prevent Skeate from selling his goods and that he only owed Skeate £3 7s 6d in total.

LORD DENMAN CJ

... We consider the law to be clear, and founded on good reason, that an agreement is not void because made under duress of goods. There is no distinction in this respect between a deed and an agreement not under seal; and, with regard to the former, the law is laid down in 2 Inst. 483, and Sheppard's Touchstone, p. 61, and the distinction pointed out between duress of, or menace to, the person, and duress of goods. The former is a constraining force, which not only takes away the free agency, but may leave no room for appeal to the law for a remedy: a man, therefore, is not bound by the agreement which he enters into under such circumstances: but the fear that goods may be taken or injured does not deprive any one of his free agency who possesses that ordinary degree of firmness which the law requires all to exert. ...

Skeate v Beale has since been strongly criticised (obiter) by Kerr J in *Occidental Worldwide Investment Corp v Skibs A/S Avanti (The Sibeon and The Sibotre)* [1976] 1 Lloyd's Rep 293 (see p.5 infra) and duress of goods is now recognised as a valid form of duress. Note that there is an interesting correspondence here between the 'ordinary degree of firmness' Lord Denman CJ expects of the usual businessman facing duress of goods and the reluctance of the courts to find economic duress unless pressure substantially greater than commercial hard bargaining can be proven. This is very much in line with the *laissez faire* approach of the courts towards commercial bargains generally.

The defendants gave the plaintiffs the option to revert to the original hire rate or of cancelling the charters. When the plaintiffs refused both options the defendants withdrew the vessels in May 1973. The plaintiffs claimed damages from the defendants on the ground that the vessels had been wrongfully withdrawn. The defendants claimed that they were entitled to the rescission of the addenda on the ground of fraudulent and innocent misrepresentation or duress. The court found that the plaintiffs were liable for fraudulent and innocent misrepresentation but that although the defendants were acting under pressure when they signed the addenda this was not such coercion as to amount to duress.

7.3   Economic Duress

The most influential decision on economic duress currently is that of Dyson J in *DSND Subsea Ltd v Petroleum Geo Services ASA* [2000] BLR 530. In this case, Dyson J formulates a test for economic duress that pulls together the law on economic duress into a coherent whole.

DSND Subsea Limited (Formerly known as DSND Oceantech Limited) v Petroleum Geo Services ASA, PGS Offshore Technology AS [2000] BLR 530

Panel: Dyson J

Facts: Petroleum Geo Services ('PGS') engaged DSND Subsea Limited ('DSND'), a professional diving operation, to carry out works in the North Sea constructing subsea structures. The contract was based on an assumption that the risers (pipes used to transfer produced fluids from the seabed to the surface facilities or lift gas), would have already been installed by PGS. DSND was to have full responsibility for the rest of the subsea system. Later, it transpired that the risers would have to be installed after the subsea system was in place. DSND was concerned about several issues and in particular, about the insurance that was in place. They thought that they would not be covered if they proceeded with the installation without further changes to the insurance and refused to continue with the work. Eventually, a memorandum of understanding ('MOU') and a memorandum of agreement ('MOA') were entered into which set out various changes to DSND's payment and acknowledged that the risers were to be installed after the subsea system which brought DSND within insurance cover. After the risers were installed, PGS then informed DSND the contract was terminated on the basis of DSND's 'serious breach of contract'. PGS argued that both the MOU and MOA should be set aside for economic duress. The economic duress point was considered as a preliminary issue by the court.

MR JUSTICE DYSON

… Was the MOU [Memorandum of Understanding] entered into under duress?

The Law

The ingredients of actionable duress are that there must be pressure, (a) whose practical effect is that there is compulsion on, or a lack of practical choice for, the victim, (b) which is illegitimate, and (c) which is a significant cause inducing the claimant to enter into the contract: see *Universal Tanking of Monrovia v ITWF* [1983] AC 336, 400B–E, and *The Evia Luck* [1992] 2 AC 152, 165G. In determining whether there has been illegitimate pressure, the court takes into account a range of factors. These include whether there has been an actual or threatened breach of contract; whether the person allegedly exerting the pressure has acted in good or bad faith; whether the victim had any realistic practical alternative but to submit to the pressure; whether the victim protested at the time; and whether he affirmed and sought to rely on the contract. These are all relevant factors. Illegitimate pressure must be distinguished from the rough and tumble of the pressures of normal commercial bargaining.

I do not believe that any of the above is controversial.

Alert

Mr Justice Dyson then turns to the issue of good faith where, in his opinion, DSND were 'justified' in refusing to carry out their contractual obligations because insurance issues had not been finalised with PGS.

Discussion

The position at the start of the meeting of 24 September was that there were two principal problems facing the parties: the question of insurance/indemnity, and the issue of compensation for the riser installation. DSND were in my view entirely justified in being reluctant to go offshore without at least a reliable assurance that, if there were a problem with the … [riser installation], PGS' all risks policy would cover it. … [If such a problem with riser installation] were to happen, the consequences might well be disastrous for DSND, unless that contingency was adequately covered by insurance/indemnity arrangements. That is why there were negotiations during the meetings of 24 and 25 September in relation to liability for the RTIAs, and amendments to the insurance and indemnity provisions of the Contract.

The Contract did not contain a provision which entitled DSND to suspend work. The Contract simply did not make provision for a situation such as occurred. If it were necessary so to hold, I would say that the suspension of work on the …[riser installation] pending resolution of the insurance/indemnity question, even if it was a breach of contract, and even if it amounted to pressure, did not amount to illegitimate pressure. It was reasonable behaviour by a contractor acting bona fide in a very difficult situation. …

Alert

Then Dyson J considered whether or not 'pressure' applied by DSND was 'illegitimate'.

I am not persuaded that PGS were subjected to pressure in the sense that they had no realistic practical alternative but to concede DSND's demands. ...Mr Wilson is a careful and intelligent person. I believe that, if he had felt that he was being blackmailed, he would at least have explored the possibility of alternative vessels. The fact that he did not do so strongly suggests that did not feel that he was being blackmailed...

There are a number of features of the case which are very difficult to explain if Mr Wilson was blackmailed into signing the MOU. First, there is the fact that there was plainly a reasonably amicable atmosphere between the parties. This is most obviously evidenced by the fact that the parties went out to dinner together during their stay in Oslo. ...

Having concluded that the MOU was not entered into under duress, the question of it having been subsequently affirmed was no longer at issue, Dyson J then went on to briefly consider the question of affirmation. His comments in this respect are *obiter*.

Affirmation

...

It is not in dispute that a contract entered into under duress is voidable. ... Lapse of time in itself does not seem to constitute a bar to relief, but it will provide evidence of acquiescence if the victim fails to take any steps to set aside the transaction within a reasonable time after he is freed from the undue influence. And where he has himself failed to commence proceedings in this way during his lifetime, his personal representatives cannot do so after his death.'

In my judgment, even if PGS were subjected to illegitimate pressure on 25 September, they were free from it by late October when Mr Darby had his conversation with Mr Greville... .I infer that, since Mr Darby raised the issue of duress with Mr Greville on 21 October, PGS must have been aware of their right to avoid the MOU on that ground. Instead of taking that course, they continued to rely on the MOU, and complained that DSND were not observing its terms. Eventually, they decided to terminate the Contract on the grounds that DSND were in breach of the terms of the MOU.

Accordingly, if I had held that PGS entered into the MOU under duress, I would have declined to set aside the agreement on the grounds that they affirmed it. Another way of putting it is to say that it would be inequitable to allow PGS to avoid the MOU after they had relied on it in the way that I have mentioned for their own benefit, after (as I have held) they ceased to be subject to any duress.

Carillion Construction Limited v Felix (UK) Limited [2001] BLR 1

Panel: Dyson, J

Facts: Carillion Construction Ltd ('Carillion') was the main contractor employed to carry out the construction of an office building. Carillion subcontracted the design, manufacture and supply of the cladding to Felix UK Ltd ('Felix'). Although Felix started work on the design in about September 1998, negotiations for the terms of the subcontract were not concluded until about December 1999. In November 1999, and notwithstanding that the subcontract works were several months away from completion, Felix suggested that an attempt should be made to agree a draft final account for Felix' works. Negotiations ensued, and culminated in an agreement reached at a meeting on 13 March 2000 that the final account sum should be £3.2 million plus VAT. This agreement was then embodied in a formal Settlement Agreement dated 17 March. Carillion contended that it was compelled to enter into the agreement by a threat made on behalf of Felix that it would not continue to supply cladding units in accordance with the subcontract unless a final account sum of £3.2 million was agreed. Carillion claimed that the agreement should be set aside for duress.

MR JUSTICE DYSON

The Law

This is not in dispute. It is common ground that the following summary of the relevant principles that I set out in *DSND Subsea Ltd v Petroleum Geo-services ASA* [unreported, 28 July 2000] is an accurate statement of the law...

Mr Justice Dyson then cited his test from *DSND Subsea Ltd* and continued:

Accordingly, Carillion must show that there was (a) pressure or a threat, (b) which was illegitimate, (c) the practical effect of which was that it had no practical choice but to enter into the agreement, and (d) which was a significant cause inducing it to enter into the contract. ...

Mr Justice Dyson went on to consider whether the pressure applied by Felix in threatening to withhold deliveries had been 'illegitimate'. It is possible to see echoes of the judgment in *DSND Subsea v Petroleum Geo Services* in Dyson J's consideration of the circumstances of the case such as the possibility, which he discounts, of Felix having genuinely believed it was entitled to take such action.

Illegitimate pressure

The threat to withhold deliveries was a threat to commit a clear breach of contract. Felix was already in breach of its obligation to complete by 17 January 2000. There was also an express term of the subcontract (clause 11.8) that it would '... *use constantly its best endeavours to prevent delay in the progress of the Sub-Contract Works ... and to prevent any such delay, resulting in the completion of the Sub-Contract Works being delayed or further delayed ...'*

Nor has it been suggested that Felix genuinely (but mistakenly) believed that it was contractually entitled to withhold deliveries lending agreement of the final account. There was no contractual entitlement to insist on agreement of the final account before completion of the Subcontract Works; still less was there any contractual right to suspend deliveries until the account was agreed.

In any event, as Mr Sears points out, even if Felix was entitled to have its final account agreed at this stage, then it could and should have referred the matter to arbitration under the subcontract.

The threat was made at a time when Felix knew that there was a number of trades which were dependent on Felix completing its work, or at least completing the outstanding work at ground floor level in order to make the building watertight. Felix knew that Carillion was becoming increasingly concerned about progress. It knew that Carillion had to complete the main contract works by 5th June, and that this would not be possible unless Felix completed the cladding works. Felix must also have known that it would be impossible for Carillion to find an alternative supplier in time to meet the main contract completion date.

For all these reasons, in my judgment, the pressure that Felix applied to Carillion by its threat to withhold deliveries until the final account was agreed was illegitimate. There was no justification for it. ...

Adam Opel GmbH v Mitras Automotive (UK) Ltd Costs [2007] EWHC 3481 (QB)

Panel: Mr Justice Donaldson QC

Facts: Mitras had agreed to be Adam Opel's sole supplier in the United Kingdom of bumper mounts for a particular model of van that Adam Opel manufactured. Adam Opel gave notice to Mitras that the contract would be terminated. Mitras then threatened to suspend supplies immediately unless it was paid compensation, comprising an increased price for each bumper, payment of certain development costs incurred by Mitras and the reversal of price concessions agreed at the start of the contract. Eventually Adam Opel agreed to Mitras's terms in order to ensure continued supply. Once the final bumper had been supplied, Adam Opel claimed recovery of the monies paid to Mitras under the compensation agreement. Opel submitted that the agreement was unenforceable because it had been made under duress and because there had been no consideration for it. Mitras argued that its claim to compensation was made in good faith, being based on a genuine belief that it was entitled to it. Judgment was given for Adam Opel. The agreement had been made under economic duress.

MR JUSTICE DONALDSON QC

The general principles of the law relating to economic duress have been elaborated over the last forty years in a number of decided cases, and were not in issue before me. It was common ground that they are accurately summarised by Dyson J in DSND Subsea Ltd v Petroleum Geo Services ASA, [2000] … and repeated in his later decision in Carillion Construction Ltd v Felix (UK) Ltd, [2001] …

26 I do not understand that summary to have been presented as a precise analytic tool, nor would it be possible to use it as such. There is plainly scope for overlap between the three ingredients of pressure, illegitimacy, and causative effect. The list of matters to be considered in assessing legitimacy is not exhaustive, and the weight to be attached to each of them will depend on the facts of the individual case. And the decision on the fundamental question whether the pressure has crossed the line from that which must be accepted in normal robust commercial bargaining involves at least some element of value judgment. …

7.4 Illegitimate Pressure

A threat to breach contract may constitute duress.

B & S Contracts and Design Ltd v Victor Green Publications Ltd [1984] ICR 419

Panel: Eveleigh, Griffiths and Kerr LJJ

Facts: The plaintiff contracted to erect stands at Olympia for the defendant. A week before the exhibition the plaintiff's workman went on strike, refusing to return to work until a pay demand was met. The plaintiff told the defendant that unless the defendant paid an additional £4,500 the contract would be cancelled. The plaintiff made it clear that the amount to be paid was to be in addition to the contract price. The defendant paid the amount demanded as the cancellation of the contract would have caused serious damage to the defendant's economic interests. At the end of the contract, the defendant deducted the £4,500 from the contract price. The plaintiff claimed the balance. It was held that the plaintiff had agreed to make the extra payment under duress.

LORD JUSTICE GRIFFITHS

…The law on economic pressure creating a situation which will be recognised as duress is in the course of development, and it is clear that many difficult decisions lie ahead of the courts. Many commercial contracts are varied during their currency because the parties are faced with changing circumstances during the performance of the contract, and it is certainly not on every occasion when one of the parties unwillingly agrees to a variation that the law would consider that he had acted by reason of duress. The cases will have to be examined in the light of their particular circumstances. But two recent decisions of the highest authority — the decision of the Privy Council in *Pao On v. Lau Yiu Long* [1980] AC 614 and *Universe Tankships Inc. of Monrovia v. International Transport Workers Federation* [1982] ICR 262 — establish that a threatened breach of contract may impose such economic pressure that the law will recognise that a payment made as a result of the threatened breach is recoverable on the grounds of duress.

The facts of this case appear to me to be as follows. The plaintiffs intended to break their contract, subject to the effect of the force majeure clause, by allowing their workforce to walk off the job in circumstances in which they could not possibly replace it with another workforce. The defendants offered to advance the sum of £4,500 on the contract price, which would have enabled the plaintiffs to pay the men a sufficient extra sum of money to induce them to remain on the job. The plaintiffs refused this sum of money. There is no question that they refused to pay as a matter of principle. They refused to pay because they did not want to reduce the sum they would receive for the contract. They said to the defendants, If you will give us £4,500 we will complete the contract. The defendants, faced with this demand, were in an impossible position. If they refused to hand over the sum of £4,500 they would not be able to erect the stands in this part of the exhibition, which would have clearly caused grave damage to their reputation and I would have thought might have exposed them to very heavy claims from the exhibitors who had leased space from them and hoped to use those stands in the ensuing exhibition. They seem to me to have been placed in the position envisaged by Lord Scarman in the Privy Council decision, *Pao On v. Lau Yiu Long* [1980] A.C. 614, in which they were faced with no alternative course of action but to pay the sum demanded of them. … I can see no reason why they [the plaintiffs] should not have accepted the money and paid the workforce save their own immediate economic interests, and they chose not to do that but to put pressure on the defendants by refusing the offer and indicating that the only way out was for the defendants to hand over the £4,500 as a gift rather than as an advance.

I think that was thoroughly unreasonable behaviour, and that being so they are not entitled to rely upon the force majeure clause, and for these reasons I agree this appeal fails.

Although breach of contract is not always grounds for duress, in this instance Griffiths LJ is clearly influenced by the plaintiff's 'unreasonable behaviour'.

Lord Justice Kerr emphasised the importance of the defendant's refusal to pay.

LORD JUSTICE KERR

… In the light of the authorities it is perhaps important to emphasise that there is no question in this case of the defendants having subsequently approbated this payment or failed to seek to avoid it, which in some cases (such as the *North Ocean Shipping Co Ltd v Hyundai Construction Co Ltd* [1979] QB 705, a decision of Mocatta J., to which Eveleigh L.J. has referred) would be fatal. In the present case the defendants took immediate action by deducting that £4,500 from the invoice price.

I also bear in mind that a threat to break a contract unless money is paid by the other party can, but by no means always will, constitute duress. It appears from the authorities that it will only constitute duress if the consequences of a refusal would be serious and immediate so that there is no reasonable alternative open, such as by legal redress, obtaining an injunction, etc. I think that this is implicit in the authorities to which we have been referred, of which the most recent one is *Universe Tankships Inc. of Monrovia v. International Transport Workers Federation* [1982] ICR. 262. I would only refer to one passage from the speech of Lord Scarman, not because he states anything that differs from what was stated elsewhere, but because I wonder whether this passage may not contain a typographical error. Lord Scarman is reported at pp. 288–289 as having said — and it applies to the facts of this case:

'The classic case of duress is, however, not the lack of will to submit but the victim's intentional submission arising from the realisation that there is no other practical choice open to him.'

I wonder whether the lack of will to submit should not have been the lack of will to resist or the lack of will in submitting. However that may be, there was no other practical choice open to the defendants in the present case, and accordingly I agree that this is a case where money has been paid under duress, which was accordingly recoverable by the defendants provided they acted promptly as they did, and which they have recovered by deducting it from the contract price. In these circumstances the plaintiffs' claim for this additional sum must fail.

In both *B&S Contracts & Design* above and the following case, the victims of the duress really had no practicable choice but to submit. As is made clear by Kerr LJ above, had they had an adequate remedy available to them other than entering into the new contract with the other party, e.g. obtaining an injunction, then the pressure being applied would not have qualified as duress.

Atlas Express Ltd v Kafco (Importers and Distributors) Ltd [1989] QB 833

Panel: Tucker J

Facts: The plaintiff, a firm of road hauliers, contracted with the defendants to deliver cartons of basket ware to various branches of Woolworths throughout the UK. A manager of the plaintiff's firm fixed the contract price at a rate of £1.10 per carton, based on an estimate that each load would consist of between 400 and 600 cartons. The first load fell significantly below his estimates, comprising of only 200 cartons. The manager then refused to take any further loads unless the defendant agreed to renegotiate the contract price to a minimum of £440 per load. The defendant, a small organisation, was heavily reliant on the Woolworths contract and unable to find another carrier, so reluctantly agreed to pay the imposed minimum charge. At a later stage, the defendant refused to pay. The plaintiff sued and the defendant argued economic duress as a defence. It was held that where a party has no alternative but to accept revised terms that were detrimental to its interest, this amounted to economic duress that vitiated the apparent consent to the re-negotiated terms.

MR JUSTICE TUCKER

The defendants were a small company and their three directors were personally committed to its success. They had secured a large order from Woolworth and had obtained a large quantity of goods in order to fulfil it. It was essential to the defendants' success and to their commercial survival that they should be in a position to make deliveries. I find that this was obvious to Mr. Hope, and was known by him. It was now early November, a time of year when demands on road hauliers and deliverers are heaviest.

It would have been difficult, if not impossible, for the defendants to find alternative carriers in time to meet their delivery dates.

I find that the meeting between Mr. Hope and Mr. Armiger took place on Friday, 14 November. …The following day, 18 November, one of the plaintiffs' drivers arrived at the defendants' premises with an empty trailer. He brought with him a document entitled Amended/Transferred Account Details. Mr. Hope had written in the new rates, which now specified a minimum charge of £440 per trailer. …

I find that when Mr. Armiger signed that agreement he did so unwillingly and under compulsion. He believed on reasonable grounds that it would be very difficult if not impossible to negotiate with another contractor. He did not regard the fact that he had signed the new agreement as binding the defendants to its terms. He had no bargaining power. He did not regard it as a genuine arm's length re-negotiation in which he had a free and equal say and, in my judgment, that view was fully justified.

In the words of the co-director, Mr. Fox, he felt that he was over a barrel. …

The issue which I have to determine is whether the defendants are bound by the agreement signed on their behalf on 18 November 1986. The defendants contend that they are not bound, for two reasons: first because the agreement was signed under duress; second because there was no consideration for it.

The first question raises a particularly interesting point of law - whether economic duress is a concept known to English law. Economic duress must be distinguished from commercial pressure, which on any view is not sufficient to vitiate consent.

...It is clear to me that in a number of English cases judges have acknowledged the existence of this concept.

Thus, in *D & C Builders Ltd v Rees* [1966] 2 QB 617 Lord Denning M.R. said, at p. 625F-G: 'No person can insist on a settlement procured by intimidation.' and in *Occidental Worldwide Investment Corporation v. Skibs A/S Avanti* [1976] Lloyd's Rep. 293, 336 Kerr J. appeared to accept that economic duress could operate in appropriate circumstances. A similar conclusion was reached by Mocatta J in North Ocean Shipping Co Ltd v Hyundai Construction Co Ltd [1979] QB 705, 719E.

In particular, there are passages in the judgment of Lord Scarman in *Pao On v. Lau Yiu Long* [1980] A.C. 614 , which clearly indicate the recognition of the concept.

Mr Justice Tucker read Lord Scarman's advice as set out above and continued:

A further case, which was not cited to me, was *B & S Contracts and Design Ltd v Victor Green Publications Ltd* [1984] ICR 419. At p. 423 Eveleigh L.J. referred to the speech of Lord Diplock in another uncited case - *Universe Tankships Inc of Monrovia v International Transport Workers Federation* [1983] 1 AC 366, 384:

'The rationale is that his apparent consent was induced by pressure exercised upon him by that other party which the law does not regard as legitimate, with the consequence that the consent is treated in law as revocable unless approbated either expressly or by implication after the illegitimate pressure has ceased to operate on his mind.'

In commenting on this Eveleigh LJ said of the word 'legitimate':

...For the purpose of this case it is sufficient to say that if the claimant has been influenced against his will to pay money under the threat of unlawful damage to his economic interest he will be entitled to claim that money back ...'

Reverting to the case before me, I find that the defendants' apparent consent to the agreement was induced by pressure which was illegitimate and I find that it was not approbated. In my judgment that pressure can properly be described as economic duress, which is a concept recognised by English law, and which in the circumstances of the present case vitiates the defendants' apparent consent to the agreement.

In any event, I find that there was no consideration for the new agreement. The plaintiffs were already obliged to deliver the defendants' goods at the rates agreed under the terms of the original agreement. There was no consideration for the increased minimum charge of £440 per trailer.

Accordingly, I find that the plaintiffs' claim fails ...

A more recent example of an illegitimate threat can be seen in *Carillion Construction Ltd v Felix (UK)* discussed above.

7.5 Legitimate Pressure

The following three cases are examples of claims of economic duress that have been dismissed by the courts and alleged illegitimate pressure that was determined to be lawful and legitimate.

CTN Cash and Carry Limited v Gallaher Limited [1994] 4 All ER 714

Panel: Sir Donald Nicholls V-C, Farquharson and Steyn LJJ

Facts: CTN bought cigarettes from Gallaher under a long-standing contract, with each purchase being a separate transaction. Gallaher regularly gave credit to CTN. A consignment of cigarettes worth £17,000 due to be delivered was stolen from a warehouse and there was a disagreement about which party bore the risk. It later became clear that the risk was in fact with Gallaher but before this a representative of Gallaher informed CTN that if CTN did not the pay the £17,000 all credit facilities would be withdrawn. CTN decided that paying was the lesser of two evils. CTN later sought to recover the money paid on the grounds of economic duress. It was held that the threat to remove credit facilities was coercive but not improper. The defendants were using the threat as a means of getting money they believed was due to them and not as a means of extorting money they knew not to be due.

LORD JUSTICE STEYN

A buyer paid a sum of money to his supplier. The sum of money was in truth not owed by the buyer to the supplier. The buyer paid the sum as a result of the supplier's threat to stop the buyer's credit facilities in their future dealings if the sum was not paid. The supplier acted in the *bona fide* belief that the sum was owing. Does the doctrine of economic duress enable the buyer to recover the payment? ...The fact that the defendants were in a monopoly position cannot therefore by itself convert what is not otherwise duress into duress.

A second characteristic of the case is that the defendants were in law entitled to refuse to enter into any future contracts with the plaintiffs for any reason whatever or for no reason at all. Such a decision not to deal with the plaintiffs would have been financially damaging to the defendants, but it would have been lawful. A fortiori it was lawful for the defendants, for any reason or for no reason, to insist that they would no longer grant credit to the plaintiffs. The defendants' demand for payment of the invoice, coupled with the threat to withdraw credit, was neither a breach of contract nor a tort.

A third, and critically important, characteristic of the case is the fact that the defendants bona fide thought that the goods were at the risk of the plaintiffs and that the plaintiffs owed the defendants the sum in question. The defendants exerted commercial pressure on the plaintiffs in order to obtain

Alert

payment of a sum which they bona fide considered due to them. The defendants' motive in threatening withdrawal of credit facilities was commercial self-interest in obtaining a sum that they considered due to them...

Lord Justice Steyn then considers the possibility of lawful act duress and concludes that whether or not a threatened act constitutes duress is more to do with whether the threat is made in good or bad faith than the lawfulness of the act itself. In the following extracts he suggests that the courts are more concerned with unconscionability than with legal technicalities.

...I also readily accept that the fact that the defendants have used lawful means does not by itself remove the case from the scope of the doctrine of economic duress. Professor Birks, in his 'Introduction to the Law of Restitution', at 177, lucidly explains:

'Can lawful pressures also count? This is a difficult question, because, if the answer is that they can, the only viable basis for discriminating between acceptable and unacceptable pressures is not positive law but social morality. In other words, the judges must say what pressures (though lawful outside the restitutionary context) are improper as contrary to prevailing standards. That makes the judges, not the law or the legislature, the arbiters of social evaluation. On the other hand, if the answer is that lawful pressures are always exempt, those who devise outrageous but technically lawful means of compulsion must always escape restitution until the legislature declares the abuse unlawful. It is tolerably clear that, at least where they can be confident of a general consensus in favour of their evaluation, the courts are willing to apply a standard of impropriety rather than technical unlawfulness. ...'

Outside the field of protected relationships, and in a purely commercial context, it might be a relatively rare case in which 'lawful-act duress' can be established. And it might be particularly difficult to establish duress if the defendant *bona fide* considered that his demand was valid. In this complex and changing branch of the law I deliberately refrain from saying 'never'. But as the law stands, I am satisfied that the defendants' conduct in this case did not amount to duress.

It is an unattractive result, inasmuch as the defendants are allowed to retain a sum which at the trial they became aware was not in truth due to them. But in my view the law compels the result.

For these reasons, I would dismiss the appeal

For a further example of an unlawful threat that did not constitute duress, see *DSND Subsea Ltd v Petroleum Geo Services ASA* above.

In *Alec Lobb (Garages) Ltd. and Others v Total Oil Great Britain Ltd.* [1983] 1 WLR 87, the first instance decision is considered here rather than the later appeal as the plaintiffs subsequently dropped their claim for duress and continued instead with a claim for undue influence.

Alec Lobb (Garages) Ltd. and Others v Total Oil Great Britain Ltd. [1983] 1 WLR 87

Panel: Peter Millett QC

Facts: The plaintiffs carried on the business of a garage and petrol filling station. In 1969 the plaintiffs were in financial difficulties and subject to a contract whereby they had to accept petrol supplies exclusively from the defendants. Contrary to the independent advice of their solicitors, the plaintiffs entered into a transaction with the defendants whereby the plaintiffs granted a lease of their property to the defendants at a peppercorn rent plus a lump sum of £35,000, representing the market value of the lease. As part of the agreement, the defendants granted a lease-back of the property to the plaintiffs for 21 years at a rent of £2,250 per annum, subject to a right to terminate after seven or fourteen years and requiring the plaintiffs to accept all the petrol for their business from the defendants. With the plaintiffs' concurrence the defendants converted the property into a self-service filling station at a cost of £19,000. In 1979, the plaintiffs claimed a declaration that the transaction was voidable for duress (amongst other claims). It was held that there was no duress.

PETER MILLETT QC

...The plaintiffs next contended that the transaction of lease and leaseback was obtained by economic duress and should be set aside accordingly. This is a branch of the law which is still developing in this country, but I accept that commercial pressure may constitute duress and render a transaction voidable, provided that the pressure amounts to a coercion of the will which vitiates consent: see *Pao On v. Lau Yiu Long* [1980] A.C. 614. Economic duress, however, is still a form of duress. A plaintiff who seeks to set aside a transaction on the grounds of economic duress must therefore establish that he entered into it unwillingly (not necessarily under protest, though the absence of protest will be highly relevant) that he had no realistic alternative but to submit to the defendant's demands; that his apparent consent was exacted from him by improper pressure exerted by or on behalf of the defendant; and that he repudiated the transaction as soon as the pressure was relaxed.

In my judgment, the plaintiffs have completely failed to establish such a case. It is possible that Mr. Lobb had no realistic alternative (though even this is doubtful); but he certainly did not enter into the transaction under any compulsion on the part of the defendants. He was under no pressure from them to accept their terms. The plaintiff company was in great financial difficulties, but these were of its own making. It was under considerable financial pressure, but this came from the bank and, to a lesser extent, from another creditor, United Dominions Trust Ltd., not from the defendants. The defendants drove a hard bargain; their terms were offered virtually on a take-it-or-leave-it basis. But this proceeded from their reluctance to enter into the transaction, which they did not consider particularly attractive. Had Mr. Lobb

 Alert

found some other means of solving his problems, and broken off the discussions, Mr. Story at least would have been delighted. If there was any pressure to conclude the deal, it came from Mr. Lobb and, indirectly, from his bank. Nor was Mr. Lobb under such compelling necessity that he was forced to submit to whatever demands the defendants might choose to make; on the contrary, he was able to and did, refuse their attempts to obtain the freehold.

... In my judgment, to set the transaction aside in those circumstances on the ground of economic duress is out of the question. ...

R v Attorney General of England and Wales [2003] UKPC 22, [2003] EMLR 24

Panel: Lord Bingham of Cornhill, Lord Steyn, Lord Hoffmann, Lord Millett, Lord Scott of Foscote

Facts: The defendant was a member of 22 SAS Regiment. His squadron was told that all members who wanted to remain in the regiment would be required to sign confidentiality contracts, failing which they would be returned to unit ('RTU'). Involuntary RTU was normally imposed as a penalty for some disciplinary offence or on the ground of professional unsuitability for the SAS. It involved exclusion from the social life of the regiment and loss of its higher rates of pay. The defendant asked a colleague whether he could obtain legal advice on the contract and had been told that he could not. He signed the contract. The defendant later left the army and entered into a contract with a publisher to publish his story. As a result the Attorney-General commenced proceedings in New Zealand for breach of contract, claiming an injunction, damages and an account of profits. In his defence the defendant pleaded amongst other things that he had signed the contract under military orders and that it had been obtained by duress. It was held that the threat of RTU was lawful and justifiable as anyone unwilling to accept the obligation of confidentiality was unsuitable for the SAS in any event.

LORD HOFFMANN

Duress

In *Universe Tankships Inc of Monrovia v International Transport Workers Federation* [1983] 1 AC 366, 400 Lord Scarman said that there were two elements in the wrong of duress. One was pressure amounting to compulsion of the will of the victim and the second was the illegitimacy of the pressure. R says that to offer him the alternative of being returned to unit, which was regarded in the SAS as a public humiliation, was compulsion of his will. It left him no practical alternative. Their Lordships are content to assume that this was the case. ...

The legitimacy of the pressure must be examined from two aspects: first, the nature of the pressure and secondly, the nature of the demand which the pressure is applied to support: see Lord Scarman in the *Universe Tankships* case, at p 401. Generally speaking, the threat of any form of unlawful action will be regarded as illegitimate. On the other hand, that fact that the threat is lawful does not necessarily make the pressure legitimate. As Lord Atkin said in *Thorne v Motor Trade Association* [1937] AC 797, 806:

'The ordinary blackmailer normally threatens to do what he has a perfect right to do — namely, communicate some compromising conduct to a person whose knowledge is likely to affect the person threatened … What he has to justify is not the threat, but the demand of money.'

In this case, the threat was lawful. Although return to unit was not ordinarily used except on grounds of delinquency or unsuitability and was perceived by members of the SAS as a severe penalty, there is no doubt that the Crown was entitled at its discretion to transfer any member of the SAS to another unit. Furthermore, the judge found, in para 123:

 Alert

'The MOD could not be criticised for its motivation in introducing the contracts. They were introduced because of the concerns about the increasing number of unauthorised disclosures by former UKSF personnel and the concern that those disclosures were threatening the security of operations and personnel and were undermining the effectiveness and employability of the UKSF. Those are legitimate concerns for the MOD to have. …'

If R had signed the contract because as a matter of military law he had been obliged to do so, their Lordships would see much force in this reasoning. But they agree with the Court of Appeal that this was not the case. There was no order in the sense of a command which created an obligation to obey under military law. Instead, R was faced with a choice which may have constituted 'overwhelming pressure' but was not an exercise by the MOD of its legal powers over him. The legitimacy of the pressure therefore falls to be examined by normal criteria and as neither of the courts in New Zealand considered either the threat to be unlawful or the demand unreasonable, it follows that the contract was not obtained by duress.

7.5.1 Taking Steps to Avoid the Contract

North Ocean Shipping Co Ltd v Hyundai Construction Co Ltd and Another (The Atlantic Baron) [1979] QB 705

Panel: Mocatta J

Facts: By a shipbuilding contract the builders agreed to build a tanker for the owners, for $30,950,000 payable in five instalments. The contract required the builders to open a reverse letter of credit for the repayment of instalments in the event of their default. After the first instalment had been paid, the dollar was devalued and the builders threatened not to deliver unless the remaining instalments were increased by 10 per cent. The owners were advised that there was no legal basis for the claim, but were anxious that they might lose a favourable charter with Shell if the ship were not finished on time, and in a telex dated 28 June 1973, they agreed to the increased payments, 'to maintain an amicable relationship and without prejudice to our rights.' The builders did this and delivered the tanker; the owners took delivery without protest. Some eight months later the owners claimed the return of the 10 per cent extra. It was suggested that they did not seek the return of the money sooner because they were concerned about the delivery of a sister ship (The Atlantic Baroness) also being built for them. However, the arbitrators found that this fear was groundless. It was held that although the agreement to pay the extra money might initially have been voidable for economic duress, the fact that the shipping company waited eight months before taking any action, meant they had affirmed it.

MR JUSTICE MOCATTA

There has been considerable discussion in the books whether, if an agreement is made under duress of goods to pay a sum of money and there is some consideration for the agreement, the excess sum can be recovered. The authority for this suggested distinction is *Skeate v. Beale* (1841) 11 Ad. & El. 983. It was there said by Lord Denman C.J. that an agreement was not void because made under duress of goods, the distinction between that case and the cases of money paid to recover goods wrongfully seized being said to be obvious in that the agreement was not compulsorily but voluntarily entered into. ... Kerr J. in *Occidental Worldwide Investment Corporation v. Skibs A/S Avanti (The Siboen and The Sibotre)* [1976] 1 Lloyd's Rep. 293, 335, gave strong expression to the view that the suggested distinction based on *Skeate v. Beale* would not be observed today. He said, though obiter, that *Skeate v. Beale* would not justify a decision: ...

Mr Justice Mocatta then read an extract from Kerr J's judgment in *The Sibeon and The Sibotre* regarding duress of goods and continued:

... Before proceeding further it may be useful to summarise the conclusions I have so far reached. First, I do not take the view that the recovery of money paid under duress other than to the person is necessarily limited to duress to goods falling within one of the categories hitherto established by the English eases. I would respectfully follow and adopt the broad statement of principle laid down by Isaacs J. cited earlier and frequently quoted and applied in the Australian cases. Secondly, from this it follows that the compulsion may take the form of economic duress if the necessary facts are proved. A threat to break a contract may amount to such economic duress. Thirdly, if there has been such a form of duress leading to a contract for consideration, I think that contract is a voidable one which can be avoided and the excess money paid under it recovered.

I think the facts found in this ease do establish that the agreement to increase the price by 10 per cent. reached at the end of June 1973 was caused by what may be called economic duress. The Yard were adamant in insisting on the increased price without having any legal justification for so doing and the owners realised that the Yard would not accept anything other than an unqualified agreement to the increase. The owners might have claimed damages in arbitration against the Yard with all the inherent unavoidable uncertainties of litigation, but in view of the position of the Yard vis-à-vis their relations with Shell it would be unreasonable to hold that this is the course they should have taken. … I do not consider the Yard's ignorance of the Shell charter material. It may well be that had they known of it they would have been even more exigent.

If I am right in the conclusion reached with some doubt earlier that there was consideration for the 10 per cent. increase agreement reached at the end of June 1973, and it be right to regard this as having been reached under a kind of duress in the form of economic pressure, then what is said in *Chitty on Contracts*, 24th ed. (1977), vol. 1, para. 442, p. 207, to which both counsel referred me, is relevant, namely, that a contract entered into under duress is voidable and not void:

> … Consequently a person who has entered into a contract under duress, may either affirm or avoid such contract after the duress has ceased; and if he has so voluntarily acted under it with a full knowledge of all the circumstances he may be held bound on the ground of ratification, or if, after escaping from the duress, he takes no steps to set aside the transaction, he may be found to have affirmed it. …

The owners were … free from the duress on November 27, 1974, and took no action by way of protest or otherwise between their important telex of June 28, 1973, and their formal claim for the return of the excess 10 per cent. paid of July 30, 1975, when they nominated their arbitrator… [B]y the time the *Atlantic Baron* was due for delivery in November 1974, market conditions had changed radically, as is found in paragraph 39 of the special case and the owners must have been aware of this. The special case finds in paragraph 40, as stated earlier, that the owners did not believe that if they made any protest in the protocol of delivery and acceptance that the Yard would have refused to deliver the vessel or the *Atlantic Baroness* and had no reason so to believe. …I have come to the conclusion that the important points here are that since there was no danger at this time in registering a protest, the final payments were made without any qualification and were followed by a delay until July 31, 1975, before the owners put forward their claim, the correct inference to draw, taking an objective view of the facts, is that the action and inaction of the owners can only be regarded as an affirmation of the variation in June 1973 of the terms of the original contract by the agreement to pay the additional 10 per cent. …

Note that, in *The Atlantic Baron,* when Macotta J states that there was no protest from North Ocean Shipping on 28 June 1973 or after, until its claim was formally served, he is stating that North Ocean Shipping neither argued the point when Hyundai first made its demand, nor did North Ocean Shipping try to take steps to avoid the contract when it was free from the duress, i.e. from 27th November 1974 onwards. This is the sense in which Mocatta J is using the concept of 'protest' as opposed to the narrower sense of negative utterances which might be made at the point the duress is first imposed.

In subsequent cases, for instance, *Pao On and Others Appellants v Lau Yiu Long and Others Respondents* [1980] AC 614 and *DSND Subsea Limited (Formerly known as DSND Oceantech Limited) v Petroleum Geo Services ASA, PGS Offshore Technology AS* [2000] BLR 530 (discussed below), a distinction is made between these two concepts i.e. protesting at the time of the exertion of the pressure and taking steps to avoid the contract as soon as the pressure has ceased. Consequently, the current position is that these represent two separate aspects to be considered.

An example of taking prompt steps to avoid the contract can be seen in *B & S Contracts and Design Ltd v Victor Green Publications Ltd* [1984] ICR 419 (see below). The victim avoided the new agreement immediately by refusing to make the payment that had been agreed under duress. This satisfied the requirement of taking steps to avoid the contract.

7.6 Causation and Economic Duress

As previously discussed in relation to causation and duress of the person, the test for causation as regards economic duress is the 'but for' test. The duress must be 'a significant cause' of the alleged victim's entry into the disputed contract.

Huyton SA v Peter Cremer GmbH & Co [1999] 1 Lloyd's Rep 620

Panel: Mance J

Facts: Under the terms of a contract by which Cremer was to deliver wheat to Huyton, Huyton was required to pay Cremer on presentation of documents in a particular form. Huyton accepted delivery of the goods but his bank refused to make payment to Cremer on the basis that the documents were not in the approved form. Before going to arbitration, the matter was resolved by Huyton agreeing to pay Cremer on condition that Cremer gave up its claims to various shipping expenses that Cremer would normally have been able to claim back from Huyton. Cremer later contended that it had entered into the agreement on grounds of economic duress. It was held that even if Cremer could show illegitimate pressure (which was doubted) it could not show that the pressure was a significant cause of its entering into the agreement. There was therefore no duress.

MR JUSTICE MANCE

I start with the requirement that the illegitimate pressure must, in cases of economic duress, constitute 'a significant cause' (cf. per Lord Goff in *The Evia Luck* ...). This is contrasted in Goff and Jones on Law of Restitution (4th edn), p. 251, footnote 59 with the lesser requirement that it should be 'a' reason which applies in the context of duress to the person. The relevant authority in the latter context is *Barton v Armstrong* [1976] AC 104 (PC) (a case of threats to kill). ...

The use of the phrase 'a significant cause' by Lord Goff in *The Evia Luck*, supported by the weighty observation in the footnote in Goff & Jones, suggests that this relaxed view of causation in the special context of duress to the person cannot prevail in the less serious context of economic duress. The minimum basic test of subjective causation in economic duress ought, it appears to me, to be a 'but for' test. The illegitimate pressure must have been such as actually caused the making of the agreement, in the sense that it would not otherwise have been made either at all or, at least, in the terms in which it was made. In that sense, the pressure must have been decisive or clinching. …

Further Reading

Hamish, L., 2005. *Construction Law Journal* 'Commercial exploitation in construction contracts: the role of economic duress and unjust enrichment'

Daniel Tan, D., 2002. *Construction Law Journal* 'Constructing a doctrine of economic duress'

Bigwood, R., 2001. *Law Quarterly Review*. Case Comment: 'Economic duress by (threatened) breach of contract'

Beale H. 2011. *Chitty on Contracts* Sweet & Maxwell. 30th ed. Vol.1 - General Principles, Part 2 – Formation of Contract, Chapter 7 - Duress and Undue Influence, Sections 1 and 2 – Duress

McKendrick, E., *Contract Law* (2017) 12th ed. Ch.17

8

Privity of Contract

Topic List

Introduction

The doctrine of privity determines who is legally affected by a contract. Until recently, only the parties to a contract could sue or be sued upon it, a legacy from classical Roman law. Privity in English law was reaffirmed in the late nineteenth century by the seminal case of *Tweddle v Atkinson* (1861) 121 ER 762 (QB), later confirmed by the House of Lords in *Dunlop Pneumatic Tyre Co. v Selfridge & Co.* [1915] AC 847.

After prolonged judicial and academic criticism of the doctrine, the position was finally altered by The Contracts (Rights of Third Parties) Act 1999 which came into force on 11 November 1999. As its name would suggest, under this legislation a third party, who is neither privy to the agreement, nor has provided consideration, is able, subject to certain qualifications, to enforce a term of the contract. However, s 7 states that the right of enforcement given to a third party in s 1 'does not affect any right or remedy of a third party that exists or is available apart from this Act.' Consequently, the common law mechanisms employed by the judiciary to circumvent privity may still be utilised and may well give superior rights to the third party concerned, as they will not be subject to the limitations in the Act.

This chapter begins by considering the narrowness of the doctrine at common law and will then examine the ways in which the doctrine has been side-stepped. Finally, the discussion culminates in an examination of the impact of the Act in relaxing the application of the principle.

8.1 The Constraints of Privity

The extent to which the doctrine of privity has constrained the courts is clearly demonstrated in the cases of *Beswick v Beswick* [1967] 3 WLR 932 and *Tweddle v Atkinson* (1861) 121 ER 762. While a just end was achieved in *Beswick v Beswick* through an order for specific performance – a discretionary remedy – the case facts demonstrate the potential for injustice arising from the doctrine.

Beswick v Beswick [1968] AC 58

Panel: Lord Reid, Lord Hodson, Lord Guest, Lord Pearce and Lord Upjohn

Facts: Peter Beswick agreed to sell his business to his nephew John in return for the undertaking (amongst others) that, if Peter died before his wife, John would pay her an annuity of £5 weekly. Peter died intestate in November 1963. In 1964 his widow became his administratrix. After Peter's death, John made one payment of £5 to Peter's widow and then refused to make any more payments. The widow sued John in her capacity as administratrix of her husband's estate and also in her personal capacity under The Law of Property Act 1925 s 56(1), which was argued to be an exception to the doctrine of privity. It was held that she was entitled to specific performance of the agreement to which her deceased husband was a contracting party because she was standing in his shoes as administratrix but the statute gave her no right of action in her personal capacity against John.

LORD REID

...For clarity I think it best to begin by considering a simple case where, in consideration of a sale by A to B, B agrees to pay the price of £1,000 to a third party X. Then the first question appears to me to be whether the parties intended that X should receive the money simply as A's nominee so that he would hold the money for behoof of A and be accountable to him for it, or whether the parties intended that X should receive the money for his own behoof and be entitled to keep it. ... {T]he next question appears to me to be: Where the intention was that X should keep the £1,000 as his own, what is the nature of B's obligation and who is entitled to enforce it? It was not argued that the law of England regards B's obligation as a nullity, and I have not observed in any of the authorities any suggestion that it would be a nullity. There may have been a time when the existence of a right depended on whether there was any means of enforcing it, but today the law would be sadly deficient if one found that, although there is a right, the law provides no means for enforcing it. So this obligation of B must be enforceable either by X or by A. I shall leave aside for the moment the question whether section 56 (1) of the Law of Property Act, 1925 , has any application to such a case, and consider the position at common law.'

...

Lord Denning's view, expressed in this case not for the first time, is that X could enforce this obligation. But the view more commonly held in recent times has been that such a contract confers no right on X and that X could not sue for the £1,000. ... It is true that a strong Law Revision Committee recommended so long ago as 1937 (Cmd. 5449):

'That where a contract by its express terms purports to confer a benefit directly on a third party it shall be enforceable by the third party in his own name ...' (p. 31).

And, if one had to contemplate a further long period of Parliamentary procrastination, this House might find it necessary to deal with this matter.

...

But if legislation is probable at any early date I would not deal with it in a case where that is not essential. So for the purposes of this case I shall proceed on the footing that the commonly accepted view is right. ... The respondent's second argument is that she is entitled in her capacity of administratrix of her deceased husband's estate to enforce the provision of the agreement for the benefit of herself in her personal capacity, and that a proper way of enforcing that provision is to order specific performance. That would produce a just result, and, unless there is some technical objection, I am of opinion that specific performance ought to be ordered. For the reasons given by your Lordships I would reject the arguments submitted for the appellant that specific performance is not a possible remedy in this case. I am therefore of opinion that the Court of Appeal reached a correct decision and that this appeal should be dismissed.

Lord Reid expresses the clear view that privity requires reform but also holds back from taking that action himself on the basis that such reform was expected imminently. He therefore takes a side-step from the issue and achieves the desired result by exercising his discretion and recommending an order for specific performance. Privity remains unchanged.

In a later case, *Woodar Investment Development Ltd v Wimpey Construction U.K. Ltd* HL [1980] 1 WLR 277 Lord Scarman refers to Lord Reid's statement in *Beswick v Beswick* and urges the House of Lords towards judicial intervention in the face of Parliament's perceived reluctance to act – see below.

8.1.1 Consideration and Privity

In *Tweddle v Atkinson*, the decision of the court was in fact based upon the issue of consideration. The outcome would have been no different had the court directed its mind to the issue of privity instead. Two fathers, John Tweddle and Guy Atkinson, both promised to pay John Tweddle's son £100 upon his marriage to Guy Atkinson's daughter. Guy Atkinson died before making the payment and the groom, John Tweddle's son, sued Guy Atkinson's estate. It was held that the plaintiff had no right to sue as he had not provided consideration for the promise. He was also not party to the contract. Note that there is no indication as to whether John Tweddle himself had made his promised payment, which could explain why he had not himself sued the estate of Guy Atkinson as he would have been entitled to do as the other party to the contract.

Link
See Further Reading, 'Privity - the end of an era (error)', Robert Flannigan *Law Quarterly Review*, 1987.

As is clear from the above case, the principle that consideration must move from the promisee is obviously closely related to the wider doctrine of privity of contract. There has been a great deal of academic debate on this subject but the two principles are to be treated separately as was made clear by Viscount Haldane LC in *Dunlop Pneumatic Tyre Co. v Selfridge & Co.* [1915] AC 847.

***Dunlop Pneumatic Tyre Company, Limited Appellants; v Selfridge and Company, Limited Respondents* [1915] AC 847**

Panel: Viscount Haldane LC, Lord Dunedin, Lord Atkinson, Lord Parker of Waddington, Lord Sumner and Lord Parmoor

Facts: Please see Chapter 5, Consideration.

VISCOUNT HALDANE LC

...My Lords, in the law of England certain principles are fundamental. One is that only a person who is a party to a contract can sue on it. Our law knows nothing of a jus quaesitum tertio arising by way of contract. Such a right may be conferred by way of property, as, for example, under a trust, but it cannot be conferred on a stranger to a contract as a right to enforce the contract in personam. A second principle is that if a person with whom a contract not under seal has been made is to be able to enforce it consideration must have been given by him to the promisor or to some other person at the promisor's request. These two principles are not recognized in the same fashion by the jurisprudence of certain Continental countries or of Scotland, but here they are well established. A third proposition is that a principal not named in the contract may sue upon it if the promisee really contracted as his agent. But again, in order to entitle him so to sue, he must have given consideration either personally or through the promisee, acting as his agent in giving it.

My Lords, in the case before us, I am of opinion that the consideration, the allowance of what was in reality part of the discount to which Messrs. Dew, the promisees, were entitled as between themselves and the appellants, was to be given by Messrs. Dew on their own account, and was not in substance, any more than in form, an allowance made by the appellants. The case for the appellants is that they permitted and enabled Messrs. Dew, with the knowledge and by the desire of the respondents, to sell to the latter on the terms of the contract of January 2, 1912. But it appears to me that even if this is so the answer is conclusive. Messrs. Dew sold to the respondents goods which they had a title to obtain from the appellants independently of this contract. The consideration by way of discount under the contract of January 2 was to come wholly out of Messrs. Dew's pocket, and neither directly nor indirectly out of that of the appellants. If the appellants enabled them to sell to the respondents on the terms they did, this was not done as any part of the terms of the contract sued on.

...

If it were necessary to express an opinion on this further question [the agency point], a difficulty as to the position of Messrs. Dew would have to be considered. Two contracts—one by a man on his own account as principal, and another by the same man as agent—may be validly comprised in the same piece of paper. But they must be two contracts, and not one as here. I do not think that a man can treat one and the same contract as made by him in two capacities. He cannot be regarded as contracting for himself and for another uno flatu.

My Lords, the form of the contract which we have to interpret leaves the appellants in this dilemma, that, if they say that Messrs. Dew contracted on their behalf, they gave no consideration, and if they say they gave consideration in the shape of a permission to the respondents to buy, they must set up further stipulations, which are neither to be found in the contract sued upon nor are germane to it, but are really inconsistent with its structure. That contract has been reduced to writing, and it is in the writing that we must look for the whole of the terms made between the parties. These terms cannot, in my opinion consistently with the settled principles of English law, be construed as giving to the appellants any enforceable rights as against the respondents.

Lord Dunedin, on the other hand, was of the view that the agreement was made by Dew as agent for Dunlop. As undisclosed principal, Dunlop would be privy to the agreement and could theoretically sue to enforce it. Nonetheless, in order to do so it would have been necessary to have shown that consideration moved from Dunlop to Selfridge.

LORD DUNEDIN

...Now the agreement sued on is an agreement which on the face of it is an agreement between Dew and Selfridge. But speaking for myself, I should have no difficulty in the circumstances of this case in holding it proved that the agreement was truly made by Dew as agent for Dunlop, or in other words that Dunlop was the undisclosed principal, and as such can sue on the agreement. None the less, in order to enforce it he must show consideration, as above defined, moving from Dunlop to Selfridge.

In the circumstances, how can he do so? The agreement in question is not an agreement for sale. It is only collateral to an agreement for sale; but that agreement for sale is an agreement entirely between Dew and Selfridge.'

Both privity and consideration were the subject of discussion in the Law Commission Report of 1996, *Privity of Contract: Contracts for the Benefit of Third Parties*.

8.2   Legal Mechanisms for Circumventing Privity

Circumstances where privity is in conflict with other legal principles have given rise to certain methods of circumventing the privity requirement.

8.2.1   Agency

An agency relationship occurs where one party, the agent, is authorised by another, the principal, to negotiate and enter into contract on behalf of the principal. Where a person acts as an agent for the principal, the principal will be bound by any contract made that falls within that authority. Moreover, where an agent contracts without authority on behalf of a named principal, the person named as principal may ratify the contract so that it becomes binding as between himself and the third party. In both circumstances the principal can enforce the contract as they are treated as having privity of contract.

The agency argument has arisen in the case law in the context of whether a third party can enforce a provision (such as an exemption clause) in a contract to which he is not a party when he is sued in tort by one of the contractual parties.

Scruttons Ltd. v Midland Silicones Ltd. **[1962] AC 446**

Panel: Viscount Simonds, Lord Reid, Lord Keith of Avonholm, Lord Denning and Lord Morris of Borth-Y-Gest.

Facts: A drum of chemicals belonging to Midland Silicones was shipped from the United States to England. The contract of carriage limited the liability of the carrier to $500 (£179) per package. The drum was damaged and its contents (valued at £593) lost as a result of the negligence of Scruttons, a company of stevedores whom the carriers had employed to unload the ship. It was held by the House of Lords that Scruttons could not rely on the limitation clause in the contract of carriage because it was not a party to that contract. The court found that there was nothing in the clause that expressly or impliedly indicated that the benefit of the limitation therein was to extend to the stevedores and, further, that the carrier did not contract as agent for the stevedores for the benefit of the clause. In the extract below, Lord Reid sets out his famous four conditions for agency.

LORD REID

My Lords, the case for the respondents is simple. Goods which they had bought were damaged by the negligence of stevedores, who are the appellants. Before the damage occurred the property in the goods had passed to the respondents and they sue in tort for the amount of the loss to them caused by that damage. The appellants seek to take advantage of provisions in the bill of lading made between the sellers of the goods and the carrier. Those provisions in the circumstances of this case would limit liability to $500. They are expressed as being in favour of the carrier but the appellants maintain on a number of grounds that they can rely on these provisions with the result that, though the damage to the respondents' goods considerably exceeded $500, the respondents cannot recover more than the equivalent of that sum from them as damages. We were informed that questions of this kind frequently arise and that this action has been brought as a test case.

In considering the various arguments for the appellants, I think it is necessary to have in mind certain established principles of the English law of contract. Although I may regret it, I find it impossible to deny the existence of the general rule that a stranger to a contract cannot in a question with either of the contracting parties take advantage of provisions of the contract, even where it is clear from the contract that some provision in it was intended to benefit him. That rule appears to have been crystallised a century ago in Tweddle v. Atkinson and finally established in this House in *Dunlop Pneumatic Tyre Co. Ltd. v. Selfridge & Co. Ltd*. There are, it is true, certain well-established exceptions to that rule - though I am not sure that they are really exceptions and do not arise from other principles. But none of these in any way touches the present case. ... The appellants in this case seek to get round this rule in three different ways. In the first place, they say that the decision in *Elder, Dempster & Co. Ltd. v. Paterson, Zochonis & Co. Ltd.*

establishes an exception to the rule sufficiently wide to cover the present case. I shall later return to consider this case. Secondly, they say that through the agency of the carrier they were brought into contractual relation with the shipper and that they can now found on that against the consignees, the respondents and thirdly, they say that there should be inferred from the facts an implied contract, independent of the bill of lading, between them and the respondent It was not argued that they had not committed a tort in damaging the respondents' goods.

Having dismissed the first and third arguments, Lord Reid considered the question of agency:

I can see a possibility of success of the agency argument if (first) the bill of lading makes it clear that the stevedore is intended to be protected by the provisions in it which limit liability, (secondly) the bill of lading makes it clear that the carrier, in addition to contracting for these provisions on his own behalf, should apply to the stevedore, (thirdly) the carrier has authority from the stevedore to do that, or perhaps later ratification by the stevedore would suffice, and (fourthly) that any difficulties about consideration moving from the stevedore were overcome.

...

I agree with your Lordships that 'carrier' in the bill of lading does not include stevedore, and if that is so I can find nothing in the bill of lading which states or even implies that the parties to it intended the limitation of liability to extend to stevedores. Even if it could be said that reasonable men in the shoes of these parties would have agreed that the stevedores should have this benefit, that would not be enough to make this an implied term of the contract. and even if one could spell out of the bill of lading an intention to benefit the stevedore, there is certainly nothing to indicate that the carrier was contracting as agent for the stevedore in addition to contracting on his own behalf. So it appears to me that the agency argument must fail ... if they [the consignees] read the bill of lading they would find nothing to show that the shippers had agreed to limit the liability of the stevedores. There is nothing to show that they ever thought about this or that if they had they would have agreed or ought as reasonable men to have agreed to this benefit to the stevedores. I can find no basis in this for implying a contract between them and the stevedores. It cannot be said that such a contract was in any way necessary for business efficiency.

Lord Reid's conditions of agency from *Scruttons v Midland Silicones* were then considered in the Privy Council case, *New Zealand Shipping Co. Ltd v A.M. Satterthwaite & Co. Ltd. (The Eurymedon)* [1975] AC 154. In this case, the stevedore was successful in arguing that the benefit of the exemption clause in a contract between the shipper and the carrier extended to it also. As you will see, this was due to the fact that a) the stevedore was expressly referred to in the clause and b) the court's willingness to find consideration in order to achieve a commercially satisfactory end.

New Zealand Shipping Co. Ltd v A.M. Satterthwaite & Co. Ltd. (The Eurymedon) [1975] AC 154

Panel: Lord Wilberforce, Lord Hodson, Viscount Dilhorne, Lord Simon of Glaisdale and Lord Salmon

Facts: An exemption clause in a contract of carriage between a shipper and a carrier discharged the carrier from all liability for loss or damage unless a claim was brought within one year. The contract documentation further stipulated that the exemption clause also extended to the carrier's servants or agents, including independent contractors, deeming the carrier to be acting as agent for them for the purpose of extending the exemption clause to them. The carrier was a wholly owned subsidiary company of the stevedore used by the shipper in the case. The carrier had authority to enter into the contract on behalf of the stevedore. As a result of the stevedore's negligence the shipment was damaged in unloading. The consignee of the shipment brought an action in tort after the lapse of one year against the stevedore for damages. At first instance, the stevedore successfully pleaded that the claim was subject to the time limit but the Court of Appeal allowed an appeal by the plaintiff consignee. It was held that the stevedore was not able to take the benefit of the exemption clause in the contract between the shipper and the carrier because at the time when the contract was signed no consideration moved from the stevedore to the shipper. The Privy Council held by a majority that the benefit of the exemption clause could be claimed by the stevedore, provided that the four conditions stipulated by Lord Reid in *Scruttons v Midland Silicones* were satisfied.

LORD WILBERFORCE

On the back of the bill of lading a number of clauses were printed in small type. It is only necessary to set out the following. The ... third paragraph of clause 1 provided:

'It is hereby expressly agreed that no servant or agent of the carrier (including every independent contractor from time to time employed by the carrier) shall in any circumstances whatsoever be under any liability whatsoever to the shipper, consignee or owner of the goods or to any holder of this bill of lading for any loss or damage or delay of whatsoever kind arising or resulting directly or indirectly from any act neglect or default on his part while acting in the course of or in connection with his employment and ... for the purpose of all the foregoing provisions of this clause the carrier is or shall be deemed to be acting as agent or trustee on behalf of and for the benefit of all persons who are or might be his servants or agents from time to time (including independent contractors as aforesaid) and all such persons shall to this extent be or be deemed to be parties to the contract in or evidenced by this bill of lading.'

The question in the appeal is whether the stevedore can take the benefit of the time limitation provision. The starting point, in discussion of this question, is provided by the House of Lords decision in *Midland Silicones Ltd. v. Scruttons Ltd.* [1962] AC. 446. There is no need to question or even to qualify that case in so far as it affirms the general proposition that a contract between two parties cannot be sued on by a third person even though the contract is expressed to be for his benefit. ... But Midland Silicones left open the case where one of the parties contracts as agent for the third person: in particular Lord Reid's speech spelt out, in four propositions, the prerequisites for the validity of such an agency contract. There is of course nothing unique to this case in the conception of agency contracts: well known and common instances exist in the field of hire purchase, of bankers' commercial credits and other transactions. Lord Reid said,...'

Lord Wilberforce then set out Lord Reid's statement of agency and continued:

...The question in this appeal is whether the contract satisfies these propositions.

Clause 1 of the bill of lading, whatever the defects in its drafting, is clear in its relevant terms. ... The carrier as agent for, inter alios, independent contractors stipulates for the same exemptions.

Much was made of the fact that the carrier also contracts as agent for numerous other persons; the relevance of this argument is not apparent. It cannot be disputed that among such independent contractors, for whom, as agent, the carrier contracted, is the appellant company which habitually acts as stevedore in New Zealand by arrangement with the carrier and which is, moreover, the parent company of the carrier. The carrier was, indisputably, authorised by the appellant to contract as its agent for the purposes of clause 1. All of this is quite straightforward and was accepted by all the judges in New Zealand. The only question was, and is, the fourth question presented by Lord Reid, namely that of consideration.

...The exemption is designed to cover the whole carriage from loading to discharge, by whomsoever it is performed: the performance attracts the exemption or immunity in favour of whoever the performer turns out to be. There is possibly more than one way of analysing this business transaction into the necessary components; that which their Lordships would accept is to say that the bill of lading brought into existence a bargain initially unilateral but capable of becoming mutual, between the shipper and the appellant [the stevedores], made through the carrier as agent. This became a full contract when the appellant performed services by discharging the goods. The performance of these services for the benefit of the shipper was the consideration for the agreement by the shipper that the appellant should have the benefit of the exemptions and limitations contained in the bill of lading. ...

The following points require mention. 1. In their Lordships' opinion, consideration may quite well be provided by the appellant, as suggested,

Alert

even though (or if) it was already under an obligation to discharge to the carrier. (There is no direct evidence of the existence or nature of this obligation, but their Lordships are prepared to assume it.) An agreement to do an act which the promisor is under an existing obligation to a third party to do, may quite well amount to valid consideration and does so in the present case: the promisee obtains the benefit of a direct obligation which he can enforce. This proposition is illustrated and supported by *Scotson v. Pegg* (1861) 6 H. & N. 295 which their Lordships consider to be good law.

Consequently, the court decided that all Lord Reid's conditions of agency were satisfied and that the carrier was therefore proven to be acting as agent for the stevedore. This brought the stevedore into the contract containing the exemption clause between the shipper and the carrier as the carrier's principal and allowed the stevedore to take the benefit of the exemption clause.

8.2.2 Assignment

Where A is under a contractual obligation to B and B assigns his contractual right to C, it may be possible for C to sue A on his promise to B. Problems arise where the contract between A and B contains a prohibition on assignment. Assignment is considered later in the section on 'Judicial Attempts to Avoid The Doctrine' and more particularly in the discussion there of *Linden Gardens Trust v Lenesta Sludge Disposals Ltd. and others; St. Martins Property Corporation Ltd and another v Sir Robert McAlpine & Sons Ltd* [1994] 1 AC 85.

8.2.3 Guarantor's Right of Subrogation

Where a guarantor has paid the principal creditor, he is subrogated to the rights of the principal creditor against the debtor, ie the guarantor 'stands in the principal creditor's shoes.' The action then proceeds as if it were between the original contracting parties.

8.2.4 Trusts

A right under a contract is a chose in action and thus may be the subject of a trust. The possibility is raised therefore that the promisee, under a contract, might declare himself trustee of the benefit of the promise in question on behalf of a third party and by that means avoid the privity doctrine. Where a trust of a contractual right is found to have been created, the principle effect is to permit the third party to enforce the benefit. This is merely an apparent exception to the common law doctrine of privity because the rights of the third party are those of the beneficiary and, as such, are equitable.

In *Re Schebsman* [1944] Ch 83, Lord Greene MR stressed that 'it is not legitimate to import into the contract the idea of a trust when the parties have given no indication that such was their intention'.

8.2.5 Collateral Contract

A collateral contract is an associated but independent contract which runs parallel to the main contract and may override or supplant one or more of the main contract's terms. If the court can establish the existence of a separate collateral contract between the promisor and the third party, it can avoid the difficulties of privity.

Shanklin Pier LD. v Detel Products LD **[1951] 2 KB 854**

Panel: McNair J

Facts: Shanklin Pier employed contractors to paint the pier. It was a term of the contract that Shanklin Pier was to specify the paint to be used. Detel informed Shanklin Pier that their paint would last for at least seven years. Shanklin Pier instructed the contractors to buy and use Detel's paint. The paint lasted three months. Shanklin Pier sued for breach of contract. However, the contract was between Shanklin Pier and the contractors. Mr Justice McNair held that there was a collateral contract between Shanklin Pier and Detel, the consideration for which was, on the one hand, the warranty by Detel that the paint would last for seven years and on the other, the instruction by Shanklin Pier to the contractors to buy the paint.

MR JUSTICE MCNAIR

This case raises an interesting and comparatively novel question whether or not an enforceable warranty can arise as between parties other than parties to the main contract for the sale of the article in respect of which the warranty is alleged to have been given. ... I am satisfied that, if a direct contract of purchase and sale of the D.M.U. [the paint] had then been made between the plaintiffs and the defendants, the correct conclusion on the facts would have been that the defendants gave to the plaintiffs the warranties substantially in the form alleged in the statement of claim. In reaching this conclusion, I adopt the principles stated by Holt, C.J., in Crosse v. Gardner [1] and Medina v. Stoughton [2] that an affirmation at the time of sale is a warranty, provided it appear on evidence to have been so intended.

Counsel for the defendants submitted that in law a warranty could give rise to no enforceable cause of action except between the same parties as the parties to the main contract in relation to which the warranty was given. In principle this submission seems to me to be unsound. If, as is elementary, the consideration for the warranty in the usual case is the entering into of the main contract in relation to which the warranty is given, I see no reason why there may not be an enforceable warranty between A and B supported by the consideration that B should cause C to enter into a contract with A or that B should do some other act for the benefit of A.

8.2.6   Actions in Tort

Where there is no contractual relationship between the aggrieved party and the wrongdoer, tort will often provide an alternative remedy. In the case of *Donoghue v Stevenson* [1932] AC 562, the plaintiff was a third party in relation to the contract of sale between the manufacturer of the bottle of ginger beer and the retailer and also in relation to the contract of sale between the retailer and the purchaser of the bottle of ginger beer. They were therefore denied a remedy in contract because of the doctrine of privity. However, as the ultimate consumer of the goods, the plaintiff could bring a claim in the tort of negligence directly against the manufacturer.

8.3   Recovery of a Loss Sustained by a Third Party – Judicial Attempts to Avoid Privity

8.3.1   Specific Types of Contract

Jackson v Horizon Holidays Ltd [1975] 1 WLR 1468

Panel: Lord Denning MR, Orr and James LJJ

Facts: The plaintiff booked a holiday for himself, his wife and twin boys through the defendants, a travel company. He stated his precise requirements and was assured that they would be met. Shortly before the departure date, the defendants informed him that the hotel he had chosen would not be ready and offered him a substitute which he accepted, after being assured that it would be as good as his original choice. In the event the accommodation, food, services, facilities and general standard of the hotel proved so unsatisfactory that the whole family suffered discomfort, vexation, inconvenience and distress and went home disappointed. The plaintiff brought an action against the travel company, claiming damages for misrepresentation and breach of contract. The trial judge awarded the plaintiff £1,100. He did not divide up that sum in any way; but he stated specifically that the damages were the plaintiff's and that though he could consider the effect on the plaintiff's mind of his wife's discomfort and the like, he could not award a sum which represented her own vexation. The defendants appealed. Lord Denning MR concluded that if the award was to compensate for the damage suffered by Mr Jackson alone it would indeed have been excessive but it could not be deemed to be so when extended to his wife and children. Lord Justice Orr agreed with Lord Denning MR's judgment while James LJ confined his comments to a statement that this was a contract for a family holiday and the plaintiff had not received this.

LORD DENNING MR

...In *Jarvis v. Swans Tours Ltd.* [1973] Q.B. 233, it was held by this court that damages for the loss of a holiday may include not only the difference in value between what was promised and what was obtained, but also damages for mental distress, inconvenience, upset, disappointment and frustration caused by the loss of the holiday. The judge directed himself in accordance with the judgments in that case. He eventually awarded a sum of £1,100. Horizon Holidays Ltd. appealed. They [the defendants] say it was far too much.

…The judge took the cost of the holidays at £1,200. The family only had about half the value of it. Divide it by two and you get £600. Then add £500 for the mental distress.

On this question a point of law arises. The judge said that he could only consider the mental distress to Mr. Jackson himself, and that he could not consider the distress to his wife and children. He said:

'The damages are the plaintiff's … I can consider the effect upon his mind of the wife's discomfort, vexation, and the like, although I cannot award a sum which represents her own vexation.'

Mr. Davies, for Mr. Jackson, disputes that proposition. He submits that damages can be given not only for the leader of the party — in this case, Mr. Jackson's own distress, discomfort and vexation — but also for that of the rest of the party.

We have had an interesting discussion as to the legal position when one person makes a contract for the benefit of a party. In this case it was a husband making a contract for the benefit of himself, his wife and children. Other cases readily come to mind. A host makes a contract with a restaurant for a dinner for himself and his friends. The vicar makes a contract for a coach trip for the choir. In all these cases there is only one person who makes the contract. It is the husband, the host or the vicar, as the case may be. Sometimes he pays the whole price himself. Occasionally he may get a contribution from the others. But in any case it is he who makes the contract. It would be a fiction to say that the contract was made by all the family, or all the guests, or the entire choir, and that he was only an agent for them. Take this very case. It would be absurd to say that the twins of three years old were parties to the contract or that the father was making the contract on their behalf as if they were principals. It would equally be a mistake to say that in any of these instances there was a trust. The transaction bears no resemblance to a trust. There was no trust fund and no trust property. No, the real truth is that in each instance, the father, the host or the vicar, was making a contract himself for the benefit of the whole party. In short, a contract by one for the benefit of third persons.

What is the position when such a contract is broken? At present the law says that the only one who can sue is the one who made the contract. None of the rest of the party can sue, even though the contract was made for their benefit. But when that one does sue, what damages can he recover? Is he limited to his own loss? Or can he recover for the others? Suppose the holiday firm puts the family into a hotel which is only half built and the visitors have to sleep on the floor? Or suppose the restaurant is fully booked and the guests have to go away, hungry and angry, having spent so much on fares to get there? Or suppose the coach leaves the choir stranded halfway and they have to hire cars to get home? None of them individually can sue. Only the father, the host or the vicar can sue. He can, of course, recover his own damages. But can he not recover for the others? I think he can. The case comes within the principle stated by Lush L.J. in *Lloyd's v. Harper* (1880) 16 Ch.D. 290, 321:

'I consider it to be an established rule of law that where a contract is made with A for the benefit of B., A. can sue on the contract for the benefit of B ., and recover all that B could have recovered if the contract had been made with B. himself.'

It has been suggested that Lush L.J. was thinking of a contract in which A was trustee for B. But I do not think so. He was a common lawyer speaking of common law. His words were quoted with considerable approval by Lord Pearce in *Beswick v. Beswick* [1968] A.C. 58 , 88. I have myself often quoted them. I think they should be accepted as correct, at any rate so long as the law forbids the third persons themselves from suing for damages. It is the only way in which a just result can be achieved. Take the instance I have put. The guests ought to recover from the restaurant their wasted fares. The choir ought to recover the cost of hiring the taxis home. Then is no one to recover from them except the one who made the contract for their benefit? He should be able to recover the expense to which he has been put, and pay it over to them. Once recovered, it will be money had and received to their use. (They might even, if desired, be joined as plaintiffs). If he can recover for the expense, he should also be able to recover for the discomfort, vexation and upset which the whole party have suffered by reason of the breach of contract, recompensing them accordingly out of what he recovers.

Applying the principles to this case, I think that the figure of £1,100 was about right. It would, I think, have been excessive if it had been awarded only for the damage suffered by Mr. Jackson himself. But when extended to his wife and children, I do not think it is excessive. People look forward to a holiday. They expect the promises to be fulfilled. When it fails, they are greatly disappointed and upset. It is difficult to assess in terms of money; but it is the task of the judges to do the best they can. I see no reason to interfere with the total award of £1,100.

8.3.2   Retreat from *Jackson*

Lord Denning MR's bold move here to outflank privity and its effect upon the rights of a third party was curtailed in the later decision of *Woodar Investment Development Ltd v Wimpey Construction U.K. Ltd* [1980] 1 WLR 277 in which case the reasoning put forward in the Court of Appeal by Lord Denning was disapproved by the House of Lords.

Woodar Investment Development Ltd v Wimpey Construction U.K. Ltd [1980] 1 WLR 277

Panel: Lord Wilberforce, Lord Salmon, Lord Russell of Killowen, Lord Keith of Kinkel and Lord Scarman

Facts: Wimpey contracted to purchase land from Woodar for £850,000 and agreed as part of the contract that on completion of the purchase it would also pay a third party £150,000.

The contract allowed the purchaser (Wimpey) to repudiate the contract if, before completion, a statutory authority 'shall have commenced' to compulsorily purchase the land. At the date of the agreement both Woodar and Wimpey knew that there was a draft compulsory purchase order hanging over the land. Wimpy attempted to terminate relying on the above provision and Woodar claimed wrongful repudiation. As well as claiming the £850,000 for itself, Woodar also tried to claim the £150,000 for the third party. It was held that there was no wrongful repudiation. However, the majority chose to comment (obiter) on the damages issue in light of the decision in *Jackson v Horizon Holidays.*

LORD WILBERFORCE

...The second issue in this appeal is one of damages. Both courts below have allowed Woodar to recover substantial damages in respect of condition I under which £150,000 was payable by Wimpey to Transworld Trade Ltd. on completion. ... in view of the unsatisfactory state in which the law would be if the Court of Appeal's decision were to stand I must add three observations:

1. The majority of the Court of Appeal followed, in the case of Goff L.J. with expressed reluctance, its previous decision in *Jackson v. Horizon Holidays Ltd.* [1975] I W.L.R. 1468. I am not prepared to dissent from the actual decision in that case. It may be supported either as a broad decision on the measure of damages (*per* James L.J.) or possibly as an example of a type of contract — examples of which are persons contracting for family holidays, ordering meals in restaurants for a party, hiring a taxi for a group — calling for special treatment. As I suggested in *New Zealand Shipping Co. Ltd. v. A. M. Satterthwaite & Co. Ltd.* [1975] A.C. 154, 167, there are many situations of daily life which do not fit neatly into conceptual analysis, but which require some flexibility in the law of contract. *Jackson's* case may well be one.

    I cannot however agree with the basis on which Lord Denning M.R. put his decision in that case. The extract on which he relied from the judgment of Lush L.J. in *Lloyd's v. Harper* (1880) 16 Ch.D. 290, 321 was part of a passage in which the Lord Justice was stating as an 'established rule of law' that an agent (sc. an insurance broker) may sue on a contract made by him on behalf of the principal (sc. the assured) if the contract gives him such a right, and is no authority for the proposition required in *Jackson's* case, still less for the proposition, required here, that, if Woodar made a contract for a sum of money to be paid to Transworld, Woodar can, without showing that it has itself suffered loss or that Woodar was agent or trustee for Transworld, sue for damages for non-payment of that sum. That would certainly not be an established rule of law, nor was it quoted as such authority by Lord Pearce in *Beswick v. Beswick* [1968] A.C. 58.

2.   Assuming that *Jackson's* case was correctly decided (as above), it does not carry the present case, where the factual situation is quite different. I respectfully think therefore that the Court of Appeal need not, and should not have followed it.

3.   Whether in a situation such as the present — viz. where it is not shown that Woodar was agent or trustee for Transworld, or that Woodar itself sustained any loss, Woodar can recover any damages at all, or any but nominal damages, against Wimpey, and on what principle, is, in my opinion, a question of great doubt and difficulty — no doubt open in this House — but one on which I prefer to reserve my opinion.

LORD KEITH OF KINKEL

…It is desirable, however, that I should express my agreement with my noble and learned friend, Lord Wilberforce, that the decision in favour of the respondents upon this issue, arrived at by the majority of the Court of Appeal, was not capable of being supported by *Jackson v. Horizon Holidays Ltd.* [1975] 1 W.L.R. 1468. That case is capable of being regarded as rightly decided upon a reasonable view of the measure of damages due to the plaintiff as the original contracting party, and not as laying down any rule of law regarding the recovery of damages for the benefit of third parties. There may be a certain class of cases where third parties stand to gain indirectly by virtue of a contract, and where their deprivation of that gain can properly be regarded as no more than a consequence of the loss suffered by one of the contracting parties. In that situation there may be no question of the third parties having any claim to damages in their own right, but yet it may be proper to take into account in assessing the damages recoverable by the contracting party an element in respect of expense incurred by him in replacing by other means benefits of which the third parties have been deprived or in mitigating the consequences of that deprivation. The decision in *Jackson v. Horizon Holidays Ltd.* is not, however, in my opinion, capable of being supported upon the basis of the true ratio decidendi in *Lloyd's v. Harper,* 16 Ch.D. 29, which rested entirely on the principles of agency. …

LORD SCARMAN

It being the view of the majority of the House that there was no repudiation, the appeal must be allowed, with the result that there is no need to consider the other issues raised. But, because of its importance, I propose to say a few words on the question of damages.

…It [the contract at issue] is simply a case of B agreeing with A to pay a sum of money to C.

B, in breach of his contract with A, has failed to pay C. C, it is said, has no remedy, because the English law of contract recognises no 'jus quaesitum tertio': *Tweddle v. Atkinson* (1861) 1 B. & S. 393. No doubt, it was for this reason that Transworld Trade is not a party to the suit. A, it is acknowledged, could in certain circumstances obtain specific performance of the promise to pay C: *Beswick v. Beswick* [1968] AC 58. But, since the contract in the present case is admitted (for reasons which do not fall to be considered by the House) to be no longer in existence, specific performance is not available. A's remedy lies only in an award of damages to himself. It is submitted that, in the absence of any evidence that A has suffered loss by reason of B's failure to pay C, A is only entitled to nominal damages.

I wish to add nothing to what your Lordships have already said about the authorities which the Court of Appeal cited as leading to the conclusion that the plaintiff company is entitled to substantial damages for the defendants' failure to pay Transworld Trade I agree that they do not support the conclusion. But I regret that this House has not yet found the opportunity to reconsider the two rules which effectually prevent A or C recovering that which B, for value, has agreed to provide.

First, the 'jus quaesitum tertio.' I respectfully agree with Lord Reid that the denial by English law of a 'jus quaesitum tertio' calls for reconsideration. In *Beswick v. Beswick* [1968] A.C. 58, 72 Lord Reid, after referring to the Law Revision Committee's recommendation in 1937 (Cmnd. 5449) p. 31 that the third party should be able to enforce a contractual promise taken by another for his benefit, observed:

'And, if one had to contemplate a further long period of Parliamentary procrastination, this House might find it necessary to deal with this matter.'

The committee reported in 1937: *Beswick v. Beswick* was decided in 1967. It is now 1979: but nothing has been done. If the opportunity arises, I hope the House will reconsider *Tweddle v. Atkinson*, 1 B. & S. 393 and the other cases which stand guard over this unjust rule.

Likewise, I believe it open to the House to declare that, in the absence of evidence to show that he has suffered no loss, A, who has contracted for a payment to be made to C, may rely on the fact that he required the payment to be made as prima facie evidence that the promise for which he contracted was a benefit to him and that the measure of his loss in the event of non-payment is the benefit which he intended for but which has not been received. Whatever the reason, he must have desired the payment to be made to C and he must have been relying on to make it. If B fails to make the payment, A must find the money from other funds if he is to confer the benefit which he sought by his contract to confer upon C. Without expressing a final opinion on a question which is clearly difficult, I think the point is one which does require consideration by your Lordships' House.

Certainly the crude proposition for which the defendants contend, namely that the state of English law is such that neither C for whom the benefit was intended nor A who contracted for it can recover it, if the contract is terminated by B's refusal to perform, calls for review: and now, not forty years on.

8.3.3 The Albazero Principle

Although Lord Denning MR's exception in *Jackson v Horizon Holidays* was expressly limited by *Woodar v Wimpey* to contracts of 'a special type' – namely where the contracting party enters into a contract for the enjoyment or pleasure of third parties – the courts were happy to adopt a principle from another case as a means of providing a third party with a remedy.

***Linden Gardens Trust v Lenesta Sludge Disposals Ltd. and others and St. Martins Property Corporation Ltd and another v Sir Robert McAlpine & Sons Ltd* [1994] 1 AC 85**

Panel: Lord Keith of Kinkel, Lord Bridge of Harwich, Lord Griffiths, Lord Ackner and Lord Browne-Wilkinson

Facts: In this case, known as the '*St Martin's Property Appeal*' two actions were 'joined' by the courts due to the similarity of the facts and legal issues in both cases. In both cases a property owner entered into a contract with a contractor for work to be carried out to their property. The property was intended to be leased to a third party on completion of the work (this was known to the contractor) and in both cases there was a prohibition of assignment in the contract preventing the owner of the property from assigning his rights under the contract to another party. Again, in both cases, the work carried out by the contractor was defective and the loss occasioned by the defective work fell upon the third party who, in each case, had by then become the lessor of the property. In *Linden Gardens v Lenesta Sludge*, the first case to be heard, the original contracting party, the property owner, had assigned its right to sue the contractors to the third party (Linden Gardens), the current lessee. The lessee's action failed. The court held the lessee had no right to sue due to the prohibition of assignment contained within the original contract between the property owner and the contractor (Lenesta Sludge). In *St. Martins Property Corporation Ltd and another v McAlpine,* again, the third party, the eventual lessee, was suing the contractor and again, the court held that the third party should fail on the same point as above, ie the prohibition against assignment. However, in this case, the lessee and the original contracting party, the property owner (St Martin's Property Corporation) were both named as plaintiffs in the action and in relation to the St Martin's Corporation's appeal a principle arising from a shipping case *The Albazero* [1977] AC 224 was cited before the court.

LORD BROWNE-WILKINSON

…On any view, the facts of this case bring it within the class of exceptions to the general rule to which Lord Diplock referred in The Albazero.

In *The Albazero* Lord Diplock said [1977] A.C. 774, 846:

'Nevertheless, although it is exceptional at common law that a plaintiff in an action for breach of contract, although he himself has not suffered any loss, should be entitled to recover damages on behalf of some third person who is not a party to the action for a loss which that third person has sustained, the notion that there may be circumstances in which he is entitled to do so was not entirely unfamiliar to the common law and particularly to that part of it which, under the influence of Lord Mansfield and his successors, Lord Ellenborough and Lord Tenterden, had been appropriated from the law merchant. 'I have already mentioned the right of the bailee, which has been recognised from the earliest period of our law, to sue in detinue or trespass for loss or damage to his bailor's goods although he cannot be compelled by his bailor to do so and he is not himself liable to the bailor for the loss or damage: *The Winkfield* [1902] P. 42. Nevertheless, he becomes accountable to his bailor for the proceeds of the judgment in an action by his bailor for money had and received. So too the doctrine of subrogation in the case of insurers, which was adopted from the law merchant by the common law in the eighteenth century, involved the concept of the nominal party to an action at common law suing for a loss which he had not himself sustained and being accountable to his insurer for the proceeds to the extent that he had been indemnified against the loss by the insurer. In this instance of a plaintiff being able to recover as damages for breach of contract for the benefit of a third person a loss which that person had sustained and he had not, the insurer is entitled to compel an assured to whom he has paid a total or partial indemnity to bring the action. A third example, once again in the field of mercantile law, is the right of an assured to recover in an action on a policy of insurance upon goods the full amount of loss or damage to them, on behalf of anyone who may be entitled to an interest in the goods at the time when the loss or damage occurs, provided that it appears from the terms of the policy that he intended to cover their interests.'

In addition, the decision in *The Albazero* itself established a further exception. This House was concerned with the status of a long-established principle based on the decision in *Dunlop v. Lambert* (1839) 6 Cl. & F. 600 that a consignor of goods who had parted with the property in the goods before the date of breach could even so recover substantial damages for the failure to deliver the goods. Lord Diplock, identified, at p. 847, the rationale of that rule as being:

'The only way in which I find it possible to rationalise the rule in Dunlop v. Lambert so that it may fit into the pattern of the English law is to treat it as an application of the principle, accepted also in relation to policies of insurance upon goods, that in a commercial contract concerning goods where it is in the contemplation of the parties that the proprietary interests in the goods may be transferred from one owner to another after the contract has been entered into and before the breach which causes loss or damage to the goods, an original party to the contract, if such be the intention of them both, is to be treated in law as having entered into the contract for the benefit of all persons who have or may acquire an interest in the goods before they are lost or damaged, and is entitled to recover by way of damages for breach of contract the actual loss sustained by those for whose benefit the contract is entered into.'

 Alert

The House of Lords held, applying *The Albazero*, that the first claimant, the property owner, could sue to recover the lessee's, the contemplated third party's, loss. This is known as the 'narrow ground' of the decision and is thought to be confined to the very specific situation where it was in the contemplation of the original contracting parties that the ownership of the property was going to be transferred to a third party who may wish to exercise rights under the original contract and that otherwise, the third party would have no remedy. The so-called 'broad ground', as favoured by Lord Griffiths, is the far more general proposition that a party to a contract does not need to own the subject matter of the contract to claim compensation for defective work done. He has suffered an expectation loss and should be able to recover for that.

LORD GRIFFITHS

I cannot accept that in a contract of this nature, namely for work, labour and the supply of materials, the recovery of more than nominal damages for breach of contract is dependent upon the plaintiff having a proprietary interest in the subject matter of the contract at the date of breach. In everyday life contracts for work and labour are constantly being placed by those who have no proprietary interest in the subject matter of the contract. To take a common example, the matrimonial home is owned by the wife and the couple's remaining assets are owned by the husband and he is the sole earner. The house requires a new roof and the husband places a contract with a builder to carry out the work. The husband is not acting as agent for his wife, he makes the contract as principal because only he can pay for it. The builder fails to replace the roof properly and the husband has to call in and pay another builder to complete the work. Is it to be said that the husband has suffered no damage because he does not own the property? Such a result would in my view be absurd and the answer is that the husband has suffered loss because he did not receive the bargain for which he had contracted with the first builder and the measure of damages is the cost of securing the performance of that bargain by completing the roof repairs properly by the second builder. To put this simple example closer to the facts of this appeal - at the time the husband employs the builder he owns the house but just after the builder starts work the couple are advised to divide their assets so the husband transfers the house to his wife. This is no concern of the builder whose bargain is with the husband. If the roof turns out to be defective the husband can recover from the builder the cost of putting it right and thus obtain the benefit of the bargain that the builder had promised to deliver. It was suggested in argument that the answer to the example I have given is that the husband could assign the benefit of the contract to the wife. But what if, as in this case, the builder has a clause in the contract forbidding assignment without his consent and refuses to give consent as McAlpine has done. It is then said that neither husband nor wife can recover damages; this seems to me to be so unjust a result that the law cannot tolerate it. ... In cases such as the present the person who places the contract has suffered financial loss

 Alert

because he has to spend money to give him the benefit of the bargain which the defendant had promised but failed to deliver. I therefore cannot accept that it is a condition of recovery in such cases that the plaintiff has a proprietary right in the subject matter of the contract at the date of breach.

As stated above, Lords Keith, Bridge, Ackner and Browne-Wilkinson decided for St Martin's on the 'narrow ground' that the case was one of the allowed exceptions under *The Albazero*. The idea of compensating a party because they did not get the bargain they paid for is the broad ground as favoured by Lord Griffiths.

In *Darlington BC v Wiltshier Northern Ltd* [1995] 1 WLR 68, *St. Martins Property Corporation Ltd and another v McAlpine* and *The Albazero* were applied.

Darlington Borough Council v Wiltshier Northern Ltd. and Another [1995] 1 WLR 68

Panel: Dillon, Steyn and Waite LJJ

Facts: Wiltshier Northern contracted with Morgan Grenfell to build a recreation centre on the Council's land. The Council had employed Morgan Grenfell to contract with Wiltshire as there were restrictions on Local Authority spending at the time which prevented the Council from contracting for the recreation centre directly. Wiltshier Northern was aware from the outset that the building was for the benefit of the Council. At the end of the contract, Morgan Grenfell validly assigned its contractual rights to the Council. It then transpired the Wiltshier Northern had breached the contract leaving £2m of remedial works requiring to be carried out. At first instance it was successfully argued that although the Council had Morgan Grenfell's rights under the contract, because Morgan Grenfell had never had a beneficial interest in the property, its loss was nominal. Accordingly, as the assignment placed the Council in Morgan Grenfell's position, the Council also had suffered only a nominal loss. The Court of Appeal held that, applying the *'St Martin's property'* exception, Morgan Grenfell would have been able to recover substantial damages on behalf of the Council. Therefore, the Council would be able to sue for its own losses as Morgan Grenfell, suing on its, the Council's, behalf.

LORD JUSTICE STEYN

The 'no loss' point

I turn to the more substantial point. The [first instance] judge regarded it as fatal to the claim that Morgan Grenfell had not paid for the cost of remedying the defects and had no intention of doing so. Mr. Blackburn [Counsel for Wiltshier Northern] supports the judge's reasoning. He says that a prima facie meritorious claim has indeed disappeared down a legal black hole. He says that if Morgan Grenfell had done the repairs or had undertaken to do so, or if there was evidence that it intended to do so, Morgan Grenfell would have been able effectively to assign a claim for substantial damages to the council.

As a mere financier of the transaction Morgan Grenfell, of course, had no interest in taking such action. Accordingly, Mr. Blackburn submits that Morgan Grenfell, the party in contractual relationship with Wiltshier, suffered no loss and could transfer no claim for substantial damages; and the council, which suffered the loss, is precluded by the privity rule from claiming the damages which it suffered. He submits that established doctrine deprives the council of a remedy and allows the contract-breaker to go scot-free. Recognising that this is hardly an attractive result, he reminds us of our duty to apply the law as it stands.

Lord Justice Steyn then commented on the speech of Lord Browne-Wilkinson in the *Linden Garden's* case and cited Lord Diplock's speech in *The Albazero* (as set out above).

…The relevant passage from Lord Diplock's speech in *The Albazero* reads, at p. 847: ' … an original party to the contract, if such be the intention of them both, is to be treated in law as having entered into the contract for the benefit of all persons who have or may acquire an interest in the goods before they are lost or damaged, and is entitled to recover by way of damages for breach of contract the actual loss sustained by those for whose benefit the contract is entered into.'

Clearly, this passage did not exactly fit the material facts in the *Linden Gardens* case. But Lord Browne-Wilkinson extracted the rationale of the decision and by analogy applied it to the purely contractual situation in *Linden Gardens*. He particularly justified this extension of the exception in *The Albazero* by invoking Lord Diplock's words in *The Albazero*:

'there may still be occasional cases in which the rule would provide a remedy where no other would be available to a person sustaining loss which under a rational legal system ought to be compensated by the person who has caused it.'

Lord Browne-Wilkinson's conclusion was supported by all members of the House of Lords, although, it is right to say, Lord Griffiths wished to go further. Relying on the exception recognised in the *Linden Gardens* case, as well as on the need to avoid a demonstrable unfairness which no rational legal system should tolerate, I would rule that the present case is within the rationale of Lord Browne-Wilkinson's speech. I do not say that the relevant passages in his speech precisely fit the material facts of the present case. But it involves only a very conservative and limited extension to apply it by analogy to the present case. For these reasons I would hold that the present case is covered by an exception to the general rule that a plaintiff can only recover damages for his own loss.

The exception contained in Lord Griffiths's speech. [The 'broad ground']

The rationale of Lord Griffiths's wider principle is essentially that, if a party engages a builder to perform specified work and the builder fails to render the contractual service, the employer suffers a loss. He suffers a loss of bargain

Decipher
Lords Keith, Bridge and Ackner supported the narrow ground following Lord Browne-Wilkinson. Lord Griffiths was alone in his championing of the broad ground.

or of expectation interest. And that loss can be recovered on the basis of what it would cost to put right the defects. ... [I]t will be clear from what I said earlier that I am in respectful agreement with the wider principle. It seems to me that Lord Griffiths based his principle on classic contractual theory.

Obviously the decision in *Darlington Borough Council v Wiltshier Northern Ltd* represents a further step toward establishing firm precedent for the acknowledgement of a common law third party right. However, this adventurous judicial foray has been firmly corralled by the decision in *Alfred McAlpine Construction Ltd v Panatown Ltd* [2001] 1 AC 518, where their Lordships reversed the Court of Appeal decision and prevented a claim for a third party where they had their own right of appeal by alternative routes.

Alfred McAlpine Construction Ltd v Panatown Ltd [2000] 3 WLR 946

Panel: Lord Clyde, Lord Goff of Chieveley, Lord Jauncey of Tullichettle, Lord Browne-Wilkinson and Lord Millett

Facts: A contractor, McAlpine, entered into a contract with an employer for the construction of an office block and car park on a site which was owned by Panatown, a third party to the construction contract. In addition to its contract with the employer, McAlpine also entered into a duty of care deed with Panatown. By that deed Panatown acquired a direct remedy against McAlpine in respect of any failure by McAlpine to exercise reasonable skill, care and attention. The deed was expressly assignable by the Panatown to its successors in title. Serious defects were found in the building and the employer served notice of arbitration claiming damages for defective work and delay. The arbitrator rejected McAlpine's preliminary objection that the employer, having suffered no loss (as it was not the owner of the property), was not entitled to recover substantial damages under the contract and made an interim award. The Court of Appeal applied *St Martin's Property* and held that the employer could recover substantial damages for Panatown based on the narrow ground ie that it did not matter that the claimant was no longer the owner. The court also held that the duty of care deed did not affect the application of the *St Martin's Property* principle. However, it was held by the House of Lords that the Court of Appeal was wrong in its decision that Panatown's direct remedy against McAlpine, as provided by the duty of care deed, was not an issue. The right to seek a remedy directly precluded Panatown from relying upon the *St Martin's Property* principle as this should only be available where there is no other possible remedy.

LORD CLYDE

...

The justification for the exception to the general rule that one can only sue for damages for a loss which he has himself suffered was explained by Lord Diplock in *The Albazero* [1977] AC 774, 847. His Lordship noted that the scope and utility of what he referred to as the rule in *Dunlop v Lambert*, 6 Cl & F 600 in its application to carriage by sea under a bill of lading had been much reduced by the passing of the Bills of Lading Act 1855 and the subsequent development of the law, but that the rule extended to all forms of carriage, including carriage by sea where there was no bill of lading:

'and there may still be occasional cases in which the rule would provide a remedy where no other would be available to a person sustaining loss which under a rational legal system ought to be compensated by the person who has caused it.'

The justification for *The Albazero* exception is thus the necessity of avoiding the disappearance of a substantial claim into what was described by Lord Stewart in *GUS Property Management Ltd v Littlewoods Mail Order Stores Ltd*, 1982 SC(HL) 157, 166 as a legal black hole, an expression subsequently taken up by Lord Keith of Kinkel in this House, at p 177.

Lord Clyde then stated that '*The Albazero* exception' should be considered as a rule of law rather than something to be established by examination of the intention of the parties. Having made this point, he goes on to explain in what circumstances the 'exception' will apply and why it did not apply to Panatown:

...In my view it is preferable to regard it as a solution imposed by the law and not as arising from the supposed intention of the parties, who may in reality not have applied their minds to the point. On the other hand if they deliberately provided for a remedy for a third party it can readily be concluded that they have intended to exclude the operation of the solution which would otherwise have been imposed by law. The terms and provisions of the contract will then require to be studied to see if the parties have excluded the operation of the exception.

That appears to have been the conclusion adopted in *Linden Gardens Trust Ltd v Lenesta Sludge Disposals Ltd; St Martins Property Corpn Ltd v Sir Robert McAlpine Ltd* [1994] 1 AC 85 (the *St Martins* case), where my noble and learned friend, Lord Browne-Wilkinson, observed, at p 115:

'In such a case, it seems to me proper, as in the case of the carriage of goods by land, to treat the parties as having entered into the contract on the footing that Corporation would be entitled to enforce contractual rights for the benefit of those who suffered from defective performance but who, under the terms of the contract, could not acquire any right to hold McAlpine liable for breach.'

In that case the point was made that the contractor and the employer were both aware that the property was going to be occupied and possibly purchased by third parties so that it could be foreseen that a breach of the contract might cause loss to others than the employer. But such foresight may be an unnecessary factor in the applicability of the exception. So also an intention of the parties to benefit a third person may be unnecessary. ....

The Albazero exception will plainly not apply where the parties contemplate that the carrier will enter into separate contracts of carriage with the later owners of the goods, identical to the contract with the consignor. Even more clearly, as Lord Diplock explained [1977] AC 774, 848, will the exception be excluded if other contracts of carriage are made in terms different from those in the original contract. In *The Albazero* the separate contracts which were mentioned were contracts of carriage. That is understandable in the context of carriage by sea involving a charterparty and bills of lading. But the counterpart in a building contract to a right of suit under a bill of lading should be the provision of a direct entitlement in a third party to sue the contractor in the event of a failure in the contractor's performance. In the context of a building contract one does not require to look for a second building contract to exclude the exception. It would be sufficient to find the provision of a right to sue. Thus as my noble and learned friend, Lord Browne-Wilkinson, observed in the *St Martins* case [1994] 1 AC 85 115:

'If, pursuant to the terms of the original building contract, the contractors have undertaken liability to the ultimate purchasers to remedy defects appearing after they acquired the property, it is manifest the case will not fall within the rationale of *Dunlop v Lambert* 6 Cl & F 600. If the ultimate purchaser is given a direct cause of action against the contractor (as is the consignee or endorsee under a bill of lading) the case falls outside the rationale of the rule.'

In the *St Martins* case the employer started off as the owner of the property and subsequently conveyed it to another company. In the present case the employer never was the owner. But that has not featured as a critical consideration in the present appeal and I do not see that that factor affects the application of the exception. In the *St Martins* case there was a contractual bar on the assignment of rights of action without the consent of the contractor. In the present case the extra qualification was added that the consent should not be unreasonably withheld. But again I do not see that difference as of significance. It does not follow that the presence of a provision enabling assignment without the consent of the contractor excludes the exception. As was held in *Darlington Borough Council v Wiltshier Northern Ltd* [1995] 1 WLR 68 where there is a right to have an assignment of any cause of action accruing to the employer against the contractor, the exception may still apply so as to enable the assignee to recover substantial damages. It may be that the exception could be excluded through some contractual arrangement between the employer and the third party who sustained the actual loss, but the law would probably be slow to find such an intention established where it would leave the black hole. At least an express provision for assignment of the employer's rights will not suffice.

I have no difficulty in holding in the present case that the exception cannot apply. As part of the contractual arrangements entered into between Panatown and McAlpine there was a clear contemplation that separate contracts would be entered into by McAlpine, the contracts of the deed of duty of care and the collateral warranties. The duty of care deed and the collateral warranties were of course not in themselves building contracts. But they did form an integral part of the package of arrangements which the employer and the contractor agreed upon and in that respect should be viewed as reflecting the intentions of all the parties engaged in the arrangements that the third party should have a direct cause of action to the exclusion of any substantial claim by the employer, and accordingly that the exception should not apply. There was some dispute upon the difference in substance between the remedies available under the contract and those available under the duty of care deed. Even if it is accepted that in the circumstances of the present case where the eventual issue may relate particularly to matters of reasonable skill and care, the remedies do not absolutely coincide, the express provision of the direct remedy for the third party is fatal to the application of *The Albazero* exception. On a more general approach the difference between a strict contractual basis of claim and a basis of reasonable care makes the express remedy more clearly a substitution for the operation of the exception. Panatown cannot then in the light of these deeds be treated as having contracted with McAlpine for the benefit of the owner or later owners of the land and the exception is plainly excluded.

8.3.4 Statutory Exceptions

As well as the 1999 Act, there are several statutory exceptions to the privity doctrine. These include The Road Traffic Act 1972, which permits an injured third party to make a claim directly against an insurance company and The Married Women's Property Act 1882 whereby a husband can take out a policy of insurance on his own life for the benefit of his wife and children. There are further specific exceptions in The Companies Act 2006 and The Bills of Exchange Act 1882 (relevant to shareholder actions and the rights of the 'end holder' of a bill of exchange respectively). Finally, there is the exception contained in The Law of Property Act 1925 as discussed in *Beswick v Beswick* (see above).

8.4 The Contracts (Rights of Third Parties) Act 1999

The Act allows a third party, in limited circumstances, to enforce a term of a contract he is not party to. It does not, however, allow a third party to have a contract to which he is not a party enforced against him.

The Act explicitly states in s 7 that it does nothing to alter the existing common law rights as examined above.

Nisshin Shipping Co. Ltd. v Cleaves & Company Ltd. and Others [2004] 1 Lloyd's Rep. 38

Panel: Colman J

Statute: Contracts (Rights of Third Parties) Act 1999 s 1(1), (2)

Facts: Cleaves sought to enforce a clause in a charterparty under the Contracts (Rights of Third Parties) Act 1999 s 1(1). Cleaves argued that the clause conferred on it a benefit of one per cent commission since the charterparty did not express any intention contrary to Cleave's entitlement to enforce the commission clause.

MR JUSTICE COLMAN

…Do Cleaves fall within s. 1 of the 1999 Act?

10. It is accepted on behalf of Cleaves that in none of the charters did the commission clauses expressly provide that Cleaves could enforce such clauses directly against the owners. However the real issues are (i) whether those clauses purported to confer a benefit on Cleaves within sub-s. (1)(b) of s. 1 and (ii) whether sub-s. 1(b) is disapplied by sub-s. (2) because 'on a proper construction of the contact it appears that the parties did not intend the term to be enforceable by the third party'.

    …The relevant wording for all four charter-parties [there were four contracts at issue] is thus as follows:

    A commission of two per cent for equal division is payable by the vessel and owners to Messrs Ifchor S.A. Lausanne and Messrs Cleaves and Company Ltd., London on hire earned and paid under this Charter, and also upon any continuation or extension of this charter.

12. It is argued that the phraseology is such that the benefit conferred by the clause is to be subsequently divided between the two firms as distinct from a provision which specifies that a particular percentage should be paid to a particular broker.

13. I cannot accept this argument. These provisions leave no doubt as to the identity of the broker to whom payment is to be made and as to the amount to be paid. It is in substance exactly the same as if the clause had provided that there was to be a commission of two per cent. of which one per cent. was to be paid to Ifchor and one per cent. to Cleaves. There is nothing in this clause to suggest that the total two per cent commission is to be paid to Ifchor and that Ifchor will then pay half of that to Cleaves. …

14. Accordingly, I hold that the effect of the clause was to confer a benefit to the extent of one per cent commission on Cleaves alone.

…

22. Secondly, it is argued by Mr. Ashcroft on behalf of Nisshin that there is no positive indication in the charter-parties that the parties did intend the brokers to have enforceable rights. …

23. It is to be noted that s. 1(2) of the 1999 Act does not provide that sub-s. 1(b) is disapplied unless on a proper construction of the contract it appears that the parties intended that the benefit term should be enforceable by the third party. Rather it provides that sub-s. 1(b) is disapplied if, on a proper construction, it appears that the parties did not intend third party enforcement. In other words, if the contract is neutral on this question, sub-s. (2) does not disapply sub-s. 1(b). Whether the contract does express a mutual intention that the third party should not be entitled to enforce the benefit conferred on him or is merely neutral is a matter of construction having regard to all relevant circumstances. The purpose and background of the Law Commission's recommendations in relation to sub-s. (2) are explained in a paper by Professor Andrew Burrows who, as a member of the Law Commission, made a major contribution to the drafting of the bill as enacted. He wrote at [2000] L.M.C.L.Q. 540 at p. 544:

    The second test therefore uses a rebuttable presumption of intention. In doing so, it copies the New Zealand Contracts (Privity) Act, 1982, s. 4, which has used the same approach. It is this rebuttable presumption that provides the essential balance between sufficient certainty for contracting parties and the flexibility required for the reform to deal fairly with a huge range of different situations. The presumption is based on the idea that, if you ask yourself, 'When is it that parties are likely to have intended to confer rights on a third party to enforce a term, albeit that they have not expressly conferred that right', the answer will be: 'Where the term purports to confer a benefit on an expressly identified third party'. That then sets up the presumption. But the presumption can be rebutted if, as a matter of ordinary contractual interpretation, there is something else indicating that the parties did not intend such a right to be given.

24. In the present case, apart from Mr. Ashcroft's third point, the charter-parties are indeed neutral in the sense that they do not express any intention contrary to the entitlement of the brokers to enforce the commission term….

…

33. It follows that Cleaves are entitled to enforce the commission clauses in their own right by reason of s. 1 of the 1999 Act.

The following case deals with who may take the benefit of s 1, as stipulated by s 1(3).

Avaraamides v Colwill [2006] EWCA Civ 1533, [2007] BLR 76

Panel: Waller and Levenson LJJ

Statute: Contracts (Rights of Third Parties) Act 1999 s 1(3)

Facts: A contractor had refurbished Mr. and Mrs. Avaraamides' bathroom. The contractor then transferred all their rights and liabilities under the contract between themselves and Mr. and Mrs. Avaraamides' to Colwill. Paragraph 3 of the agreement between the contractor and Colwill provided that Colwill would: '...undertake to complete outstanding customers' orders...and to pay in the normal course of time any liabilities properly incurred by the company...' The contractor failed to complete the work and Colwill refused to do so. At first instance it was held that Mr. and Mrs. Avaraamides were third parties on whom paragraph 3 of the above transfer agreement had conferred a benefit. The defendants, Colwill, appealed.

LORD JUSTICE WALLER

...

... By section 1(3) of the 1999 Act 'The third party must be expressly identified in the contract by name, as a member of a class or as answering a particular description...'. The second part of the third paragraph ['and to pay in the normal course of time any liabilities properly incurred by the company'] simply does not identify any third party or class of third parties.

The temptation in the circumstances of a case such as this, to find a route which renders the appellants liable, is great. They have taken over the assets of the company and agreed with the company to meet liabilities. The remedy of the respondents if the 1999 Act does not apply seems to be to pursue the company which, according to the evidence, now has no assets, with the possibility of persuading the liquidator of the company to then pursue the appellants for failing to discharge the liabilities which under the transfer agreement they have agreed to do. Why not save the appellants that exercise by use of the 1999 Act?

The answer I am afraid is that section 1(3), by use of the word 'express', simply does not allow a process of construction or implication. I considered whether it would be possible for Mr Mills to rely on the fact that 'customers' are identified in the contract as beneficiaries of the first part of paragraph 3, even if liabilities in the second part includes persons other than customers. Could he submit that even though others are included within the liabilities under the second part, 'customers' as a class are identified and that is sufficient. The difficulty is that the section is concerned with the benefit conferred on a third party, and with the identification of that person. The benefit from the obligation to pay liabilities properly incurred would benefit third parties but of a large number of unidentified classes.

I should add that, although both parties have fought the appeal on the basis that the written agreement evidences an agreement between the company and the appellants, the fact is that the written contract is between the appellants and the shareholders, and when one adds that point to the failure to identify, I am actually doubtful whether it can be said that this agreement, on its true construction, was one under which it was intended that any persons with rights against the company were to be able to enforce them directly against the appellants.'

Further Reading

Flannigan, R., 1987. 'Privity - the end of an era (error)', Law Quarterly Review.

'Law Commission Report of 1996, Privity of Contract: Contracts for the Benefit of Third Parties'

'The Contracts (Rights of Third Parties) Act 1999 and its implications in commercial contracts' [2000] LMCLQ 540

McKendrick, E., Contract Law (2017) 12th ed. Ch.7

9

Terms I

Topic List

Introduction

The contract embodies the agreement of the parties. The terms of the contract constitute the specific obligations of the parties. In order to identify whether and how the parties have failed to comply with their obligations, it is first necessary precisely to identify those obligations.

There are two 'sources' of terms. The parties may expressly state the terms of the contract, either orally or in writing. Additionally, the court may 'imply' terms into the contract. Generally, this will be done in an effort to ensure that the contract properly reflects the intentions of the parties (terms implied in fact), or some necessary aspect of their relationship (terms implied in law).

The terms of the contract can be contrasted with representations and 'mere puffs'. If a party to the contract makes a misrepresentation, that may result in rescission of the contract and/or an award of damages; but it will not result in a breach of the contract. This has important consequences when considering the remedies available to a claimant. A statement that is mere puff has no force whatsoever, whether as a term of the contract, or as a representation.

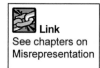
Link
See chapters on Misrepresentation

9.1 Distinguishing between a Term and a Representation

Whether any particular statement is a term of the contract will depend, ultimately, on the court's assessment of what reasonable persons in the position of the parties would have intended.

Nevertheless, there are a number of factors that will indicate whether the parties intended to make a particular statement a binding part of their agreement. These factors include the importance of the statement, whether it was put down in writing, the time at which the statement was made, and the level of expertise of the person making it.

9.1.1 Importance

Bannerman v White (1861) 142 ER 685

Panel: Erle CJ, Williams, Willes and Byles JJ

Facts: A prospective buyer of hops asked the seller whether any sulphur had been used in their preparation. The buyer warned that he did not want the goods if sulphur had been used. The seller insisted that no sulphur had been used. After taking delivery of the hops, the buyer discovered that sulphur had in fact been used in the cultivation of a portion of the hops. One of the questions for the court was whether the seller's undertaking that no sulphur had been used was a term of the contract.

ERLE CJ

Thus, the question was,—'Was the affirmation that no sulphur had been used intended between the parties to be part of the contract of sale, and a warranty by the plaintiff?'

...

As to this, it was contended on one side that the conversation relating to the sulphur was preliminary to entering on the contract, and no part thereof, both from the form of expression and also from the written guarantee which was shewn to have been given. On the other side it was contended that the whole interview was one transaction, that the intention of the parties was alone to be regarded, that the defendants had declared the importance they attached to the inquiry, and that the plaintiff must have known it.

...

This undertaking was a preliminary stipulation; and if it had not been given, the defendants would not have gone on with the treaty which resulted in the sale. In this sense it was the condition upon which the defendants contracted; and it would be contrary to the intention expressed by this stipulation that the contract should remain valid if sulphur had been used.

In the view of Erle CJ, the fact that the undertaking was the fundamental basis on which the defendants entered into the transaction demonstrated that it must have been a term of the contract. Ultimately, however, there is no definitive test other than asking what the parties objectively intended.

9.1.2   Timing and the Reduction to Writing

The closer the statement is in time to the actual point of agreement, the more likely it is to be a contractual term. As noted above, if the statement is also reduced to writing as part of a written contract, that is a powerful indicator that it is a term rather than a mere representation or puff.

Routledge v McKay **[1954] 1 WLR 615**

Panel: Lord Evershed MR, Denning and Romer LJJ

Facts: The seller of a motorcycle stated that it was a 1941 or 1942 model and pointed to a statement to that effect in the motorcycle's registration documents. In fact, the motorcycle was a 1930 model. This statement was made some time before the written contract was entered into. The critical issue was whether this statement could amount to a binding contractual term.

LORD EVERSHED MR

On the oral evidence, all there is and all the judge found, or I think intended to find, was that on the first meeting of [the buyer] and [the seller] (and before, be it noted, the bargain was eventually made), and in answer to a question, [the seller] specifically stated that it was a 1942 model, and pointed to the corroboration of that statement found in the book.

...

[The written memorandum of sale] represents prima facie the record of what the parties intended to agree when the actual transaction took place. [Counsel for the seller] has contended that the terms of it necessarily exclude any warranty — that is to say, any collateral bargain, either contemporary or earlier in date. I am not sure that I would go as far with [counsel for the seller] in that respect. But I think that, as a matter of construction, it would be extremely difficult to say that such an agreement was consistent with a warranty being given at the same time and so as to be intended to form a part of the bargain then made. ...

Now if the earlier representation is to be a warranty, then it has got to be contractual in form. In other words, so far as I can see, once the existence of a warranty as part of the actual bargain is excluded, it must be a separate contract; and the difficulty, and I think the overwhelming difficulty, which faces [the buyer] here is that when the representation was made there was then no bargain, and it is therefore, in my view, impossible to say that it could have been collateral to some other contract.

...

I have felt compelled to the conclusion that the judge here had not before him any evidence which entitled him to conclude that there was given, and intended to be given, a warranty (in the proper sense of that word) when the reference to the date of origin of the motor-cycle was made by [the seller]; and I only add that the written agreement tends to support that view rather than to controvert it.

As the statement about the model year of the motorcycle had not been included in the written contract, it would be very difficult to show that it was intended to be a term of the contract. In addition, the longer the period of time prior to contracting a statement is made, the more difficult it will be to say that the statement was the basis on which the final contract was entered into.

9.1.3 Special Knowledge or Skill

The relative expertise of each party will necessarily affect the importance that the other party gives to their statements, and will therefore be a relevant consideration in determining whether a statement is a term of the contract.

***Dick Bentley v Harold Smith* [1965] 1 WLR 623**

Panel: Lord Denning MR, Danckwerts and Salmon LJJ

Facts: The plaintiff was planning to purchase a car, and asked the defendant car dealers to find him a 'quality', well-vetted, Bentley car. The defendant located a car and the plaintiff came to inspect it. At the time of inspection, the defendant told him that the car had done only 20,000 miles since being fitted with a new engine. The defendant later repeated this statement. The plaintiff took the car for a short trial run and then purchased it. The car soon developed problems and the plaintiff discovered that the car had in fact done more than 20,000 miles. The question for the court was whether the assertions made by the defendant about the car's mileage formed a term of the contract.

LORD DENNING MR

…The first point is whether this representation, namely, that it had done 20,000 miles only since it had been fitted with a replacement engine and gearbox, was an innocent misrepresentation (which does not give rise to damages), or whether it was a warranty. It was said by Holt CJ, and repeated in *Heilbut, Symons & Co. v. Buckleton* [1913] AC 30, 49, HL that: 'An affirmation at the time of the sale is a warranty, provided it appear on evidence to be so intended.' But that word 'intended' has given rise to difficulties. I endeavoured to explain in *Oscar Chess Ltd v Williams* [1957] 1 WLR 370, 375 that the question whether a warranty was intended depends on the conduct of the parties, on their words and behaviour, rather than on their thoughts. If an intelligent bystander would reasonably infer that a warranty was intended, that will suffice. What conduct, then? What words and behaviour lead to the inference of a warranty?

Looking at the cases once more, as we have done so often, it seems to me that if a representation is made in the course of dealings for a contract for the very purpose of inducing the other party to act upon it, and actually inducing him to act upon it, by entering into the contract, that is prima facie ground for inferring that it was intended as a warranty. It is not necessary to speak of it as being collateral. Suffice it that it was intended to be acted upon and was in fact acted on. But the maker of the representation can rebut this inference if he can show that it really was an innocent misrepresentation, in that he was in fact innocent of fault in making it, and that it would not be reasonable in the circumstances for him to be bound by it. In the *Oscar Chess* case (at 375) the inference was rebutted. There a man had bought a second-hand car and received with it a log-book which stated the year of the car, 1948. He afterwards resold the car. When he resold it he simply repeated what was in the log-book and passed it on to the buyer. He honestly believed on reasonable grounds that it was true. He was completely innocent of any fault. There was no warranty by him, but only an innocent misrepresentation. Whereas in the present case it is very different. The inference is not rebutted. Here we have a dealer, Smith, who was in a position to know, or at least to find out, the history of the car. He could get it by writing to the makers. He did not do so. Indeed, it was done later. When the history of this car was examined, his statement turned out to be quite wrong. He ought to have known better. There was no reasonable foundation for it.

In *Dick Bentley* the seller was the dealer, and the buyer could therefore be expected to rely on what he said about the model of the car. By contrast, in

Oscar Chess Ltd v Williams [1957] 1 WLR 370, the buyer was himself a car dealer and therefore was in a position to assess the veracity of the statement made. Consequently, the statement made by the seller did not form a term of the contract. In other words, if the statement maker has special knowledge or skill, his statement is more likely to be a term of the contract.

9.1.4   When do Oral Terms override Written Terms?

Where a purchaser alleges that the written terms of a contract have been 'overridden' by oral assurances, the court will take into account all of the above considerations in making its determination of which statement prevails. Although the assurance is not reduced to writing, the court will be influenced by when the statement was made, the expertise of the person making it, and the importance that a reasonable person in the position of the buyer would give to the statement.

Couchman v Hill [1947] KB 554

Panel: Scott, Tucker and Bucknill LJJ

Facts: The plaintiff purchased a heifer at an auction. The defendant had described the heifer in the auction catalogue as 'unserved'. The plaintiff sought and received reassurances of this from both the defendant and the auctioneer. However, the catalogue stated that the sale was subject to the auctioneer's usual terms and conditions. One of those conditions was that all lots were sold 'with all faults, imperfections and errors of description'. (In other words, the seller took no responsibility for any defects in the goods sold or any errors in the description of those goods.) The heifer, which was later found to be carrying a calf, suffered a miscarriage and died. The critical question was whether the defendant's statements were a term of the contract, or whether the catalogue took precedence.

 Decipher A heifer which has not been mated.

LORD JUSTICE SCOTT

There was no contract in existence until the hammer fell: the offer was defined, the auctioneer's authority was defined, but it was in law open to any would-be purchaser to intimate in advance before bidding for any particular heifer offered from the rostrum that he was not willing to bid for the lot, unless the vendor modified the terms of sale contained in the two documents in some way specified by him. There is no doubt that the plaintiff did make some attempt of the kind in order to protect himself from the risk of buying an animal that was not of the kind described.

The real question is, what did the parties understand by the question addressed to and the answer received from both vendor and auctioneer. It is contended by the defendant that the question meant: 'having regard to the onerous stipulations which I know I shall have to put up with if I bid and the lot is knocked down to me, can you give me your honourable assurance that the heifers have in fact not been served? If so, I will risk the penalties of the catalogue.' The alternative meaning is: 'I am frightened of contracting on your published terms, but I will bid if you will tell me by word of mouth that you accept full responsibility for the statement in the catalogue that the heifers have not been served, or, in other words, give me a clean warranty. That is the only condition on which I will bid.' If that was the meaning there was clearly an oral offer of a warranty which overrode the stultifying condition in the printed terms: that offer was accepted by the plaintiff when he bid, and the contract was made on that basis when the lot was knocked down to him.

Lord Justice Scott found that the statement that the heifer was unserved did constitute a term of the contract which overrode the terms in the auction catalogue. As can be seen from his Lordship's reasoning, the importance of the statement, its timing, and the expertise of the seller all contributed to this conclusion.

9.2 The Parol Evidence Rule

The parol evidence rule applies to written contracts and prevents the parties from adducing extrinsic evidence to vary or interpret the terms of the written contract. The written contract is the totality of the parties' agreement. Therefore, no evidence can be led about oral representations. However, this rule often leads to harsh results that do not properly reflect the basis on which the parties had entered into their transaction. As a consequence, the courts have developed ways to avoid the extreme effects of the parol evidence rule.

J Evans & Son (Portsmouth) Ltd v Andrea Merzario Ltd [1976] 1 WLR 1078

Panel: Lord Denning MR, Roskill and Geoffrey Lane LJJ

Facts: The plaintiffs purchased machines from Italy. They entered into a contract with the defendants for carriage of those goods by ship from Italy to England. The defendants gave the plaintiffs an oral assurance that the goods would be carried below deck and the plaintiffs agreed to the contract in reliance on that promise. The written terms of the contract contained a clause excluding the defendants' liability where goods were shipped on deck. The machines were in fact carried on deck and, during the course of the voyage, fell overboard. The central questions were whether the oral promise was an enforceable contractual promise and, if so, whether the defendant could rely on the exclusion clause in the written agreement.

LORD DENNING MR

...We have a different approach nowadays to collateral contracts. When a person gives a promise or an assurance to another, intending that he should act on it by entering into a contract, and he does act on it by entering into the contract, we hold that it is binding ... it seems to me plain that [the defendant] gave an oral promise or assurance that the goods in this new container traffic would be carried under deck. He made the promise in order to induce [the plaintiff] to agree to the goods being carried in containers. On the faith of it, [the plaintiff] accepted the quotations and gave orders for transport. In those circumstances the promise was binding. There was a breach of that promise and the forwarding agents are liable — unless they can rely on the printed conditions.

...I do not think [the printed conditions can be relied upon]. The cases are numerous in which oral promises have been held binding in spite of written exempting conditions: such as *Couchman v. Hill* [1947] KB 554; *Harling v. Eddy* [1951] 2 KB 739; *City and Westminster Properties (1934) Ltd v Mudd* [1959] Ch 129. The most recent is *Mendelssohn v Normand* [1970] 1 QB 177, 184, where I said: 'The printed condition is rejected because it is repugnant to the express oral promise or representation.' During the argument Roskill LJ put the case of the Hague Rules. If a carrier made a promise that goods would be shipped under deck, and, contrary to that promise, they were carried on deck and there was a loss, the carrier could not rely on the limitation clause. Following these authorities, it seems to me that the forwarding agents cannot rely on the condition. There was a plain breach of the oral promise by the forwarding agents. I would allow the appeal.

LORD JUSTICE ROSKILL

...The real question, as I venture to think, is not whether one calls this an assurance or a guarantee, but whether that which was said amounted to an enforceable contractual promise by the defendants to the plaintiffs that any goods thereafter entrusted by the plaintiffs to the defendants for carriage from Milan to the United Kingdom via Rotterdam and thence by sea to England would be shipped under deck. The matter was apparently argued before the judge on behalf of the plaintiffs on the basis that the defendants' promise (if any) was what the lawyers sometimes call a collateral oral warranty. That phrase is normally only applicable where the original promise was external to the main contract, that main contract being a contract in writing, so that usually parol evidence cannot be given to contradict the terms of the written contract. The basic rule is clearly stated in paragraph 742 of Benjamin's Sale of Goods, 9th ed. (1974) to which I refer but which I will not repeat. But that doctrine, as it seems to me, has little or no application where one is not concerned with a contract in writing (with respect, I cannot accept [counsel for the defendants'] argument that there was here a contract in writing) but with a contract which, as I think, was partly oral, partly in writing, and partly by conduct. In such a case the court does not require to have recourse to lawyer's devices such as collateral oral warranty in order to seek to adduce evidence which would not otherwise be admissible. The court is entitled to look at and should look at all the evidence from start to finish in order to see what the bargain was that was struck between the parties. That is what we have done in this case and what, with great respect, I think the judge did not do in the course of his judgment. I unreservedly accept [counsel for the defendant's] submission that one must not look at one or two isolated answers given in evidence; one should look at the totality of the evidence[.] When one

 Alert

 Alert

does that, one finds, first, as I have already mentioned, that these parties had been doing business in transporting goods from Milan to England for some time before; secondly, that transportation of goods from Milan to England was always done on trailers which were always under deck; thirdly, that the defendants wanted a change in the practice — they wanted containers used instead of trailers; fourthly, that the plaintiffs were only willing to agree to that change if they were promised by the defendants that those containers would be shipped under deck, and would not have agreed to the change but for that promise. The defendants gave such a promise, which to my mind against this background plainly amounted to an enforceable contractual promise. In those circumstances it seems to me that the contract was this: 'If we continue to give you our business, you will ensure that those goods in containers are shipped under deck'; and the defendants agreed that this would be so. Thus there was a breach of that contract by the defendants when this container was shipped on deck; and it seems to me to be plain that the damage which the plaintiffs suffered resulted from that breach.

These passages demonstrate two ways in which the harsh effects of the parol evidence rule can be avoided. Lord Denning MR found that the oral promise induced entry into the shipping contract and constituted a binding collateral contract. By contrast, Roskill and Geoffrey Lane LJJ found that there was only one contract, but that this contract was partly written and partly oral.

Attempts by litigants and judges to subvert the parol evidence rule have been largely successful. Indeed these exceptions have almost swallowed up the rule, and the extent to which it is now of any practical utility is doubtful. Where the contract is wholly written, oral evidence is inadmissible, but it is also irrelevant, as the entirety of the parties' agreement is contained in the written words of the contract. Where the contract is partly in writing and partly oral, of course, oral evidence is not excluded.

Nevertheless, the focus of the courts on the written agreement of the parties, and their continued unwillingness to allow them to rely on pre-contractual negotiations and subjective declarations of intent to interpret contractual terms is a legacy of the parol evidence rule which still informs the modern approach to contractual interpretation.

9.3 Unusual or Onerous Terms

While the terms of a contract primarily operate to define the positive obligations of the parties, the parties may also agree to narrow or limit the obligations of one or both of the parties. These types of term are commonly referred to as exemption clauses. The courts have adopted a sceptical approach to such terms, and have developed special rules to limit their effect.

Beginning in the 19th century, a series of decisions were handed down concerning the incorporation of exemption clauses on the back of tickets for trains. In *Parker v South Eastern Railway Co.* (1877) 2 CPD 416 it was held

Link
See chapter on Exemption Clauses I.

that, in order to incorporate such a term by notice, reasonable steps must be taken to draw the term to the other party's attention.

The question remained, however, whether a similar principle was applicable to clauses that did not purport to exclude liability but merely imposed some unusual or onerous obligation on one of the parties. This question was resolved in *Interfoto Picture Library Ltd. v Stiletto Visual Programmes Ltd* [1989] QB 433.

Interfoto Picture Library Ltd. v Stiletto Visual Programmes Ltd [1989] QB 433

Link

For a fuller explanation of this case, see the chapter on Exemption Clauses I.

Panel: Dillon and Bingham LJJ

Facts: Stiletto ordered photographic transparencies from Interfoto. The transparencies were delivered in a jiffy bag with a delivery note. This delivery note had nine printed conditions. Condition 2 stipulated that the transparencies had to be returned within 14 days of delivery or thereafter a holding fee of £5 per day plus VAT would be charged. Stiletto did not read the conditions and returned the transparencies four weeks later. Interfoto invoiced Stiletto for £3,783.50. Stiletto refused to pay.

LORD JUSTICE DILLON

At the time of the ticket cases in the last century it was notorious that people hardly ever troubled to read printed conditions on a ticket or delivery note or similar document. That remains the case now. In the intervening years the printed conditions have tended to become more and more complicated and more and more one-sided in favour of the party who is imposing them, but the other parties, if they notice that there are printed conditions at all, generally still tend to assume that such conditions are only concerned with ancillary matters of form and are not of importance. In the ticket cases the courts held that the common law required that reasonable steps be taken to draw the other parties' attention to the printed conditions or they would not be part of the contract. It is, in my judgment, a logical development of the common law into modern conditions that it should be held, as it was in *Thornton v. Shoe Lane Parking Ltd* [1971] 2 QB 163, that, if one condition in a set of printed conditions is particularly onerous or unusual, the party seeking to enforce it must show that that particular condition was fairly brought to the attention of the other party.

Thus, the more onerous or unusual a term, the greater the degree of notice that must be given.

9.4 Implied Terms (Common Law)

For various reasons the parties may fail to express all of the terms that they wish to govern their relationship. The courts have therefore developed numerous bases on which to imply terms into a contract.

Terms are generally implied in fact or in law. The difference between the two was summarised by Lord Denning MR in *Shell UK Ltd v Lostock Garage Ltd* [1976] 1 WLR 1187.

Shell UK Ltd v Lostock Garage Ltd [1976] 1 WLR 1187

Panel: Lord Denning MR, Ormrod and Bridge LJJ

Facts: Lostock entered into an agreement with Shell whereby, in return for discounts, it would exclusively sell Shell petrol. Shell also entered into similar agreements with a number of other petrol stations in the area. In 1975, a 'price war' began and competing petrol stations lowered their prices. Shell subsidised some of the petrol stations with which it had entered into agreements so that they could compete. However, it did not subsidise Lostock, which was obliged by its agreement with Shell to continue selling its petrol at a certain price. Lostock argued that there was an implied term of its agreement that Shell would not discriminate against it in favour of competing garages.

LORD DENNING MR

…[T]here are two broad categories of implied terms.

The first category [Terms implied in law]

The first category comprehends all those relationships which are of common occurrence. Such as the relationship of seller and buyer, owner and hirer, master and servant, landlord and tenant, carrier by land or by sea, contractor for building works, and so forth. In all those relationships the courts have imposed obligations on one party or the other, saying they are 'implied terms.' These obligations are not founded on the intention of the parties, actual or presumed, but on more general considerations: see *Luxor (Eastbourne) Ltd. v Cooper* [1941] AC 108, 137 by Lord Wright; *Lister v Romford Ice and Cold Storage Co Ltd* [1957] AC 555, 576 by Viscount Simonds, and at p. 594 by Lord Tucker (both of whom give interesting illustrations); and *Liverpool City Council v Irwin* [1976] 2 WLR 562, 571 by Lord Cross of Chelsea, and at p. 579 by Lord Edmund-Davies. In such relationships the problem is not to be solved by asking what did the parties intend? Or would they have unhesitatingly agreed to it, if asked? It is to be solved by asking: has the law already defined the obligation or the extent of it? If so, let it be followed. If not, look to see what would be reasonable in the general run of such cases: see by Lord Cross of Chelsea at p. 570H: and then say what the obligation shall be. The House in *Liverpool City Council v Irwin* [1976] 2 WLR 562 went through that very process. They examined the existing law of landlord and tenant, in particular that relating to easements, to see if it contained the solution to the problem: and, having found that it did not, they imposed an obligation on the landlord to use reasonable care. In these relationships the parties can exclude or modify the obligation by express words; but unless they do so, the obligation is a legal incident of the relationship which is attached by the law itself and not by reason of any implied term.

Link
See below

...

The second category [Terms implied in fact]

The second category comprehends those cases which are not within the first category. These are cases — not of common occurrence — in which from the particular circumstances a term is to be implied. In these cases the implication is based on an intention imputed to the parties from their actual circumstances: see *Luxor (Eastbourne) Ltd v Cooper* [1941] AC 108, 137 by Lord Wright. Such an imputation is only to be made when it is necessary to imply a term to give efficacy to the contract and make it a workable agreement in such manner as the parties would clearly have done if they had applied their mind to the contingency which has arisen. These are the 'officious bystander' types of case: see *Lister v. Romford Ice and Cold Storage Co Ltd* [1957] AC 555, 594, by Lord Tucker. In such cases a term is not to be implied on the ground that it would be reasonable: but only when it is necessary and can be formulated with a sufficient degree of precision.

In summary, the rationale for implying a term in fact will be to give effect to the imputed intentions of the parties, while terms are implied in law to give effect to general considerations relating to particular relationships.

Lostock did not succeed in its implied term argument. The court considered that it was not necessary to imply any term into the contract, and that such a term could not be formulated with adequate precision.

9.4.1 Terms Implied in Fact

The courts have held that terms should be implied by fact into a contract on a number of grounds. There may be a course of dealing between the parties that suggests that they always contracted on a certain basis (see *McCutcheon v McBrayne* [1964] 1 WLR 125 and *Hollier v Rambler* [1972] 2 QB 71). Or a term may be so commonly used in a particular trade that it can be assumed that it was intended to be part of a contract arising in the course of that trade (*British Crane Hire v Ipswich Plant* [1974] 1 All ER 1059).

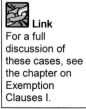
Link
For a full discussion of these cases, see the chapter on Exemption Clauses I.

The most commonly invoked basis of implication, however, is the need to give 'business efficacy' to the contract. This test has its genesis in the following case.

***The Moorcock (*1889) LR 14 PD 64**

Panel: Lord Esher MR, Bowen and Fry LJJ

Facts: The appellants owned a jetty at which they agreed to allow the respondent shipowner to moor his ship. At low tide the ship grounded. The appellants had taken no steps to ascertain whether or not this was a safe place for the vessel to lie. The ship sustained damage. The critical question was whether the appellants were responsible for the state of the bottom of the river adjoining the jetty.

LORD ESHER MR

In this case the appellants made an agreement with the respondent for the use of their wharf and jetty in such a manner as to enable them to earn money from the respondent. The use of their wharf involved the use of the river adjacent to the front of their wharf, for the owner of a vessel such as the *Moorcock* could not use their wharf without mooring that vessel alongside the jetty. It is a necessary and an immediate step to the earning profit by the use of the wharf that the vessel should be moored to the jetty. The appellants do not charge directly for the use of their wharf, but they cannot charge anything to anybody, or, under the circumstances, earn anything until the vessel moors itself to their jetty. She is moored to the jetty in order that the wharf may be used for the loading and unloading of goods into and from the vessel, and the appellants get paid for the use of their wharf by charging in respect of the goods that lie on and cross their wharf.

Such a vessel as the *Moorcock* could not be moored to this wharf without taking the ground at low water on every tide; therefore, in order that the wharf may be used so that the appellants may earn profit, a vessel must be moored to their wharf, and at the front of it, under such circumstances that she must take the ground at every tide. Now the owners of the wharf and the jetty are there always, and if anything happens in front of their wharf they have the means of finding it out, but persons who come in their ships to this wharf have no reasonable means of discovering what the state of the bed of the river is until the vessel is moored and takes the ground for the first time.

What, then, is the reasonable implication in such a contract? In my opinion honest business could not be carried on between such a person as the respondent and such people as the appellants, unless the latter had impliedly undertaken some duty towards the respondent with regard to the bottom of the river at this place. If that is so, what is the least onerous duty which can be implied? In this case we are not bound to say what is the whole of the duty. All we have got to say is whether there is not at least the duty which the learned judge in the court below has held does lie on them and to be implied as part of their contract. The appellants can find out the state of the bottom of the river close to the front of their wharf without difficulty. They can sound for the bottom with a pole, or in any way they please, for they are there at every tide, and whether they can see the actual bottom of the river at low water is not material. Supposing at low water there were two feet of water always over the mud, this would make no difference. Persons who are accustomed to the water do not see the bottom of the water with their eyes, they find out what is there by sounding, and they can feel for the bottom and find out what is there with even more accuracy than if they saw it with their eyes, and when they cannot honestly earn what they are desiring to earn without this, it is implied that they have undertaken to see that the bottom of the river is reasonably fit, or at all events that they have taken reasonable care to find out that the bottom of the river is reasonably fit for the purpose for which they agree that their jetty should be used, that is, they should take reasonable care to find out in what condition

Alert

the bottom is, and then either have it made reasonably fit for the purpose, or inform the persons with whom they have contracted that it is not so. That I think is the least that can be implied as their duty, and this is what I understand the learned judge has implied, and then he finds as a matter of fact that they did not take reasonable means in this case, and in that view also I agree. I therefore think the appellants broke their contract, and that they are liable to the respondent for the injury which his vessel sustained.

The court ultimately held that it was an implied term of the contract that the appellants take reasonable care to maintain the river bed and therefore the appeal was dismissed.

This 'business efficacy' test has undergone a number of different formulations. One of these is the 'officious bystander' test referred to by Lord Denning MR in *Lostock v Shell* (above). This formulation of the principle was classically encapsulated by MaCkinnon LJ below.

Shirlaw v Southern Foundries [1939] 2 KB 206

Panel: Sir Wilfrid Greene MR, Mackinnon and Goddard LJJ

Facts: The defendant company appointed the plaintiff as its managing director for a term of 10 years. Two years later the defendant was taken over, the company's articles of association changed and the plaintiff was removed from his position as director and, ipso facto, his position as managing director. The plaintiff alleged that it was an implied term of his contract that they would not remove him as a director during the 10 years of his appointment and that the company's articles would not be altered so as to give it a power to do so.

LORD JUSTICE MACKINNON

... I recognize that the right or duty of a Court to find the existence of an implied term or implied terms in a written contract is a matter to be exercised with care; and a Court is too often invited to do so upon vague and uncertain grounds. Too often also such an invitation is backed by the citation of a sentence or two from the judgment of Bowen LJ in *The Moorcock* (1889) 14 PD 64. They are sentences from an extempore judgment as sound and sensible as all the utterances of that great judge; but I fancy that he would have been rather surprised if he could have foreseen that these general remarks of his would come to be a favourite citation of a supposed principle of law, and I even think that he might sympathize with the occasional impatience of his successors when *The Moorcock* is so often flushed for them in that guise.

For my part, I think that there is a test that may be at least as useful as such generalities. If I may quote from an essay which I wrote some years ago, I then said: 'Prima facie that which in any contract is left to be implied and need not be expressed is something so obvious that it goes without saying; so that, if, while the parties were making their bargain, an officious bystander were to

Alert

suggest some express provision for it in their agreement, they would testily suppress him with a common 'Oh, of course!'"

At least it is true, I think, that, if a term were never implied by a judge unless it could pass that test, he could not be held to be wrong.

Applying that in this case, I ask myself what would have happened if, when this contract had been drafted and was awaiting signature, a third party reading the draft had said: 'Would it not be well to put in a provision that the company shall not exercise or create any right to remove Mr. Shirlaw from his directorship, and he have no right to resign his directorship?' I am satisfied that they would both have assented to this as implied already, and agreed to its expression for greater certainty. Mr. Shirlaw would certainly have said: 'Of course that is implied. If I am to be bound by this agreement, including the barring of my activities under clauses 11 and 12 when I cease to be managing director, obviously the company must not have, or create, the power to remove me at any moment from the Board and so disqualify me from that post'; and the company, which must be presumed to have been then desirous of binding him to serve them as managing director for ten years, would, I think, with equal alacrity have said: 'Of course that is implied. If you were tempted by some offer elsewhere, it would be monstrous for you to be able to resign your directorship and, by so disqualifying yourself from being managing director, put an end to this agreement.'

In the result, I think that the learned judge came to a right decision and this appeal fails.

The Court of Appeal ultimately held that a term should be implied that the company would not take steps to remove the plaintiff as a director during the period in which he was appointed managing director. The decision of the Court of Appeal was affirmed by the House of Lords: [1940] AC 701.

Both the 'business efficacy' test, and the 'officious bystander' test attempt to identify what the parties ultimately intended, an idea that has been recently affirmed by the Privy Council.

Attorney General of Belize and others v Belize Telecom Ltd and Anor [2009] 1 WLR 1988

Panel: Lord Hoffmann, Lord Rodger of Earlsferry, Baroness Hale of Richmond, Lord Carswell and Lord Brown of Eaton-under-Heywood

Facts: A special company was created by the Government of Belize as part of the privatisation of the telecommunication industry. A dispute arose as to the rights of various owners of shares in the company to appoint its directors. In the course of their advice, their Lordships considered the proper foundation of terms implied in fact.

LORD HOFFMANN

...There is only one question: is that what the instrument, read as a whole against the relevant background, would reasonably be understood to mean?

...

The danger lies, however, in detaching the phrase 'necessary to give business efficacy' from the basic process of construction of the instrument. It is frequently the case that a contract may work perfectly well in the sense that both parties can perform their express obligations, but the consequences would contradict what a reasonable person would understand the contract to mean. ...

The same point had been made many years earlier by Bowen LJ in his well known formulation in *The Moorcock* (1889) 14 PD 64, 68:

'In business transactions such as this, what the law desires to effect by the implication is to give such business efficacy to the transaction as must have been intended at all events by both parties who are business men ...'

Likewise, the requirement that the implied term must 'go without saying' is no more than another way of saying that, although the instrument does not expressly say so, that is what a reasonable person would understand it to mean. Any attempt to make more of this requirement runs the risk of diverting attention from the objectivity which informs the whole process of construction into speculation about what the actual parties to the contract or authors (or supposed authors) of the instrument would have thought about the proposed implication. The imaginary conversation with an officious bystander in *Shirlaw v Southern Foundries* (1926) Ltd [1939] 2 KB 206, 227 is celebrated throughout the common law world. Like the phrase 'necessary to give business efficacy', it vividly emphasises the need for the court to be satisfied that the proposed implication spells out what the contact would reasonably be understood to mean. But it carries the danger of barren argument over how the actual parties would have reacted to the proposed amendment. That, in the Board's opinion, is irrelevant. Likewise, it is not necessary that the need for the implied term should be obvious in the sense of being immediately apparent, even upon a superficial consideration of the terms of the contract and the relevant background. The need for an implied term not infrequently arises when the draftsman of a complicated instrument has omitted to make express provision for some event because he has not fully thought through the contingencies which might arise, even though it is obvious after a careful consideration of the express terms and the background that only one answer would be consistent with the rest of the instrument. In such circumstances, the fact that the actual parties might have said to the officious bystander 'Could you please explain that again?' does not matter.

The Board reiterates that, when implying terms in fact, one must ask what the reasonable person would understand the contract to mean rather than enquiring as to the subjective intentions of the parties.

Recently, in *Mediterranean Salvage and Towage Ltd v Seamar Trading and Commerce Inc.*, *The Reborn* (2009) EWCA Civ 531, Lord Clarke MR clarified Lord Hoffmann's judgment by stating that Lord Hoffmann was 'not in any way resiling from the often stated position that it must be necessary to imply the proposed term. It is never sufficient that it should be reasonable.'

9.4.2 Terms Implied in Law

The seminal consideration of terms implied by law was delivered by Lord Wilberforce in *Liverpool City Council v Irwin* [1977] AC 239.

Liverpool City Council v Irwin [1977] AC 239

Panel: Lord Wilberforce, Lord Cross of Chelsea, Lord Salmon, Lord Edmund-Davies and Lord Fraser of Tullybelton

Facts: The tenants of a council block withheld their rent as a protest against conditions in the common areas of the building. The council commenced possession proceedings and the tenants counterclaimed for damages, alleging that the council had a duty to repair and maintain the common areas of the building. They alleged, amongst other things, that the lift did not work and that the rubbish shoots were blocked. The contract of letting between the council and the tenants contained no term requiring maintenance or repair. The critical question, therefore, was whether there was an implied term that placed an obligation on the council to keep the common parts of the block in a proper state of repair.

LORD WILBERFORCE

...Where there is, on the face of it, a complete, bilateral contract, the courts are sometimes willing to add terms to it, as implied terms: this is very common in mercantile contracts where there is an established usage: in that case the courts are spelling out what both parties know and would, if asked, unhesitatingly agree to be part of the

bargain. In other cases, where there is an apparently complete bargain, the courts are willing to add a term on the ground that without it the contract will not work - this is the case, if not of *The Moorcock* (1889) 14 PD 64 itself on its facts, at least of the doctrine of *The Moorcock* as usually applied. This is, as was pointed out by the majority in the Court of Appeal, a strict test - though the degree of strictness seems to vary with the current legal trend - and I think that they were right not to accept it as applicable here. There is a third variety of implication, that which I think Lord Denning MR favours, or at least did favour in this [c]ase, and that is the implication of reasonable terms. But though I agree with many of his instances, which in fact fall under one or other of the preceding heads, I cannot go so far as to endorse his principle; indeed, it seems to me, with respect, to extend a long, and undesirable, way beyond sound authority.

The present case, in my opinion, represents a fourth category, or I would rather say a fourth shade on a continuous spectrum. The court here is simply concerned to establish what the contract is, the parties not having themselves fully stated the terms. In this sense the court is searching for what must be implied.

What then should this contract be held to be? There must first be implied a letting, that is, a grant of the right of exclusive possession to the tenants. With this there must, I would suppose, be implied a covenant for quiet enjoyment, as a necessary incident of the letting. The difficulty begins when we consider the common parts. We start with the fact that the demise is useless unless access is obtained by the staircase; we can add that, having regard to the height of the block, and the family nature of the dwellings, the demise would be useless without a lift service; we can continue that, there being rubbish chutes built into the structures and no other means of disposing of light rubbish, there must be a right to use the chutes. The question to be answered - and it is the only question in this case - is what is to be the legal relationship between landlord and tenant as regards these matters.

There can be no doubt that there must be implied (i) an easement for the tenants and their licensees to use the stairs, (ii) a right in the nature of an easement to use the lifts, (iii) an easement to use the rubbish chutes.

But are these easements to be accompanied by any obligation upon the landlord, and what obligation? There seem to be two alternatives. The first, for which the council contends, is for an easement coupled with no legal obligation, except such as may arise under the Occupiers' Liability Act 1957 as regards the safety of those using the facilities, and possibly such other liability as might exist under the ordinary law of tort. The alternative is for easements coupled with some obligation on the part of the landlords as regards the maintenance of the subject of them, so that they are available for use.

My Lords, in order to be able to choose between these, it is necessary to define what test is to be applied, and I do not find this difficult. In my opinion such obligation should be read into the contract as the nature of the contract itself implicitly requires, no more, no less: a test, in other words, of necessity. The relationship accepted by the corporation is that of landlord and tenant: the tenant accepts obligations accordingly, in relation inter alia to the stairs, the lifts and the chutes. All these are not just facilities, or conveniences provided at discretion: they are essentials of the tenancy without which life in the dwellings, as a tenant, is not possible. To leave the landlord free of contractual obligation as regards these matters, and subject only to administrative or political pressure, is, in my opinion, inconsistent totally with the nature of this relationship. The subject matter of the lease (high rise blocks) and the relationship created by the tenancy demand, of their nature, some contractual obligation on the landlord.

 Alert

I do not think that this approach involves any innovation as regards the law of contract. The necessity to have regard to the inherent nature of a contract and of the relationship thereby established was stated in this House in *Lister v Romford Ice and Cold Storage Co Ltd* [1957] AC 555. That was a case between master and servant and of a search for an 'implied term.' Viscount Simonds, at p. 579, makes a clear distinction between a search for an implied term such as might be necessary to give 'business efficacy' to the particular contract and a search, based on wider considerations, for such a term as the nature of the contract might call for, or as a legal incident of this kind of contract. If the search were for the former, he says, '... I should lose myself in the attempt to formulate it with the necessary precision.' (p. 576.) We see an echo of this in the present case, when the majority in the Court of Appeal, considering a 'business efficacy term' - i.e., a *'Moorcock'* term (*The Moorcock* 14 PD 64) - found themselves faced with five alternative terms and therefore rejected all of them. But that is not, in my opinion, the end, or indeed the object, of the search.

...

It remains to define the standard. My Lords, if, as I think, the test of the existence of the term is necessity the standard must surely not exceed what is necessary having regard to the circumstances. To imply an absolute obligation to repair would go beyond what is a necessary legal incident and would indeed be unreasonable. An obligation to take reasonable care to keep in reasonable repair and usability is what fits the requirements of the case. Such a definition involves - and I think rightly - recognition that the tenants themselves have their responsibilities. What it is reasonable to expect of a landlord has a clear relation to what a reasonable set of tenants should do for themselves.

...It has not been shown in this case that there was any breach of that obligation. On the main point therefore I would hold that the appeal fails.

My Lords, it will be seen that I have reached exactly the same conclusion as that of Lord Denning MR, with most of whose thinking I respectfully agree. I must only differ from the passage in which, more adventurously, he suggests that the courts have power to introduce into contracts any terms they think reasonable or to anticipate legislative recommendations of the Law Commission. A just result can be reached, if I am right, by a less dangerous route.

Lord Wilberforce focussed, therefore, on identifying the rights and obligations that were the necessary incident of the particular relationship in question: landlord and tenant. Terms are implied in law in relation to a number of other categories of relationship, including employers and employees. But, only such terms as are deemed 'necessary' by the nature of the contract will be capable of implication by law.

9.5   Implied Terms (Statute)

In order to understand this section, you will need to be familiar with both the Sale of Goods Act 1979 (SGA 1979) and the Supply of Goods and Services Act 1982 (SGSA 1982).

The SGA 1979 now governs the implication of terms into a sale of goods contract. The Act implies terms relating to title in the goods sold, whether those goods correspond with their description, whether they are of satisfactory quality and whether they are fit for a particular purpose. Often these implied terms will overlap.

The SGA 1979 s 14(2A) defines 'satisfactory quality' as the 'standard that a reasonable person would regard as satisfactory, taking account of any description of goods, the price (if relevant) and all other relevant circumstances'.

Section 14(2B) provides a checklist of what factors may be taken into account in assessing the quality of goods.

The SGA 1979 s 14(3) places a more stringent duty upon a seller when the buyer has made known to the seller that they plan to use the goods for a particular purpose.

Lambert v Lewis [1982] AC 225

Panel: Lord Diplock, Lord Elwyn-Jones, Lord Fraser of Tullybelton, Lord Scarman and Lord Bridge of Harwich

Statute: Sale of Goods Act 1893

Facts: A trailer carrying rubble became detached from a Land Rover belonging to a farmer. The trailer hit a car coming in the opposite direction, killing the driver of that car. The farmer brought proceedings against the seller of the coupling that joined the trailer to the vehicle and its manufacturer, alleging a breach of what are now the SGA 1979 ss 14(2) and (3).

LORD DIPLOCK

… The farmer was driven to rely upon the implied warranties under [the SGA 1979 s 14(2) and (3)] … which were clearly applicable to his contract with the dealers. It is, however, only necessary to refer to the [term in s 14(3)] that the coupling as fitted to the Land Rover should be reasonably fit for towing trailers fitted with either cup-shaped or ring-type means of attachment. Fitness in this context plainly includes a warranty that it may be so used upon a public highway without danger to other users of the road.

The implied warranty of fitness for a particular purpose relates to the goods at the time of delivery under the contract of sale in the state in which they were delivered. I do not doubt that it is a continuing warranty that the goods will continue to be fit for that purpose for a reasonable time after delivery, so long as they remain in the same apparent state as that in which they were

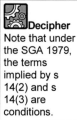**Decipher**
Note that under the SGA 1979, the terms implied by s 14(2) and s 14(3) are conditions.

delivered, apart from normal wear and tear. What is a reasonable time will depend upon the nature of the goods but I would accept that in the case of the coupling the warranty was still continuing up to the date, some three to six months before the accident, when it first became known to the farmer that the handle of the locking mechanism was missing.

The goods must therefore be durable at the time of sale and must remain fit for their particular purpose for a reasonable period of time after delivery. Of course, it is only when some defect in the goods arises later that a breach of this term will become apparent.

However, a term will not be implied under s 14(3) where the circumstances show that the buyer does not rely, or that it is unreasonable for him to rely, on the skill and judgment of the seller.

Balmoral Group Ltd v Borealis Ltd [2006] EWHC 1900 (Comm), [2006] 2 Lloyd's Rep 629

Panel: Christopher Clarke J

Facts: Borealis supplied a polymer to Balmoral for use in the making of oil tanks. The material supplied was not defective and was generally of satisfactory quality. However it was not suitable for Balmoral's particular purpose, namely the construction of above ground static tanks used to store oil over a long period. The critical question was whether this constituted a breach of the term implied by the SGA 1979 s 14(3).

MR JUSTICE CHRISTOPHER CLARKE

…A buyer will, in the absence of any terms of exclusion or restriction, have a good claim for breach of an implied warranty of fitness for purpose if:

(a)   the sales to him were in the course of a business;

(b)   he has made known to the seller, expressly or by implication, the particular purpose for which he was buying the goods;

(c)   he relied, wholly or partly, on the seller's skill and judgment and it was not unreasonable of him to do so;

(d)   the goods supplied are not reasonably fit for that purpose because of a defect lying within the sphere of expertise of the seller upon which the buyer relied; and

(e)   that unfitness is the cause of his loss.

In respect of (c) the burden is on the seller to show that the buyer did not rely on his skill and judgment, or that it was unreasonable of him to do so.

I turn, therefore to consider whether, on the assumption that no exclusionary terms are applicable, there was an implied warranty of fitness for purpose.

All the sales were made in the course of Borealis' business.

Borealis was well aware from the start of its dealings with Balmoral that Balmoral was making green oil tanks ... by rotomoulding. Borealis introduced borecene to Balmoral as a possible substitute polymer. Balmoral made known to Borealis, insofar as that was necessary, that they would be buying borecene to use to make green oil tanks in their rotomoulding machines.

Borealis indicated to Balmoral that borecene could provide a number of significant advantages as a polymer, including reduced cycle time; warpage control; improved flow properties; a broader processing window; improved mechanical properties and the potential to reduce charge weights due to even wall thickness control...

Borealis were the makers of borecene, and therefore in the best position to know its intrinsic properties, both chemical and mechanical... . But Borealis were not professional rotomoulders, let alone conversant with the particular way in which Balmoral designed, manufactured and tested oil tanks. That was within Balmoral's sphere of expertise.

In those circumstances Balmoral, in ordering borecene, reasonably relied on Borealis to supply a polymer whose properties made it reasonably suitable for the purpose of making green oil tanks by rotomoulding... .

But Balmoral could not reasonably rely on Borealis in respect of design or rotomoulding both of which were within its sphere of expertise.

...

Balmoral have, in my judgment, failed to establish that borecene was not reasonably suitable for the purpose of making green oil tanks by rotomoulding in that it was incapable of being used to make satisfactory oil tanks...

The critical issue for Christopher Clarke J, therefore, was whether it was reasonable for Balmoral to rely on Borealis in respect of the design and manufacture of the tanks. As Balmoral was in a position of greater expertise, Balmoral's claim failed.

The terms implied by the SGA 1979 are important elements of the statutory consumer protection framework. They cannot be excluded in consumer transactions.

Link
See Unfair Contract Terms Act 1977 s 6(2)

The Supply of Goods and Services Act 1982 is also an important source of implied terms. In particular, s 13 implies a term to the effect that all services supplied in the course of a business must be provided with reasonable care and skill.

Further Reading

Furmston, M., 2007. *Chesire, Fifoot & Furmston's Law of Contract*. 15th ed. pp.165–172

Low & Loi. 2005. *'The many 'tests' for terms implied in fact: welcome clarity'* *Law Quarterly Review.* 125 Oct. pp.561–567

McKendrick, E., *Contract Law* (2017) 12th ed. Ch.8

10

Terms II

Topic List

Introduction

This chapter considers what has at times been a controversial area of the law: the classification of terms of a contract as conditions, warranties and innominate terms. The relevance of this distinction is that breach of the different types of term can result in different remedies for the innocent party.

The breach of a condition entitles the innocent party to treat the contract as repudiated (in other words, to terminate the contract) and to claim damages for any loss suffered. The breach of a warranty entitles the innocent party to claim damages only. Finally, whether termination will be available on breach of an innominate term will depend on the seriousness of the consequences of the breach.

The reasoning behind this distinction has traditionally been that a condition is seen as being of such importance to the parties that it goes to the 'root' of the contract. On the other hand, a warranty is viewed as being a term of lesser importance.

Link
Terms I, Sale of Goods Act 1979 s 14(2)

Some terms implied by statute may be classified by the statute itself, for example, the term that goods will be of 'satisfactory quality' implied by the Sale of Goods Act 1979 s 14(2) is classified as a condition by s 14(6). However, when the terms are not classified by statute, the parties to a contract would be well advised to agree, prior to finalising the contract, which terms are so important that they amount to conditions and which are merely warranties. Thought should be given to these issues when negotiating the terms of a contract. If the wording used is unclear then, in the event of a breach, the parties may end up litigating over how particular terms ought to be classified. However, you will see by the end of this chapter, that the court will not necessarily agree that a term is a condition simply because it is labelled as one (see the case of *L Schuler A G v Wickman Machine Tool Sales Limited* [1974] AC 235, below).

The classification of terms is a topic which has troubled the court for many years. This is understandable given the different remedies available to innocent parties which will depend on the nature of the term breached. The right to terminate as opposed to a right simply to claim damages can be one for which it is worth fighting. While reading the cases, you should consider whether you are in agreement with the way in which the court has interpreted parties' intentions and the grounds for the interpretations at which they have arrived.

10.1 Conditions and Warranties

Two cases from the 1870s illustrate how the court may take different approaches to the classification of contractual terms in apparently quite similar circumstances.

Poussard v Spiers and Pond (1875 – 76) LR 1 QBD 410

Panel: Blackburn, Quain and Field JJ

Facts: Madame Poussard, the plaintiff's wife, entered into a written agreement with Mr Spiers and Mr Pond, the defendants, to play a role in an opera playing at their theatre.

Madame Poussard then became unwell and was unable to attend rehearsals during the week prior to the opening. As it was unclear for how long she might be unavailable, the defendants' manager booked another performer to play the part if Madame Poussard was unable to do so. Madame Poussard failed to attend the first four performances of the opera and, upon her being ready to assume the role, the defendants refused to allow this and purported to terminate the contract on the basis of her repudiatory breach. The plaintiff brought a claim for wrongful dismissal.

MR JUSTICE BLACKBURN

...We think that the question, whether the failure of a skilled and capable artiste to perform in a new piece through serious illness is so important as to go to the root of the consideration, must to some extent depend on the evidence; and is a mixed question of law and fact. ...

Now, in the present case, we must consider what were the courses open to the defendants under the circumstances. They might, it was said on the argument before us (though not on the trial), have postponed the bringing out of the piece till the recovery of Madame Poussard, and if her illness had been a temporary hoarseness incapacitating her from singing on the Saturday, but sure to be removed by the Monday, that might have been a proper course to pursue. But the illness here was a serious one, of uncertain duration, and if the plaintiff had at the trial suggested that this was the proper course, it would, no doubt, have been shewn that it would have been a ruinous course; and that it would have been much better to have abandoned the piece altogether than to have postponed it from day to day for an uncertain time, during which the theatre would have been a heavy loss.

The remaining alternatives were to employ a temporary substitute until such time as the plaintiff's wife should recover; and if a temporary substitute capable of performing the part adequately could have been obtained upon such a precarious engagement on any reasonable terms, that would have been a right course to pursue; but if no substitute capable of performing the part adequately could be obtained, except on the terms that she should be permanently engaged at higher pay than the plaintiff's wife, in our opinion it follows, as a matter of law, that the failure on the plaintiff's part went to the root of the matter and discharged the defendants.

The Divisional Court here held that the breach of Madame Poussard's obligation to attend the first performances of the opera went to the root of the agreement and was consequently a breach of condition, entitling the defendants to terminate. The court seems to have laid emphasis upon the importance of Madame Poussard's attendance in the particular circumstances of this case. You will note how the outcome differs in the following case and should consider how the facts of the two cases can be distinguished.

Bettini v Gye [1874-80] (1875-76) LR 1 QBD 183

Panel: Blackburn, Quain and Archibald JJ

Facts: An opera singer, Mr Bettini, was engaged by an operatic director, Mr Gye, to sing for him at his theatre in London during the 1875 season of concerts. The opera was to start on 30 March and end on 13 July of that year and Mr Bettini agreed that he would be in London at least six days prior to 30 March to participate in rehearsals. Mr Bettini did not arrive in London until 28 March 1875 due to illness and Mr Gye refused to employ him as a result.

MR JUSTICE BLACKBURN

...The question raised by the demurrer is, not whether the plaintiff has any excuse for failing to fulfil this part of his contract, which may prevent his being liable in damages for not doing so, but whether his failure to do so justified the defendant in refusing to proceed with the engagement, and fulfil his, the defendant's part. And the answer to that question depends on whether this part of the contract is a condition precedent to the defendant's liability, or only an independent agreement, a breach of which will not justify a repudiation of the contract, but will only be a cause of action for a compensation in damages. ...

We think the answer to this question depends on the true construction of the contract taken as a whole.

Parties may think some matter, apparently of very little importance, essential; and if they sufficiently express an intention to make the literal fulfilment of such a thing a condition precedent, it will be one; or they may think that the performance of some matter, apparently of essential importance and primâ facie a condition precedent, is not really vital, and may be compensated for in damages, and if they sufficiently expressed such an intention, it will not be a condition precedent. ...

In the absence of such an express declaration, we think that we are to look to the whole contract, and applying the rule stated by Parke., B, to be acknowledged, see whether the particular stipulation goes to the root of the matter, so that a failure to perform it would render the performance of the rest of the contract by the plaintiff a thing different in substance from what the defendant has stipulated for; or whether it merely partially affects it and may be compensated for in damages. Accordingly, as it is one or the other, we think it must be taken to be or not to be intended to be a condition precedent. ...

As far as we can see, the failure to attend at rehearsals during the six days immediately before the 30th of March could only affect the theatrical performances and, perhaps, the singing in duets or concerted pieces during the first week or fortnight of this engagement, which is to sing in theatres, halls, and drawing-rooms, and concerts for fifteen weeks.

We think, therefore, that it does not go to the root of the matter so as to require us to consider it a condition precedent. ...

It was held that the stipulation that Mr Bettini be present at least six days prior to the first performance to participate in rehearsals was not intended by the parties to be a condition; it did not go to the root of the contract. Consequently, Mr Gye was not entitled to treat the contract as being at an end by refusing to employ him but could instead claim damages.

It would seem that the distinction between the two cases lies in the importance of the requirement of the parties to attend the specified events. Madame Poussard's attendance at the first four performances went to the root of the contract whereas Mr Bettini's attendance of the first four days of rehearsals was of lesser importance and was consequently a warranty.

10.2   The Twentieth Century Approach

The strict distinction between conditions and warranties has been criticised for being overly rigid since every breach of a condition will allow the innocent party to terminate no matter how insignificant the breach. Consequently, the courts have constructed a middle ground. Some terms are neither conditions nor warranties at the point of creation of the contract; instead, the court looks at the seriousness of the consequences of the breach to determine whether termination is available. Such clauses are called 'innominate terms'.

Hong Kong Fir Shipping Company Limited v Kawasaki Kisen Kaisha Limited [1962] 2 QB 26

Panel: Sellers, Upjohn and Diplock LJJ

The claimant owned a ship, *The Hong Kong Fir*, which was chartered to the defendant under an agreement dated 26 December 1956 for a period of two years.

The agreement contained a term that the ship was to be delivered in a seaworthy condition. This was set out in clause 1 of the agreement; 'she being in every way fitted for ordinary cargo service'. The ship was delivered to the defendant on 13 February 1957 but she was discovered to be in an unseaworthy condition as her engines were old and her engine room staff were insufficiently competent to maintain them. This led to her requiring substantial repairs.

The defendant argued that this was a breach of a condition, meaning that the claimant had committed a repudiatory breach and that the defendant could treat the contract as being at an end. The court did not agree. In reaching its decision, the court moved away from the traditional distinction between conditions or warranties. Instead, it held that there are some terms which are known as 'innominate terms' which cannot be classified as conditions or warranties from the outset. Instead, one must look to the consequences of the breach to determine the effect thereof.

LORD JUSTICE UPJOHN

...Why is this apparently basic and underlying condition of seaworthiness not, in fact, treated as a condition? It is for the simple reason that the seaworthiness clause is breached by the slightest failure to be fitted 'in every way' for service. Thus, to take examples from the judgments in some of the cases I have mentioned above, if a nail is missing from one of the timbers of a wooden vessel or if proper medical supplies or two anchors are not on board at the time of sailing, the owners are in breach of the seaworthiness stipulation. It is contrary to common sense to suppose that in such circumstances the parties contemplated that the charterer should at once be entitled to treat the contract as at an end for such trifling breaches. ...

It is open to the parties to a contract to make it clear either expressly or by necessary implication that a particular stipulation is to be regarded as a condition which goes to the root of the contract, so that it is clear that the parties contemplate that any breach of it entitles the other party at once to treat the contract as at an end. That matter is to be determined as a question of the proper interpretation of the contract...

Where, however, on the true construction of the contract, the parties have not made a particular stipulation a condition, it would be unsound and misleading to conclude that, being a warranty, damages is a sufficient remedy.

In my judgment, the remedies open to the innocent party for breach of a stipulation which is not a condition strictly so called, depend entirely on the nature of the breach and its foreseeable consequences. ...[T]he question to be answered is, does the breach of the stipulation go so much to the root of the contract that it makes further commercial performance of the contract impossible, or in other words is the whole contract frustrated? If yea, the innocent party may treat the contract as at an end. If nay, his claim sounds in damages only.

If I have correctly stated the principles, then as the stipulation as to the seaworthiness is not a condition in the strict sense the question to be answered is, did the initial unseaworthiness as found by the judge, and from which there has been no appeal, go so much to the root of the contract that the charterers were then and there entitled to treat the charterparty as at an end? The only unseaworthiness alleged, serious though it was, was the insufficiency and incompetence of the crew, but that surely cannot be treated as going to the root of the contract for the parties must have contemplated that in such an event the crew could be changed and augmented. In my judgment, on this part of his case [Counsel for the defendant] necessarily fails.

LORD JUSTICE DIPLOCK

There are, however, many contractual undertakings of a more complex character which cannot be categorised as being 'conditions' or 'warranties'... . Of such undertakings, all that can be predicated is that some breaches will, and others will not, give rise to an event which will deprive the party not in default of substantially the whole benefit which it was intended that he should obtain from the contract; and the legal consequences of a breach of such an undertaking, unless provided for expressly in the contract, depend on the nature of the event to which the breach gives rise and do not follow automatically from a prior classification of the undertaking as a 'condition' or a 'warranty'.

Alert

The importance of *Hong Kong Fir* is therefore to make it clear that, in circumstances where the term cannot be said to be a condition or warranty at the outset, the effect of the breach will need to be considered in determining whether the innocent party has the right to treat the contract as being at an end. If the breach deprives the innocent party of substantially the whole benefit of the contract, the breach will have the same effect as breach of a condition and allow the innocent party to terminate the contract and claim damages; if not, the innocent party will be limited to a claim for damages only.

10.3   The Effect of Prior Classification by the Parties

Parties will often attempt to classify terms themselves. However, even where parties do label terms as 'conditions', this does not necessarily mean that the court will interpret the word as having the specific legal meaning discussed above. This is demonstrated by the following case.

L Schuler A G v Wickman Machine Tool Sales Limited [1974] AC 235

Panel: Lord Reid, Lord Morris of Borth-Y-Gest, Lord Wilberforce, Lord Simon of Glaisdale and Lord Kilbrandon

Facts: Schuler was a manufacturing company which entered into a written agreement giving Wickman an exclusive right to sell Schuler products in certain territories (including the UK). Clause 7(b) of the agreement stated that it was a condition of the agreement that Wickman should send named representatives to particular firms at least once a week, in order to take orders for panel presses, and that the same representative should visit on each occasion, unless there were unavoidable reasons preventing this. Clause 11 of the agreement allowed either party to terminate it by notice in writing, in the event that the other committed a material breach of its obligations and failed to remedy this within 60 days of being required to do so in writing by the innocent party.

Wickman's representatives did not in fact visit the listed firms every week and Schuler argued that they were entitled to terminate the agreement because Wickman was in breach of a condition of the contract. Wickman's main argument in response was that Schuler was only entitled to terminate the agreement for the reasons and in the manner set out in clause 11.

LORD REID

Schuler maintain that the word 'condition' has now acquired a precise legal meaning; ... a term of a contract any breach of which by one party gives to the other party an immediate right to rescind the whole contract. ... But it is frequently used with a less stringent meaning. One is familiar with printed 'conditions of sale' incorporated into a contract and with the words 'For conditions see back' printed on a ticket. There it simply means that the 'conditions' are terms of the contract. ...

Sometimes a breach of a term gives [the option to rescind] ... to the aggrieved party because it is of a fundamental character going to the root of the contract, sometimes it gives that option because the parties have chosen to stipulate that it shall have that effect. ...

In the present case it is not contended that Wickman's failures to make visits amounted in themselves to fundamental breaches. What is contended is that the terms of cl 7 'sufficiently express an intention' to make any breach, however small, of the obligation to make visits a condition so that any breach shall entitle Schuler to rescind the whole contract if they so desire.

Schuler maintain that the use of the word 'condition' is in itself enough to establish this intention. No doubt some words used by lawyers do have a rigid inflexible meaning. But we must remember that we are seeking to discover intention as disclosed by the contract as a whole. Use of the word 'condition' is an indication - even a strong indication - of such an intention but it is by no means conclusive. The fact that a particular construction leads to a very unreasonable result must be a relevant consideration. The more unreasonable the result the more unlikely it is that the parties can have intended it, and if they do intend it the more necessary it is that they shall make that intention abundantly clear.

 Alert

Clause 7(b) requires that over a long period each of the six firms shall be visited every week by one or other of two named representatives. It makes no provision for Wickman being entitled to substitute others even on the death or retirement of one of the named representatives. Even if one could imply some right to do this, it makes no provision for both representatives being ill during a particular week. And it makes no provision for the possibility that one or other of the firms may tell Wickman that they cannot receive Wickman's representatives during a particular week. So if the parties gave any thought to the matter at all they must have realised the probability that in a few cases out of the 1,400 required visits a visit as stipulated would be impossible. But if Schuler's contention is right failure to make even one visit entitles them to terminate the contract however blameless Wickman might be. This is so unreasonable that it must make me search for some other possible meaning of the contract. If none can be found then Wickman must suffer the consequences. But only if that is the only possible interpretation.

If I have to construe cl 7 standing by itself then I do find difficulty in reaching any other interpretation. But if cl 7 must be read with cl 11 the difficulty disappears. The word 'condition' would make any breach of cl 7(b), however excusable, a material breach. That would then entitle Schuler to give notice under clause 11(a)(i) requiring the breach to be remedied. There would be no point in giving such a notice if Wickman were clearly not in fault but if it were given Wickman would have no difficulty in showing that the breach had been remedied. If Wickman were at fault then on receiving such a notice they would have to amend their system so that they could show that the breach had been remedied. If they did not do that within the period of the notice then Schuler would be entitled to rescind.

In my view, that is a possible and reasonable construction of the contract and I would therefore adopt it. The contract is so obscure that I can have no confidence that this is its true meaning but for the reasons which I have given I think that it is the preferable construction. It follows that Schuler was not entitled to rescind the contract as it purported to do. So I would dismiss this appeal. ...

The House of Lords here reiterates the traditional judicial view that their role is to give effect to the intention of the parties by way of an 'objective' analysis of the words used in the agreement itself. It is acknowledged by the majority that the use of the word 'condition' would normally indicate that the parties intended the term in question to have the particular legal consequences associated with this (i.e. ability to treat the contract as at an end rather than merely claim damages for breach of the term).

However, as per Lord Reid, the House of Lords clearly took the view that use of the word 'condition' was not conclusive, particularly when interpreting the word in that way would lead to what they felt was an unreasonable result, i.e. that each and every failure to attend by Wickman would give Schuler the right to terminate the contract.

The other key feature was that there was another clause relating to termination of the contract (clause 11). The existence of this clause meant that it was open to Schuler to require Wickman to remedy the breach, failing which they could terminate the agreement. This being the case, there was no need to treat clause 7(b) as a condition, as any breach of this term would in any event be 'material' and entitle Schuler to require this to be made good. The question of how this could be done, once the visits had already been missed, is something that Lord Reid considers elsewhere in the judgment.

Lord Wilberforce dissented from the majority, taking the view that clause 7(b) was in fact a condition and that the words used by the parties in the agreement clearly indicated this. He was also concerned that treating the clause as a warranty would effectively deny Schuler a remedy for Wickman's breaches of the agreement.

It might be argued that the majority here opted to 'rewrite' the agreement in the way that the parties might themselves have done, had they given more careful consideration to the words being used. Regardless of your views on this point, it should be noted that the word 'condition' is used in many different senses, both in everyday life and in law, and that where parties use this without sufficient precision, the court will draw its own conclusions as to what was intended by this.

Further Reading

Bojczuk, W., 1987. *When is a condition not a condition?*. *J B L* 1987, Sep. pp.353–362

McKendrick, E., *Contract Law*. (2017) 12th ed. Ch.10

11

Exemption Clauses I

Topic List

Introduction

As a general definition, an exemption clause is a contract term seeking to exclude or limit liability arising from contract or tort. In *Photo Production Ltd v Securicor Transport Ltd* [1980] AC 827, Lord Diplock defined an exemption clause as:

'One which excludes or modifies an obligation, whether primary [primary obligations are those contained in the contract], general secondary or anticipatory secondary [secondary obligations are those which arise automatically by law when a contract term is breached], that would otherwise arise under the contract by implication of law. Parties are free to agree to whatever exclusion or modification of all three types of obligations as they please within the limits that the agreement must retain the legal characteristics of a contract; and must not offend against the equitable rule against penalties...'

Exemption clauses are common in contracts and critical in contractual disputes. Traditionally, exemption clauses have been viewed as unfair as they have often been misused, usually to the detriment of consumers. The courts have responded to this by looking for ways in which to limit their effect and to encourage parties to use them genuinely to allocate risk between them. At common law, since the courts cannot simply negate unreasonable exemption clauses, they have instead chosen to limit their effect by restricting the incorporation and interpretation or construction of such clauses. Now that there are statutory controls which provide the courts with a direct means of rendering an exemption clause unenforceable if it is held to be unfair or unreasonable, the common law controls imposed by the courts can seem rather artificial. The common law controls are still, however, of vital importance and will be considered by the courts prior to considering the statutory controls.

This chapter focuses on the common law controls in place; the statutory controls will be considered in the next chapter. The first level of control at common law is incorporation and the second is construction of the term. The common law controls represent an interesting area of law, demonstrating the tension between the court's desire for justice on the one hand and certainty of contract on the other.

11.1   Incorporation

There are three key methods of incorporation: (i) by signature, (ii) by reasonable notice and (iii) by consistent and regular course of dealing. As a preliminary issue, it needs to be considered whether the exemption clause has been incorporated on time and whether it was contained in a contractual document.

11.1.1   Timing

Olley v Marlborough Court Limited [1949] 1 KB 532

Panel: Bucknill, Singleton and Denning LJJ

Facts: Mr and Mrs Olley entered into a contract when they paid in advance at the reception desk for a week's stay at a hotel. When they then went upstairs to their room, there was a notice which said: 'The Proprietors will not hold themselves responsible for articles lost or stolen, unless handed to the manageress for safe custody. Valuables should be deposited for safe custody in a sealed package and a receipt obtained'. On one occasion, Mrs Olley closed her self-locking bedroom door behind her and left the key behind the reception desk on the appropriate hook. While she was out, someone managed to get into their room and steal certain items.

LORD JUSTICE DENNING

...The first question is whether that notice [in the bedroom] formed part of the contract. Now people who rely on a contract to exempt themselves from their common law liability must prove that contract strictly. Not only must the terms of the contract be clearly proved, but also the intention to create legal relations - the intention to be legally bound - must also be clearly proved. The best way of proving it is by a written document signed by the party to be bound. Another way is by handing him before or at the time of the contract a written notice specifying its terms and making it clear to him that the contract is on those terms. A prominent public notice which is plain for him to see when he makes the contract or an express oral stipulation would, no doubt, have the same effect. But nothing short of one of these three ways will suffice. It has been held that mere notices put on receipts for money do not make a contract. (See *Chapelton v. Barry Urban District Council* [1940] 1 K.B. 532.) So, also, in my opinion, notices put up in bedrooms do not of themselves make a contract. As a rule, the guest does not see them until after he has been accepted as a guest. The hotel company no doubt hope that the guest will be held bound by them, but the hope is vain unless they clearly show that he agreed to be bound by them, which is rarely the case.

Lord Justice Denning made the logical point that notice of terms must be given *before or at the time the contract is made*. As the contract was made at the reception desk, the terms of the notice in the bedroom came too late and were not incorporated into the contract.

Thornton v Shoe Lane Parking Ltd [1971] 2 QB 163

Panel: Lord Denning MR, Megaw LJ and Sir Gordon Willmer

Facts: Mr Thornton drove his car into a multi-storey car park that he had never used before. At the entrance of the car park there was a notice that stated that all cars were: 'Parked at owner's risk'. It was an automatic machine that gave him his ticket when he drove up beside it. Mr Thornton took the ticket, read the time on the front and put it in his pocket before driving into the car park and parking his car. On his return to collect the car later, there was an accident and he was severely injured. The defendants contended that the ticket incorporated a condition exempting them from liability. On the bottom left hand corner of the ticket it was written in small print that it was: '[I]ssued subject to conditions … displayed on the premises'. On a pillar opposite the ticket machine there was a display panel setting out eight printed conditions. The second condition stated that the car park would not be liable for any injury to the customer occurring when his car was on the premises.

LORD DENNING MR

We have been referred to the ticket cases of former times from *Parker v. South Eastern Railway Co.* (1877) 2 C.P.D. 416 to *McCutcheon v. David MacBrayne Ltd.* [1964] 1 W.L.R. 125. They were concerned with railways, steamships and cloakrooms where booking clerks issued tickets to customers who took them away without reading them. In those cases the issue of the ticket was regarded as an offer by the company. If the customer took it and retained it without objection, his act was regarded as an acceptance of the offer: see *Watkins v. Rymill* (1833) 10 Q.B.D. 178, 188 and *Thompson v. London, Midland and Scottish Railway Co.* [1930] 1 K.B. 41, 47. These cases were based on the theory that the customer, on being handed the ticket, could refuse it and decline to enter into a contract on those terms. He could ask for his money back. That theory was, of course, a fiction. No customer in a thousand ever read the conditions. If he had stopped to do so, he would have missed the train or the boat.

None of those cases has any application to a ticket which is issued by an automatic machine. The customer pays his money and gets a ticket. He cannot refuse it. He cannot get his money back. He may protest to the machine, even swear at it. But it will remain unmoved. He is committed beyond recall. He was committed at the very moment when he put his money into the machine. The contract was concluded at that time. It can be translated into offer and acceptance in this way: the offer is made when the proprietor of the machine holds it out as being ready to receive the money. The acceptance takes place when the customer puts his money into the slot. The terms of the offer are contained in the notice placed on or near the machine stating what is offered for the money. The customer is bound by those terms as long as they are sufficiently brought to his notice before-hand, but not otherwise. He is not bound by the terms printed on the ticket if they differ from the notice, because the ticket comes too late. The contract has already been made: see *Olley v. Marlborough Court Ltd.* [1949] 1 K.B. 532. The ticket is no more than a voucher or receipt for the money that has been paid (as in the deckchair case, *Chapelton v Barry Urban District Council* [1940] 1 KB 532) on terms which have been offered and accepted before the ticket is issued.

In the present case the offer was contained in the notice at the entrance giving the charges for garaging and saying 'at owner's risk', i.e., at the risk of

Decipher
Note Lord Denning MR's explanation of the process of offer and acceptance when purchasing a ticket from a clerk.

Decipher
Note the point at which offer and acceptance occur when a ticket is purchased from an automatic machine.

Alert

the owner so far as damage to the car was concerned. The offer was accepted when Mr Thornton drove up to the entrance and, by the movement of his car, turned the light from red to green, and the ticket was thrust at him. The contract was then concluded, and it could not be altered by any words printed on the ticket itself. In particular, it could not be altered so as to exempt the company from liability for personal injury due to their negligence.

...All I say is that it [the exempting condition on the pillar opposite the ticket machine] is so wide and so destructive of rights that the court should not hold any man bound by it unless it is drawn to his attention in the most explicit way. It is an instance of what I had in mind in J. Spurling Ltd. v. Bradshaw [1956] 1 W.L.R. 461, 466. In order to give sufficient notice, it would need to be printed in red ink with a red hand pointing to it - or something equally startling...

Link
See Interfoto v Stiletto

SIR GORDON WILLMER

I have reached the same conclusion... . It seems to me that the really distinguishing feature of this case is the fact that the ticket on which reliance is placed was issued out of an automatic machine. ...In all the previous so-called 'ticket cases' the ticket has been proffered by a human hand, and there has always been at least the notional opportunity for the customer to say - if he did not like the conditions - 'I do not like your conditions: I will not have this ticket.' But in the case of a ticket which is proffered by an automatic machine there is something quite irrevocable about the process. ...It seems to me that any attempt to introduce conditions after the irrevocable step has been taken of causing the machine to operate must be doomed to failure. ...

This case supports the rule set out in *Olley v Marlborough Court* that a clause cannot be incorporated after a contract has been concluded. It also sets out when the contract is deemed concluded in the case of ticket transactions. Both Lord Denning MR and Sir Gordon Willmer make a distinction between face-to-face ticket transactions and tickets issued from automatic machines. Lord Denning MR re-iterates that in face-to-face ticket sales, the offer is made when the ticket is issued and acceptance takes place when the customer takes it and retains it without objection. As there is no opportunity to reject a ticket when it is issued from a ticket machine, he states that the offer takes place when the proprietor of the machine holds it out as ready to accept money and that acceptance takes place when the customer puts money into the machine. Consequently, in such cases, terms on a ticket are introduced too late to be incorporated.

The terms of the offer contained in the notice on the pillar next to the machine would have been incorporated if Mr Thornton had been given reasonable notice of them. Lord Denning MR points out that the nature of the clause should be taken into account when assessing the degree of notice required. In this case, he states that the exemption clause was 'so wide and so destructive of rights' that the court could not hold anyone bound by it unless it had been drawn to their attention in an explicit way. He re-iterates what he said in *Spurling Ltd v Bradshaw* [1956] 1 WLR 461 about the clause needing 'to be printed in red ink with a red hand pointing to it' before it can be held to be sufficient notice.

11.1.2   Contractual Document

Chapelton v Barry Urban District Council [1940] 1 KB 532

Panel: Slesser, Mackinnon and Goddard LJJ

Facts: Mr Chapelton wanted to hire a deck chair at a beach. There was a notice next to a pile of deck chairs stating the hire charges and that tickets were obtainable from the deck chair attendant. The notice itself did not contain an exemption clause. Mr Chapelton paid the assistant for two chairs and was given two tickets. He put them into his pocket without reading them. On the reverse side of the ticket were the words: 'The council will not be liable for any accident or damage arising from the hire of the chair'. The canvas on the chair that Mr Chapelton was sitting on gave way due to the negligence of the defendant council. The council argued that the clause on the ticket excluded it from liability.

LORD JUSTICE SLESSER

…I do not think that the notice excluding liability was a term of the contract at all[.]… Mellish L.J. in *Parker v. South Eastern Ry. Co.* 2 C.P.D. 416, 422, … points out that it may be that a receipt or ticket may not contain terms of the contract at all, but may be a mere voucher… . I think the object of the giving and the taking of this ticket was that the person taking it might have evidence at hand by which he could show that the obligation he was under to pay 2d. for the use of the chair for three hours had been duly discharged, and I think it is altogether inconsistent, in the absence of any qualification of liability in the notice put up near the pile of chairs, to attempt to read into it the qualification contended for. In my opinion, this ticket is no more than a receipt, and is quite different from a railway ticket which contains upon it the terms upon which a railway company agrees to carry the passenger.

LORD JUSTICE MACKINNON

…If a man does an act which constitutes the making of a contract, such as taking a railway ticket, or depositing his bag in a cloak-room, he will be bound by the terms of the document handed to him by the servant of the carriers or bailees; but if he merely pays money for something and receives a receipt for it, or does something which clearly only amounts to that, he cannot be deemed to have entered into a contract in the terms of the words that his creditor has chosen to print on the back of the receipt, unless, of course, the creditor has taken reasonable steps to bring the terms of the proposed contract to the mind of the man.

Both Slesser and Mackinnon LJJ make the distinction between train tickets which have terms on them and tickets that are given in return for payment and are therefore more like 'receipts'. Unless reasonable notice of the terms is given, a 'mere receipt' will not have contractual force.

LORD JUSTICE GODDARD

I cannot imagine that anybody paying 2d. ... for the privilege of sitting in a chair on the beach would think for one moment that some conditions were being imposed upon him which would limit his ordinary rights, or that the document he received when paying his 2d. was a contractual document in any shape or form. I think the ticket he received was nothing but a receipt for his 2d. – a receipt which showed him how long he might use the chair.

Lord Justice Goddard makes the point that a document will be deemed to be a contractual one if it is obvious to a reasonable person that it is intended to have this effect. In this case, no reasonable person would have expected that terms were being imposed on him and that the document he was given was contractual.

In summary, the Court of Appeal held that the ticket was a 'mere receipt', given out so that a deck chair user could prove that he had paid for his chair. It was held that it was not reasonable to expect people to check such a receipt for notification of terms. Note that not all receipts will fail to incorporate terms into the contract; it depends on the facts and whether it is reasonable to expect to find terms of the contract on the particular receipt in question.

11.1.3 Methods of Incorporation

11.1.3.1 Signature

L'Estrange v F. Graucob Limited [1934] 2 KB 394

Panel: Scrutton and Maugham LJJ

Facts: Harriet L'Estrange bought an automatic cigarette machine from the defendant. She signed an order form which had the essential terms of the contract in ordinary print and special terms in small print. One of these special terms was that: '[A]ny express or implied condition, statement, or warranty, statutory or otherwise not stated herein is hereby excluded.' When the machine was delivered it did not work properly and L'Estrange brought an action against the defendant claiming (amongst other things) damages for breach of an implied warranty that the machine was fit for the purpose for which it was sold. The defendant referred to the exemption clause but L'Estrange replied that she had not read the order form and did not know what it contained.

LORD JUSTICE SCRUTTON

In the course of the argument in the county court reference was made to the railway passenger and cloak-room ticket cases... . In the present case the learned judge asked himself the three questions appropriate to these cases, and in answering them has found as facts: (i.) that the plaintiff knew that there was printed material on the document which she signed, (ii.) that she did not know that the document contained conditions relating to the contract, and (iii.) that the defendants did not do what was reasonably sufficient to bring these conditions to the notice of the plaintiff.

The present case is not a ticket case, and it is distinguishable from the ticket cases. ...In cases in which the contract is contained in a railway ticket or other unsigned document, it is necessary to prove that an alleged party was aware, or ought to have been aware, of its terms and conditions. These cases have no application when the document has been signed. When a document containing contractual terms is signed, then, in the absence of fraud, or, I will add, misrepresentation, the party signing it is bound, and it is wholly immaterial whether he has read the document or not.

Alert

...[W]hether the plaintiff was or was not told that the document was an order form, it was in fact an order form, and an order form is a contractual document. It may be either an acceptance or a proposal which may be accepted, but it always contains some contractual terms. There is no evidence that the plaintiff was induced to sign the contract by misrepresentation.

LORD JUSTICE MAUGHAM

I regret the decision to which I have come, but I am bound by legal rules and cannot decide the case on other considerations.

...I deal with this case on the footing that when the order confirmation was signed by the defendants confirming the order form which had been signed by the plaintiff, there was then a signed contract in writing between the parties. If that is so, then, subject to certain contingencies, there is no doubt that it was wholly immaterial whether the plaintiff read the small print or not.

...In this case it is, in my view, an irrelevant circumstance that the plaintiff did not read, or hear of, the parts of the sales document which are in small print, and that document should have effect according to its terms. I may add, however, that I could wish that the contract had been in a simpler and more usual form. It is unfortunate that the important clause excluding conditions and warranties is in such small print. I also think that the order confirmation form should have contained an express statement to the effect that it was exclusive of all conditions and warranties.

Lord Justice Scrutton sets out the rule clearly: when a document containing contractual terms is signed then, in the absence of fraud or misrepresentation, the party signing it is bound. No enquiry will be made into whether the party signing had read the document or understood what the terms meant. The reasoning for this lies in the objective approach to intention. If a party has signed a document then it is reasonable to conclude that he has read the document and agrees to all the terms in that document. The rule is clearly important for contractual certainty but the harsh effect of its strict application was noted by Maugham LJ who had some sympathy for L'Estrange.

Curtis v Chemical Cleaning and Dyeing Co [1951] 1 KB 805

Panel: Somervell, Singleton and Denning LJJ

Facts: Mrs Curtis took a white satin wedding dress to the defendant drycleaners to be cleaned, and on handing it over an assistant asked Mrs Curtis to sign a receipt. When Mrs Curtis asked why she had to sign, the assistant replied that the defendants would not accept liability for damage to the beads and sequins on the trimming of the dress. She signed the receipt without reading it but the receipt did in fact contain a term excluding the defendants' liability for any damage howsoever arising. When the dress was returned to Mrs Curtis it was stained. The defendants tried to rely on their exclusion clause.

LORD JUSTICE DENNING

This case is of importance because of the many cases nowadays when people sign printed forms without reading them, only to find afterwards that they contain stringent clauses exempting the other side from their common-law liabilities. … If the party affected signs a written document, knowing it to be a contract which governs the relations between them, his signature is irrefragable evidence of his assent to the whole contract, including the exempting clauses, unless the signature is shown to be obtained by fraud or misrepresentation: *L'Estrange v. Graucob* [1934] 2 K.B 394. …

In my opinion any behaviour, by words or conduct, is sufficient to be a misrepresentation if it is such as to mislead the other party about the existence or extent of the exemption. If it conveys a false impression, that is enough. … When one party puts forward a printed form for signature, failure by him to draw attention to the existence or extent of the exemption clause may in some circumstances convey the impression that there is no exemption at all, or at any rate not so wide an exemption as that which is in fact contained in the document. The present case is a good illustration. The customer said in evidence: 'When I was asked to sign the document I asked why? The assistant said I was to accept any responsibility for damage to beads and sequins. I did not read it all before I signed it'. In those circumstances, by failing to draw attention to the width of the exemption clause, the assistant created the false impression that the exemption only related to the beads and sequins, and that it did not extend to the material of which the dress was made. It was done perfectly innocently, but nevertheless a false impression was created.

This case is a good example of when a term contained in a signed contractual document will not be binding due to an overriding oral assurance. Lord Justice Denning supports what Scrutton LJ said in *L'Estrange v F. Graucob Limited*, in that a party is bound by an exemption clause if he signs a written

Link
See Chapter 13 on Misrepresentation

contractual document, unless the signature is obtained by misrepresentation. It is not required that the misrepresentation be one that falls within the definition set out in Chapter 13, below; it is sufficient that a false impression is conveyed as to the extent or existence of the term. Therefore when someone asks why he is signing a document and he is given an oral assurance which does not correspond to the exemption clause in the document, the exemption clause will not be held incorporated and the oral assurance will override its effect.

11.1.3.2   Reasonable notice

***Parker v South Eastern Railway Company* (1876-77) LR 2 CPD 416**

Panel: Mellish, Baggallay and Bramwell LJJ

Facts: Mr Parker left a bag in a cloakroom belonging to the defendant. He paid two pence and was given a ticket which he did not read but assumed it to be a receipt. On the front of the ticket it stated: 'See Back'. On the back of the ticket was a printed notice stating that the defendant would not be responsible for loss of any item whose value was more than £10. A notice containing the same condition was displayed in the cloakroom. Mr Parker's bag was lost or stolen and he claimed its value, which was more than £10. The defendant pleaded the exemption clause.

LORD JUSTICE MELLISH

The question then is, whether the plaintiff was bound by the conditions contained in the ticket. In an ordinary case, where an action is brought on a written agreement which is signed by the defendant, the agreement is proved by proving his signature, and, in the absence of fraud, it is wholly immaterial that he has not read the agreement and does not know its contents. The parties may, however, reduce their agreement into writing, so that the writing constitutes the sole evidence of the agreement, without signing it; but in that case there must be evidence independently of the agreement itself to prove that the defendant has assented to it. In that case, also, if it is proved that the defendant has assented to the writing constituting the agreement between the parties, it is, in the absence of fraud, immaterial that the defendant had not read the agreement and did not know its contents. Now if in the course of making a contract one party delivers to another a paper containing writing, and the party receiving the paper knows that the paper contains conditions which the party delivering it intends to constitute the contract, I have no doubt that the party receiving the paper does, by receiving and keeping it, assent to the conditions contained in it, although he does not read them, and does not know what they are...

Now, I am of [the] opinion that we cannot lay down, as a matter of law, either that the plaintiff was bound or that he was not bound by the conditions printed on the ticket, from the mere fact that he knew there was writing on the ticket, but did not know that the writing contained conditions. I think there may be cases in which a paper containing writing is delivered by one party to another in the course of a business transaction, where it would be quite reasonable that the party receiving it should assume that the writing contained in it no condition, and should put it in his pocket unread. For instance, if a person driving through a turnpike-gate received a ticket upon paying the toll, he might reasonably assume that the object of the ticket was that by producing it he might be free from paying toll at some other turnpike-gate, and might put it in his pocket unread. On the other hand, if a person who ships goods to be carried on a voyage by sea receives a bill of lading signed by the master, he would plainly be bound by it, although afterwards in an action against the shipowner for the loss of the goods, he might swear that he had never read the bill of lading, and that he did not know that it contained the terms of the contract of carriage, and that the shipowner was protected by the exceptions contained in it. Now the reason why the person receiving the bill of lading would be bound seems to me to be that in the great majority of cases persons shipping goods do know that the bill of lading contains the terms of the contract of carriage; and the shipowner, or the master delivering the bill of lading, is entitled to assume that the person shipping goods has that knowledge. It is, however, quite possible to suppose that a person who is neither a man of business nor a lawyer might on some particular occasion ship goods without the least knowledge of what a bill of lading was, but in my opinion such a person must bear the consequences of his own exceptional ignorance, it being plainly impossible that business could be carried on if every person who delivers a bill of lading had to stop to explain what a bill of lading was.

Now the question we have to consider is whether the railway company were entitled to assume that a person depositing luggage, and receiving a ticket in such a way that he could see that some writing was printed on it, would understand that the writing contained the conditions of contract, and this seems to me to depend upon whether people in general would in fact, and naturally, draw that inference. The railway company, as it seems to me, must be entitled to make some assumptions respecting the person who deposits luggage with them: I think they are entitled to assume that he can read, and that he understands the English language, and that he pays such attention to what he is about as may be reasonably expected from a person in such a transaction as that of depositing luggage in a cloak-room. The railway company must, however, take mankind as they find them, and if what they do is sufficient to inform people in general that the ticket contains conditions, I think that a particular plaintiff ought not to be in a better position than other persons on account of his exceptional ignorance or stupidity or carelessness. But if what the railway company do is not sufficient to convey to the minds of people in general that the ticket contains conditions, then they have received goods on deposit without obtaining the consent of the persons depositing them to the conditions limiting their liability. I am of opinion, therefore, that the proper direction to leave to the jury in these cases is, that if the person receiving the ticket did not see or know that there was any writing on the ticket, he is not bound by the conditions; that if he knew there was writing, and

 Alert

knew or believed that the writing contained conditions, then he is bound by the conditions; that if he knew there was writing on the ticket, but did not know or believe that the writing contained conditions, nevertheless he would be bound, if the delivering of the ticket to him in such a manner that he could see there was writing upon it, was, in the opinion of the jury, reasonable notice that the writing contained conditions.

In assessing whether the printed terms on the back of a ticket given to Mr Parker by the defendant had been incorporated into the contract between them, Mellish LJ compared different contractual scenarios. He distinguished a ticket given for a toll gate whereby the recipient would have no reason to believe it contained terms of the contract; and a bill of lading given for shipping goods, where the person ought to know (even if they do not) that it contains contractual terms. In essence, Mellish LJ states that what matters is not whether the claimant has become aware of the exemption clause but whether the person seeking to rely on the clause has taken *reasonable steps* to bring it to his attention.

What constitutes reasonable notice will vary according to the facts of each case. *Interfoto Picture Library Ltd v Stiletto Visual Programmes Ltd* [1989] QB 433 sets out the particular considerations which are relevant when the term, which is sought to be incorporated, is particularly onerous or unusual.

Interfoto Picture Library Ltd v Stiletto Visual Programmes Ltd [1989] QB 433

Panel: Dillon and Bingham LJJ

Facts: Stiletto ordered photographic transparencies from Interfoto. The transparencies were delivered in a jiffy bag with a delivery note. This delivery note had nine printed conditions. Condition 2 stipulated that the transparencies had to be returned within 14 days of delivery or thereafter a holding fee of £5 per day plus VAT would be charged. Stiletto did not read the conditions and returned the transparencies four weeks later. Interfoto invoiced Stiletto for £3,783.50. Stiletto refused to pay.

LORD JUSTICE DILLON

...The contract came into existence when the plaintiffs sent the transparencies to the defendants and the defendants, after opening the bag, accepted them by Mr. Beeching's phone call to the plaintiffs at 3.10 on 5 March. The question is whether condition 2 was a term of that contract.

There was never any oral discussion of terms between the parties before the contract was made. ... In particular there was no discussion whatever of terms in the original telephone conversation when Mr. Beeching made his preliminary inquiry. The question is therefore whether condition 2 was sufficiently brought to the defendants' attention to make it a term of the contract which was only concluded after the defendants had received, and must have known that they had received the transparencies and the delivery note.

This sort of question was posed, in relation to printed conditions, in the ticket cases, such as *Parker v. South Eastern Railway Co.* (1877) 2 C.P.D. 416, in the last century. At that stage the printed conditions were looked at as a whole and the question considered by the courts was whether the printed conditions as a whole had been sufficiently drawn to a customer's attention to make the whole set of conditions part of the contract; if so the customer was bound by the printed conditions even though he never read them.

More recently the question has been discussed whether it is enough to look at a set of printed conditions as a whole. When for instance one condition in a set is particularly onerous does something special need to be done to draw customers' attention to that particular condition? In an obiter dictum in *J. Spurling Ltd. v. Bradshaw* [1956] 1 W.L.R. 461, 466 (cited in *Chitty on Contracts*, 25th ed. (1983), vol. 1, p. 408) Denning L.J. stated:

'Some clauses which I have seen would need to be printed in red ink on the face of the document with a red hand pointing to it before the notice could be held to be sufficient.'

Then in *Thornton v. Shoe Lane Parking Ltd.* [1971] 2 Q.B. 163 both Lord Denning M.R. and Megaw L.J. held as one of their grounds of decision ... that where a condition is particularly onerous or unusual the party seeking to enforce it must show that that condition, or an unusual condition of that particular nature, was fairly brought to the notice of the other party. Lord Denning ... re-stated and applied what he had said in the *Spurling* case, and held that the court should not hold any man bound by such a condition unless it was drawn to his attention in the most explicit way. ...

Condition 2 of these plaintiffs' conditions is in my judgment a very onerous clause. The defendants could not conceivably have known, if their attention was not drawn to the clause, that the plaintiffs were proposing to charge a 'holding fee' for the retention of the transparencies at such a very high and exorbitant rate.

At the time of the ticket cases in the last century it was notorious that people hardly ever troubled to read printed conditions on a ticket or delivery note or similar document. That remains the case now. In the intervening years the printed conditions have tended to become more and more complicated and more and more one-sided in favour of the party who is imposing them, but the other parties, if they notice that there are printed conditions at all, generally still tend to assume that such conditions are only concerned with ancillary matters of form and are not of importance. In the ticket cases the courts held that the common law required that reasonable steps be taken to draw the other parties' attention to the printed conditions or they would not be part of the contract. It is, in my judgment, a logical development of the common law into modern conditions that it should be held, as it was in *Thornton v. Shoe Lane Parking Ltd.* [1971] 2 Q.B. 163, that, if one condition in a set of printed

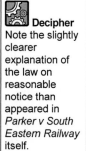
Decipher
Note the slightly clearer explanation of the law on reasonable notice than appeared in *Parker v South Eastern Railway* itself.

conditions is particularly onerous or unusual, the party seeking to enforce it must show that that particular condition was fairly brought to the attention of the other party.

In the present case, nothing whatever was done by the plaintiffs to draw the defendants' attention particularly to condition 2; it was merely one of four columns' width of conditions printed across the foot of the delivery note. Consequently condition 2 never, in my judgment, became part of the contract between the parties.

Lord Justice Dillon reminds us of the position in respect of 'ticket cases', such as *Parker v South Eastern Railway*, where the court was concerned with looking at the printed conditions as a whole in assessing whether notice of them had been sufficient. He confirms the common law approach of those 'ticket cases', in that reasonable steps must be taken to draw the other party's attention to the printed conditions. However, he makes the point that over the years, printed conditions on tickets have become more and more complicated, as well as more one-sided, and it is not enough to view the conditions as a whole to assess whether reasonable notice of them has been given. Instead, Dillon LJ states that the nature of the specific clauses, as well as the document as a whole, should be considered.

He cites Lord Denning MR's *obiter dictum* in *Spurling v Bradshaw* about a clause needing to be printed in red ink on the face of the document with a red hand pointing to it before it can be deemed sufficient notice and points out that this was re-stated and applied in *Thornton v Shoe Lane Parking*. Applying these cases, Dillon LJ concludes that a party who seeks to incorporate a term which is particularly onerous or unusual must prove that the term has been fairly and reasonably drawn to the attention of the other party. A higher degree of notice is therefore required. What constitutes reasonable notice will therefore depend on how unusual or onerous an exemption clause is; the more unusual or onerous the term, the greater the steps which need to be taken.

11.1.3.3 Consistent and regular course of dealing

Consistent

McCutcheon v David Macbrayne Ltd [1964] 1 WLR 125

Panel: Lord Reid, Lord Hodson, Lord Guest, Lord Devlin and Lord Pearce

Facts: The appellant, Mr McCutcheon, wanted his car to be shipped to the mainland from the Hebrides. He asked his brother-in-law, Mr McSporran, to organise it for him. Mr McSporran had employed the respondents to ship cars for him in the past so he delivered the car to them and paid them the money. The respondents gave him a receipt only. Normally, the respondents would provide a customer with a 'risk note' to sign. Mr McSporran had sometimes signed risk notes, but had never read the conditions. The risk note included a condition that the goods were shipped at the owner's risk. The ship sank due to the negligence of the respondents and Mr McCutcheon's car was lost. The respondents argued that the exclusion clause on the risk note was incorporated by previous course of dealing.

LORD REID

The question is, what was the contract between the parties? The contract was an oral one. No document was signed or changed hands until the contract was completed. ...The terms of the receipt ... cannot be regarded as terms of the contract. So the case is not one of the familiar ticket cases where the question is whether conditions endorsed on or referred to in a ticket or other document handed to the consignor in making the contract are binding on the consignor. If conditions not mentioned when this contract was made are to be added to or regarded as part of this contract it must be for some reason different from those principles which are now well settled in ticket cases. If this oral contract stands unqualified there can be no doubt that the respondents are liable for the damage caused by the negligence of their servants.

...The only other ground on which it would seem possible to import these conditions is that based on a course of dealing. If two parties have made a series of similar contracts each containing certain conditions, and then they make another without expressly referring to those conditions it may be that those conditions ought to be implied. ... According to Mr. McSporran, there had been no constant course of dealing; sometimes he was asked to sign and sometimes not. And, moreover, he did not know what the conditions were. This time he was offered an oral contract without any reference to conditions, and he accepted the offer in good faith.

 Alert

...I doubt whether it is possible to spell out a course of dealing in his case. In all but one of the previous cases he had been acting on behalf of his employer in sending a different kind of goods and he did not know that the respondents always sought to insist on excluding liability for their own negligence. So it cannot be said that when he asked his agent to make a contract for him he knew that this or, indeed, any other special term would be included in it. ...

'The judicial task is not to discover the actual intentions of each party; it is to decide what each was reasonably entitled to conclude from the attitude of the other' (*Gloag on Contract*, 2nd ed., p.7).

In this case I do not think that either party was reasonably bound or entitled to conclude from the attitude of the other, as known to him, that these conditions were intended by the other party to be part of this contract. ...

In order for terms to be incorporated by course of dealing, there must be a consistent course of dealing. The evidence failed to establish a consistent course of dealing because, although on some occasions Mr McSporran had been asked to sign the risk note, there were other occasions when he had not been. The House of Lords held that there was no consistent course of dealing and therefore the respondents could not rely on their exclusion clause in the risk note.

LORD DEVLIN

The fact that a man has made a contract in the same form 99 times (let alone three or four times which are here alleged) will not of itself affect the hundredth contract in which the form is not used. Previous dealings are relevant only if they prove knowledge of the terms, actual and not constructive, and assent to them. If a term is not expressed in a contract, there is only one other way in which it can come into it and that is by implication. No implication can be made against a party of a term which was unknown to him. …Without knowledge there is nothing.

Lord Devlin said that previous dealings were only relevant if they proved actual knowledge of the terms and assent to them. In other words, it was a subjective test, questioning whether the person actually knew of the terms. This view, however, was not shared by the other judges and was rejected by the House of Lords in *Henry Kendall Ltd v William Lillico Ltd* [1969] 2 AC 31. In *Henry Kendall*, the parties entered into three to four oral contracts per month over a period of three years for the sale of poultry feeding mixture. Each transaction was then evidenced by a 'sold note' which contained terms – the buyers had never read the term in question. The House of Lords held that the conditions in the sold notes were incorporated into the contract because, by continuing business (ie buying more feeding mixture), the defendants proved their assent to the incorporation of the terms. The key issue was not, therefore, whether they had knowledge of the terms, rather, the fact that they had not objected to the terms would have led the seller to believe that they were assenting to them. Consequently, the terms were incorporated.

11.1.3.4 Regular

Hollier v Rambler Motors (AMC) Ltd [1972] 2 QB 71

Panel: Salmon and Stamp LJJ and Latey J

Facts: While Mr Hollier's car was at the defendants' garage, it was damaged by a fire caused by the defendants' negligence. The defendants had repaired Mr Hollier's car on three or four occasions over a period of five years. On at least two of the occasions, Mr Hollier had signed a form but had not read it. He was therefore unaware of a clause in the form which stated: 'The Company is not responsible for damage caused by fire to customer's cars on the premises'. The defendants sought to rely on it.

LORD JUSTICE SALMON

I will deal first of all with the point as to whether the clause relied on by the defendants can properly be implied into this oral contract by reason of the course of dealing between the parties. Mr. Hollier, the plaintiff, had during the five years preceding March 1970 on many occasions bought spare parts from the defendants. As a rule, when he wanted the car to be repaired or serviced, he sent it elsewhere, but three or four times during those five years he had had the repair or service carried out by the defendants. It was the defendants' practice when they were doing repairs or servicing a motor car - but not when they were merely supplying spare parts - to have a form which is described as an 'invoice' signed by the customer. The form, which is before us, I need not read in detail, but it describes the work which is to be carried out and gives the price for carrying out the work. At the bottom of the form appear the words 'I hereby authorise the above repairs to be executed and agree to pay cash for same upon delivery of car to me. Customer's signature' – and the customer normally signed the form. Then immediately underneath the signature appear the words 'The company is not responsible for damage caused by fire to customer's cars on the premises. Customer's cars are driven by staff at owners' risk.' It is not clear whether on each of the three or four occasions when the plaintiff had work carried out he signed the form to which I have referred, but he did, at any rate, sign the form on two of those occasions... . The plaintiff did not read the forms on any occasion when he signed them, but there was nothing to have prevented him from doing so.

[Counsel for the defendants] says that there was a course of dealing which constituted the three or four occasions over five years - that is, on an average, not quite one dealing a year - from which it is to be implied that what he called 'the condition' at the bottom of the contract should be imported into the oral agreement made in the middle of March 1970. I am bound to say that, for my part, I do not know of any other case in which it has been decided or even argued that a term could be implied into an oral contract on the strength of a course of dealing (if it can be so called) which consisted at the most of three or four transactions over a period of five years. ...

Alert

It seems to me that if it was impossible to rely on a course of dealing in *McCutcheon v. David MacBrayne Led.* (*sic*), still less would it be possible to do so in this case, when the so-called course of dealing consisted only of three or four transactions in the course of five years.

While *McCutcheon v MacBrayne* set out that course of dealing must be consistent before it can incorporate a clause, this case adds that the course of dealing must also be regular. A course of dealing consisting of three to four transactions over five years was insufficient. (Note that the fact that Mr Hollier had never read the form which contained the clause was held to be immaterial because he had the opportunity to do so and he signed it on at least two occasions.)

11.2 Construction

At common law, in order to succeed in excluding the loss in question, the exemption clause, properly interpreted, must cover such loss; this is known as construction. The courts have developed specific rules to assist them with regulating the ability of the party in default to rely on the exemption clause. In general, a party seeking to rely on a clause must show that, on its plain meaning, it covers the particular incident in question. Ambiguous terms must be construed *contra proferentem* ie against the party seeking to rely on the term.

11.2.1   Contra Proferentem

Houghton v Trafalgar Insurance Co Ltd [1954] 1 QB 247

Panel: Somervell, Denning and Romer LJJ

Facts: A car carrying six passengers was involved in an accident. The car insurance policy was with the defendant insurance company. It excluded liability for damage 'caused or arising whilst the car is conveying any load in excess of that for which it was constructed'. As there was only seating space for five passengers, the defendants denied liability claiming that six passengers was an excess load and therefore fell within the exclusion clause.

LORD JUSTICE SOMERVELL

If there is any ambiguity, since it is the defendants' clause, the ambiguity will be resolved in favour of the assured. In my opinion, the words relied on ... only clearly cover cases where there is a weight load specified in respect of the motor-vehicle, be it lorry or van. I agree that the earlier words in the clause obviously are applicable to an ordinary private car in respect of which there is no such specified weight load. But there was - and I think that it would have been inadmissible - no evidence whether this was a form which was used for lorries as well as for ordinary private motor-cars. I do not think that that matters. We have to construe the words in their ordinary meaning, and I think that those words only clearly cover the case which I have put. If that is right, they cannot avail the insurance company in the present case.

I would only add that the present suggestion of their application is, to me, a remarkable one. I think that it would need the plainest possible words if it were desired to exclude the insurance cover by reason of the fact that there was at the back one passenger more than the seating accommodation. ...

This judgment supports the view that the person responsible for including an exemption clause in the contract has the opportunity to make the wording clear and so should be the one to be deprived if there is any ambiguity. In this case, the clause was held to be ambiguous because it was not clear whether 'load in excess' referred to the weight or number of people the car was carrying. The defendants could not therefore rely on their exclusion clause. It is a good illustration of the effect of construing a term *contra proferentem*. The case of *Ailsa Craig Fishing Co. Ltd v Malvern Fishing Co. Ltd and Another* [1983] 1 WLR 964 demonstrates the difference in application of the rule to exclusion clauses as opposed to limitation clauses.

Ailsa Craig Fishing Co. Ltd. v Malvern Fishing Co Ltd and Another [1983] 1 WLR 964

Panel: Lord Wilberforce, Lord Elwyn-Jones, Lord Salmon, Lord Fraser of Tullybelton and Lord Lowry

Facts: The appellants, Ailsa Craig, were owners of a fishing vessel which sank while berthed at Aberdeen Harbour. While the ship sank, she damaged the vessel moored next to her, causing that one also to sink. The loss of both vessels was caused by breach of contract and negligence on the part of the respondents, Securicor, who had been contracted to provide security at the harbour. Clause 2(f) of this security contract purported to limit Securicor's liability to £1,000. The trial judge awarded damages of £55,000 but Securicor successfully appealed to the First Division of the Court of Session against this seeking to rely on the limitation clause. Ailsa Craig appealed to the House of Lords.

LORD WILBERFORCE

Whether a clause limiting liability is effective or not is a question of construction of that clause in the context of the contract as a whole. If it is to exclude liability for negligence, it must be most clearly and unambiguously expressed, and in such a contract as this, must be construed *contra proferentem*. … The relevant words must be given, if possible, their natural, plain meaning. Clauses of limitation are not regarded by the courts with the same hostility as clauses of exclusion: this is because they must be related to other contractual terms, in particular to the risks to which the defending party may be exposed, the remuneration which he receives, and possibly also the opportunity of the other party to insure.

LORD FRASER OF TULLYBELTON

The question whether Securicor's liability has been limited falls to be answered by construing the terms of the contract in accordance with the ordinary principles applicable to contracts of this kind. The argument for limitation depends upon certain special conditions attached to the contract prepared on behalf of Securicor and put forward in their interest. There is no doubt that such conditions must be construed strictly against the proferens, in this case Securicor, and that in order to be effective they must be 'most clearly and unambiguously expressed'... .

In my opinion these principles are not applicable in their full rigour when considering the effect of clauses merely limiting liability. Such clauses will of course be read *contra proferentem* and must be clearly expressed, but there is no reason why they should be judged by the specially exacting standards which are applied to exclusion and indemnity clauses. The reason for imposing such standards on these clauses is the inherent improbability that [t]he other party to a contract including such a clause intended to release the proferens from a liability that would otherwise fall upon him. But there is no such high degree of improbability that he would agree to a limitation of the liability of the proferens, especially when ... the potential losses that might be caused by the negligence of the proferens or its servants are so great in proportion to the sums that can reasonably be charged for the services contracted for. It is enough in the present case that the clause must be clear and unambiguous. ...

Having considered ... criticisms of clause (f) the question remains whether in its context it is sufficiently clear and unambiguous to receive effect in limiting the liability of Securicor for its own negligence or that of its employees. In my opinion it is. It applies to any liability 'whether under the express or implied terms of this contact, or at common law, or in any other way.' Liability at common law is undoubtedly wide enough to cover liability including the negligence of the proferens itself, so that even without relying on the final words 'any other way,' I am clearly of opinion that the negligence of Securicor is covered.

Lord Wilberforce makes the point that the courts do not look at limitation clauses with the same hostility as exclusion clauses. Lord Fraser agrees with this, stating that the *contra proferentem* rule should not be applied as strictly to limitation clauses as it would be to exclusion and indemnity clauses. This of course makes sense as an agreed limitation clause is more likely to accord with the true intentions of the parties.

In this case, it was held that the limitation clause 2(f) was sufficiently clear and therefore Securicor successfully limited their liability.

11.2.2 Excluding Liability for Negligence

The courts apply the *contra proferentem* rule with particular rigour when a party is attempting to exclude liability for his own negligence. These rules are set out in *Canada Steamship Lines v The King* [1952] AC 192.

Canada Steamship Lines v The King [1952] AC 192

Panel: Lord Porter, Lord Normand, Lord Morton of Henryton, Lord Asquith of Bishopstone and Lord Cohen

Facts: The Crown leased a freight shed to Canada Steamship Lines (the appellants). Clause 7 of the lease purported to exclude liability for any damage to the contents of the shed and clause 8 stated that the Crown would keep the shed in repair. A fire broke out, due to the negligence of the Crown's employees, which destroyed the shed and all of its contents. The Crown sought to rely on their exclusion clause.

LORD MORTON OF HENRYTON

Their Lordships think that the duty of a court in approaching the consideration of such clauses [exemption clauses] may be summarized as follows:-

(1) If the clause contains language which expressly exempts the person in whose favour it is made (hereafter called 'the proferens') from the

consequence of the negligence of his own servants, effect must be given to that provision. ...

(2) If there is no express reference to negligence, the court must consider whether the words used are wide enough, in their ordinary meaning, to cover negligence on the part of the servants of the proferens. If a doubt arises at this point, it must be resolved against the proferens... .

(3) If the words used are wide enough for the above purpose, the court must then consider whether 'the head of damage may be based on some ground other than that of negligence,' to quote again Lord Greene in ... [*Alderslade v Hendon Laundry Limited* [1945] K.B. 189, 192.] The 'other ground' must not be so fanciful or remote that the proferens cannot be supposed to have desired protection against it; but subject to this qualification, which is no doubt to be implied from Lord Greene's words, the existence of a possible head of damage other than that of negligence is fatal to the proferens even if the words used are prima facie wide enough to cover negligence on the part of his servants. ...

So far, clause 7 has been considered apart from clause 8, but these two clauses must be read together, according to the ordinary principles of construction. So reading them, it appears to their Lordships most unlikely that clause 7 was intended to protect the Crown from claims for damage resulting from the negligence of its servants in carrying out the very obligations which were imposed on the Crown by clause 8. ...

In this case, Lord Morton of Henryton set out a construction test that he considered was the correct approach for the court to take when ascertaining whether a clause exempts negligence liability. The first rule is that if a clause expressly mentions negligence then effect must be given to the clause. We know from later cases that this test is satisfied if a synonym for negligence is used instead but the safest option is to use the word 'negligence' expressly.

If the first rule is not satisfied, then the court should look at both the second and third. The second rule is that the court must consider whether the words are wide enough, in their ordinary meaning, to exempt negligence on the part of the party relying on the exemption clause. If any doubt arises, the wording must be construed against the party relying on the clause.

If the clause is wide enough, the court must then apply the third rule and consider whether the exemption clause may cover some other head of liability other than negligence. The alternative head of liability must not be too 'fanciful or remote'. If there is such a head of liability, the exemption clause will only operate to exclude or limit that liability and negligence will not be exempted.

White v John Warwick & Co Ltd [1953] 1 WLR 1285 provides a good example of a case in which there was an alternative head of liability; therefore, it was this alternative head of liability which was excluded, and not negligence.

White v John Warwick & Co Ltd [1953] 1 WLR 1285

Panel: Singleton, Denning and Morris LJJ

Facts: Mr White hired a tradesman's bike from the defendants. He was thrown off the bike and injured when the saddle tipped up. Clause 11 of the agreement provided that the defendants would not be liable for any: '[P]ersonal injuries to the riders of the machines hired...' Mr White brought an action claiming damages for personal injuries. In his claim he alleged two causes of action: (i) that the defendants were strictly liable under the Sale of Goods (Implied Terms) Act 1973 s 3 (re-enacted by the Sale of Goods Act 1979 s 14(2)) to supply a bike which was reasonably fit for the purpose for which it was required, and (ii) that the defendants were negligent in that they had not taken care to ensure the bike was in a proper working condition. Counsel for Mr White argued that, while the defendants might be able to rely on Clause 11 in respect of the breach of the strict duty to provide him with a bicycle which was reasonably fit for purpose, they could not exclude their liability for negligence.

LORD JUSTICE DENNING

In this type of case two principles are well settled. The first is that if a person desires to exempt himself from a liability which the common law imposes on him, he can only do so by a contract freely and deliberately entered into by the injured party in words that are clear beyond the possibility of misunderstanding. The second is: if there are two possible heads of liability on the part of defendant, one for negligence, and the other a strict liability, an exemption clause will be construed, so far as possible, as exempting the defendant only from his strict liability and not as relieving him from his liability for negligence.

Lord Justice Denning stated that when someone is liable not only for an act of negligence but also for breach of a strict contractual duty then the exclusion clause would not operate to exclude the negligence liability but would only exclude the strict liability instead.

In this case, it was held that Clause 11 protected the defendants from their strict contractual duty (to provide a bike which was reasonably fit for the purpose for which it was required) but it would not exempt them from their liability for negligence.

Link
See Poole's *Textbook on Contract Law* at 8.2.1 for an explanation of strict and qualified duties.

Alderslade v Hendon Laundry limited [1945] KB 189 provides an example of a case where negligence liability was the only plausible head.

Alderslade v Hendon Laundry limited [1945] KB 189

Panel: Lord Greene MR, Mackinnon LJ and Uthwatt J

Facts: Mr Alderslade left ten large handkerchiefs with the defendant laundry to be washed. They were never returned so Mr Alderslade bought some replacement ones and sought to claim back the expense. In their defence, the defendants relied on Condition 3 of the conditions on which the handkerchiefs had been accepted: 'The maximum amount allowed for lost or damaged articles is twenty times the charge made for laundering'. The defendants offered this amount to Mr Alderslade but he refused and brought an action against them as it was not nearly as much as he had spent replacing the lost handkerchiefs.

LORD GREENE MR

...Where the head of damage in respect of which limitation of liability is sought to be imposed by such a clause is one which rests on negligence and nothing else, the clause must be construed as extending to that head of damage, because it would otherwise lack subject-matter. Where, on the other hand, the head of damage may be based on some other ground than that of negligence, the general principle is that the clause must be confined in its application to loss occurring through that other cause, to the exclusion of loss arising through negligence. The reason is that if a contracting party wishes in such a case to limit his liability in respect of negligence, he must do so in clear terms in the absence of which the clause is construed as relating to a liability not based on negligence. ...

Alert

It was argued by counsel for the plaintiff that the clause must be construed in the present case so as to exclude loss by negligence... . It was said that the loss of a customer's property might take place for one of two reasons, namely, negligence and mere breach of contract, and that in the absence of clear words referring to negligence, loss through negligence cannot be taken to be covered by the clause. In my opinion that argument fails. It is necessary to analyse the legal relationship between the customer and the defendants. What I may call the hard core of the contract, the real thing to which the contract is directed, is the obligation of the defendants to launder. That is the primary obligation. It is the contractual obligation which must be performed according to its terms, and no question of taking due care enters into it. The defendants undertake, not to exercise due care in laundering the customer's goods, but to launder them, and if they fail to launder them it is no use their saying, 'We did our best, we exercised due care and took reasonable precautions, and we are very sorry if as a result the linen is not properly laundered.' That is the essence of the contract, and in addition there are certain ancillary obligations into which the defendants enter if they accept goods from a customer to be laundered. The first relates to the safe custody of the goods while they are in the possession of the defendants. The customer's goods may have to wait for a time in the laundry premises to be washed, and while they are so waiting there is an obligation to take care of them, but it is in my opinion not the obligation of an insurer but the obligation to take reasonable care for the protection of the goods. If while they are waiting to be washed in the laundry a thief, through no fault of the defendants, steals them, the defendants are not liable. The only way in which the defendants could be made liable for the loss of articles awaiting their turn to

Decipher
In fact, in light of the Supply of Goods and Services Act 1982 s 13, the obligation would be to provide the service with reasonable care and skill.

be washed would, I think, quite clearly be if it could be shown that they had been guilty of negligence in performing their duty to take care of the goods. That is one ancillary obligation which is inherent in a contract of this kind. Another relates to the delivery of the goods. The laundry company in most cases, and indeed in this case, make a practice of delivering the goods to the customer, and in the ordinary way the customer expects to receive that service. But what is the precise obligation of the laundry in respect of the return of the goods after the laundering has been completed? In my opinion it stands on the same footing as the other ancillary obligation that I have mentioned, namely, the obligation to take reasonable care in looking after and safeguarding the goods. It cannot I think be suggested that the obligation of the laundry company in the matter of returning the goods after they have been laundered is the obligation of an insurer. To say that they have undertaken by contract an absolute obligation to see that they are returned seems to me to go against common sense. Supposing the defendants are returning the goods by van to their customer and while the van is on its way a negligent driver of a lorry drives into it and overturns it with the result that it is set on fire and the goods destroyed. No action would lie by the customer for damages for the loss of those goods any more than it would lie against any ordinary transport undertaking which was not a common carrier. To hold otherwise would mean that in respect of that clearly ancillary service the defendants were undertaking an absolute obligation that the goods would, whatever happened, be returned to the customer. It seems to me that the only obligation on the defendants in the matter of returning the goods is to take reasonable care.

In the present case all that we know about the goods is that they are lost. There seems to me to be no case of lost goods in respect of which it would be necessary to limit liability, unless it be a case where the goods are lost by negligence. ...[I]f my view is right, the obligation of the defendants is an obligation to take reasonable care and nothing else. Therefore, the claim of a customer that the defendants are liable to him in respect of articles that have been lost must, I think, depend on the issue of due care on their part. If that be right, to construe this clause, so far as it relates to loss, in such a way as to exclude loss occasioned by lack of proper care, would be to leave the clause so far as loss is concerned - I say nothing about damage - without any content at all. The result is in my opinion is [sic] that the clause must be construed as applying to the case of loss through negligence. Therefore this appeal succeeds, and the appropriate reduction in damages must be made in the order.

Lord Greene MR stated that when the basis of liability lies in negligence only, an exemption clause must be construed to cover that negligence. In this case, the only obligation on the defendant laundry was to take reasonable care not to lose the handkerchiefs. Breach of a duty to take reasonable care is of course negligence so when they lost the handkerchiefs, their liability effectively rested in negligence only. If the clause did not apply to limit liability for negligence, it would be redundant or as Lord Greene MR states: 'lack subject matter'. The Court of Appeal therefore held that the defendant was able to rely on Condition 3.

Persimmon Homes Ltd v Ove Arup & Partners Ltd [2017] EWCA Civ 373.

Panel: Jackson LJ, Beatson LJ and Moylan LJ

Facts: The claimant Persimmon Homes Ltd claimed that the defendant engineers, Ove Arup & Partners Ltd, had negligently failed to identify and report on the presence of asbestos on a site the claimant was developing. The defendant relied on exclusion clauses in the contract, which were repeated using the same wording in associated warranties.

The exemption clauses and warranties were found in a section of the relevant contract headed "Professional indemnity insurance"; these provided that the defendant would maintain professional indemnity insurance of not less than £5 million per event. The relevant clauses stated that the defendant's liability for pollution and contamination would be limited to £5 million in the aggregate. The exclusion stated that:

"Liability for any claim in relation to asbestos is excluded."

The question of whether the exclusion clauses excluded liability for the claims was tried as a preliminary issue.

Held: The High Court found that the exclusion clauses did exclude liability for the claims, as the clauses represented an agreed allocation of risks between the parties. The High Court found that the meaning of the clauses was clear, and the courts should give effect to that meaning. The claimants appealed.

On appeal: dismissed.

The claimant relied on the *contra proferentem* rule and the *Canada Steamship* guidelines to argue that, even if the exclusion clauses were not limited to causing the spread of asbestos, they were not wide enough to exempt the defendant from liability. These arguments were rejected by the Court of Appeal.

The court commented that, when applying the *contra proferentem* rule has a very limited role when applied to commercial contracts, negotiated between parties of equal bargaining power. The court considered that the words used, commercial sense and the documentary and factual context should normally be enough to determine the meaning of a contract term. In this contract the court concluded that the meaning of the clauses was clear, and the *contra proferentem* rule had no impact.

Further, the court commented that since the decision in *Canada Steamship Lines v The King*, there had been a long running debate as to how to apply that decision to commercial contracts and the extent to which it was still good law. The court commented that, in commercial contracts, as far as the *Canada Steamship* rules still exist, they are now more relevant to indemnity clauses than exemption clauses

LORD JUSTICE JACKSON

.....Over the last 66 years there has been a long running debate about the effect of that passage and the extent to which it is still good law. In hindsight we can see that it is not satisfactory to deal with exemption clauses and indemnity clauses in one single compendious passage.

In recent years, and especially since the enactment of UCTA, the courts have softened their approach to both indemnity clauses and exemption clauses: see *Lictor Anstalt v MIR Steel UK* [2012] EWCA Civ 1397; [2013] 2 All ER (Comm) 54 at [31] to [34]. Although the present judgment is not the place for a general review of the law of contract, my impression is that, at any rate in commercial contracts, the *Canada Steamships* guidelines (in so far as they survive) are now more relevant to indemnity clauses than to exemption clauses.

As previously noted, the exemption clauses in the present case form part of the contractual arrangements concerning professional indemnity insurance. In clause 6 of the 2009 agreement and in clause 4 of the warranties, the parties agreed (a) what risks Arup would accept and insure against and (b) what risks Arup would not accept and would not insure against. Self-evidently, the fees which Arup charged and which the Consortium agreed to pay allowed for the cost of that professional indemnity insurance, even though that cost was not separately identified.

In my view, the canons of construction elucidated in the *Canada Steamships* line of cases are of very little assistance in the present case.

If I am wrong, however, and if Lord Morton's principles are applicable, the two exemptions clauses still exclude liability for the breaches of duty alleged in the particulars of claim. I reach that conclusion for the following reasons:

(i) The words of the two clauses in their ordinary meaning are wide enough to cover negligence by Arup in advising about the extent of asbestos on site.

(ii) It is not possible to think of any non-negligent ground of claim relating to asbestos which the parties might have had in mind. The suggested non-negligent breaches put forward by the claimants, namely breaches of various regulations, fall into Lord Morton's "fanciful or remote" category. The parties cannot sensibly have been agreeing that Arup's only liability in relation to asbestos would be for non-negligent breaches of those regulations.

Let me now draw the threads together. The meaning of the two exemption clauses is clear. Neither the *contra proferentem* rule nor the case law on exemption clauses can come to the rescue of the claimants. Clause 6.3 of the 2009 agreement and clause 4.3 of the warranties exclude liability for all the Consortium's pleaded claims in respect of asbestos. I therefore reject the third and fourth grounds of appeal.

If my Lords agree, this appeal will be dismissed.

There is a difference between excluding liability for your own negligence and agreeing to compensate another party for the consequences of its negligence. The guidelines were, he concluded, of very little assistance in the present case. But even if that was wrong, it did not help the claimant. There was no non-negligent ground of claim relating to asbestos that the parties might realistically have had in mind in agreeing the clause.

Further Reading

McKendrick, E., *Contract Law* (2017) 12th ed. Ch.9 and 11

12

Exemption Clauses II

Topic List

Introduction

Even if exemption clauses are deemed incorporated into the contract and capable of being construed in such a way that under common law they are effective, there are statutory controls in place which must also be considered. The Unfair Contract Terms Act 1977 (UCTA) renders many exemption clauses ineffective.

12.1 Unfair Contract Terms Act 1977

12.1.1 The question of reasonableness

***George Mitchell (Chesterhall) Ltd v Finney Lock Seeds Ltd* [1983] 2 AC 803**

Panel: Lord Diplock, Lord Scarman, Lord Roskill, Lord Bridge of Harwich and Lord Brightman

Statute: Unfair Contract Terms Act 1977 s 11

Facts: The respondents bought some Finney's Late Dutch Special cabbage seeds from the appellant seed merchants. The respondents had purchased seeds from the appellants for many years and were aware of the relevant conditions of sale. The conditions of sale were on the back of the invoice and limited liability to replacement of the goods or a refund of the purchase price. The respondents planted the seeds in 63 acres, but rather than being Finney's Late Dutch Special cabbage, they were autumn cabbage; the crop was commercially useless and had to be ploughed in. The seeds had cost £201.60 but the loss to the respondents was over £61,000. The appellants tried to rely on their limitation clause.

LORD BRIDGE OF HARWICH

This is the first time your Lordships' House has had to consider a modern statutory provision giving the court power to override contractual terms excluding or restricting liability, which depends on the court's view of what is 'fair and reasonable.'. ...[T]he several provisions of the Unfair Contract Terms Act 1977 which depend on 'the requirement of reasonableness,' defined in section 11 by reference to what is 'fair and reasonable,' albeit in a different context, are likely to come before the courts with increasing frequency. It may, therefore, be appropriate to consider how an original decision as to what is 'fair and reasonable' made in the application of any of these provisions should be approached by an appellate court. It would not be accurate to describe such a decision as an exercise of discretion. But a decision under any of the provisions referred to will have this in common with the exercise of a discretion, that, in having regard to the various matters to which ... section 11 of the Act of 1977 direct attention, the court must entertain a whole range of considerations, put them in the scales on one side or the other, and decide at the end of the day on which side the balance comes down. There will

Alert

sometimes be room for a legitimate difference of judicial opinion as to what the answer should be, where it will be impossible to say that one view is demonstrably wrong and the other demonstrably right. It must follow, in my view, that, when asked to review such a decision on appeal, the appellate court should treat the original decision with the utmost respect and refrain from interference with it unless satisfied that it proceeded upon some erroneous principle or was plainly and obviously wrong. ...

The decisive factor, however, appears from the evidence of four witnesses called for the appellants, two independent seedsmen, the chairman of the appellant company, and a director of a sister company (both being wholly-owned subsidiaries of the same parent). They said that it had always been their practice, unsuccessfully attempted in the instant case, to negotiate settlements of farmers' claims for damages in excess of the price of the seeds, if they thought that the claims were 'genuine' and 'justified.' This evidence indicated a clear recognition by seedsmen in general, and the appellants in particular, that reliance on the limitation of liability imposed by the relevant condition would not be fair or reasonable.

Two further factors, if more were needed, weight the scales in favour of the respondents. The supply of autumn, instead of winter, cabbage seeds was due to the negligence of the appellants' sister company. Irrespective of its quality, the autumn variety supplied could not, according to the appellants' own evidence, be grown commercially in East Lothian. Finally, as the trial judge found, seedsmen could insure against the risk of crop failure caused by supplying the wrong variety of seeds without materially increasing the price of seeds.

My Lords, even if I felt doubts about the statutory issue, I should not, for the reasons explained earlier, think it right to interfere with the unanimous original decision of that issue by the Court of Appeal. As it is, I feel no such doubts. If I were making the original decision, I should conclude without hesitation that it would not be fair or reasonable to allow the appellants to rely on the contractual limitation of their liability. ...

In his judgment, Lord Bridge gives guidance as to how the question of reasonableness raised in UCTA s 11 should be approached by the courts. He emphasises that it is a matter of weighing up a range of considerations and therefore whether an exemption clause is reasonable or not depends on a certain amount of judicial discretion. Lord Bridge recognises that this approach can lead to differences of judicial opinion but qualifies this by stating that if the question of reasonableness reaches an appellate court, the court should adhere to the original decision unless it is clearly wrong. In this case, he weighs up the considerations and finds in favour of the respondents, which is in line with the original decision.

Further Reading

McKendrick, E., *Contract Law* (2017). 12th ed. Ch.11

13

Misrepresentation I (Actionability)

Topic List

Introduction

A 'misrepresentation' is a false representation ie a false statement of fact (or law). It can be distinguished from a 'mere puff' (see *Dimmock v Hallett* (1866) LR 2 Ch App 21). It is also distinct from a term, which has been incorporated into the contract (see Chapter 8 'Terms of a Contract I' in your Contract Law Manual). Note that if the court decides that a representation is a term, and it is false, this will give rise to an action for both breach of contract and potentially for misrepresentation (if the misrepresentation is actionable).

In order for a misrepresentation to be sued upon i.e. for it to be 'actionable', it must have all the following characteristics: it must be unambiguous; false; a statement of fact; addressed to the party misled; an inducement to contract and the cause of loss. All elements of this definition must be present for an action in misrepresentation to succeed.

The effect of a misrepresentation is, subject to limitations, to make the contract voidable but not void. In order to avoid the contract, the wronged party must take action to rescind the contract.

This chapter will examine the elements of an actionable misrepresentation; Misrepresentation II considers the different categories of misrepresentation and the remedies available under those categories.

13.1 Elements of an Actionable Misrepresentation

13.1.1 Unambiguous

The representation must be unambiguous. The representor will not be liable if the representee has placed an unreasonable construction on the representation.

McInerny v Lloyd's Bank Ltd [1974] 1 Lloyd's Rep 246

Panel: Lord Denning MR, Megaw and James LJJ

Facts: McInerny agreed to sell companies to Mackay on condition that Mackay's bank would provide a guarantee. The bank wrote to Mackay stating that it was unable to provide a guarantee and that Mackay could only pay using an irrevocable credit which should be sufficient for McInerny's purposes. Mackay forwarded this letter to McInerny who entered into the contract with Mackay. Mackay subsequently defaulted and McInerny sued Mackay's bank, Lloyds, on the basis that their letter was a negligent misrepresentation which suggested that they were willing to step in and pay Mackay's liabilities. The court held that McInerny had placed his own interpretation on the letter which on a reasonable construction did not give the assurances that McInerny had asked for.

LORD DENNING MR

In considering whether a statement was made negligently, its meaning should be considered in the sense in which the maker intended it, or in which he knew or ought to have known the recipient would understand it. In saying this I have in mind the rule in regard to statements said to be made fraudulently, see *Akerhielm v. De Mare*, [1959] A.C. 789; *Gross v. Lewis Hillman Limited*, [1970] 1 Ch. 449; and I apply it suitably in regard to statements said to be made negligently. In most cases, of course, the meaning is plain enough. It means the same both to the maker and to the recipient. If the maker should deny its plain meaning, he would not be believed. But, where the meaning is not clear, it should be given the meaning intended by the maker, or which he knew or ought to have known the recipient would put upon it....

 Alert

Turning now to the present case, it seems to me that the bank manager's reply of Oct. 5, 1967, can be criticized for its drafting, but not for the substance of what it said. It was so ill-drafted that Mr. McInerny thought it gave the assurance that was asked for. But a careful reading of it shows, I think, that the bank manager gave no such assurance. He never accepted the 'irrevocable instructions' of Mr. Mackay. He never promised to apply each year to the Bank of England for exchange control permission. He never agreed to guarantee any of the instalments falling due on Sept. 30, 1969, 1970 and 1971. Those were the assurances which were requested of him. He gave none of them. Nor did he intend to give any of them. True his letter was so drafted that Mr. McInerny interpreted it as giving them. But the bank manager is not responsible for that interpretation. Nor did the bank manager know that Mr. McInerny would put that interpretation on it. Nor ought he to have known it.

13.1.2 False

The statement must be false. It will not be false if it is substantially correct.

Avon Insurance plc v Swire Fraser Ltd [2000] 1 All ER (Comm) 573

Panel: Rix J

Facts: The claimants were insurers of a large number of Lloyd's names. The defendants were insurance brokers authorised by the claimants to issue stop loss policies to Lloyd's names on their behalf. The claimants were shown and taken through a presentation document which had been prepared by the defendants and which described how the underwriting of the stop loss policies would be undertaken. The claimants argued that the presentation document contained the misrepresentation that each risk, that is to say each of the names who proposed to take out an insurance policy from the claimants, would be individually assessed by the leading underwriter, Mr Victor Broad. It was claimed that Mr Broad did not in fact assess each name and that the defendants were negligent (but not dishonest) in representing that he would.

It was held that the statement made by the defendants was 'substantially true' and therefore not a misrepresentation.

MR JUSTICE RIX

…Thus a representation may be true without being entirely correct, provided it is substantially correct and the difference between what is represented and what is actually correct would not have been likely to induce a reasonable person in the position of the claimants to enter into the contracts….

13.1.3 Statement of Fact

A representation must be a statement of fact. A statement of fact can be made by words or by conduct and is not a statement of opinion or of future intention. Silence cannot be a statement of fact.

A statement of law is a statement of fact.

13.1.4 Is Conduct a Statement of Fact?

Conduct may be treated as a statement of fact.

Gordon and Teixeira v Selico Ltd. and Select Managements Ltd (1986) 18 **HLR 219**

Panel: Slade and Woolf LJJ and Sir Denys Buckley

Facts: An independent contractor employed by the defendant was told to 'sort out' some dry rot in a flat. The contractor covered up the dry rot rather than eradicating it. The claimants purchased the flat and then discovered the concealed dry rot. It was held that in concealing the dry rot, the independent contractor had knowingly made a false representation to the claimants.

LORD JUSTICE SLADE

In these circumstances, the learned judge [the first instance judge, Goulding J] felt able to dispose of the issue of deceit quite shortly. Having found as a fact that Mr. Azzam was guilty of the dishonest cover-up alleged, he continued:

'Is it, however, actionable at law? The law must be careful not to run ahead of popular morality by stigmatising as fraudulent every trivial act designed to make buildings or goods more readily saleable, even if a highly scrupulous person might consider it dishonest. But it is to my mind quite a different matter for an intending vendor to hide so sinister and menacing a defect as active dry rot. The case is fairly comparable, in my view, with the concealment of cracks indicating the settlement of foundations, considered in *Ridge v. Crawley*, (1958) 172 E.G. 637 and, in the Court of Appeal, (1959) 173 E.G. 959. There the plaintiff relied on a combination of words and conduct, but I believe it to be the law that conduct alone can constitute a fraudulent misrepresentation. (See *Horsfall v. Thomas 1 H. and C.* 90, and *Smith v. Hughes* L.R. 6 Q.B. 597). In my judgment the concealment of dry rot by Mr.

Alert

Azzam was a knowingly false representation that Flat C did not suffer from dry rot, which was intended to deceive purchasers, and did deceive the plaintiffs to their detriment. I am satisfied that the plaintiffs would not have entered into a contract or accepted the lease had they known there was dry rot inside Flat C.'

Spice Girls Limited v Aprilia World Service BV [2002] EMLR 27

Panel: Chadwick LJ, Sir Andrew Morritt VC and Rix LJ

Facts: Aprilia sponsored a Spice Girls concert tour in return for promotional work by the band. Geri, one of the group, had told the others that she intended to leave prior to the conclusion of the promotional work. The trial judge held that there had been a misrepresentation by conduct in that all the girls took part in a photo shoot. The Court of Appeal agreed but on a wider basis; namely that the claimants had, by their conduct, conveyed to the defendants the impression that all members of the group were committed to the contract with the defendants and that none of them had an existing, declared intention, to leave the group.

LORD JUSTICE CHADWICK V-C (delivering the judgment of the court)

On 4th May 1998 the second instalment of £150,000 was paid by AWS to SGL. On the same day the commercial shoot, postponed from 25th April, took place in London and was attended by all five Spice Girls. Arden J [the first instance judge] concluded:

'Given that the benefits of the commercial shoot could not be enjoyed by Aprilia if one of the Spice Girls left the group before March 1999, participation in the shoot in my judgment carried with it a representation by conduct that SGL did not know, and had no reasonable ground to believe, that any of the Spice Girls had an existing declared intention to leave the group before that date. Nothing was done to correct that representation which was a continuing representation. It was on the facts found material to Aprilia's decision to enter into the agreement that none of the Spice Girls was intending to leave in the contract period. Accordingly, SGL had a duty to correct its misrepresentation. What I have said about the commercial shoot must equally apply to other promotional material depicting the five Spice Girls which was intended to be used at any time during the period of the agreement.' ...

In our view the judge was entitled to conclude that the representations, express or implied, in both the fax of 30th March 1998, which continued, and participation in the commercial shoot on 4th May 1998 were material inducements to AWS to enter into the Agreement on 6th May 1998. ... For all these reasons, while we consider that the judge took too narrow a view as to what representations were made and when, we do not accept the submissions for SGL that s.2(1) Misrepresentation Act 1967 is inapplicable. Subject to proof of damage, we conclude that SGL is liable to AWS under that provision.

13.1.5 Is Opinion a Statement of Fact?

A statement of opinion is not a statement of fact if honestly offered by a layman who has no greater or expert knowledge than the addressee.

Bisset v Wilkinson [1927] AC 177

Panel: Viscount Dunedin, Lord Atkinson, Lord Phillimore, Lord Carson, and Lord Merrivale

Facts: The vendor of a sheep farm told the purchaser that, in his judgment, the land could carry 2,000 sheep. This turned out to be untrue. The court held that the purchaser could not set the purchase aside as the statement was not a false statement of fact but a statement of opinion which he honestly held *and* the purchaser knew that the vendor had never farmed sheep on the farm and was therefore expressing an opinion.

LORD MERRIVALE

In the present case, ... the material facts of the transaction, the knowledge of the parties respectively, and their relative positions, the words of representation used, and the actual condition of the subject-matter spoken of, are relevant to the two inquiries necessary to be made: What was the meaning of the representation? Was it true?

In ascertaining what meaning was conveyed to the minds of the now respondents by the appellant's statement as to the two thousand sheep, the most material fact to be remembered is that, as both parties were aware, the appellant had not and, so far as appears, no other person had at any time carried on sheep-farming upon the unit of land in question. That land as a distinct holding had never constituted a sheep-farm. The two blocks comprised in it differed substantially in character. Hogan's block was described by one of the respondents' witnesses as 'better land.' 'It might carry,' he said, 'one sheep or perhaps two or even three sheep to the acre.' He estimated the carrying capacity of the land generally as little more than half a sheep to the acre. And Hogan's land had been allowed to deteriorate during several years before the respondents purchased. As was said by Sim J.: 'In ordinary circumstances, any statement made by an owner who has been occupying his own farm as to its carrying capacity would be regarded as a statement of fact. .... This, however, is not such a case. The defendants knew all about Hogan's block and knew also what sheep the farm was carrying when they inspected it. In these circumstances .... the defendants were not justified in regarding anything said by the plaintiff as to the carrying capacity as being anything more than an expression of his opinion on the subject.' In this view of the matter their Lordships concur.

Whether the appellant honestly and in fact held the opinion which he stated remained to be considered. This involved examination of the history and condition of the property. If a reasonable man with the appellant's knowledge could not have come to the conclusion he stated, the description of that conclusion as an opinion would not necessarily protect him against rescission

 Alert

for misrepresentation. But what was actually the capacity in competent hands of the land the respondents purchased had never been, and never was, practically ascertained.

Where the opinion is given by one with greater knowledge and is one that could not have been reasonably held, it may be treated as a statement of fact

 Alert

Smith v Land and House Property Corporation (1885) LR 28 Ch D 7

Panel: Baggallay, Bowen and Fry LJJ

Facts: This was a contract for the sale of a hotel. The owners of the hotel described the present lessee, a Mr Fleck, as 'a most desirable tenant'. In fact, Mr Fleck was in arrears and had to be pursued regularly for payment of his rent. The purchasers agreed to buy for £4,700 but before the sale was completed Mr Fleck went into liquidation. The purchasers refused to complete on the sale. The plaintiffs sued for specific performance. The chairman of the purchasers was orally examined, and deposed most positively, that the company would not have bought but for the representation in the particulars that Mr Fleck was a most desirable tenant. Mr Justice Denman held that there was a material misrepresentation and that the contract had been entered into in reliance upon it. He accordingly dismissed the action, and on a counter-claim by the defendants, rescinded the contract.

LORD JUSTICE BOWEN

In considering whether there was a misrepresentation, I will first deal with the argument that the particulars only contain a statement of opinion about the tenant. It is material to observe that it is often fallaciously assumed that a statement of opinion cannot involve the statement of a fact. In a case where the facts are equally well known to both parties, what one of them says to the other is frequently nothing but an expression of opinion. The statement of such opinion is in a sense a statement of a fact, about the condition of the man's own mind, but only of an irrelevant fact, for it is of no consequence what the opinion is. But if the facts are not equally known to both sides, then a statement of opinion by the one who knows the facts best involves very often a statement of a material fact, for he impliedly states that he knows facts which justify his opinion.

 Alert

Where the opinion is given by an expert it may be treated as a statement of fact.

Esso Petroleum Co. Ltd. v Mardon [1976] QB 801

Panel: Lord Denning MR, Ormrod and Shaw LJJ

Facts: Mardon took a lease of a petrol station after being assured by an Esso representative that the annual throughput would be 200,000 gallons of petrol per year. In the meantime, the local planning authority refused permission for the pumps to front on to the main street and the station had to be built back to front. The estimate of the Esso representative, made on the basis of original plans, was not revised in the light of the changed planning. The estimated gallonage was never reached and, as a result, the petrol station was uneconomic. Consequently, Mardon was unable to repay the sums due to Esso on the loan. Esso sued for possession of the petrol station and Mardon counter-claimed on the basis of negligent misrepresentation. Esso argued that, as there had not previously been a petrol station on that site, the estimated throughput was merely a statement of opinion. It was held by the Court of Appeal that the statement as to the maximum sales was one of fact. Esso had substantial skill and expertise in estimating the potential sales of a petrol station in a specific location. The case could be distinguished from that of *Bisset v Wilkinson* where the land had never been used as a sheep farm and both parties were equally able to form an opinion as to its carrying capacity.

LORD DENNING MR

if a man, who has or professes to have special knowledge or skill, makes a representation by virtue thereof to another - be it advice, information or opinion - with the intention of inducing him to enter into a contract with him, he is under a duty to use reasonable care to see that the representation is correct, and that the advice, information or opinion is reliable. If he negligently gives unsound advice or misleading information or expresses an erroneous opinion, and thereby induces the other side to enter into a contract with him, he is liable in damages. This proposition is in line with what I said in *Candler v. Crane, Christmas & Co.* [1951] 2 K.B. 164, 179-180, which was approved by the majority of the Privy Council in *Mutual Life and Citizens' Assurance Co. Ltd. v. Evatt* [1971] A.C. 793. and the judges of the Commonwealth have shown themselves quite ready to apply *Hedley Byrne* [1964] A.C. 465, between contracting parties. ...

Applying this principle, it is plain that Esso professed to have - and did in fact have - special knowledge or skill in estimating the throughput of a filling station. They made the representation - they forecast a throughput of 200,000 gallons - intending to induce Mr. Mardon to enter into a tenancy on the faith of it. They made it negligently. It was a 'fatal error.' and thereby induced Mr. Mardon to enter into a contract of tenancy that was disastrous to him. For this misrepresentation they are liable in damages.

13.1.6 Is Intention a Statement of Fact?

A statement of fact is a statement about something that exists or an action that has happened. A statement of future intention cannot therefore be a statement of fact.

Beattie v Ebury (1871-72) LR 7 Ch App 777

Panel: Mellish and James LJJ

Facts: Three directors of a railway company opened, on behalf of the company, an account with a bank, and sent a letter signed by the three as directors requesting the bank to honour cheques signed by two of the directors and countersigned by the secretary. The directors then proceeded to draw cheques on the account until it was substantially overdrawn. The bank claimed against the directors personally as the account could not satisfy the debt. It was held that the statements in the letter given by the directors were not guarantees but mere statements of intention and therefore there was no misrepresentation.

LORD JUSTICE MELLISH

I am not quite certain whether the Vice-Chancellor did not think that there was a representation that the company would pay, so as to make them liable upon the misrepresentation simply because they have not paid. I do not say that with certainty, for after reading his judgment I am not quite clear what the ground was on which he really proceeded. If he did proceed on that ground, I should remark that there is a clear difference between a misrepresentation in point of fact, a representation that something exists at that moment which does not exist, and a representation that something will be done in the future. Of course, a representation that something will be done in the future cannot either be true or false at the moment it is made, and although you may call it a representation, if it is anything, it is a contract or promise. The directors cannot be liable on the ground that the company have made default, and have not paid the amount, unless according to the true construction of this document it amounts to a guarantee. It is perfectly plain that it does not amount to a guarantee, and moreover I think it perfectly plain that the Union Bank never considered it to amount to a guarantee, for when they wanted a guarantee from the directors (and for a very considerable part of the sum they did require the guarantee of the directors), they asked them to give a separate guarantee, which shews that unquestionably they never relied on this document as a guarantee.

 Alert

A representor may change his mind without having to inform the original addressee whom he told of his future intention.

Wales v Wadham [1977] 1 WLR 199

Panel: Tudor Evans J

Facts: A husband left his wife to live with another woman. Prior to, and during, divorce proceedings the wife asserted that she would not remarry after the divorce as she had a conscientious objection to remarriage. The divorce settlement was negotiated on the more generous basis that she would remain single. Prior to the conclusion of the settlement the wife agreed to marry another and did not communicate this change of intention to the husband. The husband sought to rescind the agreement on the ground of his wife's non-disclosure of her intention to remarry. The court upheld the settlement, and dismissed the husband's claim. The wife had not misrepresented her then current intention when she told her husband that she would not remarry; and non-disclosure of her change of intention did not avoid the agreement.

MR JUSTICE TUDOR EVANS

I must now consider the husband's submission that the wife's statement to him that she would not remarry amounts to a misrepresentation which induced him to enter the contract. It is the husband's case that had he been aware of the true facts he would never have made the offer to pay £13,000. This was intended to commute his liability for periodical payments, a liability which, in the event, he would never have had. In order to prove a fraudulent misrepresentation, the husband must show that the wife made a statement of fact which was false to her knowledge or that she was reckless as to its truth, and that such misrepresentation was intended to, and did cause the husband to enter the contract. It is submitted that even if the wife's statement that she would never remarry was honestly held, she was under a duty to tell the husband of her changed circumstances, but that she failed to do so. Counsel has referred me to *With v. O'Flanagan* [1936] Ch. 575, in the Court of Appeal. … Lord Wright M.R., at p. 582, quoted, with approval, observations of Fry J. in *Davies v. London & Provincial Marine Insurance Co.* (1878) 8 Ch.D. 469, 475, where he said:

'So, again, if a statement has been made which is true at the time, but which during the course of negotiations becomes untrue, then the person who knows that it has become untrue is under an obligation to disclose to the other the changed circumstances.'

The representations in both of these cases related to existing fact and not to a statement of intention in relation to future conduct. A statement of intention is not a representation of existing fact, unless the person making it does not honestly hold the intention he is expressing, in which case there is a misrepresentation of fact in relation to the state of that person's mind. That does not arise on the facts as I have found them. On the facts of this case, the wife made an honest statement of her intention which was not a representation of fact, and I can find no basis for holding that she was under a duty in the law of contract to tell the husband of her change of mind.

 Alert

Note however that if a statement of future intention is made by a representor who at the time he makes it knows that he cannot or will not keep to it, he misrepresents his existing intention. This may be treated as a statement of fact.

Edgington v Fitzmaurice (1885) LR 29 Ch D 459

Panel: Cotton, Bowen and Fry LJJ

Facts: A company issued a prospectus inviting the public to purchase debentures in the company. The prospectus said that the money would be used to improve the company's premises and expand its business. This can be seen as a statement of future intention. However, at the time this statement was made, the directors of the company knew that the money would not be used in this way and would be used to pay off existing company debts. Lord Justice Bowen noted that a representation as to the future would not normally form the basis of an action for misrepresentation but also said, 'The state of a man's mind is as much a fact as the state of his digestion'.

LORD JUSTICE BOWEN

This is an action for deceit, in which the Plaintiff complains that he was induced to take certain debentures by the misrepresentations of the Defendants, and that he sustained damage thereby. The loss which the Plaintiff sustained is not disputed. In order to sustain his action he must first prove that there was a statement as to facts which was false; and secondly, that it was false to the knowledge of the Defendants, or that they made it not caring whether it was true or false. ...

The alleged misrepresentations were three. First, it was said that the prospectus contained an implied allegation that the mortgage for £21,500 could not be called in at once, but was payable by instalments. I think that upon a fair construction of the prospectus it does so allege; and therefore that the prospectus must be taken to have contained an untrue statement on that point; but it does not appear to me clear that the statement was fraudulently made by the Defendants. It is therefore immaterial to consider whether the Plaintiff was induced to act as he did by that statement.

Secondly, it is said that the prospectus contains an implied allegation that there was no other mortgage affecting the property except the mortgage stated therein. I think there was such an implied allegation, but I think it is not brought home to the Defendants that it was made dishonestly; accordingly, although the Plaintiff may have been damnified by the weight which he gave to the allegation, he cannot rely on it in this action: for in an action of deceit the Plaintiff must prove dishonesty. Therefore if the case had rested on these two allegations alone, I think it would be too uncertain to entitle the Plaintiff to succeed.

But when we come to the third alleged misstatement I feel that the Plaintiff's case is made out. I mean the statement of the objects for which the money was to be raised. These were stated to be to complete the alterations and additions to the buildings, to purchase horses and vans, and to develop the supply of fish. A mere suggestion of possible purposes to which a portion of the money might be applied would not have formed a basis for an action of deceit. There must be a misstatement of an existing fact: but the state of a man's mind is as much a fact as the state of his digestion. It is true that it is very difficult to prove what the state of a man's mind at a particular time is, but if it can be ascertained it is as much a fact as anything else. A misrepresentation as to the state of a man's mind is, therefore, a misstatement of fact. Having applied as careful consideration to the evidence as I could, I have reluctantly come to the conclusion that the true objects of the Defendants in raising the money were not those stated in the circular. I will not go through the evidence, but looking only to the cross-examination of the Defendants, I am satisfied that the objects for which the loan was wanted

 Alert

were misstated by the Defendants, I will not say knowingly, but so recklessly as to be fraudulent in the eye of the law.

Then the question remains—Did this misstatement contribute to induce the Plaintiff to advance his money. Mr. Davey's argument has not convinced me that they did not. He contended that the Plaintiff admits that he would not have taken the debentures unless he had thought they would give him a charge on the property, and therefore he was induced to take them by his own mistake, and the misstatement in the circular was not material. But such misstatement was material if it was actively present to his mind when he decided to advance his money. The real question is, what was the state of the Plaintiff's mind, and if his mind was disturbed by the misstatement of the Defendants, and such disturbance was in part the cause of what he did, the mere fact of his also making a mistake himself could make no difference. ... Therefore I think that the statement is material, and that the Plaintiff would be unlike the rest of his race if he was not influenced by the statement of the objects for which the loan was required. The learned Judge in the Court below came to the conclusion that the misstatement did influence him, and I think he came to a right conclusion.

 Alert

13.1.7 Is Silence a Statement of Fact?

Mere silence is not a statement of fact. There is no duty to disclose material facts.

Keates v The Earl of Cadogan (1851) 10 Common Bench Reports 591

Panel: Jervis CJ

Facts: The defendant let a house to the plaintiff knowing that the plaintiff wanted it for immediate occupation. The defendant did not tell the plaintiff that the house was uninhabitable and the plaintiff made no enquiries concerning the state of the property. It was held that in the absence of fraud, the defendant was under no implied duty to disclose the state of the house.

JERVIS CJ

I think this declaration does not disclose a sufficient cause of action. It is not pretended that there was any warranty, express or implied, that the house was fit for immediate occupation: but it is said, that, because the defendant knew that the plaintiff wanted it for immediate occupation, and knew that it was in an unfit and dangerous state, and did not disclose that fact to the plaintiff, an action of deceit will lie. The declaration does not allege that the defendant made any misrepresentation, or that he had reason to suppose that the plaintiff would not do what any man in his senses would do, viz. make proper investigation, and satisfy himself as to the condition of the house before he entered upon the occupation of it. There is nothing amounting to deceit: it was a mere ordinary transaction of letting and hiring. The defendant is entitled to judgment.

The question before the court in each case will first be to define what the duty of disclosure was on the facts.

Sykes v Taylor-Rose [2004] 2 P& CR 30

Panel: Peter Gibson and Mantell LJJ and Sir William Aldous

Facts: The respondents purchased a house in 1998. They subsequently became aware that a horrific murder had been committed at the property in the early 1980s. Their solicitor advised them that the vendor had been under no obligation to disclose the history of the property and that they would be under no such obligation when they came to sell it. They continued to live in the house for another 18 months and then sold it to the appellants for £83,000. Prior to the sale, the respondents completed a 'Seller's Property Information Form'. In response to question 13 'Is there any other information which you think the buyer may have a right to know?' the respondents answered 'No' having first consulted their solicitor. The sale was completed in December 2000 and in July 2001 the appellants saw a TV documentary about the house and the murder. The appellants moved out and put the house on the market, revealing the history of the house to potential buyers with the result that the house sold for £75,000 which the appellants contended was £25,000 below its market value. It was held that question 13 was confined to information which the purchaser *might be* entitled to know. If all that was needed was an honest answer, then there could be no breach of duty. Further, given that the respondents had acted on the advice of their solicitor, it could not be said that they had acted negligently.

SIR WILLIAM ALDOUS

The questions in the form were directed to the vendors. If the questions had required them to have reasonable grounds for their belief, difficult matters would arise as to what would amount to reasonable grounds for a belief in the variety of circumstances that could arise. Clearly vendors would, before answering the questions, need to seek professional advice. The answer 'no' would open up endless scope for dispute. In any case the question itself makes no reference to a requirement for the belief to be based upon reasonable grounds and (for reasons which I will give later) I can see no reason why such an obligation should be imported. The question is intended to be answered by persons with no legal training and its words should be given their normal and ordinary meaning. In my view the judge was correct. As there was no dispute that the answer to question 13 was honestly given, there was no misrepresentation.

… It was accepted in this court that there was no legal obligation upon the vendors to disclose the history of the property. That was the decision of the judge on the first issue. The words 'have a right to know' must limit the type of information that needs to be considered and seem to expand the general duty, which is agreed did not include a duty to disclose the circumstances of the murder. …

LORD JUSTICE PETER GIBSON

I feel a good deal of sympathy for the appellants. ... However, the question for this court is a dry question of law as to whether the respondents incurred a liability to the appellants in answering question 13 of the Seller's Property Information Form in the negative. The answer to that question cannot be affected by my sympathy for the appellants.

Because the *caveat emptor* rule can work harshly on purchasers, whose knowledge of material facts affecting the property they are purchasing is almost certain to be considerably less than that of the vendors, the practice of sending pre-contract enquiries has become standard and the scope of the enquiries has been extended over a period of time. It is for the buyer to decide what enquiries to raise and in what form. It cannot be doubted that a more specific and less subjective question going to the value of the property or to the ability of the purchaser to enjoy the property could have been asked. Unhappily, question 13 in the Law Society's form at that time (we are told that it is no longer in use) did allow the answer to be given in a way which only required, in my view, the vendor to answer the question honestly.

For the reasons given by Sir William Aldous, I too would hold that this court cannot interfere with the conclusion of the judge on the main issue in the light of his finding that the vendors were honest in answering that question.

13.1.8 Exceptions to the General Rule in *Keates v Cadogan*: Half Truth

It is a misrepresentation (ie a false statement of fact) to make statements which are true but which are misleading because they do not reveal the whole facts.

Dimmock v Hallett (1866-67) LR 2 Ch App 21

Panel: Turner and Cairns LJJ

Facts: A vendor of land told the purchaser that all the farms on the land were fully let, but omitted to inform him that the tenants had given notice to quit. This was held to be a misrepresentation by half truth.

LORD JUSTICE CAIRNS

The purchaser further grounds his case on misrepresentations in the particulars. Some of the instances alleged appear to me to be unimportant. Thus I think that a mere general statement that land is fertile and improvable, whereas part of it has been abandoned as useless, cannot, except in extreme cases—as, for instance, where a considerable part is covered with water, or otherwise irreclaimable—be considered such a misrepresentation as to entitle a purchaser to be discharged. In the present case, I think the statement is to be looked at as a mere flourishing description by an auctioneer. ...

Lord Justice Cairns went on to consider other untruthful representations as to the amount of rent that various properties were worth and continued:

I am of opinion, therefore, that the particulars contain representations which were untrue, and calculated materially to increase the apparent value of the property. The Court requires good faith in conditions of sale, and looks strictly at the statements contained in them.

Again, Creyke's Hundreds, containing 115 acres, is described as let to R. Hickson, a yearly Lady Day tenant, at £130 per annum; and another farm, Misson Springs, containing 131 acres, is mentioned as let to Wigglesworth, a yearly Lady Day tenant, at £160 per annum. Now the sale took place on the 25th of January, 1866, and there is no reference made in the particulars to the fact that each of these tenants had given a notice to quit, which would expire at Lady Day. The purchaser, therefore, would be led to suppose, as to these farms, that he was purchasing with continuing tenancies at fixed rents, whereas he would, in fact, have to find tenants immediately after the completion of his purchase. I refer particularly to this, because as to some of the other farms it is stated in the particulars that the tenants had given notice to quit; so that the purchaser must have been led to believe that the tenants of Creyke's Hundreds and Misson Springs were continuing tenants. This again, as it seems to me, is a material misrepresentation.

The vendor contends that these are only errors, entitling the purchaser to compensation under the thirteenth condition of sale. I think that such a condition applies to accidental slips, but not to a case like the present, where, though I do not mean to impute actual fraud, there is what, in the view of a Court of equity, amounts to fraud—a misrepresentation calculated materially to mislead a purchaser.

13.1.8.1 Exceptions to the General Rule in *Keates v Cadogan*: Continuing Representation

A statement of fact which is true but which, prior to entering into the contract becomes false, may be a misrepresentation if the representor does not correct it and allows the other party to enter into the contract on the basis of the original representation.

With v O'Flanagan [1936] Ch 575

Panel: Lord Wright MR, Romer LJ and Clauson J

Facts: A doctor was selling his medical practice. At the beginning of negotiations he stated that the income of the practice was at a certain level but during the course of negotiations he became ill and the income had fallen to virtually nothing by the time of the sale. He did not reveal this fact. It was held that by remaining silent he had made a continuing representation, holding out his original statement as still being true. There was a duty to disclose the change in circumstances and the consequent change in income to the representee.

LORD WRIGHT MR

As to the law, which has been challenged, I want to say this. I take the law to be as it was stated by Fry J. in *Davies v. London and Provincial Marine Insurance Co.* where it is perhaps most fully expressed. ... The learned judge points out

'Where parties are contracting with one another, each may, unless there be a duty to disclose, observe silence even in regard to facts which he believes would be operative upon the mind of the other; and it rests upon those who say that there was a duty to disclose, to shew that the duty existed.'

Then the learned judge points out that in many cases there is such a duty as between persons in a confidential or a fiduciary relationship where the preexisting relationship involves the duty of entire disclosure. Then his Lordship says:

'In the next place, there are certain contracts which have been called contracts uberrimae fidei where, from their nature, the Court requires disclosure from one of the contracting parties.'

The learned judge refers to contracts of partnership and marine insurance. Then he goes on:

'Again, in ordinary contracts the duty may arise from circumstances which occur during the negotiation. Thus, for instance, if one of the negotiating parties has made a statement which is false in fact, but which he believes to be true and which is material to the contract, and during the course of the negotiation he discovers the falsity of that statement, he is under an obligation to correct his erroneous statement; although if he had said nothing he very likely might have been entitled to hold his tongue throughout.' ...

Lord Wright MR then goes on to refer to other authorities which state the same principle:

...The matter, however, may be put in another way though with the same effect, and that is on the ground that a representation made as a matter of inducement to enter into a contract is to be treated as a continuing representation. That view of the position was put in *Smith v. Kay* by Lord Cranworth. He says of a representation made in negotiation some time before the date of a contract: 'It is a continuing representation. The representation does not end for ever when the representation is once made; it continues on. ...'

Lord Wright MR refers to another case which also raises the question of what type of misrepresentation a continuing representation may be:

The underlying principle is also stated again in a slightly different application by Lord Blackburn in *Brownlie v. Campbell*. I need only quote a very short passage. Lord Blackburn says:

'when a statement or representation has been made in the *bonâ fide* belief that it is true, and the party who has made it afterwards comes to find out that it is untrue, and discovers what he should have said, he can no longer honestly keep up that silence on the subject after that has come to his knowledge, thereby allowing the other party to go on, and still more, inducing him to go on, upon a statement which was honestly made at the time when it was made, but which he has not now retracted when he has become aware that it can be no longer honestly persevered in. ...'

The learned Lord goes on to say that would be fraud, though nowadays the Court is more reluctant to use the word 'fraud' and would not generally use the word 'fraud' in that connection because the failure to disclose, though wrong and a breach of duty, may be due to inadvertence or a failure to realize that the duty rests upon the party who has made the representation not to leave the other party under an error when the representation has become falsified by a change of circumstances.

13.1.9 Addressed to the Party Misled

The misrepresentation must be addressed to the party misled, either by the misrepresentor themselves or through a third party.

Commercial Banking Co of Sydney v RH Brown & Co [1972] 2 Lloyd's Rep 360

Panel: Barwick CJ, Mctiernan, Menzies, Owen and Gibbs JJ

Facts: The plaintiffs agreed to sell wool to a buyer.   Just before delivery of the wool, the plaintiffs heard rumours that the buyer was in financial trouble. The plaintiffs asked their bank manager to make enquiries about the buyer which he did by contacting the buyer's bank. In response to his enquiry, the buyers' bank (the defendants), replied, *inter alia*, that '[The buyer] is capably managed by directors well experienced in the wool trade…had always met its engagements, is trading satisfactorily and we consider that it would be safe for its trade engagements generally.' The plaintiffs' bank manager passed on this response to the plaintiffs.   Accordingly, the plaintiffs delivered the wool but then received no payment. The plaintiffs brought an action against the buyer's bank for fraudulent misrepresentation. The trial judge found that the opinion was not honestly held by the buyer's bank manager who knew that the plaintiffs' bank had asked for the opinion on behalf of a customer likely to enter into trade relations with the buyer, that it was likely to be relied upon by the plaintiffs; and that it was given with the intent to deceive.   The judgment was upheld on appeal by the High Court of Australia.

BARWICK CJ

A person who makes a false and fraudulent misrepresentation is only liable to the persons to whom it is made, i.e., to the persons whom it is intended should act upon it: *Peek v. Gurney*, (1873) L.R. 6 H.L. 377. It is not necessary for liability that the misrepresentation should be made directly, it can be made to one, to be passed on to another; it is not necessary that it should be made to a particular person; it can be made to a group to which the plaintiff belongs so that the plaintiff is one of those intended to be deceived. The representation must, however, in one way or another, be made to the plaintiff to induce him to act upon it. Here the Perth manager of the defendant's bank was aware that the manager of the Bank of New South Wales at Cranbrook did not want the information which was sought merely for the purposes of the bank itself. The information was obviously sought for a customer or customers of the bank proposing to deal with Wool Exporters Pty. Ltd. and, it appears to me, that it was open to his Honour to hold, as he did, that it was supplied to be passed on to such customers.

13.1.10 Materiality and Inducement to Enter the Contract

In order to be actionable, the representation must have caused (induced) the representee to enter into the contract. The misrepresentation has to play a 'real and substantial' part in inducing the misrepresentee to enter the contract (*JEB Fasteners v Mark Bloom* [1983] 1 All ER ER 583). However, the misrepresentation need not be the only reason as to why the claimant entered into the contract (see *Edgington v Fitzmaurice* (1885) LR 29 Ch D 459 above).

When considering the issue of inducement, the first question for the court is whether the representation was material. The test for materiality is an objective one: did the statement relate to an issue that would have influenced a reasonable man?

Pan Atlantic Insurance Co. Ltd. and Another Appellants v Pine Top Insurance Co. Ltd. Respondents [1995] 1 AC 501

Panel: Lord Templeman, Lord Goff of Chieveley, Lord Mustill, Lord Slynn of Hadley and Lord Lloyd of Berwick

Facts: This is a complex case involving renewal of reinsurance contracts. The main issue before the courts was that of non-disclosure by the plaintiffs of certain losses they had sustained when applying for renewal of a reinsurance policy. The question was whether the losses were 'material circumstances', non-disclosure of which was a misrepresentation of the plaintiff's position such as to render the renewed reinsurance policy voidable.

LORD MUSTILL

The judgment is very specific to the specialist area of insurance law. However, the statement that may be extrapolated from it to form the general objective test for materiality comes from Lord Mustill's speech and his conclusion that:

The test was whether the information would have influenced a reasonable insurer to decline the risk or to have stipulated for a higher premium.

If the statement is found to be objectively material, inducement will generally be presumed. This is a rebuttable presumption. This was confirmed in the case of *Smith v Chadwick* (1881-82) LR 20 Ch D 27 (later affirmed by the House of Lords (1883-84) L.R. 9 App. Cas. 187) The Court of Appeal judgment is more instructive as the main principles to arise from this case are discussed in greater detail.

Smith v Chadwick (1881-82) LR 20 Ch D 27

Panel: Sir George Jessell MR, Cotton and Lindley LJJ

Facts: A prospectus contained a false statement that a certain important person was on the board of directors. The plaintiff admitted under cross-examination that this had not influenced him in entering into the contract as he had never heard of that person.

SIR GEORGE JESSELL MR

...The real questions which we have to try are, whether there were representations false in fact; whether if any of those representations were false in fact, they were false to the knowledge of the Defendants, or recklessly made by them; whether, if there were any such, they were material to induce the Plaintiff to enter into the contract.

Now, without repeating at full length what I have said in a recent case, I think the law on this subject is clear. A man may issue a prospectus, or make any other statement to induce another to enter into a contract, believing that his statement is true, and not intending to deceive; but he may through carelessness have made statements which are not true, and which he ought to have known were not true, and if he does so he is liable in an action for deceit; he cannot be allowed to escape merely because he had good intentions, and did not intend to defraud. Again, on the question of the materiality of the statement, if the Court sees on the face of it that it is of such a nature as would induce a person to enter into the contract, or would tend to induce him to do so, or that it would be a part of the inducement, to enter into the contract, the inference is, if he entered into the contract, that he acted on the inducement so held out, and you want no evidence that he did so act; but even then you may shew that in fact he did not so act in one of two ways, either by shewing that he knew the truth before he entered into the contract, and therefore, could not rely on the mis-statements; or else by shewing that he avowedly did not rely upon them, whether he knew the facts or not. He may by contract have bound himself not to rely upon them, that is to take the matter at his own risk whether they were true or false (which was the conclusion to which the House of Lords came in the recent case of *Brownlie v. Campbell*, or he may state that he did not rely upon them in the witness-box, which I think is so in one instance here. But unless it is shewn in one way or the other that he did not rely on the statement the inference follows.

If the statement is found *not* to be objectively material, it is presumed that the statement did *not* induce the contract. This is a rebuttable presumption.

Museprime Properties Ltd. v Adhill Properties Ltd. (1991) 61 P & CR 111

Panel: Scott J

Facts: A parcel of property comprising several let properties was sold at auction. The auction particulars identified the rents payable and at the auction, the auctioneers read out a statement that notices had been served and the tenants had made offers of new rent all of which had been rejected by the freeholders. The plaintiff made a successful bid of £490,000, signed the contract and paid a deposit of £49,000 believing that all the rents were still negotiable. It subsequently became clear that the notices had each specified a rent and that no effective counter-notices had been served within the month provided by the lease so that agreement on the rents must be deemed to have been reached. The plaintiff purchasers refused to complete on the sale. The defendants purported to terminate the contract and also to forfeit the deposit. The properties were re-sold at a price £110,000 less than the £490,000. The plaintiff claimed the right to rescind based on misrepresentation. It was held that the representations on which the plaintiff relied were misrepresentations which were material in that they induced the plaintiff to enter into the contract and, at the time when the defendant purported to terminate the contract, the plaintiff was entitled to rescind for misrepresentation. This was so even if it was unreasonable of the plaintiff to suppose that he could negotiate higher rents for the properties, putting the onus of proof upon him to satisfy the court that the misrepresentations had induced him to enter into the contract, as he had satisfied the court on this matter.

MR JUSTICE SCOTT

Accordingly, in my judgment, the representations on which the plaintiff relies were misrepresentations. Mr. Primost, as a final fling by way of defence, contended that the representations, even if misrepresentations, were not material ones. ...

A representation is material, in my opinion, if it is something that induces the person to whom it is made, whether solely or in conjunction with other inducements, to contract on the terms on which he does contract. ...

In our view any misrepresentation which induces a person to enter into a contract should be a ground for rescission of that contract. If the misrepresentation would have induced a reasonable person to enter into the contract then the court will, as we have seen, presume that the representee was so induced and the onus will be on the representor to show that the representee did not rely on the misrepresentation either wholly or in part. If, however, the misrepresentation would not have induced a reasonable person to contract, the onus will be on the representee to show that the misrepresentation induced him to act as he did. But these considerations relate to the onus of proof. To disguise them under the cloak of materiality is misleading and unnecessary.

 Alert

If the representee was not aware of the misrepresentation it will not have induced the contract.

Horsfall v Thomas (1862) 1 Hurlstone and Coltman 158 ER 813

Panel: Bramwell and Pollock JJ

Facts: The claimant purchased a gun from the defendant which blew apart after six shots had been fired. The vendor had fraudulently concealed the defect by inserting a metal plug into the weak spot in the gun. However, the buyer had not inspected the gun prior to the purchase. The case was dismissed. As the purchaser did not inspect the gun or form any opinion as to whether or not it was sound, the concealment did not affect him. Without doubt there was a misrepresentation but it did not induce the purchaser to enter into the contract.

MR JUSTICE BRAMWELL

This was an action by the drawer against the acceptor of a bill of exchange: and there was a plea that the bill was obtained by the fraud of the plaintiffs. The facts, opened by the defendant's counsel and partly proved (so far as is necessary to refer to them), were these: The plaintiffs contracted with the defendant to make for him a gun, which he was to pay for by two bills of exchange, one at six, the other at twelve months' date. The gun was made, and delivered at Woolwich in pursuance of the defendant's directions, but he made no examination of it. The plaintiff drew on him the bills of exchange, one of which was paid, and on the other this action is brought. According to the opening of the defendant's counsel (and it may be assumed, for the purpose of this decision), there was such a defect in the gun as would have justified the defendant, had he known it, in refusing to accept the gun. Further, that the plaintiffs or their workmen had done something to the gun which would conceal the defect from any person who did not carefully inspect it. The gun was received by the defendant, and fired several times. At first it answered extremely well, but afterwards, as it was said, in consequence of the defect, it burst and became worthless.

… One matter relied on by the defendant (and which struck me forcibly on the application to me at Chambers to stay the execution) was, that the plaintiffs or their workmen had done something to the gun which concealed the defect in it; and had it turned out, upon the defendant's inspection of the gun, that what was done to it was done for the express purpose of concealing, and did in fact conceal, the defect from him; there might have been evidence of a fraudulent intent. But the defendant never examined the gun, and therefore it is impossible that an attempt to conceal the defect could have had any operation on his mind or conduct.

 Alert

13.1.11　　Investigation and Inducement

If the representee did not rely on the statement but relied instead on some other factor, it will not have induced the contract e.g. where the representee chooses to test the validity of the representor's statement by making his own investigations.

John Attwood v Robert Small (1838) VI Clark & Finnelly 232

Panel: The Earl of Devon, Lord Cottenham, Lord Brougham, Lord Lyndhurst and Lord Wynford

Facts: The vendor of a mine made widely exaggerated statements about its earning capacity. The intending purchaser did not believe the glowing reports made by the vendor and therefore sent his own agents to make an independent report. The agents produced a similarly glowing report to that of the vendor. The mine then turned out to be virtually worthless and the purchaser brought a claim maintaining that the prospects of the mine had been misrepresented to him. The claim was dismissed. The purchaser had not relied on the statement of the vendor but had been induced to purchase the mine on the strength of his own agent's report. The fact that the agent had failed to discover the truth did not make the seller liable.

THE EARL OF DEVON

In this case the purchasers having doubts as to the accuracy of the representations made to them, and prudently resolving to examine for themselves, go to the spot where the works were carried on and where the books were kept. ... Accordingly it appears that the members of the deputation did occupy several hours in examining and comparing those papers with the books, and did certify such examination by their signatures; if they did not examine them thoroughly, the fault was their own. If, after they were told that no regular furnace books were kept of late years—an important part of the case,—they did not call for and expect such books or accounts as were in fact kept for the carrying on of the business, the fault was their own; in such case they lost sight altogether of the purpose for which they went down to Corngreaves, for they might have received the deputation papers in London just as well as in Staffordshire [the location of the mine to be purchased]. If on the other hand they did examine and test those accounts by comparison with the documents in existence, but found they did not give a satisfactory or sufficient view of the present state of the works, then the fault was equally their own, in reporting to their constituents [employers] that they were satisfied, and in proceeding to complete this purchase upon the ground of such satisfaction. The only answer to this part of the case appears to be that James or Edwards (for the evidence is put in that way), the agents of Attwood, made a statement as to the yields of the then present time, which was false in fact, and misled the deputation. ...

LORD BROUGHAM

… My Lords, when we apply to this case the principles which I stated at the outset, we find the facts are wanting; we find there is no misrepresentation which gave rise to the contract. We find that the purchasers did not rely upon the representation, but said, we will inquire ourselves …

From 6 June 1825, downwards, they constantly proceeded upon the plan of satisfying themselves, first by sending their agents, then by going down themselves, then by inquiring themselves, then even afterwards by sending other agents to inquire, and those agents reporting that the representation was true, and that those parties finding by their own inquiries that the agents had reported accurately, and that the representation was corroborated by the result of the inquiry, and that even when their own interest, when everything in the commercial world was down, when shares were falling, when money was not to be had, when they were asking time for a prolongation of the term of payment to Mr Attwood, and when it was their interest to discover a flaw in the contract, they then inquire again and send a new agent to inquire, Mr Foster, an engineer, and they state to him their own opinion to be in favour of Mr Attwood's representations; and Mr Foster, in answer as late as 26 April, less than a month before the bill was put upon the file, reports in favour of Mr Attwood's representations.

Such being the facts, even if no observation arose as to the delay, as to the adoption and affirmance of the contract, purging it of all objections which might be made, and supposing that they had come in time, instead of delaying so many months; then I ask myself this question, In these circumstances have these parties a right to be released from their contract by the interposition of a Court of Equity, according to those principles which I have stated? When I ask myself that question upon which alone my judgment must turn, I am bound to say No …

Is there a duty to investigate a representation?

Redgrave v Hurd (1881) 20 Ch D 1

Panel: Sir George Jessel MR, Baggallay and Lush LJJ

Facts: The plaintiff, a solicitor, offered his business and property for part sale. The defendant replied and had two interviews. He was told the business was bringing in approximately £3,400 per year. The defendant read the summaries of the accounts and saw only £200. He asked where the rest was. The plaintiff provided letters and papers as evidence of other work done. Once the deal was done the defendant put down £100. The defendant then found that the practice was worthless and refused to complete. The plaintiff sued for specific performance and the defendant claimed rescission on the basis of misrepresentation. The Court of Appeal held that the misrepresentation was material and calculated to induce the contract. Even though the representee was unable to prove that he had not relied on the statement this was not enough to prove that he had. If a material representation calculated to induce has been made, then the inference of law is that it did so induce and only positive proof that the representee had not relied on the statement would refute the inference of inducement.

SIR GEORGE JESSEL MR

There is another proposition of law of very great importance which I think it is necessary for me to state, because, with great deference to the very learned Judge from whom this appeal comes, I think it is not quite accurately stated in his judgment. If a man is induced to enter into a contract by a false representation it is not a sufficient answer to him to say, 'If you had used due diligence you would have found out that the statement was untrue. You had the means afforded you of discovering its falsity, and did not choose to avail yourself of them.' I take it to be a settled doctrine of equity, not only as regards specific performance but also as regards rescission that this is not an answer unless there is such delay as constitutes a defence under the Statute of Limitations. ... Nothing can be plainer, I take it, on the authorities in equity than that the effect of false representation is not got rid of on the ground that the person to whom it was made has been guilty of negligence. One of the most familiar instances in modern times is where men issue a prospectus in which they make false statements of the contracts made before the formation of a company, and then say that the contracts themselves may be inspected at the offices of the solicitors. It has always been held that those who accepted those false statements as true were not deprived of their remedy merely because they neglected to go and look at the contracts. ...

Alert

It has been apparently supposed by the learned Judge in the Court below that the case of *Attwood v. Small* conflicts with that proposition. He says this: 'He inquired into it to a certain extent, and if he did that carelessly and inefficiently it is his own fault. As in *Attwood v. Small*, those directors and agents of the company who made ineffectual inquiry into the business which was to be sold to the company were nevertheless held by their investigation to have bound the company, so here, I think, the Defendant who made a cursory investigation into the position of things on the 17th of February must be taken to have accepted the statements which were in those papers.' I think that those remarks are inaccurate in law, and are not borne out by the case to which the learned Judge referred. ...

Sir George Jessel MR then goes on to discuss *Attwood v Small*. He explains that *Attwood v Small* is different on the facts from *Redgrave v Hurd* in that the plaintiffs in *Attwood v Small* did not rely on the statements made to them but enquired into them for themselves:

I therefore confine myself for this purpose to the opinions of the three Lords who decided the case [*Attwood v Small*] in favour of the Appellants. The first opinion is that of Earl Devon, who had been a Master in Chancery, and although of course his opinion is entitled to great respect, yet I do not attach so much importance to it as I do to that of Lord Cottenham. His Lordship says: ...: 'The whole course of the proceeding from its commencement to its close tends to shew that the purchasers did not rely upon any statements made to them, but resolved to examine and judge for themselves.' Now, that is a good ground if borne out by the evidence. It is a different ground from that taken by the other Lords, but it cannot be objected to in point of law. ...

Is it reasonable for the representee to check the validity of the statements made?

Smith Respondent v Eric S. Bush Appellants Harris and Another Appellants v Wyre Forest District Council and Another Respondents [1990] 1 AC 831

Panel: Lord Keith of Kinkel, Lord Brandon of Oakbrook, Lord Templeman, Lord Griffiths and Lord Jauncey of Tullichettle

Facts: The plaintiff, Smith, applied for a mortgage. The defendant carried out the valuation on behalf of the mortgage company. Smith signed a form which contained a clause stating that neither the mortgage provider nor the defendant warranted that the valuation would be accurate and that there was no acceptance of responsibility. The valuation stated that no essential repairs were required. This was untrue. Smith sued the defendant for negligence. It was held that a duty of care was owed by the defendant to the prospective purchaser.

LORD GRIFFITHS

I believe that it is impossible to draw up an exhaustive list of the factors that must be taken into account when a judge is faced with this very difficult decision. Nevertheless, the following matters should, in my view, always be considered.

1. Were the parties of equal bargaining power. If the court is dealing with a one-off situation between parties of equal bargaining power the requirement of reasonableness would be more easily discharged than in a case such as the present where the disclaimer is imposed upon the purchaser who has no effective power to object.

2. In the case of advice would it have been reasonably practicable to obtain the advice from an alternative source taking into account considerations of costs and time. In the present case it is urged on behalf of the surveyor that it would have been easy for the purchaser to have obtained his own report on the condition of the house, to which the purchaser replies, that he would then be required to pay twice for the same advice and that people buying at the bottom end of the market, many of whom will be young first-time buyers, are likely to be under considerable financial pressure without the money to go paying twice for the same service. ...

 Alert

Lord Griffiths then went on to consider two further factors for consideration. The first of these was the difficulty of the task (and concluded a valuation is 'fairly elementary'). The final element he thought to be relevant was the practical consequences of allowing the surveyor's liability to be excluded (and concluded that it would be 'unlikely to cause significant hardship' for the surveyor but would be 'a financial catastrophe' for the purchaser). As can be seen from all of the above, the concern here is to protect the ordinary purchaser without professional expertise. Lord Griffiths goes on:

> ... It must, however, be remembered that this is a decision in respect of a dwelling house of modest value in which it is widely recognised by surveyors that purchasers are in fact relying on their care and skill. It will obviously be of general application in broadly similar circumstances. But I expressly reserve my position in respect of valuations of quite different types of property for mortgage purposes, such as industrial property, large blocks of flats or very expensive houses. In such cases it may well be that the general expectation of the behaviour of the purchaser is quite different. With very large sums of money at stake prudence would seem to demand that the purchaser obtain his own structural survey to guide him in his purchase and, in such circumstances with very much larger sums of money at stake, it may be reasonable for the surveyors valuing on behalf of those who are providing the finance either to exclude or limit their liability to the purchaser.

Note that if the representee has partly relied on the representation and partly on their own investigation, they may still be able to prove inducement, as in the case of *Edgington v Fitzmaurice* (1885) LR 29 Ch D 459 where Bowen LJ said:

> The real question is, what was the state of the Plaintiff's mind, and if his mind was disturbed by the misstatement of the Defendants, and such disturbance was in part the cause of what he did, the mere fact of his also making a mistake himself could make no difference.

 Alert

Any investigation carried out by the misrepresentee will not be taken into account by the court where the misrepresentation is proven to be fraudulent.

S. Pearson & Son Ltd v Dublin Corporation [1907] AC 351

Panel: Lord Loreburn LC, Earl of Halsbury, Lord Ashbourne, Lord Macnaghten, Lord James of Hereford, Lord Robertson, Lord Atkinson and Lord Collins

Facts: The appellants brought an action of deceit against the defendants, Dublin Corporation, claiming damages for false representations as to the position, dimensions and foundations of a wall, whereby the appellants were compelled to execute more costly works than would otherwise have been required. The plans, drawings and specifications were prepared by engineers employed by the corporation. The first instance judge, Palles CB, refused to leave any question to the jury, and entered judgment for the respondents on the ground that the contractors were bound by a clause by their contract to verify for themselves all the information given in the plans and other documents. The King's Bench Division reversed the decision of Palles CB, and the Court of Appeal reversed that decision and restored the decision of

Palles CB. On appeal from the Court of Appeal it was held by the House of Lords that the clause in the contract was only valid where both parties were dealing honestly which was not the case here.

LORD LOREBURN LC

The plaintiffs' case is that they were induced to enter into a Contract for the construction of certain sewage works by statements made by and on behalf of the defendants as to the existence to a depth of nine feet below ordnance datum of an old wall. Undoubtedly evidence was adduced at the trial from which the jury might, if they thought right, conclude that the plaintiffs were so induced by statements made on behalf of the defendants. Also, there was evidence for the jury that those statements were made either with a knowledge of their falsity, or (which is the same thing) with a reckless indifference whether they were true or false, on the part of the engineers employed by the defendants to make the plans which were submitted to plaintiffs as the basis of the tender. And had the case rested there I gather that the Chief Baron would have left the case to the jury, and that the learned judges who subsequently had this litigation before them would have approved this course.

But another feature of the case was considered fatal to the plaintiffs' claim. The contract contained clauses, which I need not cite at length, to the effect that the contractors must not rely on any representation made in plans or elsewhere, but must ascertain and judge of the facts for themselves. And, therefore, the Chief Baron withdrew the case from the jury. As I understand it, the view he held, in substance confirmed by the Court of Appeal, was that the plaintiffs, so forewarned, had no right to rely on any representation, and could not be heard to say they were induced by statements on which by contract they were not to rely. Or, at all events, it was said that the defendants, being themselves innocent, are protected by such clauses against the consequence of contractors acting on false statements made by defendants' agents, however fraudulent those agents might be.

Now it seems clear that no one can escape liability for his own fraudulent statements by inserting in a contract a clause that the other party shall not rely upon them. I will not say that a man himself innocent may not under any circumstances, however peculiar, guard himself by apt and express clauses from liability for the fraud of his own agents. It suffices to say that in my opinion the clauses before us do not admit of such a construction. They contemplate honesty on both sides and protect only against honest mistakes. The principal and the agent are one, and it does not signify which of them made the incriminated statement or which of them possessed the guilty knowledge.

 Alert

Further Reading

Koh, P., (2008). *Some issues in misrepresentation*. Journal of Business Law. 2008, 2, 123-138

Peel, E., 2008. Chitty on Contracts. 30th ed. Sweet & Maxwell. Ch.2. Vol.1– General Principles, Part 2 – Formation of Contract, Chapter 6– Misrepresentation, Sections 1–5

McKendrick, E., *Contract Law* (2017) 12th ed. Ch.13

14

Misrepresentation II (Categories & Remedies)

Topic List

1. Categories of Misrepresentation
2. Remedies
3. Rescission
4. Indemnity
5. Damages

Introduction

Misrepresentation II will examine the different categories of misrepresentation and the remedies available under those categories.

14.1 Categories of Misrepresentation

Prior to the introduction of the Misrepresentation Act 1967 ('MA 67') only two common law categories of misrepresentation were recognised: fraudulent and innocent. The MA 67 has brought in statutory claims for negligent and innocent misrepresentation under s 2(1), (2). There is also the option of a tortious claim in negligent misstatement at common law.

The definitions of each of the above categories are discussed below.

14.1.1 Fraudulent Misrepresentation

The definition of fraudulent misrepresentation was made by Lord Herschell in *Derry v Peek* (1889) LR 14 App Cas 337 in the House of Lords.

Derry v Peek (1889) LR 14 App Cas 337

Panel: Lord Halsbury LC, Lord Watson, Lord Bramwell, Lord Fitzgerald and Lord Herschell

Facts: A tramway company was empowered by a special Act of Parliament to operate certain tramways by using animal power. The Act further provided that, with the consent of the Board of Trade, mechanical power might be used. The directors of the company, wishing to raise more capital, included the following statement in a prospectus: '...[T]he company has the right to use steam or mechanical motive power instead of horses, and it is fully expected that by means of this a considerable saving will result...' The plaintiff, Peek, relying on this representation, bought shares. The company was later wound up because the Board of Trade refused to allow the use of mechanical power over the whole of the company's tramway. Peek contended that there was fraud. It was held that the false statement in the prospectus was not fraudulent.

LORD HERSCHELL

'This action is one which is commonly called an action of deceit, a mere common law action.' This is the description of it given by Cotton L.J. in delivering judgment.

...In the Court below Cotton L.J. said: 'What in my opinion is a correct statement of the law is this, that where a man makes a statement to be acted upon by others which is false, and which is known by him to be false, or is made by him recklessly, or without care whether it is true or false, that is, without any reasonable ground for believing it to be true, he is liable in an action of deceit at the suit of anyone to whom it was addressed or anyone of the class to whom it was addressed and who was materially induced by the misstatement to do an act to his prejudice.' About much that is here stated there cannot, I think, be two opinions.

The above encapsulates the definition of fraudulent misrepresentation: knowingly, without belief or recklessly. In the following, Lord Herschell pre-empts the MA 67 s 2(1) and the statutory claim in negligent misrepresentation with his discussion of 'reasonable grounds' for belief. It took nearly another hundred years for this to be codified by statute.

But when the learned Lord Justice speaks of a statement made recklessly or without care whether it is true or false, *that is* without any reasonable ground for believing it to be true, I find myself, with all respect, unable to agree that these are convertible expressions. To make a statement careless whether it be true or false, and therefore without any real belief in its truth, appears to me to be an essentially different thing from making, through want of care, a false statement, which is nevertheless honestly believed to be true. And it is surely conceivable that a man may believe that what he states is the fact, though he has been so wanting in care that the Court may think that there were no sufficient grounds to warrant his belief. I shall have to consider hereafter whether the want of reasonable ground for believing the statement made is sufficient to support an action of deceit. I am only concerned for the moment to point out that it does not follow that it is so, because there is authority for saying that a statement made recklessly, without caring whether it be true or false, affords sufficient foundation for such an action.

... I may state at once that, in my opinion, without proof of fraud no action of deceit is maintainable. When I examine the cases which have been decided upon this branch of the law, I shall endeavour to shew that there is abundant authority to warrant this proposition. ... This renders a close and critical examination of the earlier authorities necessary.

The next issue that Lord Herschell considers is whether a fraudulent statement has to be made with the intention of defrauding the misrepresentee.

I may pass now to *Foster v. Charles.* It was there contended that the defendant was not liable, even though the representation he had made was false to his knowledge, because he had no intention of defrauding or injuring the plaintiff. This contention was not upheld by the Court, Tindal C.J. saying: 'It is fraud in law if a party makes representations which he knows to be false, and injury ensues, although the motives from which the representations proceeded may not have been bad.'...

Recklessness was defined in *Thomas Witter Ltd v TBP Industries Ltd* [1996] 2 All ER 573 as a 'flagrant disregard for the truth'.

Thomas Witter Ltd v TBP Industries Ltd [1996] 2 All ER 573

Panel: Jacob J

Facts: The defendant was a carpet manufacturer. The plaintiff wanted to buy the defendant's company. At a meeting the defendant gave the plaintiff figures which were handed to him by his accountant which were at best a rough approximation and which overestimated substantially the income of the company. The defendant was found to be negligent in that he had believed the figures that he stated to the plaintiff but had no reasonable grounds to do so. He was not however, so reckless as to have a total disregard for the truth. It was held that this was not a fraudulent misrepresentation.

MR JUSTICE JACOB

Mr Justice Jacob stated that for a misrepresentation to be considered fraudulent:

... It must be made with the intention that it should be acted on and it is, in fact, acted upon. Male fides are not a prerequisite for a fraudulent misrepresentation to be proven ... Recklessness is only evidence of fraud – not proof, unless it amounts to a flagrant disregard for the truth and so is also dishonest.

 Alert

14.1.2 Negligent Misrepresentation (Misrepresentation Act 1967)

Howard Marine and Dredging Co. Ltd. v A. Ogden & Sons (Excavations) Ltd. [1978] 2 WLR 515

Panel: Lord Denning MR, Bridge and Shaw LJJ

Statute: Misrepresentation Act 1967 s 2(1)

Facts: The defendants hired two barges from the claimants. The claimants told the defendants that the barges' capacity was 1600 tonnes when in fact it was 1055 tonnes. The figure had been derived from Lloyd's Register which was wrong. The Court of Appeal held that it was a negligent misrepresentation under MA 67 s 2(1). The true figures were in the ships' documents and the claimants had failed to show any 'objectively reasonable ground' for disregarding the figure in the documents and relying instead on the Register.

LORD JUSTICE BRIDGE

...Accordingly, in my judgment, Ogdens establish no claim against Howards in contract. But the remaining, and to my mind the more difficult, question raised in this appeal is whether Mr. O'Loughlin's undoubted misrepresentation gives rise to any liability in tort either under the provisions of the Misrepresentation Act 1967 or at common law for breach of a duty of care owed to Ogdens with respect to the accuracy of the information given. I will consider first the position under the statute. The Misrepresentation Act 1967, by section 2 (1), provides. ...

Lord Justice Bridge read out s 2(1) and continued:

The first question then is whether Howards would be liable in damages in respect of Mr. O'Loughlin's misrepresentation if it had been made fraudulently, that is to say, if he had known that it was untrue. An affirmative answer to that question is inescapable. The judge found in terms that what Mr. O'Loughlin said about the capacity of the barges was said with the object of getting the hire contract for Howards, in other words, with the intention that it should be acted on. This was clearly right. Equally clearly the misrepresentation was in fact acted on by Ogdens. It follows, therefore, on the plain language of the statute that, although there was no allegation of fraud, Howards must be liable unless they proved that Mr. O'Loughlin had reasonable ground to believe what he said about the barges' capacity.

Alert

It is unfortunate that the judge never directed his mind to the question whether Mr. O'Loughlin had any reasonable ground for his belief. The question he asked himself, in considering liability under the Misrepresentation Act 1967, was whether the innocent misrepresentation was negligent. He concluded that if Mr. O'Loughlin had given the inaccurate information in the course of the April telephone conversations he would have been negligent to do so but that in the circumstances obtaining at the Otley interview in July there was no negligence. I take it that he meant by this that on the earlier occasions the circumstances were such that he would have been under a duty to check the accuracy of his information, but on the later occasions he was exempt from any such duty. I appreciate the basis of this distinction, but it seems to me, with respect, quite irrelevant to any question of liability under the statute. If the representee proves a misrepresentation which, if fraudulent, would have sounded in damages, the onus passes immediately to the representor to prove that he had reasonable ground to believe the facts represented. In other words the liability of the representor does not depend upon his being under a duty of care the extent of which may vary according to the circumstances in which the representation is made. In the course of negotiations leading to a contract the statute imposes an absolute obligation not to state facts which the representor cannot prove he had reasonable ground to believe.

Alert

Although not specifically posing the question of whether he had reasonable ground for his belief, the judge made certain findings about Mr. O'Loughlin's state of mind. He said:

'Mr. O'Loughlin looked at the documents of the ships he was in charge of including HB2 and HB3's German documents. He is not a master of maritime German. He saw, but did not register, the deadweight figure of 1,055.135 tonnes. Being in the London office he went to the City and looked up Lloyd's Register. There he noted that the summer loading deadweight figure for B41 and B45, described as TM sand carriers, was 1,800 tonnes. This figure stayed in his mind. But it was one of Lloyd's Register's rare mistakes.'

...The question remains whether his [Mr O'Loughlin's] evidence, however benevolently viewed, is sufficient to show that he had an objectively reasonable ground to disregard the figure in the ship's documents and to prefer the Lloyd's Register figure. I think it is not. The fact that he was more interested in cubic capacity could not justify reliance on one figure of deadweight capacity in preference to another. The fact that the deadweight figure in the ship's documents was a freshwater figure was of no significance since, as he knew, the difference between freshwater and sea water deadweight capacity was minimal. Accordingly I conclude that Howards failed to prove that Mr. O'Loughlin had reasonable ground to believe the truth of his misrepresentation to Mr. Redpath.

14.1.3 Damages in lieu of Rescission

The remedy of damages in lieu of rescission is available only at the discretion of the court. Where damages in lieu of rescission are awarded, the damages awarded under MA 67 s 2(1) will be reduced to reflect those awarded under s 2(2).

Must there be an existing right to rescind for damages in lieu to be awarded?

Until recently, there was conflicting authority on this issue. In **Thomas Witter Ltd v TBP Industries Ltd.** [1996] 2 All ER 573 (for facts, see above) it was held that, as long as the right to rescind had existed at some point, then damages in lieu could be awarded under MA 67 s 2(2), even if that right had be lost. In **Government of Zanzibar v British Aerospace (Lancaster House) Ltd** [2000] 1 WLR 2333 it was held that the court did not have power to award damages in lieu under MA 67 s 2(2) if the right to rescind was no longer available.

The position has now been settled by the Court of Appeal.

Salt v Stratstone Specialist Ltd [2015] EWCA Civ 745

Panel: Longmore LJ, Patten LJ, Roth J

Statute: Misrepresentation Act 1967 s 2(2)

Facts: In 2007, Mr Salt purchased a Cadillac car from Stratstone for £21,895. Stratstone had described the car as brand new. After the purchase a number of defects emerged. In 2008, Salt tried to reject the car and asked for his money back. Stratstone refused. In 2009, Salt sued Stratstone, claiming that the car was not of merchantable quality and seeking damages. On disclosure it was discovered that the car was, in fact, two years old and had been involved in a collision. Salt amended his claim to make a claim for misrepresentation, and rescission of the contract. Stratstone argued that any right to rescind had been lost due to i) it being impossible to restore the parties to their previous position; and ii) lapse of time. Stratstone further argued that, because the right to rescind had been lost, no damages were payable in lieu of rescission under MA 67 s2(2). It was held that the parties could be restored to their previous positions, and that contract could be rescinded for misrepresentation (as the car could be returned). Further, it was held that an award of damages in lieu of rescission under MA 67 s 2(2) was only available if rescission was available (therefore approving the approach in Government of Zanzibar v British Aerospace).

LONGMORE LJ

This raises the much discussed question whether section 2(2) is available at all if there is a bar to rescission; it is a question on which there is a conflict of authority at first instance…

The point appears to be open at the level of the Court of Appeal. The words of the statute are "if it is claimed … that the contract ought to be or has been rescinded the court … may declare the contract subsisting and award damages in lieu of rescission". No doubt a claimant can be said to make a claim even if he is subsequently held not to be entitled to do so. But the words "in lieu of rescission" must, in my view, carry with them the implication that rescission is available (or was available at the time the contract was rescinded). If it is not (or was not available in law) because e.g. the contract has been affirmed, third party rights have intervened, an excessive time has elapsed or restitution has become impossible, rescission is not available and damages cannot be said to be awarded "in lieu of rescission".

14.1.4 Innocent Misrepresentation (Misrepresentation Act 1967)

As stated above, until 1967 at common law any misrepresentation which was not made fraudulently was automatically deemed to be innocent (see *Redgrave v Hurd in the previous chapter*). The definition of an innocent misrepresentation, now derived from the MA 67 s 2(1), is a statement made where the representor proves that not only did he believe that what he was saying was true but where he also proves that he had reasonable grounds for belief in the truth of his statement.

14.1.5 Negligent Misstatement at Common Law (Tort of Negligence)

Hedley Byrne v Heller & Partners [1964] AC 465

Facts: Hedley Byrne were advertising agents. They asked their bank to check a prospective client's (Easipower Ltd's) financial status. Heller & Partners were Easipower's bank and they replied 'without responsibility' that Easipower was 'considered good for its ordinary business engagements'. Hedley Byrne went ahead and booked advertising space on Easipower's behalf although the terms of the contract were that Hedley Byrne assumed liability for any default. Easipower then went into liquidation and Hedley Byrne sued Heller & Partners for negligence. It was held that the type of statement Heller & Partners had made to Hedley Byrne could give rise to an action in tort where a duty of care was owed due to a special relationship between the parties. The special relationship must be such that reasonable reliance by the wronged party on the special skill of the other was reasonably foreseeable and that there was proximity between the two. Note that damages will be assessed according to the 'reasonable foreseeablity' test in *The Wagon Mound* [1967] 1 AC 617. For further on this type of action see tort law.

14.2   Remedies

The positive remedies afforded in relation to misrepresentation are those of rescission, damages and indemnity, the exact combination of remedies being dependent upon the category of misrepresentation.

14.3   Rescission

The effect of misrepresentation is to render the contract voidable but not void. The contract therefore subsists until the representee decides to set it aside (rescind the contract). The remedy of rescission is available for any type of misrepresentation.

14.3.1 Communication of Intention to Rescind

The general rule is that, in order to rescind, the representee must communicate the intention to do so to the representor. It is possible for the representee to record an intention to rescind by way of some overt act which is deemed to be reasonable in the circumstances.

Car & Universal Finance Co v Caldwell [1965] 1 QB 525

Panel: Lord Denning MR (sitting as an additional judge of the Queen's Bench Division)

Facts: Caldwell sold his car to a rogue on the basis of a fraudulent misrepresentation. The rogue then sold it to Car & Universal Finance and promptly disappeared. The issue before the court was which of these two innocent parties, Car & Universal Finance or Caldwell, owned the car? It was held that Caldwell owned the car having taken reasonable steps to show his intention to rescind the contract (by alerting the police amongst other actions) before the rogue had sold the car on to Car & Universal Finance. The extract is taken from Lord Denning MR's judgment in the Queen's Bench Division, which was upheld on Appeal.

LORD DENNING MR

I hold, therefore, that where a seller of goods has a right to avoid a contract for fraud, he sufficiently exercises his election if he at once, on discovering the fraud, takes all possible steps to regain the goods even though he cannot find the rogue or communicate with him. That is what Caldwell did here by going to the police and asking them to get back the car. I, therefore, hold that on January 13 the contract of sale to these rogues was avoided and Caldwell then became the owner of the car again. It was only after he avoided it (so that it was once again his property), that these rogues purported to sell it to Motobella and Motobella purported to sell it to G. & C. Finance. Those sales were ineffective to pass the property because it had already been re-vested in Caldwell.

 Alert

Rescission is available to a party misled by an innocent misrepresentation notwithstanding that the misrepresentation has become a term of the contract: MA 67
s 1.

14.3.2 Bars to Rescission: Affirmation

A misrepresentee may not rescind a contract if they are deemed to have affirmed it.

A contract is affirmed if the representee declares his intention to proceed with the contract or does some act from which such an intention may reasonably be inferred. Once an election is unequivocally made it is determined forever and cannot be revived.

Long v Lloyd [1958] 1 WLR 753

Panel: Jenkins, Parker and Pearce LJJ

Facts: Long bought a lorry advertised as being in 'exceptional condition'. Lloyd, the seller, stated it was capable of 40 miles per hour at 11 miles to the gallon. Two days after the purchase the dynamo ceased to function, the oil seal was found to be defective, a crack in one of the wheels was discovered and the vehicle had consumed 8 gallons after doing 40 miles. Lloyd offered to pay half for a new dynamo and Long accepted. The lorry went off on a journey and broke down irrevocably. Long claimed rescission of the contract for misrepresentation but the court held that by the time the lorry left for the journey, Long had affirmed the contract and accepted the lorry in full knowledge of the condition and performance of the vehicle.

LORD JUSTICE PEARCE

Thus, to recapitulate the facts, after the trial run the plaintiff drove the lorry home from Hampton Court to Sevenoaks, a not inconsiderable distance. After that experience he took it into use in his business by driving it on the following day to Rochester and back to Sevenoaks with a load. By the time he returned from Rochester he knew that the dynamo was not charging, that there was an oil seal leaking, that he had used 8 gallons of fuel for a journey of 40 miles, and that a wheel was cracked. He must also, as we think, have known by this time that the vehicle was not capable of 40 miles per hour. As to oil consumption, we should have thought that, if it was so excessive that the sump was practically dry after 300 miles, the plaintiff could have reasonably been expected to discover that the rate of consumption was unduly high by the time he had made the journey from Hampton Court to Sevenoaks and thence to Rochester and back.

On his return from Rochester the plaintiff telephoned to the defendant and complained about the dynamo, the excessive fuel consumption, the leaking oil seal and the cracked wheel. The defendant then offered to pay half the cost of the reconstructed dynamo which the plaintiff had been advised to fit, and the plaintiff accepted the defendant's offer. We find this difficult to reconcile with the continuance of any right of rescission which the plaintiff might have had down to that time.

But the matter does not rest there. On the following day the plaintiff, knowing all that he did about the condition and performance of the lorry, dispatched it, driven by his brother, on a business trip to Middlesbrough. That step, at all events, appears to us to have amounted, in all the circumstances of the case, to a final acceptance of the lorry by the plaintiff for better or for worse, and to have conclusively extinguished any right of rescission remaining to the plaintiff after completion of the sale.

Accordingly, even if the plaintiff should be held, notwithstanding *Seddon v. North Eastern. Salt Co. Ltd.*, to have had a right to rescission which survived the completion of the contract, we think that on the facts of this case he lost any such right before his purported exercise of it.

14.3.3 Bars to Rescission: Lapse of Time

The general rule is that an action for rescission must be brought promptly, as rescission is an equitable remedy and delay defeats the equities. Note that in the case of fraudulent misrepresentation, time runs from the date when the fraud was, or ought reasonably to have been discovered.

Leaf v International Galleries [1950] 2 KB 86

Panel: Evershed MR, Denning and Jenkins LJJ

Facts: Leaf bought a painting of Salisbury Cathedral, described by the sellers as a genuine Constable. Five years later, Leaf discovered that the painting was not a genuine Constable and he brought this action for rescission on the grounds of innocent misrepresentation. The Court of Appeal dismissed Leaf's appeal.

LORD JUSTICE DENNING

No claim for damages is before us at all. The only question is whether the plaintiff is entitled to rescind.

First, Denning LJ explained why the contract for the sale of the picture was not void for mistake.

...There was no mistake at all about the subject-matter of the sale. It was a specific picture, 'Salisbury Cathedral.' The parties were agreed in the same terms on the same subject-matter, and that is sufficient to make a contract: see *Solle v. Butcher*...

He then went on to consider that an action for breach of contract was time-barred:

The circumstances in which a buyer is deemed to have accepted goods in performance of the contract are set out in s. 35 of the [Sale of Goods] Act, which says that the buyer is deemed to have accepted the goods, amongst other things, 'when, after the lapse of a reasonable time, he retains the goods without intimating to the seller that he has rejected them.' In this case the buyer took the picture into his house and, apparently, hung it there, and five years passed before he intimated any rejection at all. That, I need hardly say, is much more than a reasonable time. ...

Finally, Denning LJ turned to the issue of misrepresentation:

Is it to be said that the buyer is in any better position by relying on the representation, not as a condition, but as an innocent misrepresentation? I agree that on a contract for the sale of goods an innocent material misrepresentation may, in a proper case, be a ground for rescission even after the contract has been executed. ...

Although rescission may in some cases be a proper remedy, it is to be remembered that an innocent misrepresentation is much less potent than a breach of condition; and a claim to rescission for innocent misrepresentation must at any rate be barred when a right to reject for breach of condition is barred. A condition is a term of the contract of a most material character, and if a claim to reject on that account is barred, it seems to me a fortiori that a claim to rescission on the ground of innocent misrepresentation is also barred.

So, assuming that a contract for the sale of goods may be rescinded in a proper case for innocent misrepresentation, the claim is barred in this case for the self-same reason as a right to reject is barred. The buyer has accepted the picture. He had ample opportunity for examination in the first few days after he had bought it. Then was the time to see if the condition or representation was fulfilled. Yet he has kept it all this time. Five years have elapsed without any notice of rejection. In my judgment he cannot now claim to rescind. His only claim, if any, as the county court judge said, was one for damages, which he has not made in this action. In my judgment, therefore, the appeal should be dismissed.

Note that if the misrepresentation had been fraudulent, the time would have run from the date of discovery of the fraud (or the date it ought reasonably to have been discovered) and not from the date of purchase of the painting.

14.3.4 Bars to Rescission: Impossibility

The right to rescind is lost if restitution in integrum is no longer possible i.e. if it is impossible to restore the parties to their previous position before the contract was made.

***Clarke v Dickson* (1858) 120 ER 463**

Panel: Crompton J

Facts: The representee was induced to take shares in a partnership which was later converted into a limited liability company. Rescission was excluded since the existing shares were wholly different in nature and status from those originally received.

MR JUSTICE CROMPTON

When once it is settled that a contract induced by fraud is not void, but voidable at the option of the party defrauded, it seems to me to follow that, when that party exercises his option to rescind the contract, he must be in a state to rescind; that is, he must be in such a situation as to be able to put the parties into their original state before the contract. Now here I will assume, what is not clear to me, that the plaintiff bought his shares from the defendants and not from the Company, and that he might at one time have had a right to restore the shares to the defendants if he could, and demand the price from them. But then what did he buy? Shares in a partnership with others. He cannot return those; he has become bound to those others. Still stronger, he has changed their nature: what he now has and offers to restore are shares in a quasi corporation now in process of being wound up. That is quite enough to decide this case. The plaintiff must rescind in toto or not at all; he cannot both keep the shares and recover the whole price. That is founded on the plainest principles of justice. If he cannot return the article he must keep it, and sue for his real damage in an action on the deceit. ... The true doctrine is, that a party can never repudiate a contract after, by his own act, it has become out of his power to restore the parties to their original condition.

However, as rescission is an equitable remedy the court will not allow minor imperfections in the restoration of the original position to stand in the way of a remedy. The court will do 'what is practically just':

Emile Erlanger and Others v The New Sombrero Phosphate Company and Others (1877-78) LR 3 App Cas 1218

Panel: Lord Penzance, The Lord Chancellor (Lord Cairns), Lord Hatherley, Lord O'Hagan, Lord Selborne, Lord Blackburn, and Lord Gordon

Facts: A lease of an island in the West Indies was sold to an agent for a group of speculators. The speculators then created a company to purchase the same mine they had bought at twice the price they had paid. It was held that they were in a fiduciary position towards the company they formed to buy the mine and therefore should have disclosed the facts which apply to the property, and which would influence the company in deciding on the reasonableness of acquiring it. The innocent shareholders in the newly formed company were allowed to rescind even though the mine had been worked to an extent and profits taken from it. The mine was returned into its original ownership and any profits made from the mine in the interim were repaid.

LORD BLACKBURN

It would be obviously unjust that a person who has been in possession of property under the contract which he seeks to repudiate should be allowed to throw that back on the other party's hands without accounting for any benefit he may have derived from the use of the property, or if the property, though not destroyed, has been in the interval deteriorated, without making compensation for that deterioration. But as a Court of Law has no machinery at its command for taking an account of such matters, the defrauded party, if he sought his remedy at law, must in such cases keep the property and sue in an action for deceit, in which the jury, if properly directed, can do complete justice by giving as damages a full indemnity for all that the party has lost: see *Clarke v. Dixon*, and the cases there cited.

But a Court of Equity could not give damages, and, unless it can rescind the contract, can give no relief. And, on the other hand, it can take accounts of profits, and make allowance for deterioration. And I think the practice has always been for a Court of Equity to give this relief whenever, by the exercise of its powers, it can do what is practically just, though it cannot restore the parties precisely to the state they were in before the contract. And a Court of Equity requires that those who come to it to ask its active interposition to give them relief, should use due diligence, after there has been such notice or knowledge as to make it inequitable to lie by. And any change which occurs in the position of the parties or the state of the property after such notice or knowledge should tell much more against the party *in morâ* [in default], than a similar change before he was *in morâ* should do.

 Alert

14.3.5 Bars to Rescission: Third Party Rights

The right to rescind will also be lost if a third party has acquired rights to the subject matter of the contract entered into as a result of the misrepresentation.

Phillips v Brooks [1919] 2 KB 243

Panel: Horridge J

Facts: See chapter 15

MR. JUSTICE HORRIDGE

The rule laid down by Lord Cairns L.C. in *Cundy v. Lindsay* is as follows:

'If it turns out that the chattel has been stolen by the person who has professed to sell it, the purchaser will not obtain a title. If it turns out that the chattel has come into the hands of the person who professed to sell it, by a de facto contract, that is to say, a contract which has purported to pass the property to him from the owner of the property, there the purchaser will obtain a good title, even although afterwards it should appear that there were circumstances connected with that contract which would enable the original owner of the goods to reduce it, and to set it aside, because these circumstances so enabling the original owner of the goods, or of the chattel, to reduce the contract and to set it aside, will not be allowed to interfere with a title for valuable consideration obtained by some third party during the interval while the contract remained unreduced.'

Crystal Palace FC (2000) Limited v Iain Dowie [2008] EWHC 240 (QB), [2008] All ER (D) 254 (Feb)

Panel: Tugendhat J

Facts: Dowie was the manager of Crystal Palace football club. He informed Crystal Palace that he wished to terminate his contract. It was alleged that he had lied to Crystal Palace about his reasons for leaving and his future plans in order to induce Crystal Palace to enter into a compromise agreement releasing Dowie from his employment contract with the club including a very onerous compensation clause which was payable by Dowie on termination of his contract. The issues to be decided by Tugendhat J were (i) whether or not Dowie had in fact made false representations to Crystal Palace upon which they relied in entering the compromise agreement and, if so, (ii) whether or not the compromise agreement should be rescinded.

MR JUSTICE TUGENDHAT

...Mr McParland submits that the remedy of rescission is not available to the Club, and never has been, because it is impossible to return the parties to the position in which they were before the Compromise Agreement was signed. Mr Dowie cannot be returned to the employment of the Club, and the Club cannot restore to him his job at Palace. Mr Dowie is under contract to

 Alert

Coventry, and the Club has another manager in place. The rights of third parties are therefore engaged. ...

Mr McParland's argument is based on the rule of law that a contract induced by fraud is not void, but voidable at the option of the party defrauded. It follows that when that party exercises his option to rescind, he must be in a state to rescind, that is he must be in a state to put the parties into their original state before the contract. This used to be called a requirement for restitutio in integrum and is now said to be for counter restitution. In none of the cases cited to me by counsel did the court have to consider a case where rescission would have the effect of putting the parties back into a contractual relationship which they had previously agreed to terminate. ...

Alert

The most recent case, relied on by Mr Davies QC, is *Halpern v Halpern* [2007] EWCA Civ 291. The court did not have to reach a conclusion on the facts of that case, but the principles are discussed in the judgment of Carnwath LJ. He said:

'. ... The classic statement ... is in *Erlanger v New Sombrero Phosphate Company* (1878) 3 App.Cas.1218, 1278, per Lord Blackburn:

'...[A] Court of Equity could not give damages, and, unless it can rescind the contract, can give no relief. And, on the other hand, it can take accounts of profits, and make allowance for deterioration. And I think the practice has always been for a Court of Equity to give this relief whenever, by the exercise of its powers, it can do what is practically just, though it cannot restore the parties precisely to the state they were in before the contract.'...

...The rights of Coventry City FC under that club's contract of employment of Mr Dowie seem to be a significant point that is not of a kind that is normally considered under the heading counter restitution. Counter restitution is what the representee (the Club) would have to give in exchange for Mr Dowie giving up his release from the Compensation Clause and returning to the Club's employment. It would in principle include the salary and bonuses (if any) due to Mr Dowie under the revived Contract of Employment. In my judgment it would not be just to Coventry City FC that this court should make an order the effect of which is to place Mr Dowie under an employee's obligations to the Club. A manager cannot perform two Employment Contracts at the same time. And if the Club envisages, as it apparently does, that it will not call for Mr Dowie to perform any obligations under the Employment Contract other than the obligations under the Compensation Clause, then that does not seem to me to be rescission in any practical sense at all. It is not possible to sever one term of the Employment Contract from all the others. It is either revived by rescission of the Compromise Agreement, or it is not.

In my judgment practical justice in this case means the making of appropriate orders for damages or other financial relief. It might at some point be necessary to categorise the claims as either damages in tort, or damages in lieu of rescission, or in other ways. That is not necessary at this stage.

Practical justice does not require that the Compensation Clause be revived on its own, severed from all the other obligations the Employment Contract placed on Mr Dowie. The financial remedies available to the court can be adapted to the circumstances of the case.

In my judgment the Compromise Agreement should not be rescinded.

14.4   Indemnity

An indemnity may be awarded in respect of legal obligations assumed as a direct result of the contract. Where an action for misrepresentation will give a right to damages (ie an action for fraudulent or negligent misrepresentation), an indemnity will generally not be awarded. As no damages as of right are available for an innocent misrepresentation, an indemnity is more likely to be awarded in this type of action.

Whittington v Seale-Hayne (1900) 82 LT 49

Panel: Farwell J

Facts: The plaintiff took a lease of a farm to breed prize poultry. The defendant misrepresented the condition of the farm which was not sanitary. As a result the plaintiff became ill and many of the poultry died. There was no negligent misrepresentation available as the case was prior to the MA 67 and on the facts there was no fraud. Consequently, the only available action was for innocent misrepresentation for which there is no automatic right of damages. However, an indemnity to recover money paid due to legal obligations arising from the transaction is available together with rescission. The plaintiff was therefore able to claim the rent he had paid under the lease and the cost of repair work he was obliged to carry out under the terms of the lease. He was not however, able to claim damages for the death of the poultry.

14.5   Damages

14.5.1 Damages for Fraudulent Misrepresentation

The damages available for fraudulent misrepresentation are damages for the tort of deceit.

Doyle v Olby (Ironmongers) [1969] 2 QB 158

Panel: Lord Denning MR, Winn and Sachs LJJ

Facts: The plaintiff purchased an ironmonger's business from the defendant. Prior to sale, the company's director produced accounts for the preceding three years which showed considerable annual profits. The director's brother told the plaintiff that all the trade was over the counter. The plaintiff agreed to buy and went into occupation under a new lease at a higher rent, but with a covenant that the vendors would not engage in a similar business within a 10-mile radius for five years. He soon found that the turnover had been misrepresented and, in particular, that half the trade had been obtained by the director's brother acting as part-time traveller. Also, shortly after he took over, an associated company began to canvass the vendors' former customers in the district. The plaintiff was awarded all losses directly flowing regardless of foreseeability as equivalent to the cost of making good the representation or the reduction in the value of the goodwill.

LORD DENNING MR

The object of damages is to compensate the plaintiff for all the loss he has suffered, so far, again, as money can do it. In contract, the damages are limited to what may reasonably be supposed to have been in the contemplation of the parties. In fraud, they are not so limited. The defendant is bound to make reparation for all the actual damages directly flowing from the fraudulent inducement. The person who has been defrauded is entitled to say:

'I would not have entered into this bargain at all but for your representation. Owing to your fraud, I have not only lost all the money I paid you, but, what is more, I have been put to a large amount of extra expense as well and suffered this or that extra damages.'

All such damages can be recovered: and it does not lie in the mouth of the fraudulent person to say that they could not reasonably have been foreseen. For instance, in this very case Mr. Doyle has not only lost the money which he paid for the business, which he would never have done if there had been no fraud: he put all that money in and lost it; but also he has been put to expense and loss in trying to run a business which has turned out to be a disaster for him. He is entitled to damages for all his loss, subject, of course to giving credit for any benefit that he has received. There is nothing to be taken off in mitigation: for there is nothing more that he could have done to reduce his loss. He did all that he could reasonably be expected to do.

Doyle v Olby (Ironmongers) Ltd was expressly approved in the following case, *Smith New Court Securities Ltd v Scrimgeour Vickers (Asset Management)* [1997] AC 254. In his judgment Lord Browne-Wilkinson outlined seven principles which he considered applicable in assessing the amount of damages payable where the plaintiff has been induced by a fraudulent misrepresentation to buy property. Five of these principles are re-statements of *Doyle v Olby (Ironmongers) Ltd* (above). In summary, the two additional principles are first, that the plaintiff must mitigate as soon as the fraud is discovered and second, that any damages awarded to the plaintiff will be reduced by the value of any benefit the plaintiff has acquired as a result of the contract.

Smith New Court Securities Ltd v Scrimgeour Vickers (Asset Management) [1997] AC 254

Panel: Lord Browne-Wilkinson, Lord Keith of Kinkel, Lord Mustill, Lord Slynn of Hadley and Lord Steyn

Facts: The plaintiff purchased shares on the basis of a fraudulent misrepresentation by the defendant. Because of the fraudulent misrepresentation, the plaintiff paid an over-inflated price for the shares. Before the plaintiff discovered the fraud, a further fraud by a third party resulted in a catastrophic drop in the price of the shares. The plaintiff was unable to sell the shares on as a result. The court awarded damages based on the difference between the actual price paid for the shares and the market value of the shares after it had fallen drastically due to the third party fraud at the time of the court action.

LORD BROWNE-WILKINSON

Lord Browne-Wilkinson first set out the facts of *Doyle v Olby (Ironmongers) Ltd* and then went on to consider the principles as to damages arising from the case:

Doyle v. Olby (Ironmongers) Ltd. establishes four points. First, that the measure of damages where a contract has been induced by fraudulent misrepresentation is reparation for all the actual damage directly flowing from (i.e. caused by) entering into the transaction. Second, that in assessing such damages it is not an inflexible rule that the plaintiff must bring into account the value as at the transaction date of the asset acquired: although the point is not adverted to in the judgments, the basis on which the damages were computed shows that there can be circumstances in which it is proper to require a defendant only to bring into account the actual proceeds of the asset provided that he has acted reasonably in retaining it. Third, damages for deceit are not limited to those which were reasonably foreseeable. Fourth, the damages recoverable can include consequential loss suffered by reason of having acquired the asset.

In my judgment *Doyle v. Olby (Ironmongers) Ltd.* was rightly decided on all these points. It is true, as to the second point, that there were not apparently cited to the Court of Appeal the 19th century cases which established the 'inflexible rule' that the asset acquired has to be valued as at the transaction date: the successful appellant was not legally represented. But in my judgment the decision on this second point is correct. The old 'inflexible rule' is both wrong in principle and capable of producing manifest injustice. The defendant's fraud may have an effect continuing after the transaction is completed, e.g. if a sale of gold shares was induced by a misrepresentation that a new find had been made which was to be announced later it would plainly be wrong to assume that the plaintiff should have sold the shares before the announcement should have been made. Again, the acquisition of the asset may, as in *Doyle v. Olby (Ironmongers) Ltd.* itself, lock the purchaser into continuing to hold the asset until he can effect a resale. To say that in such a case the plaintiff has obtained the value of the asset as at the transaction date and must therefore bring it into account flies in the face of common sense: how can he be said to have received such a value if, despite his efforts, he has been unable to sell.

Turning for a moment away from damages for deceit, the general rule in other areas of the law has been that damages are to be assessed as at the date the wrong was committed. But recent decisions have emphasised that this is only a general rule: where it is necessary in order adequately to compensate the plaintiff for the damage suffered by reason of the defendant's wrong a different date of assessment can be selected. ...

In many cases, even in deceit, it will be appropriate to value the asset acquired as at the transaction date if that truly reflects the value of what the plaintiff has obtained. Thus, if the asset acquired is a readily marketable asset and there is no special feature (such as a continuing misrepresentation or the purchaser being locked into a business that he has acquired) the transaction date rule may well produce a fair result. ... But in cases where property has been acquired in reliance on a fraudulent misrepresentation there are likely to be many cases where the general rule has to be departed from in order to give adequate compensation for the wrong done to the plaintiff, in particular where the fraud continues to influences the conduct of the plaintiff after the transaction is complete or where the result of the transaction induced by fraud is to lock the plaintiff into continuing to hold the asset acquired.

Finally, it must be emphasised that the principle in Doyle v. Olby (Ironmongers) Ltd. [1969] 2 Q.B. 158, strict though it is, still requires the plaintiff to mitigate his loss once he is aware of the fraud. So long as he is not aware of the fraud, no question of a duty to mitigate can arise. But once the fraud has been discovered, if the plaintiff is not locked into the asset and the fraud has ceased to operate on his mind, a failure to take reasonable steps to sell the property may constitute a failure to mitigate his loss requiring him to bring the value of the property into account as at the date when he discovered the fraud or shortly thereafter.

 Alert

In sum, in my judgment the following principles apply in assessing the damages payable where the plaintiff has been induced by a fraudulent misrepresentation to buy property: (1) the defendant is bound to make reparation for all the damage directly flowing from the transaction; (2) although such damage need not have been foreseeable, it must have been directly caused by the transaction; (3) is [sic] assessing such damage, the plaintiff is entitled to recover by way of damages the full price paid by him, but he must give credit for any benefits which he has received as a result of the transaction; (4) as a general rule, the benefits received by him include the market value of the property acquired as at the date of acquisition; but such general rule is not to be inflexibly applied where to do so would prevent him obtaining full compensation for the wrong suffered; (5) although the circumstances in which the general rule should not apply cannot be comprehensively stated, it will normally not apply where either (a) the misrepresentation has continued to operate after the date of the acquisition of the asset so as to induce the plaintiff to retain the asset or (b) the circumstances of the case are such that the plaintiff is, by reason of the fraud, locked into the property. (6) In addition, the plaintiff is entitled to recover consequential losses caused by the transaction; (7) the plaintiff must take all reasonable steps to mitigate his loss once he has discovered the fraud...

Loss of profits sustained as a result of a fraudulent misrepresentation may also be claimed.

East v Maurer [1991] 1 WLR 461

Panel: Mustill, Butler-Sloss and Beldam LJJ

Facts: The claimants bought a hairdressing salon from the defendant. The defendant had another shop on the same road as the salon he sold to the claimants. He informed the claimants that he would not work at the other salon. This proved to be untrue. As a result of the defendant having carried on business at such close proximity, the claimants were unable to make a profit in their salon. The court awarded loss of profits. However, the profits were awarded not on the contractual measure but on the tortious measure of what the claimants would have made if the contract had never happened and if they had instead bought another salon of the same type in a similar town.

LORD JUSTICE BELDAM

If in fact the plaintiffs lost the profits which they could reasonably have expected from running a business in the area of a kind similar to the business in this case, I can see no reason why those do not fall within the words of Lord Atkin in *Clark v. Urquhart* [1930] A.C. 28, 68, 'actual damage directly flowing from the fraudulent inducement.'

So I consider that on the facts found by the judge in the present case, the plaintiffs did establish that they had suffered a loss due to the defendants' misrepresentation which arose from their inability to earn the profits in the business which they hoped to buy in the Bournemouth area.

I would therefore reject the submission of Mr. Shawcross that loss of profits is not a recoverable head of damage in cases of this kind.

However, I am not satisfied that in arriving at the figure of £15,000 the judge approached the quantification of those damages on the correct basis. It seems to me that he was inclined to base his award on an assessment of the profits which the business actually bought by the plaintiffs might have made if the statement made by the first defendant had amounted to a warranty that customers would continue to patronise the salon in Exeter Road; further that he left out of account a number of significant factors. What he did was to found his award on an evaluation which he made of the profits of the business at Exeter Road made by the first defendant in the year preceding the purchase of the business by the plaintiffs. ...

The above calculation is based on the contractual measure which Beldam LJ disagreed with.

> It seems to me that he should have begun by considering the kind of profit which the second plaintiff might have made if the representation which induced her to buy the business at Exeter Road had not been made, and that involved considering the kind of profits which *she* might have expected to make in another hairdressing business bought for a similar sum. ...

The above is the tortious measure i.e. as if the claimant had not entered into that particular contract. Lord Justice Beldam then goes on to consider the other possible limitations to the claimant's hypothetical profits.

> The judge left out of account the fact that the second plaintiff was moving into an entirely different area and one in which she was, comparatively speaking, a stranger. Secondly, that she was going to deal with a different clientele. Thirdly, that there were almost certainly in that area of Bournemouth other smart hairdressing salons which represented competition and which, in any event, if the first defendant had, as he had represented, gone to open a salon on the Continent, could have attracted the custom of his former clients.

> ...Taking all the factors into account, I think that the judge's figure was too high; for my part I would have awarded a figure of £10,000 for that head of damage, and to this extent I would allow the appeal.

Contributory negligence is not available as a defence to a claim for fraudulent misrepresentation.

Standard Chartered Bank v Pakistan National Shipping Corporation (No.2) [2003] 1 AC 959

Panel: Lord Slynn of Hadley, Lord Mustill, Lord Hoffmann, Lord Hobhouse of Woodborough and Lord Rodger of Earlsferry

Facts: This case concerned payment under a letter of credit for bitumen. The letter of credit was subject to a time limit. If the shipment were delayed, the letter of credit would expire. Falsified bills of lading were produced in order for the payment to go ahead. The party to whom the bills of lading were given did not notice the falsification and although the documents were late, paid out on the letter of credit. When the fraud was discovered and the misrepresentors were sued, they claimed that the misrepresentee was partly to blame for the loss through its own negligence for not having noticed the falsification.

LORD HOFFMAN

... In the case of fraudulent misrepresentation, however, I agree with Mummery J in *Alliance & Leicester Building Society v Edgestop Ltd* [1993] 1 WLR 1462 that there is no common law defence of contributory negligence. (See also Carnwath J in *Corporación Nacional del Cobre de Chile v Sogemin Metals Ltd* [1997] 1 WLR 1396 and Blackburn J in *Nationwide Building*

Alert

Society v Thimbleby & Co [1999] Lloyd's Rep PN 359.) It follows that, in agreement with the majority in the Court of Appeal, I think that no apportionment under the 1945 Act is possible.

14.5.2 Damages for Negligent Misrepresentation: MA 67 s 2(1)

The correct measure of damages for negligent misrepresentation under the MA 67 must be based on the tort of deceit.

Royscot Trust v Rogerson [1991] 3 WLR 57

Panel: Balcombe and Ralph Gibson LJJ

Statute: Misrepresentation Act 1967 s 2(1)

Facts: A car dealer induced a finance company to enter into a hire-purchase agreement by misrepresenting the amount of the deposit paid by the customer, who later defaulted and sold the car to a third party. The dealer was held liable to the finance company under s 2(1) for the balance due under the agreement. The court felt bound to apply the 'plain words' of the section and accordingly, the plaintiff was entitled to recover all losses even if those losses were unforeseeable, provided they were not otherwise too remote (this being the measure of damages for fraudulent misrepresentation under *Doyle v Olby (Ironmongers)*).

LORD JUSTICE BALCOMBE

So I turn to the issue on this appeal which the dealer submits raises a pure point of law: where (a) a motor dealer innocently misrepresents to a finance company the amount of the sale price of, and the deposit paid by the intended purchaser of, the car, and (b) the finance company is thereby induced to enter into a hire-purchase agreement with the purchaser which it would not have done if it had known the true facts, and (c) the purchaser thereafter dishonestly disposes of the car and defaults on the hire-purchase agreement, can the finance company recover all or part of its losses on the hire-purchase agreement from the motor dealer?

The finance company's cause of action against the dealer is based on section 2(1) of the Misrepresentation Act 1967. [He read MA 67 s2(1)]...

[T]here is now a number of decisions which make it clear that the tortious measure of damages is the true one. ... One at least, *Chesneau v. Interhome Ltd.* ... is a decision of this court. The claim was one under section 2(1) of the Act of 1967 and the appeal concerned the assessment of damages. In the course of his judgment Eveleigh L.J. said:

'[Damages] should be assessed in a case like the present one on the same principles as damages are assessed in tort. The subsection itself says: 'if the person making the misrepresentation would be liable to damages in respect thereof had the misrepresentation been made fraudulently, that person shall be so liable . . .' By 'so liable' I take it to mean liable as he would be if the misrepresentation had been made fraudulently.'

In view of the wording of the subsection it is difficult to see how the measure of damages under it could be other than the tortious measure and, despite the initial aberrations referred to above, that is now generally accepted. Indeed counsel before us did not seek to argue the contrary.

The first main issue before us was: accepting that the tortious measure is the right measure, is it the measure where the tort is that of fraudulent misrepresentation, or is it the measure where the tort is negligence at common law? The difference is that in cases of fraud a plaintiff is entitled to any loss which flowed from the defendant's fraud, even if the loss could not have been foreseen: see *Doyle v. Olby (Ironmongers) Ltd.* [1969] 2 Q.B. 158. In my judgment the wording of the subsection is clear: the person making the innocent misrepresentation shall be 'so liable,' i.e., liable to damages as if the representation had been made fraudulently. ...

This was also the original view of the academic writers. In an article, 'The Misrepresentation Act 1967' (1967) 30 M.L.R. 369 by P. S. Atiyah and G. H. Treitel, the authors say, at pp. 373-374:

'The measure of damages in the statutory action will apparently be that in an action of deceit . . . But more probably the damages recoverable in the new action are the same as those recoverable in an action of deceit . . .'

Professor Treitel has since changed his view. In Treitel, The Law of Contract, 7th ed. (1987), p. 278, he says:

'Where the action is brought under section 2(1) of the Misrepresentation Act, one possible view is that the deceit rule will be applied by virtue of the fiction of fraud. But the preferable view is that the severity of the deceit rule can only be justified in cases of actual fraud and that remoteness under section 2(1) should depend, as in actions based on negligence, on the test of foreseeability.'

The only authority cited in support of the 'preferable' view is *Shepheard v. Broome* [1904] A.C. 342, a case under section 38 of the Companies Act 1867, which provided that in certain circumstances a company director, although not in fact fraudulent, should be 'deemed to be fraudulent.' As Lord Lindley said, at p. 346: 'To be compelled by Act of Parliament to treat an honest man as if he were fraudulent is at all times painful,' but he went on to say:

'but the repugnance which is naturally felt against being compelled to do so will not justify your Lordships in refusing to hold the appellant responsible for acts for which an Act of Parliament clearly declares he is to be held liable.'

The House of Lords so held.

It seems to me that that case, far from supporting Professor Treitel's view, is authority for the proposition that we must follow the literal wording of section

2(1), even though that has the effect of treating, so far as the measure of damages is concerned, an innocent person as if he were fraudulent.

...Professor Furmston in *Cheshire, Fifoot and Furmston's Law of Contract*, 11th ed. (1986), p. 286, says:

'It has been suggested' - and the reference is to the passage in Atiyah and Treitel's article cited above - 'that damages under section 2(1) should be calculated on the same principles as govern the tort of deceit. This suggestion is based on a theory that section 2(1) is based on a 'fiction of fraud'. We have already suggested that this theory is misconceived. On the other hand the action created by section 2(1) does look much more like an action in tort than one in contract and it is suggested that the rules for negligence are the natural ones to apply.'

...With all respect to the various learned authors whose works I have cited above, it seems to me that to suggest that a different measure of damage applies to an action for innocent misrepresentation under the section than that which applies to an action for fraudulent misrepresentation (deceit) at common law is to ignore the plain words of the subsection and is inconsistent with the cases to which I have referred. In my judgment, therefore, the finance company is entitled to recover from the dealer all the losses which it suffered as a result of its entering into the agreements with the dealer and the customer, even if those losses were unforeseeable, provided that they were not otherwise too remote.

Clearly, the Law Reform (Contributory Negligence) Act 1945 s 1 is available as a defence to a claim for negligent misstatement at common law and damages may be reduced accordingly. A claim for negligent misrepresentation under the MA 67 should also, logically, be subject to a defence of contributory negligence.

Gran Gelato Ltd v Richcliff (Group) Ltd [1992] Ch 560

Panel: Sir Donald Nicholls V-C

Statute: Misrepresentation Act 1967 s 2(1)

Facts: Gran Gelato were granted a ten-year underlease by Richcliff which would expire in 1994. The headlease had a redevelopment break clause which was exercisable after June 1989. Gran Gelato did not know this and in answer to Gran Gelato's queries prior to entering into the underlease, Richcliff's solicitor said that there were no rights to the Richcliff's knowledge that would affect Gran Gelato's enjoyment of the property. In 1988 the break clause was exercised and Gran Gelato claimed in both negligent misstatement and in negligent misrepresentation under the MA 67 s 2(1). Richcliff claimed contributory negligence on the basis that Gran Gelato did not request actual sight of the headlease before proceeding with the purchase of the underlease. It was held that, as there were concurrent claims for negligence and negligent misrepresentation under the MA 67, the defence of contributory negligence could apply to both claims.

SIR DONALD NICHOLLS V-C

Contributory negligence

Richcliff has advanced a defence of contributory negligence. Clearly, this is available as a defence to the claim against Richcliff for damages for breach of the common law duty of care; but is it available to the claim against Richcliff under section 2(1) of the Misrepresentation Act 1967? In other words, does section 1 of the Law Reform (Contributory Negligence) Act 1945 apply to a claim by a plaintiff for damages under the Misrepresentation Act 1967? So far as is material section 1(1) provides:

'Where any person suffers damage as the result partly of his own fault and partly of the fault of any other person or persons, a claim in respect of that damage shall not be defeated by reason of the fault of the person suffering the damage, but the damages recoverable in respect thereof shall be reduced to such extent as the court thinks just and equitable having regard to the claimant's share in the responsibility for the damage; . . .'

Fault is defined in section 4 as 'negligence, breach of statutory duty or other act or omission which gives rise to a liability in tort or would, apart from this Act, give rise to the defence of contributory negligence; . . .'

[Sir Donald Nicholls V-C then read MA 67 s 2 (1)]

'... that person shall be so liable notwithstanding that the misrepresentation was not made fraudulently, unless he proves that he had reasonable ground to believe and did believe up to the time the contract was made that the facts represented were true.'

Thus, in short, liability under the Misrepresentation Act 1967 is essentially founded on negligence, in the sense that the defendant, the representor, did not have reasonable grounds to believe that the facts represented were true. (Of course, if he did not believe the facts represented were true he will be liable for fraud.) This being so, it would be very odd if the defence of contributory negligence were not available to a claim under that Act. It would be very odd if contributory negligence were available as a defence to a claim for damages based on a breach of a duty to take care in and about the making of a particular representation, but not available to a claim for damages under the Act in respect of the same representation.

In my view, the answer to this point is provided by the decision of the Court of Appeal in *Forsikringsaktieselskapet Vesta v. Butcher* [1989] A.C. 852. There the court held that the Act of 1945 applies to a case where there is a claim for damages for negligence at common law even if, in addition, there is a claim in contract to the same effect. ...

In the present case the conduct of which Gran Gelato complains founds a cause of action both in negligence at common law and under the Act of 1967. As already noted, under the Act of 1967 liability is essentially founded on negligence. By parity of reasoning with the conclusion in *Forsikringsaktieselskapet Vesta v. Butcher* [1989] A.C. 852 regarding concurrent claims in negligence in tort and contract, the Act of 1945 applies in the present case where there are concurrent claims against Richcliff in negligence in tort and under the Act of 1967.

However, the judgment in *Royscot Trust v Rogerson* suggests that as a claim for negligent misrepresentation under the MA 67 should be treated as a claim for fraudulent misrepresentation, contributory negligence should therefore not be available.

14.5.3 Damages for Innocent Misrepresentation

There is no automatic right to damages for an innocent misrepresentation but as with negligent misrepresentation (above), the court has the discretion under s 2(2) to award damages in lieu of rescission.

14.5.4 Damages for Negligent Misstatement at Common Law

The measure of damages is that utilised for the tort of negligence. Consequently, damages will be assessed on the basis of all losses which are reasonably foreseeable and are not too remote: *The Wagon Mound* [1967] 1 AC 617.

Further reading

McKendrick, E., *Contract Law* (2017) 12th ed. Ch.13

15

Mistake

Topic List

Introduction

The courts are generally unwilling to allow the parties to succeed in a claim for mistake, as the effect is to render the contract void *ab initio*, ie the agreement between the parties is invalid from the outset. This can be contrasted with a successful action for misrepresentation which will only render the contract voidable requiring the court to make an order for rescission to avoid the contract.

This chapter will examine cases regarding unilateral mistake as to identity.

15.1 Unilateral Mistake as to Identity: Face to Face Contracts

The manner in which the mistake as to identity occurred is an important factor for the courts. They have been more willing to treat mistakes of identity as operative where the contract has been made at a distance. As will be seen in the cases that follow, the courts are far more reluctant to declare a contract void for mistake when it has been made face to face.

Phillips v Brooks, Limited [1919] 2 KB 243

Panel: Horridge J

Facts: A rogue, representing himself to be Sir George Bullough of St James Square, bought a ring from a jeweller, Brooks. After verifying in a telephone directory that a Sir George Bullough did indeed live at that address, the jeweller allowed the rogue to take the ring away with him, whereupon the rogue promptly pledged the ring at a pawn brokers. The jeweller traced the ring to the pawn brokers and sued for the return of the ring on the basis that the contract with the rogue was void for mistake.

MR JUSTICE HORRIDGE

...I have carefully considered the evidence of the plaintiff, and have come to the conclusion that, although he believed the person to whom he was handing the ring was Sir George Bullough, he in fact contracted to sell and deliver it to the person who came into his shop, and who was not Sir George Bullough, but a man of the name of North, who obtained the sale and delivery by means of the false pretence that he was Sir George Bullough. It is quite true the plaintiff in re-examination said he had no intention of making any contract with any other person than Sir George Bullough; but I think I have myself to decide what is the proper inference to draw where a verbal contract is made and an article delivered to an individual describing himself as somebody else.

After obtaining the ring the man North pledged it in the name of Firth with the defendants, who bona fide and without notice advanced 350l. upon it. The question, therefore, in this case is whether or not the property had so passed to the swindler as to entitle him to give a good title to any person who gave value and acted bona fide without notice. This question seems to have been decided in an American case of *Edmunds v. Merchants' Despatch Transportation Co.* ...

The following expressions used in the judgment of Morton C.J. seem to me to fit the facts in this case: 'The minds of the parties met and agreed upon all the terms of the sale, the thing sold, the price and time of payment, the person selling and the person buying. The fact that the seller was induced to sell by fraud of the buyer made the sale voidable, but not void. He could not have supposed that he was selling to any other person; his intention was to sell to the person present, and identified by sight and hearing; it does not defeat the sale because the buyer assumed a false name or practised any other deceit to induce the vendor to sell. ...'

...

The court held that although the plaintiff believed he was contracting with Sir George Bullough, the contract was in fact concluded with the person who came into his shop, identified by sight and hearing. The contract, therefore, was not void for mistake, but only voidable for misrepresentation, and as the goods had passed onto the third party who was unaware of the fraud, before the contract was avoided, the third party obtained good title to the ring. This principle is set out in the Sale of Goods Act 1979 s 23.

The next case to be considered has proven exceptionally difficult to reconcile with *Phillips v Brooks*.

Ingram and Others v Little [1961] 1 QB 31

Panel: Sellers, Pearce and Devlin LJJ

Facts: The plaintiffs were elderly sisters who had advertised a car for sale. The man who came to view the car introduced himself as Hutchinson. They agreed a price but when he took out his cheque book to pay, the plaintiffs called off the deal saying they would only take cash. He then assured them that he was indeed Mr P.G.M. Hutchinson, a respectable businessman from Caterham, Surrey. After checking his name and address in a nearby post office, the plaintiffs accepted the cheque and allowed him to drive the car away. The cheque was later dishonoured by which time the rogue had traded in the car with a car dealer who bought it in good faith. The plaintiffs sued the third party car dealer for the return of the car, or alternatively for damages for its conversion. Mr Justice Slade gave judgment for the plaintiffs, and the defendant appealed.

LORD JUSTICE SELLERS

...

The decision in the present case turns solely on whether 'Hutchinson' entered into a contract which gave him a title to the car which would subsist until it was avoided on the undoubted fraud being discovered.

...The judge, treating the plaintiffs as the offerors and the rogue 'Hutchinson' as the offeree, found that the plaintiffs in making their offer to sell the car not for cash but for a cheque (which in the circumstances of the Bank Holiday week-end could not be banked before the following Tuesday, August 6, 1957) were under the belief that they were dealing with, and therefore making their offer to, the honest P. G. M. Hutchinson of Caterham, whom they had reason to believe was a man of substance and standing.

'Hutchinson,' the offeree, knew precisely what was in the minds of the two ladies for he had put it there and he knew that their offer was intended for P. G. M. Hutchinson of Caterham and that they were making no offer to and had no intention to contract with him, as he was. There was no offer which he 'Hutchinson' could accept and, therefore, there was no contract.

The judge pointed out that the offer which the plaintiffs made was one which was capable of being accepted only by the honest P. G. M. Hutchinson of Caterham and was incapable of acceptance by 'Hutchinson'. In all the circumstances of the present case I would accept the judge's findings. Indeed the conclusion so reached seems self-evident.

Is the conclusion to be held wrong in law? If it is, then, as I see it, it must be on the sole ground that as 'Hutchinson' was present, albeit making fraudulent statements to induce the plaintiffs to part with their car to him in exchange for his worthless cheque and was successful in so doing, then a bargain must have been struck with him personally, however much he deceived the plaintiffs into thinking they were dealing with someone else. ...

The mere presence of an individual cannot, however, be conclusive that an apparent bargain he may make is made with him. ...

[*Phillips v Brooks*] is not an authority to establish that where an offer or acceptance is addressed to a person (although under a mistake as to his identity) who is present in person, then it must in all circumstances be treated as if actually addressed to him. I would regard the issue as a question of fact in each case depending on what was said and done and applying the elementary principles of offer and acceptance in the manner in which Slade J directed himself.

The question in each case should be solved in my opinion, by applying the test, which Slade J applied, 'How ought the promisee to have interpreted the promise' in order to find whether a contract has been entered into.

I am in agreement with the judge when he quotes, accepts and applies the following passage from Dr. Goodhart's article ('Mistake as to identity in the Law of Contract' (1941) 57 LQR 228, 231): 'It is the interpretation of the promise which is the essential thing. This is usually based on the interpretation which a reasonable man, in the promisee's position, would place on it, but in those cases where the promisor knows that the promisee has placed a peculiar interpretation on his words, then this is the binding one. ...'

The legal position is, I think, well illustrated by Dr. Goodhart in the article (57 L.Q.R. 228, 241) already referred to. There is a difference between the case where A makes an offer to B in the belief that B is not B but is someone else, and the case where A makes an offer to B in the belief that B is X. In the first case B does in fact receive an offer, even though the offeror does not know that it is to B he is making it, since he believes B to be someone else. In the second case, A does not in truth make any offer to B at all; he thinks B is X, for whom alone the offer is meant. There was an offer intended for and available only to X. B cannot accept it if he knew or ought to have known that it was not addressed to him. ...

If it is the formation of a contract which calls for consideration, as it is here, 'How ought the promisee to have interpreted the promise' is, in my opinion, the correct approach, as the judge has held; but I recognise that the correct answer may not always prove as ascertainable as I believe it to be in the present case.

I would dismiss the appeal.

LORD JUSTICE PEARCE

...

An apparent contract made orally inter praesentes raises particular difficulties. The offer is apparently addressed to the physical person present. Prima facie, he, by whatever name he is called, is the person to whom the offer is made. His physical presence identified by sight and hearing preponderates over vagaries of nomenclature... .Yet clearly, though difficult, it is not impossible to rebut the prima facie presumption that the offer can be accepted by the person to whom it is physically addressed. To take two extreme instances. If a man orally commissions a portrait from some unknown artist who had deliberately passed himself off, whether by disguise or merely by verbal cosmetics, as a famous painter, the impostor could not accept the offer. For though the offer is made to him physically, it is obviously, as he knows, addressed to the famous painter. The mistake in identity on such facts is clear and the nature of the contract makes it obvious that identity was of vital importance to the offeror. At the other end of the scale, if a shopkeeper sells goods in a normal cash transaction to a man who misrepresents himself as being some well-known figure, the transaction will normally be valid. For the shopkeeper was ready to sell goods for cash to the world at large and the particular identity of the purchaser in such a contract was not of sufficient importance to override the physical presence identified by sight and hearing. Thus the nature of the proposed contract must have a strong bearing on the question of whether the intention of the offeror (as understood by his offeree) was to make his offer to some other particular identity rather than to the physical person to whom it was orally offered. In our case, the facts lie in the debatable area between the two extremes. At the beginning of the negotiations, always an important consideration, the name or personality of the false Hutchinson were of no importance and there was no other identity competing with his physical presence. The plaintiffs were content to sell the car for cash to any purchaser. The contractual conversation was orally addressed to the physical identity of the false Hutchinson. The identity was the man present, and his name was merely one of his attributes. Had matters continued thus, there would clearly have been a valid but voidable contract.

…

…But, even if there had been a concluded agreement before discussion of a cheque, it was rescinded. The man tried to make Miss Ingram take a cheque. She declined and said that the deal was off. He did not demur but set himself to reconstruct the negotiations. For the moment had come, which he must all along have anticipated, as the crux of the negotiations, the vital crisis of the swindle. He wanted to take away the car on credit against his worthless cheque, but she refused. Thereafter, the negotiations were of a different kind from what the vendor had mistakenly believed them to be hitherto. The parties were no longer concerned with a cash sale of goods where the identity of the purchaser was prima facie unimportant. They were concerned with a credit sale in which both parties knew that the identity of the purchaser was of the utmost importance. …

…

LORD JUSTICE DEVLIN

The point on which the present case turns is the effect of deception about the identity of a contracting party. It is a difficult point on which I have the misfortune to differ from my brethren. …

…

In the textbooks, cases of mistaken identity are to be found both in the chapters that deal with the formation of contract and in those that deal with the effect of mistake. Whichever way it is looked at, the essential question is the same: has a contract been made? If the fatal defect goes to form, the question is answered with a simple negative and the case is put under the head of formation. If the defect is one of substance, that is, where the outward form is complete but the necessary consensus is vitiated by mistake, the question is answered by saying that the contract is void. …

…

The fact that Miss Ingram refused to contract with H. until his supposed name and address had been 'verified' goes to show that she regarded his identity as fundamental. In this she was misguided. She should have concerned herself with creditworthiness rather than with identity. The fact that H. gave P. G. M. Hutchinson's address in the directory was no proof that he was P. G. M. Hutchinson; and if he had been, that fact alone was no proof that his cheque would be met. Identity, therefore, did not really matter. Nevertheless, it may truly be said that to Miss Ingram, as she looked at it, it did. In my judgment, Miss Ingram's state of mind is immaterial to this question. When the law avoids a contract ab initio, it does so irrespective of the intentions or opinions or wishes of the parties themselves. … In my judgment, in the present case

H.'s identity was immaterial. His creditworthiness was not, but creditworthiness in relation to contract is not a basic fact; it is only a way of expressing the belief that each party normally holds that the other will honour his promise.

...

...There can be no doubt, as all this difference of opinion shows, that the dividing line between voidness and voidability, between fundamental mistake and incidental deceit, is a very fine one. That a fine and difficult distinction has to be drawn is not necessarily any reproach to the law. But need the rights of the parties in a case like this depend on such a distinction? The great virtue of the common law is that it sets out to solve legal problems by the application to them of principles which the ordinary man is expected to recognise as sensible and just; their application in any particular case may produce what seems to him a hard result, but as principles they should be within his understanding and merit his approval. But here, contrary to its habit, the common law, instead of looking for a principle that is simple and just, rests on theoretical distinctions. Why should the question whether the defendant should or should not pay the plaintiff damages for conversion depend upon voidness or voidability, and upon inferences to be drawn from a conversation in which the defendant took no part? The true spirit of the common law is to override theoretical distinctions when they stand in the way of doing practical justice. For the doing of justice, the relevant question in this sort of case is not whether the contract was void or voidable, but which of two innocent parties shall suffer for the fraud of a third. The plain answer is that the loss should be divided between them in such proportion as is just in all the circumstances. If it be pure misfortune, the loss should be borne equally; if the fault or imprudence of either party has caused or contributed to the loss, it should be borne by that party in the whole or in the greater part.... I believe it would be useful if Parliament were now to consider whether or not it is practicable by means of a similar act of law reform to provide for the victims of a fraud a better way of adjusting their mutual loss than that which has grown out of the common law.

The question of apportioning loss on a statutory basis was considered by the Law Reform Committee in its Twelfth Report 'Transfer of Title to Chattels' (1966) (Cmnd 2958). The committee rejected Devlin LJ's apportionment suggestion as impracticable.

In *Lewis v Averay* [1972] 1 QB 198 the court struggled to reconcile the decisions reached in *Phillips v Brooks* and *Ingram v Little*.

Lewis v Averay [1972] 1 QB 198

Panel: Lord Denning MR, Phillimore and Megaw LJJ

Facts: The plaintiff advertised his car for sale and a rogue, posing as the well-known television actor, Richard Greene, called to view the car. He agreed to buy the car and presented a cheque book to pay. On being asked by the plaintiff for proof of identity, he produced a Pinewood Studios film pass, with the name Richard Greene and the rogue's photo. The plaintiff let him take the car away whereupon he sold it to a music student, who bought it unaware of the fraud. The cheque was dishonoured and the plaintiff brought an action against the third party for the return of the car. The rogue could not be traced. Deputy Judge Ellison in the county court held that here was no contract between the plaintiff and the rogue, therefore the rogue was unable to pass a valid title to the car on to the third party. He awarded the plaintiff damages. The defendant appealed.

LORD DENNING MR

This is another case where one of two innocent persons has to suffer for the fraud of a third. It will no doubt interest students and find its place in the textbooks.

...

The real question in the case is whether on May 8, 1969, there was a contract of sale under which the property in the car passed from Mr. Lewis to the rogue. If there was such a contract, then, even though it was voidable for fraud, nevertheless Mr. Averay would get a good title to the car. But if there was no contract of sale by Mr. Lewis to the rogue - either because there was, on the face of it, no agreement between the parties, or because any apparent agreement was a nullity and void ab initio for mistake, then no property would pass from Mr. Lewis to the rogue. Mr. Averay would not get a good title because the rogue had no property to pass to him.

There is no doubt that Mr. Lewis was mistaken as to the identity of the person who handed him the cheque. He thought that he was Richard Greene, a film actor of standing and worth: whereas in fact he was a rogue whose identity is quite unknown. It was under the influence of that mistake that Mr. Lewis let the rogue have the car. He would not have dreamed of letting him have it otherwise.

What is the effect of this mistake? There are two cases in our books which cannot, to my mind, be reconciled the one with the other. One of them is *Phillips v. Brooks Ltd.* [1919] 2 K.B. 243, where a jeweller had a ring for sale. The other is *Ingram v. Little* [1961] 1 Q.B. 31, where two ladies had a car for sale. In each case the story is very similar to the present. A plausible rogue comes along. The rogue says he likes the ring, or the car, as the case may be. He asks the price. The seller names it. The rogue says he is prepared to buy it at that price. He pulls out a cheque book. He writes, or prepares to write, a cheque for the price. The seller hesitates. He has never met this man before. He does not want to hand over the ring or the car not knowing whether the cheque will be met. The rogue notices the seller's hesitation. He is quick with his next move. He says to the jeweller, in *Phillips v. Brooks*: 'I am Sir George Bullough of 11 St. James's Square'; or to the ladies in *Ingram v. Little* 'I am P. G. M. Hutchinson of Stanstead House, Stanstead Road, Caterham'; or to the post-graduate student in the present case: 'I am Richard Greene, the film actor of the Robin Hood series.' Each seller checks up the information. The jeweller looks up the directory and finds there is a Sir George Bullough at 11 St. James's Square. The ladies check up too. They look at the telephone directory and find there is a 'P. G. M. Hutchinson of Stanstead House, Stanstead Road, Caterham.' The post-graduate student checks up too. He examines the official pass of the Pinewood Studios and finds that it is a pass for 'Richard A. Green' [sic] to the Pinewood Studios with this man's photograph on it. In each case the seller feels that this is sufficient confirmation of the man's identity. So he accepts the cheque signed by the rogue and lets him have the ring, in the one case, and the car and logbook in the other two cases. The rogue goes off and sells the goods to a third person who buys them in entire good faith and pays the price to the rogue. The rogue disappears. The original seller presents the cheque. It is dishonoured. Who is entitled to the goods? The original seller? Or the ultimate buyer? The courts have given different answers. In *Phillips v. Brooks*, the ultimate buyer was held to be entitled to the ring. In *Ingram v. Little* the original seller was held to be entitled to the car. In the present case the deputy county court judge has held the original seller entitled.

It seems to me that the material facts in each case are quite indistinguishable the one from the other. In each case there was, to all outward appearance, a contract: but there was a mistake by the seller as to the identity of the buyer. This mistake was fundamental. In each case it led to the handing over of the goods. Without it the seller would not have parted with them.

…In *Ingram v. Little* [1961] 1 Q.B. 31 the majority of the court suggested that the difference between *Phillips v. Brooks* [1919] 2 K.B. 243 and *Ingram v. Little* was that in *Phillips v. Brooks* the contract of sale was concluded (so as to pass the property to the rogue) before the rogue made the fraudulent misrepresentation: see [1961] 1 Q.B.

31, 51, 60: whereas in *Ingram v. Little* the rogue made the fraudulent misrepresentation before the contract was concluded. My own view is that in each case the property in the goods did not pass until the seller let the rogue have the goods.

Again it has been suggested that a mistake as to the identity of a person is one thing: and a mistake as to his attributes is another. A mistake as to identity, it is said, avoids a contract: whereas a mistake as to attributes does not. But this is a distinction without a difference. A man's very name is one of his attributes. It is also a key to his identity. If then, he gives a false name, is it a mistake as to his identity? or a mistake as to his attributes? These fine distinctions do no good to the law.

...I do not, therefore, accept the theory that a mistake as to identity renders a contract void.

I think the true principle is that which underlies the decision of this court in *King's Norton Metal Co. Ltd. v. Edridge Merrett & Co. Ltd.* (1897) 14 T.L.R. 98 and of Horridge J. in *Phillips v. Brooks* [1919] 2 K.B. 243, which has stood for these last 50 years. It is this: when two parties have come to a contract - or rather what appears, on the face of it, to be a contract - the fact that one party is mistaken as to the identity of the other does not mean that there is no contract, or that the contract is a nullity and void from the beginning. It only means that the contract is voidable, that is, liable to be set aside at the instance of the mistaken person, so long as he does so before third parties have in good faith acquired rights under it.

Although I very much regret that either of these good and reliable gentlemen should suffer, in my judgment it is Mr. Lewis who should do so. I think the appeal should be allowed and judgment entered for the defendant.

LORD JUSTICE MEGAW

For myself, with very great respect, I find it difficult to understand the basis, either in logic or in practical considerations, of the test laid down by the majority of the court in *Ingram v. Little* [1961] 1 Q.B. 31. ...

...

...The well-known textbook Cheshire and Fifoot on the Law of Contract 7th ed. (1969), 213 and 214, deals with the question of invalidity of a contract by virtue of unilateral mistake, and in particular unilateral mistake relating to mistaken identity. The editors describe what in their submission are certain facts that must be established in order to enable one to avoid a contract on the basis of unilateral mistake by him as to the identity of the opposite party. The first of those facts is that all the time when he made the offer he regarded the identity of the offeree as a matter of vital importance. To translate that into the facts of the present case, it must he established that at the time of offering to sell his car to the rogue, Mr. Lewis regarded the identity of the rogue as a matter of vital importance. In my view, Mr. Titheridge is abundantly justified, on the notes of the evidence and on the findings of the judge, in his submission that the mistake of Mr. Lewis went no further than a mistake as to the attributes of the rogue. It was simply a mistake as to the creditworthiness of the man who was there present and who described himself as Mr. Green...

...[I]t is, I think, clear, as Mr. Titheridge submits, that there was not here any evidence that would justify the finding that he, Mr. Lewis, regarded the identity of the man who called himself Mr. Green as a matter of vital importance.

I agree that the appeal should be allowed.

 Alert

The current position in relation to face to face contracts remains as outlined by Megaw LJ in *Lewis v Averay,* that is, it is presumed that the seller intended to deal with the person in front of them identified by sight and hearing, thus rendering the contract voidable for misrepresentation but not void for mistake.

This presumption will only be rebutted, and the contract held void for mistake, if the seller is able to establish that identity, rather than attributes, was of 'vital importance'. This would seem a very difficult burden to overcome.

15.2 Unilateral Mistake as to Identity: Non Face to Face (Distance Selling) Contracts

As a general rule, it is easier to establish that a contract is void for mistake when the parties are not dealing face to face.

Cundy v Lindsay (1878) 3 App Cas 459

Panel: Lord Cairns LC, Lord Hatherley, Lord Penzance and Lord Gordon

Facts: A rogue by the name of Mr Blenkarn rented a room at 37, Wood Street, Cheapside. He sent an order to the plaintiffs for handkerchiefs, signing his name to look like Blenkiron. Blenkiron & Co were in fact an established company at 123, Wood Street, Cheapside. Believing they were dealing with Blenkiron & Co, the plaintiffs dispatched the order. The rogue then sold most of the goods on to a third party, Cundy, who had bought them unaware of the fraud. The plaintiffs sued for return of the goods.

LORD CAIRNS LC

My Lords, you have in this case to discharge a duty which is always a disagreeable one for any Court, namely, to determine as between two parties, both of whom are perfectly innocent, upon which of the two the consequences of a fraud practised upon both of them must fall. …

My Lords, the question, therefore, in the present case, as your Lordships will observe, really becomes the very short and simple one which I am about to state. Was there any contract which, with regard to the goods in question in this case, had passed the property in the goods from the Messrs. Lindsay to Alfred Blenkarn? If there was any contract passing that property, even although, as I have said, that contract might afterwards be open to a process of reduction, upon the ground of fraud, still, in the meantime, Blenkarn might have conveyed a good title for valuable consideration to the present Appellants.

…The principal parties concerned, the Respondents and Blenkarn, never came in contact personally - everything that was done was done by writing. What has to be judged of, and what the jury in the present case had to judge of, was merely the conclusion to be derived from that writing, as applied to the admitted facts of the case.

Now, my Lords, discharging that duty and answering that inquiry, what the jurors have found is in substance this: it is not necessary to spell out the words, because the substance of it is beyond all doubt. They have found that by the form of the signatures to the letters which were written by Blenkarn, by the mode in which his letters and his applications to the Respondents were made out, and by the way in which he left uncorrected the mode and form in which, in turn, he was addressed by the Respondents; that by all those means he led, and intended to lead, the Respondents to believe, and they did believe, that the person with whom they were communicating was not Blenkarn, the dishonest and irresponsible man, but was a well known and solvent house of Blenkiron & Co., doing business in the same street. My Lords, those things are found as matters of fact, and they are placed beyond the range of dispute and controversy in the case.

If that is so, what is the consequence? It is that Blenkarn—the dishonest man, as I call him—was acting here just in the same way as if he had forged the signature of Blenkiron & Co., the respectable firm, to the applications for goods, and as if, when, in return, the goods were forwarded and letters were sent, accompanying them, he had intercepted the goods and intercepted the letters, and had taken possession of the goods, and of the letters which were addressed to, and intended for, not himself but, the firm of Blenkiron & Co. Now, my Lords, stating the matter shortly in that way, I ask the question, how is it possible to imagine that in that state of things any contract could have arisen between the Respondents and Blenkarn, the dishonest man? Of him they knew nothing, and of him they never thought. With him they never intended to deal. Their minds never, even for an instant of time rested upon him, and as between him and them there was no consensus of mind which could lead to any agreement or any contract whatever. As between him and them there was merely the one side to a contract, where, in order to produce a contract, two sides would be required. With the firm of Blenkiron & Co. of course there was no contract, for as to them the matter was entirely unknown, and therefore the pretence of a contract was a failure.

The result, therefore, my Lords, is this, that your Lordships have not here to deal with one of those cases in which there is de facto a contract made which may afterwards be impeached and set aside, on the ground of fraud; but you have to deal with a case which ranges itself under a completely different chapter of law, the case namely in which the contract never comes into existence. My Lords, that being so, it is idle to talk of the property passing. The property remained, as it originally had been, the property of the Respondents, and the title which was attempted to be given to the Appellants was a title which could not be given to them.

My Lords, I therefore move your Lordships that this appeal be dismissed with costs, and the judgment of the Court of Appeal affirmed.

The case of *Cundy v Lindsay* can be contrasted with the decision in *Kings Norton Metal v Edridge Merrett & Co Ltd* (1897) 14 TLR 98. In this case, the rogue created a bogus entity called Hallam & Co. He created some headed note-paper, adding in subsidiary branches of the company to give the impression that it was a well-established business. The rogue then ordered goods which he sold on to a third party before the fraud was discovered. In this case, the contract was not held to be void for mistake as the plaintiff had merely mistaken the customer's attributes (notably his creditworthiness) rather than his identity.

These two cases were discussed in the following case, as was the distinction between face to face and non face to face contracts. An opportunity was presented for their Lordships to clarify the area of mistake, although as you will see, their Lordships were not united in their approach.

Shogun Finance Ltd v Hudson [2004] 1 AC 919

Panel: Lord Nicholls of Birkenhead, Lord Hobhouse of Woodborough, Lord Millett, Lord Phillips of Worth Matravers and Lord Walker of Gestingthorpe

Facts: A fraudster visited a Mitsubishi showroom and agreed to buy a Mitsubishi Shogun on hire purchase. The hire purchase contract operated by way of the dealer selling the car to the finance company, who then made a contract with the customer for the hire of the car. The fraudster showed a driving licence stolen from a Mr Patel by means of identification, and signed the finance agreement. The dealer faxed over the signed agreement and a copy of the stolen driving licence to the finance company who proceeded to make the requisite credit checks on Mr Patel and approve the sale. The rogue then paid a deposit and was allowed to drive away the car. The following day, the rogue sold the car, complete with the valid paperwork, to an unsuspecting Mr Hudson.

Once the finance company discovered the fraud they brought a claim against Mr Hudson for damages in conversion and the claim ultimately went to the House of Lords. Note that Lord Nicholls and Lord Millett dissented from the majority.

LORD NICHOLLS OF BIRKENHEAD

1. My Lords, this appeal raises a difficult problem about the effect of fraudulent misrepresentation on the formation of a contract. If a crook (C) fraudulently represents to the owner of goods (O) that he is another identifiable person (X) and on that basis O parts with goods to C by way of sale, is there in law a contract between O and C? Does the answer to this question differ according to whether O and C communicated face-to-face, or by correspondence, or over the telephone, or by e-mail? The law on cases involving this type of fraudulent conduct, euphemistically described as cases of 'mistaken identity', is notoriously unsatisfactory. The reported decisions are few in number and they are not reconcilable. In the present case Sedley LJ said the law has tied itself into a Gordian knot. Brooke LJ said the law is in a 'sorry condition' which only Parliament or your Lordships' House can remedy: see [2002] QB 834, 847, 855, paras 23, 51.

...

Fraudulent misrepresentation and identity

12. ...The factual postulate now under consideration, as mentioned at the outset, is that a crook (C) fraudulently misrepresents to the owner of

goods (O) that he, C, is another identifiable person (X) whom O believes to be creditworthy. In reliance on this representation O agrees to sell the goods and he hands them over to C. Is this pursuant to a voidable contract between O and C? Or is there no contract between them at all? As between O and C the answer is of no moment. Either way O has ample remedies against C, assuming C has some money and can be traced. As already noted, however, the answer to these question may be of crucial importance to a third party who subsequently bought the goods in good faith from C.

13.   In cases of this type there are two innocent parties, O and the third party purchaser. Striking the right balance when one of two innocent parties must sustain a loss is seldom easy. ...

...

Fraudulent misrepresentation: face-to-face dealings

18.   I can now turn to the effect of a fraudulent misrepresentation made by a person about his identity. In cases of face-to-face dealings the law, as declared by the preponderance of authority, is tolerably clear. The owner of the goods believes the person in front of him is X, and in that belief he contracts with the person in front of him. The fraudulent misrepresentation by the crook C regarding his identity no more negatives O's intention to contract with C than, in my earlier example, the seller's misrepresentation about the identity of the proffered goods negatives the buyer's intention to buy the proffered goods. In each case the relevant intention is to be ascertained by looking at the position which, as a result of the misrepresentation, the other party believes to exist. On that footing there is consensus, in the relevant respect, between the parties. O believes C, the person in front of him, to be X and he deals with C in that belief. The fraud entitles O to avoid the contract, but it does not negative the formation of a contract with C.

 Alert

...

Fraudulent misrepresentation: dealing by correspondence

26.   But what of the case where a fraudulent misrepresentation is made in writing but O and C do not meet each other? C writes to O saying he is X and the deal proceeds on that basis. O parts with his goods to the person with whom he is in fact dealing, namely, C, in the belief he is X.

27.   At first sight it seems counter-intuitive to speak of a contract between O and C in cases of this type. It seems counter-intuitive because on its face a contract in writing or in correspondence expressed to be made between O and X is inconsistent, agency apart, with its being a contract between O and C. But this intuitive response is not a sound guide if it leaves out of account, as all too easily it may, the vitally important underlying fraudulent misrepresentation. In his dealings with O the crook C represented he was X, and O proceeded to deal with him (C) in that belief.

28. When this feature is kept in mind it readily becomes apparent that in principle cases of this type are no different from cases of face-to-face dealings. The existence of physical immediacy in one case, and the absence of it in the other, is immaterial. The physical immediacy of C in face-to-face cases tends to emphasise O's intention to deal with the person in front of him. With other forms of communication such as the telephone or correspondence this physical immediacy is lacking. But in each case, whatever the mode of communication, what matters is whether O agreed to sell his goods to the person with whom he was dealing, not why he did so or under what name. The latter is relevant to remedy, not to formation of a contract.

29. In this regard mention must be made of reasoning sometimes advanced here, along the lines that the identity of the person to whom a written offer is made is a question solely of construction of the document. The offer, it is said, is made to the person identified in the document and no one else. A written offer made by O to X is not capable of acceptance by C. Hence, it is said that, whatever the position in face-to-face dealings, in cases of written contracts or contracts made by correspondence there can be no contract between O and C, contradicting as this would the terms of the document.

30. The flaw in this reasoning is that it begs the crucial question: to whom was the offer made? The reasoning assumes this is a straightforward case of an offer made to the person named. Indeed the person named is X. But that is only part of the picture.

O believes that X, the person to whom he is writing and to whom he addressed the offer, is one and the same person as the person with whom he is dealing. In fact he is not dealing with X. He is dealing with C. O's misapprehension in this regard, induced by C's fraud, is no different in principle from a case where C's misrepresentation is made orally in the course of the face-to-face meeting. The legal problem is the same in both cases. The presence or absence of writing does not constitute a principled ground of distinction.

 Alert

31. Thus, when Lindsay & Co supplied linen handkerchiefs in response to a written order they were under a misapprehension regarding the identity of the person placing the order in the same way as the jeweller in the shop was under a misapprehension regarding the identity of his customer ('I am Sir George Bullough') in *Phillips v Brooks Ltd* [1919] 2 KB 243. If the approach adopted in *Phillips v Brooks Ltd* is correct, Lindsay's misapprehension no more negatived the formation of a contract with the person placing the written order for handkerchiefs than did the like misapprehension by the jeweller in *Phillips v Brooks Ltd*. The jeweller parted with his ring to the customer in his shop. Lindsay parted with their linen by sending it to the address supplied by the crook. On what terms? The answer must be, on the terms agreed between Lindsay and the person with whom they were dealing. That was a contract Lindsay could have enforced, had they wished. Or they

could have repudicated it on the grounds of fraudulent misrepresentation.

32. In *Cundy v Lindsay* 3 App Cas 459 the House reached the contrary conclusion. The reasoning of all their Lordships was to the same effect. Lord Cairns LC encapsulated this reasoning, at p 465:

'Of [the crook Blenkarn] [Lindsay] knew nothing, and of him they never thought. With him they never intended to deal. Their minds never, even for an instant of time rested upon him, and as between him and them there was no consensus of mind which could lead to any arrangement or any contract whatever.'

Lord Hatherley and Lord Penzance left open what the position would be had the crook come into personal contact with Lindsay.

The choice

33. In my view this decision is not reconcilable with *Phillips v Brooks Ltd* [1919] 2 KB 243 or with *Lewis v Averay* [1972] 1 QB 198 or with the starting point 'presumption' formulated by Devlin LJ in *Ingram v Little* [1961] 1 QB 31. The legal principle applicable in these cases cannot sensibly differ according to whether the transaction is negotiated face-to-face, or by letter, or by fax, or by e-mail, or over the telephone or by video link or video telephone. Typically today a purchaser pays for goods with a credit or debit card. He produces the card in person in a shop or provides details of the card over the telephone or by e-mail or by fax. When a credit or debit card is fraudulently misused in this way the essence of the transaction is the same in each case. It does not differ from one means of communication to the next. The essence of the transaction in each case is that the owner of the goods agrees to part with his goods on the basis of a fraudulent misrepresentation made by the other regarding his identity. Since the essence of the transaction is the same in each case, the law in its response should apply the same principle in each case, irrespective of the precise mode of communication of offer and acceptance.

 Alert

34. Accordingly, if the law of contract is to be coherent and rescued from its present unsatisfactory and unprincipled state, the House has to make a choice: either to uphold the approach adopted in *Cundy v Lindsay* and overrule the decisions in *Phillips v Brooks Ltd* and *Lewis v Averay*, or to prefer these later decisions to *Cundy v Lindsay*.

35. I consider the latter course is the right one, for a combination of reasons. It is in line with the direction in which, under the more recent decisions, the law has now been moving for some time. It accords better with basic principle regarding the effect of fraud on the formation of a contract. It seems preferable as a matter of legal policy. As between two innocent persons the loss is more appropriately borne by the person who takes the risks inherent in parting with his goods without receiving payment. This approach fits comfortably with the intention of Parliament in enacting the limited statutory exceptions to the

 Alert

proprietary principle of nemo dat quod non habet. Thus, by section 23 of the 1979 Act Parliament protected an innocent buyer from a seller with a voidable title... . In a case such as the present the owner of the goods has no interest in the identity of the buyer. He is interested only in creditworthiness. It is little short of absurd that a subsequent purchaser's rights depend on the precise manner in which the crook seeks to persuade the owner of his creditworthiness and permit him to take the goods away with him. This ought not to be so. The purchaser's rights should not depend upon the precise form the crook's misrepresentation takes.

36. *Cundy v Lindsay* has stood for a long time. But I see no reason to fear that adopting this conclusion will unsettle the law of contract. In practice the problems surrounding *Cundy v Lindsay* arise only when third parties' rights are in issue. To bring the law here into line with the law already existing in 'face-to-face' cases will rid the law of an anomaly. Devlin LJ's starting point presumption is a workable foundation which should apply in all cases. A person is presumed to intend to contract with the person with whom he is actually dealing, whatever be the mode of communication.

...

38. It follows that I would allow this appeal. ...

LORD HOBHOUSE OF WOODBOROUGH

...

47. The first point is a matter of the construction of the written document. It admits of only one conclusion. There is no mention in the document of anyone other than Mr Durlabh Patel. The language used is clear and specific, both in the substance of the identification — name and address and driving licence number and age — and in the express words of the offer and acceptance clause — 'the customer named overleaf'. ...

48. It has been suggested that the finance company was willing to do business with anyone, whatever their name. But this is not correct: it was only willing to do business with a person who had identified himself in the way required by the written document so as to enable it to check before it enters into any contractual or other relationship that he meets its credit requirements. Mr Durlabh Patel was such an identified person and met its credit requirements so it was willing to do business with him. If the applicant had been, say, Mr B Patel of Ealing or Mr G Patel of Edgbaston, it would not have been willing to deal with them if they could not be identified or did not meet with its credit requirements. Correctly identifying the customer making the offer is an essential precondition of the willingness of the finance company to deal with that person. The Rogue knew, or at least confidently expected, that the finance company would be prepared to deal with Mr Durlabh Patel but probably not with

him, the Rogue; and he was, in any event, not willing himself to enter into any contract with the finance company. This is not a case such as that categorised by Sedley LJ ([2002] QB at 846) as the use of a 'simple alias' to disguise the purchaser rather than to deceive the vendor — the situation which resembles that in *King's Norton Metal v Edridge Merrett & Co* (14 TLR 98). But, even then, in a credit agreement it would be useless to use a pseudonym as no actual verifiable person against whom a credit check could be run would have been disclosed and the offer would never be accepted. Mr Durlabh Patel is the sole hirer under this written agreement. No one else acquires any rights under it; no one else can become the bailee of the motor car or the 'debtor' 'under the agreement'. It is not in dispute that R was not Mr Durlabh Patel nor that R had no authority from Mr Patel to enter into the agreement or take possession of the motor car.

49. Mr Hudson seeks to escape from this conclusion by saying: 'but the Rogue was the person who came into the dealer's office and negotiated a price with the dealer and signed the form in the presence of the dealer who then witnessed it.' The third and fourth points address this argument. The gist of the argument is that oral evidence may be adduced to contradict the agreement contained in a written document which is the only contract to which the finance company was a party. The agreement is a written agreement with Mr Durlabh Patel. The argument seeks to contradict this and make it an agreement with the Rogue. It is argued that other evidence is always admissible to show who the parties to an agreement are. Thus, if the contents of the document are, without more, insufficient unequivocally to identify the actual individual referred to or if the identification of the party is non-specific, evidence can be given to fill any gap. ... But it is different where the party is, as here, specifically identified in the document: oral or other extrinsic evidence is not admissible. ... The rule that other evidence may not be adduced to contradict the provisions of a contract contained in a written document is fundamental to the mercantile law of this country; the bargain is the document; the certainty of the contract depends on it. The relevant principle is well summarised in Phipson on Evidence, paragraphs 42–11 and 42–12: 'When the parties have deliberately put their agreement into writing, it is conclusively presumed between themselves and their privies that they intend the writing to form a full and final statement of their intentions, and one which should be placed beyond the reach of future controversy, bad faith or treacherous memory.'

...

54. It follows that the appeal must be dismissed and the majority judgment of the Court of Appeal affirmed.

...

LORD MILLETT

56.   My Lords, A makes an offer to B. B accepts it, believing that he is dealing with C. A knows of B's mistake, and may even have deliberately caused it. What is the result of the transaction? Is there a contract at all? There is obviously no contract with C, who is not a party to the transaction and knows nothing of it. But is there a contract with A? And if so is it void or merely voidable?

57.   Generations of law students have struggled with this problem. They may be forgiven for thinking that it is contrived by their tutors to test their mettle. After all, the situation seems artificial and is one which is seldom likely to arise in practice, at least in the absence of fraud. Unfortunately fraudulent impersonation is not at all uncommon today. The growth in the number of credit transactions, often entered into electronically between persons unknown to each other, has led to a surge in what has been called 'theft of identity', that is the fraudulent assumption of another's identity by a customer in order to have the wrong account debited or to misdirect inquiries into his own creditworthiness. In the classic case A, fraudulently masquerading as C, buys goods on credit from B; B, having conducted appropriate checks to satisfy himself that C is worthy of credit and believing A to be C, lets A have possession of the goods; and A thereupon sells the goods to D, an unsuspecting purchaser, before disappearing without paying for them. Who is to bear the loss? That depends on whether D, who has paid for the goods, has obtained title to them, for if not then B can reclaim them. But D will have obtained title only if A was able to transfer title to him, and this turns on whether the transaction between A and B resulted in a voidable contract for the purchase of the goods by A (which B will have been unable to avoid in time) or no contract at all.

58.   The problem is sometimes mentioned in the textbooks in the section which deals with the formation of contract, where the question is whether a contract has been concluded; but it is more usually dealt with in the section which is concerned with the effect of mistake and in particular 'mistaken identity', where the question is said to turn on whether A's identity is (i) 'fundamental' (in which case the contract is completely void) or (ii) 'material' but not 'fundamental' (in which case the contract is merely voidable). In his dissenting judgment in *Ingram v Little* [1961] 1 QB 31, 64 Devlin LJ distinguished between the two questions and observed that it was easy to fall into error if one did not begin with the first question, whether there is sufficient correlation between offer and acceptance to bring a contract into existence. But if there is, I question whether the contract should be held to be void for mistake rather than merely voidable.

59.   As I have said, the situation is seldom likely to arise in practice in the absence of fraud, and where the fraud is not directed to the identity of the offeror the contract is only voidable, not void, for the victim of

deception ought to be able to elect to affirm the contract if he chooses to do so. It seems anomalous that a mistake which is induced by fraud should have a less vitiating effect than one which is not; and it is difficult to see why a mistake induced by fraud should make a contract altogether void if it is a mistake as to the offeror's identity (whatever that may mean) and not if it is a mistake as to some other attribute of his such as his creditworthiness which may be equally or more material.

60. As Treitel observes (The Law of Contract, 10th ed (1999), p 277) it is often difficult to say precisely what mistake has been made and, even when this is clear, it is often difficult to say whether it should be classified as a mistake of identity or of attribute. As between A and B themselves, of course, it does not normally matter whether the contract is void or merely voidable; it obviously cannot be enforced by A against B's wishes in either case. The question usually assumes importance only where an innocent third party is involved, and then it is critical. Under the law as it stands at present, his title depends on whether the fraudster obtained the goods in his own name by means of a false or forged credit reference or in the name of another by means of a genuine reference relating to that other. This is indefensible. I take the view that the law should if at all possible favour a solution which protects innocent third parties by treating the contract as voidable rather than void, whether for fraud or for mistake.

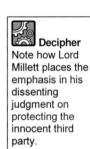

Decipher
Note how Lord Millett places the emphasis in his dissenting judgment on protecting the innocent third party.

61. My Lords, I think that the time has come to follow the lead given by Lord Denning MR more than 30 years ago in *Lewis v Averay* [1972] 1 QB 198. He roundly rejected the theory that if a party is mistaken as to the identity of the person with whom he is contracting there is no contract, or that if there is a contract it is null and void so that no property can pass under it: see pp 206-207. He thought that the doctrine, derived from the writings of Pothier, should not be admitted as part of English law but should be 'dead and buried'. As he observed, it gives rise to fine distinctions which do no good to the law, and it is unjust that an innocent third party, who knows nothing of what passed between the rogue and his vendor, should have his title depend on such refinements.

62. But it is still necessary to answer the logically anterior and more difficult question: does the transaction result in the formation of a contract between A and B? There is clearly a transaction between them, for B has let A have possession of the goods and take them away, usually with the intention that he should be free to deal with them as owner. But is the transaction contractual?

63. It is trite law, as Devlin LJ explained in the passage immediately following that cited above, that before a contract can come into existence there must be offer and acceptance, and these must correspond. The offer must be addressed to the offeree, either as an individual or as a member of a class or of the public. The acceptance must come from one who is so addressed and must itself be addressed

to the offeror. It is not possible in law for a person to accept an offer made to someone else; or to intercept an acceptance of someone else's offer and treat it as an acceptance of his own.

64. This is usually straightforward enough, at least in the absence of fraud. As my noble and learned friend, Lord Phillips of Worth Matravers, observes, there is normally no difference between the identity of the person to whom the offer or acceptance is directed and the person for whom it is intended. But what if, by reason of fraud, the two are not the same? What if A, posing as C, makes an offer to B which B purports to accept? B directs his acceptance to A, but intends it for C. It does not help to substitute the question: 'To whom was B's acceptance made?' This merely raises the question: 'What do you mean by 'made'?'

65. The outcome is said to depend on B's intention objectively ascertained, and this is usually treated as if it were a straightforward question of fact to be determined on the evidence. In *Ingram v Little* [1961] 1 QB 31 Pearce LJ said, at p 61, that 'Each case must be decided on its own facts.' This is singularly unhelpful, since it involves asking: did B intend to contract with A believing him to be C? Or with C believing him to be A? The question is meaningless. As Devlin LJ pointed out in *Ingram v Little*, at p 65:

'If Miss Ingram had been asked whether she intended to contract with the man in the room or with P G M Hutchinson, the question could have no meaning for her, since she believed them both to be one and the same. The reasonable man of the law—if he stood in Miss Ingram's shoes—could not give any better answer ... All that Miss Ingram or any other witness in her position can say is that she did in fact accept the offer made to her; and that, if she had not been tricked or deceived, she would not have accepted it.' (Emphasis added.)

66. In this situation the courts have distinguished between transactions entered into in writing and transactions entered into orally between parties who are in the presence of each other. In the former case B's intention is ascertained by construing the description of the counterparty in the contract. This naturally identifies C, the person whose identity A has fraudulently assumed, and (provided that C actually exists) invariably leads to the conclusion that there is no counterparty and therefore no contract. In the latter case, the courts have adopted a different approach. They have introduced a rebuttable presumption that, where parties deal with each other face-to-face, each of them intends to contract with the physical person to whom he addresses the words of contract. Unless the presumption is rebutted, this must lead to the conclusion that there is a contract with the impostor.

67. I do not find this satisfactory. What evidence is sufficient to rebut the presumption? As Devlin LJ stressed, it cannot be rebutted by piling up evidence that B would never have accepted the offer if he had not

thought that it had been made by C. Such evidence merely shows that the deception was material; it does not establish the identity of B's counterparty. There might perhaps be something to be said for making the presumption conclusive. ...

68.   But the real objection to the present state of the law, in my view, is that the distinction between the face-to-face contract and other contracts is unrealistic. ...My difficulty is that I cannot see that there is any difference in principle between the two situations when it comes to identifying B's counterparty. In both cases B's acceptance is directed to the impostor but intended for the person whose identity he has assumed. ...

69.   In *Ingram v Little* [1961] 1 QB 31 Devlin LJ said, at p 66, that 'the presumption that a person is intending to contract with the person to whom he is actually addressing the words of contract seems to me to be a simple and sensible one ...' I respectfully agree. But why should it be adopted only in the case of a contract entered into between persons who deal in the physical presence of each other? If the offeree's words of acceptance are taken to be addressed to the physical person standing in his presence who made the offer, what is the position where they deal with each other by telephone? Is the disembodied voice to be equated with physical presence? Is it sufficient that the parties are in the hearing of each other? Does it make a difference if the dealing is by televisual link, so that the parties are in the hearing and sight but not the presence of each other? New means of communication make the distinction untenable.

70.   But in truth the distinction was always unsound. If the offeree's words of acceptance are taken to be addressed to the physical person standing in his presence who made the offer, why is the contract entered into by correspondence different? Why is the offeree's letter of acceptance not taken to be addressed to the physical person who made the written offer which he is accepting? The offeree addresses the offeror by his assumed name in both cases. Why should this be treated as decisive in the one case and disregarded in the other? Indeed, the correlation between offer and acceptance is likely to be greater in the case of a contract entered into by correspondence, since the offeree's letter of acceptance will either be sent to the impostor at his own address or be delivered to him personally and it will almost certainly contain internal references to his offer.

71.   In my opinion there are only two principled solutions to the problem. The law must give preference, either to the person for whom the offer or acceptance is intended, or to the person to whom it is directed, and must do so in all cases as a matter of law. The difficulty is in deciding which solution should be adopted, for there is much to commend each of them.

72. The first solution, which gives preference to the person for whom the offer or acceptance is intended, possibly accords more closely to the existing authorities, which treat the face-to-face transaction as an exception to the general rule, and with the decision in *Cundy v Lindsay* 3 App Cas 459, the only case on the subject which has come before the House. It also accords more closely with the parties' subjective intentions, for B intends to deal with C, especially if he has checked his creditworthiness, and not with A, of whom he has never heard; while A has no intention of being bound by contract at all. From his point of view the supposed contract is merely a pretence to enable him to get hold of goods without paying for them. He does not need a contract, for he is content with possession without title. In the days when the law distinguished between trickery and deception, he would have obtained possession by a trick rather than title by false pretences.

73. The strongest argument in favour of this solution, I suppose, is that it could be said to be based on the parties' own assessment of what they mean by the counterparty's 'identity'. Ultimately this must refer to a physical person, but a physical person can only be identified by describing his or her attributes. For this purpose it is customary to refer to a person's name and address, which are usually though not always unique to one person. But names are merely identifying labels and can be assumed without any intention to deceive. A person is free to adopt whatever name suits his fancy, and may validly contract under an alias. Even if he has assumed a false name for the sole purpose of deceiving the counterparty, there is a contract so long, at least, as there is no real person of that name: see *King's Norton Metal Co Ltd v Edridge, Merrett & Co Ltd* 14 TLR 98.

74. But as Treitel observes (The Law of Contract, 10th ed, p 277) a person may be identified by reference to any one of his attributes. He may be identified as 'the person in the room', 'the person who spoke on the telephone', 'the person who appended the illegible signature', 'the writer of the letter under reply', or 'the person who made the offer'; but he may also be identified, and sometimes more relevantly, as 'the person whose creditworthiness has been checked and found to be satisfactory'. Any of these may be the means of identifying a unique person. ...

75. Given the equivocal nature of a person's 'identity', there is something to be said for selecting those aspects of the offeror's identity which are material in causing the other party to accept the offer. In the present case, for example, Mr Patel's name address and date of birth had no intrinsic relevance in themselves. The claimant would have entered into the transaction with anyone, whatever his name and address or date of birth, so long as it was satisfied that he was worthy of credit. Mr Patel's personal details were merely the information which enabled it to conduct inquiries into the credit of the person it assumed to be its customer. It makes commercial sense to treat a contract made in these

circumstances as purporting to be made between the finance company and the subject of its inquiries rather than with the person who merely produced the information necessary to enable it to make them.

76. Nevertheless I have come to the conclusion that it is the second solution which ought to be adopted. All the considerations which I have mentioned, and which seem to favour the first solution, when properly analysed go to the mechanics of the deception and its materiality rather than to the identity of the offeror. They ought to come into play when consideration is given to the second question, whether the contract is voidable, rather than to the first, whether there is sufficient correlation between offer and acceptance ('consensus ad idem') to bring a contract into existence. Until the fraud is exposed and it is discovered that A is not C, the existence of a contract is not in doubt. The fraud is relevant to the question whether the contract is enforceable against B rather than its existence.

77. I regard *King's Norton Metal Co. Ltd. v Edridge, Merrett & Co. Ltd.* (*supra*) as worthy of more attention than it has usually been given. In that case, where the contract was entered into by correspondence, the rogue assumed a fictitious name in order to give a spurious impression of respectability. The Court held that there was a valid (though voidable) contract. The decisive feature was thought to be that there was no one of the assumed name. A.L. Smith LJ is reported at p. 99 as follows:

'The question was, With whom, upon this evidence, which was all one way, did the plaintiffs contract to sell the goods? *Clearly with the writer of the letters.* If it could have been shown that there was a separate entity called Hallam and Co [C] and another entity called Wallis [A] then the case might have come within the decision in *Cundy v Lindsay.* In his opinion there was a contract by the plaintiffs with the person who wrote the letters, by which the property passed to him. There was only one entity, trading it might be under an alias, and there was a contract by which the property passed to him' (emphasis added).

78. It is unclear whether it would have made a difference if, unknown to the plaintiffs, there had been an entity called Hallam and Co; or if to the knowledge of both parties there were many such entities, as in the cases where a man used to book a hotel room for himself and a girlfriend under a common but fictitious name in order to give the impression (when such things mattered) that they were married. The case is different where the impostor assumes the name and address of a real person of substance when entering into a credit transaction. In such a case his purpose is to direct inquiries to that person's credit rather than his own. A better explanation of *King's Norton Metal Co. Ltd. v Edridge, Merrett & Co. Lt*d. is that the rogue merely assumed a false name and did not go further and assume another person's identity. But the distinction is a fine one which it may not always be possible to draw, and in any case depends on the nature and purpose of the deception

and is accordingly relevant to its effect on the mind of the offeree and not to the correlation between offer and acceptance.

...

83. In the Court of Appeal [2002] QB 834 both Sedley LJ (who dissented) and Brooke LJ, at p 855, para 51, expressed disquiet at 'the sorry condition' of the law. In the former's view, with which I agree, the decision in *Cundy v Lindsay* 3 App Cas 459 stands in the way of a coherent development of this branch of the law. We have the opportunity to restate the law, and cannot shirk the duty of putting it on a basis which is both just and principled, even if it means deciding that we should no longer follow a previous decision of the House.

84. We cannot leave the law as it is. It is neither fair nor principled, and not all the authorities from which it is derived can be reconciled; some, at least, must be overruled if it is to be extricated from the present quagmire. If the law is to be rationalised and placed on a proper footing, the formulation which I have proposed has the merit of according with the recommendations made in the Twelfth Report of the Law Reform Committee on the Transfer of Title to Chattels (Cmnd 2958) and in Anson's Law of Contract, 28th ed, p 332. It would also bring English law into line with the law both in the United States and in Germany. The law of the United States has not stood still. Section 2-403 of the Uniform Commercial Code, 14th ed, p 117 provides by subsection (1):

'A person with voidable title has power to transfer a good title to a good faith purchaser for value. When goods have been delivered under a transaction of purchase the purchaser has such power even though— (a) the transferor was deceived as to the identity of the purchaser ...'

Any restriction of the rule to face-to-face transactions has disappeared. In the Official Comment on the section, p 118, reference is made to 'the long-standing policy of civil protection of buyers from persons guilty of such trick or fraud'. This seems to me to be a policy which accords with good sense and justice and one which we ought to adopt for ourselves. I agree with the view of Professor Atiyah, An Introduction to the Law of Contract, 5th ed (1995), p 86 that 'a person who hands goods over to a stranger in return for a cheque is obviously taking a major risk, and it does not seem fair that he should be able to shift the burden of this risk on to the innocent third party'.

...

108. ...*Cundy v Lindsay* 3 App Cas 459, a decision of this House which has stood for more than 120 years ... cannot be regarded as authoritative on the question whether a contract otherwise properly entered into is void for mistake rather than voidable. It has had an unfortunate influence on the development of the law, leading to an unprincipled distinction between face-to-face transactions and others and the indefensible conclusion that an innocent purchaser's position depends on the nature of the mistake of

a third party or the precise mechanics of the fraud which had been perpetrated on him. In my view it should now be discarded and the law put on a simpler and more principled and defensible basis.

109. In my opinion only the decision in *Cundy v Lindsay* stands in the way of a rational and coherent restatement of the law. My noble and learned friend, Lord Phillips of Worth Matravers, has expressed the view that the conclusion to which Lord Nicholls and I have come conflicts not only with that case but with the approach in almost all the numerous cases which he has cited. If they had preceded *Cundy v Lindsay*, that would be a strong reason for not adopting it. But they were merely following a decision of this House by which they were bound. Far from applying it generally, they attempted to distinguish it by carving out an unprincipled exception from it which Lord Nicholls has shown cannot be supported. While departing from *Cundy v Lindsay* would make obsolete the reasoning in those cases, dictated as it was by that decision, it would undermine the actual decision in very few cases. There is no long line of authority to be overruled. Indeed, only two cases need to be overruled; and neither of them can be supported even on the view that *Cundy v Lindsay* was rightly decided.

110. In my opinion *Cundy v Lindsay* 3 App Cas 459 should no longer be followed and *Ingram v Little* [1961] 1 QB 31 ... should be overruled. I would allow the appeal.

LORD PHILLIPS OF WORTH MATRAVERS

111. My Lords, this appeal is a variation on a theme that has bemused courts and commentators alike for over 150 years. Two individuals conduct negotiations in which all the terms necessary to constitute a binding contract are agreed. One of those individuals has, however, been masquerading as a third party. Does a binding contract result?

...

119. The critical issue in this case is whether a hire-purchase agreement was ever concluded between Shogun and the rogue. If an agreement was concluded, then the rogue was the 'debtor' under section 27 of the 1964 Act and passed good title in the vehicle to Mr Hudson. If no agreement was concluded, then the rogue stole the vehicle by deception and passed no title to Mr Hudson.

...

Formation of contract

123. A contract is normally concluded when an offer made by one party ('the offeror') is accepted by the party to whom the offer has been made ('the offeree'). Normally the contract is only concluded when the acceptance is communicated by the offeree to the offeror. A contract will not be concluded unless the parties are agreed as to its material terms. There must be 'consensus ad idem'. Whether the parties have reached

agreement on the terms is not determined by evidence of the subjective intention of each party. It is, in large measure, determined by making an objective appraisal of the exchanges between the parties. If an offeree understands an offer in accordance with its natural meaning and accepts it, the offeror cannot be heard to say that he intended the words of his offer to have a different meaning. The contract stands according to the natural meaning of the words used. There is one important exception to this principle. If the offeree knows that the offeror does not intend the terms of the offer to be those that the natural meaning of the words would suggest, he cannot, by purporting to accept the offer, bind the offeror to a contract: *Hartog v Colin & Shields* [1939] 3 All ER 566; *Smith v Hughes* (1871) LR 6 QB 597. Thus the task of ascertaining whether the parties have reached agreement as to the terms of a contract can involve quite a complex amalgam of the objective and the subjective and involve the application of a principle that bears close comparison with the doctrine of estoppel. Normally, however, the task involves no more than an objective analysis of the words used by the parties. The object of the exercise is to determine what each party intended, or must be deemed to have intended.

...

125. Just as the parties must be shown to have agreed on the terms of the contract, so they must also be shown to have agreed the one with the other. If A makes an offer to B, but C purports to accept it, there will be no contract. Equally, if A makes an offer to B and B addresses his acceptance to C there will be no contract. Where there is an issue as to whether two persons have reached an agreement, the one with the other, the courts have tended to adopt the same approach to resolving that issue as they adopt when considering whether there has been agreement as to the terms of the contract. The court asks the question whether each intended, or must be deemed to have intended, to contract with the other. That approach gives rise to a problem where one person is mistaken as to the identity of the person with whom he is dealing, as the cases demonstrate. I propose at this point to consider those cases.

...

149. Giving the leading judgment, Lord Denning MR commented that it was impossible to distinguish between *Phillips v Brooks Ltd* [1919] 2 KB 243 and *Ingram v Little* [1961] 1 QB 31 on the facts. ...

150. Phillimore LJ agreed, though in a manner which paid due respect to the doctrine of precedent. He referred, at p 208, to the fact that *Ingram v Little* was a case of 'very special and unusual facts' and held that there was nothing that could displace the prima facie presumption that the plaintiff was dealing with the rogue. The case was on all fours with *Phillips v Brooks Ltd*, which had been good law for 50 years.

151. Megaw LJ concurred, observing that he found it difficult to understand the basis, either in logic or in practical considerations, of the test laid down in *Ingram v Little*.

152. Lord Denning MR did not apply the approach of attempting to identify the intention of the plaintiff. He proceeded on the simple basis that, to all outward appearances, the plaintiff entered into an agreement with the rogue, with whom he was dealing. Both he and Phillimore LJ considered that the case was on all fours with *Phillips v Brooks Ltd*, which had been rightly decided.

153. The difficulty in applying a test of intention to the identification of the parties to a contract arises, so it seems to me, only where the parties conduct their dealings in some form of inter-personal contact, and where one purports to have the identity of a third party. There the innocent party will have in mind, when considering with whom he is contracting, both the person with whom he is in contact and the third party whom he imagines that person to be.

154 The same problem will not normally arise where the dealings are carried out exclusively in writing. The process of construction of the written instruments, making appropriate use of extrinsic evidence, will normally enable the court to reach a firm conclusion as to the person with whom a party intends to contract. This was the position in *Boulton v Jones* 27 LJ Ex 117, *Cundy v Lindsay* 3 App Cas 459 *and King's Norton Metal Co Ltd v Edridge, Merrett & Co Ltd* 14 TLR 98. There is a substantial body of authority that demonstrates that the identity of a party to a contract in writing falls to be determined by a process of construction of the putative contract itself. ...

...

The result in the present case

167. I have had the advantage of reading in draft the opinions of my noble and learned friends who have sat with me on this appeal. Lord Hobhouse of Woodborough and Lord Walker of Gestingthorpe have concluded that, as the contract was a written document, the identity of the hirer falls to be ascertained by construing that document. Adopting that approach, the hirer was, or more accurately purported to be, Mr Patel. As he had not authorised the conclusion of the contract, it was void.

168. Lord Nicholls of Birkenhead and Lord Millett have adopted a different approach. They point out the illogicality of applying a special approach to face-to-face dealings. What of dealings on the telephone, or by videolink? There also it could be said that each of the parties to the dealings is seeking to make a contract with the other party to the dealings. And this can even be said when the dealings are conducted by correspondence. If A writes to B making an offer and B writes back

responding to that offer, B is intending to contract with the person who made that offer. If a contract is concluded in face-to-face dealings, notwithstanding that one party is masquerading as a third party, why should the result be different when the dealings are by letter?

169. Lord Nicholls of Birkenhead and Lord Millett propose an elegant solution to this illogicality. Where two individuals deal with each other, by whatever medium, and agree terms of a contract, then a contract will be concluded between them, notwithstanding that one has deceived the other into thinking that he has the identity of a third party. In such a situation the contract will be voidable but not void. While they accept that this approach cannot be reconciled with *Cundy v Lindsay* 3 App Cas 459, they conclude that *Cundy v Lindsay* was wrongly decided and should no longer be followed.

170. While I was strongly attracted to this solution, I have found myself unable to adopt it. *Cundy v Lindsay* exemplifies the application by English law of the same approach to identifying the parties as is applied to identifying the terms of the contract. In essence this focuses on deducing the intention of the parties from their words and conduct. Where there is some form of personal contact between individuals who are conducting negotiations, this approach gives rise to problems. In such a situation I would favour the application of a strong presumption that each intends to contract with the other, with whom he is dealing. Where, however, the dealings are exclusively conducted in writing, there is no scope or need for such a presumption. ...

 Alert

...

176. ...I have not found the assessment of the law easy, but nor is the application of the law to the facts. Shogun's representatives were aware of the presence of the prospective hirer in the dealer's showrooms in Leicester. To an extent the dealings were interpersonal through the medium of the dealer. Should one treat them as comparable to face-to-face dealings and conclude that there was a presumption that Shogun intended to contract with the man with whom they were dealing? Should one treat the written agreement as no more than peripheral to the dealings and conclude that it does not override that presumption? I have concluded that the answer to these questions is 'no'.

...

178. These considerations lead me to conclude that the correct approach in the present case is to treat the agreement as one concluded in writing and to approach the identification of the parties to that agreement as turning upon its construction. The particulars given in the agreement are only capable of applying to Mr Patel. It was the intention of the rogue that they should identify Mr Patel as the hirer. The hirer was so identified by Shogun. Before deciding to enter into the agreement they checked that Mr Patel existed and that he was worthy of credit. On that

> basis they decided to contract with him and with no one else. Mr Patel was the hirer under the agreement. As the agreement was concluded without his authority, it was a nullity. The rogue took no title under it and was in no position to convey any title to Mr Hudson.
>
> 179. For these reasons I would dismiss this appeal.
>
> ...

Shogun may be regarded as a missed opportunity to clarify the law of unilateral mistake as to identity. That this area of law continues to lack coherence will be evident from the above discussion. It is submitted that the position proposed in the two strong dissenting judgments of Lords Nicholls and Millett, that whenever identity is fraudulently misrepresented, whether this be conducted face to face or at a distance, the result should be to always render a contract voidable rather than void, would have marked a considerable improvement upon the current position. Instead, the majority choose to formalise the distinction between face to face and non face to face dealings. However, the reasoning of the majority differed in that Lord Hobhouse, with whom Lord Walker concurred, placed emphasis on the construction of the document and application of the parol evidence rule, whereas Lord Phillips placed the emphasis on formation of a contract regarding mistake as to identity. *Ingram v Little* was not specifically overruled, but their Lordships were clear that in face to face dealings you will be presumed to deal with the person who is physically present, which means *Ingram* is highly unlikely to be followed in the future.

Further Reading

Goodhart, (1941). *Mistake as to identity in the Law of Contract.* 57 LQR 228

Hare, (2004). *Identity mistakes: a lost opportunity.* 67. Modern Law Review 993

McLauchlan, (2005). *Mistake of Identity and Contract Formation.* 21 JCL 1

MacMillan, (2005). *Rogues, swindlers and cheats: the development of mistake of identity in English contract law.* C.L.J. 64(3), 711-744

McKendrick, E., *Contract Law* (2017) 12th ed. Ch.14

16

Discharge I

Topic List

Introduction

This chapter describes the ways in which a contract can be brought to an end (ie 'discharged') by the parties. The contract might be brought to an end amicably, by *both* parties fulfilling their obligations under the contract. This is commonly known as 'discharge by performance'. Both sides have received what they bargained for, so there is no injured party who is entitled to damages.

Sometimes the parties will *both* agree to end their obligations under the contract; this is commonly known as 'discharge by agreement'. The parties can agree at the time of contracting that the contract will be discharged in certain circumstances (these requirements are contained in a 'termination clause'). Alternatively, the parties can agree to discharge *an existing contract*; this is done by forming a new contract. All the normal requirements for contract formation must be satisfied – and importantly, the new contract must be supported by consideration. Again, both parties have received what they bargained for (ie what they bargained for under the new contract) so there is no injured party who is entitled to damages.

Finally, the contract can be brought to an end by one party's breach. The innocent party is generally entitled to damages for the loss caused by a breach. In addition, when a breach is sufficiently serious, the innocent party is *also* entitled to walk away from any future obligations under the contract. The contract breaker is said to have committed a 'repudiatory breach' and the innocent party has a 'right of election'; he may either treat the contract as repudiated (ie accept that the breach has terminated the contract) or, in certain circumstances, affirm the contract. If he chooses to treat the contract as repudiated, this is usually known as 'discharge by breach'.

Discharge of a contract by performance, agreement or breach is always the result of the choices made by the parties. It can be contrasted with 'frustration' of a contract. A contract is 'frustrated' by events that are outside of the control of either party (see Chapter 17).

 Link
See Discharge II
Chapter 17

16.1 Discharge by Performance

The starting point for determining whether a contract has been discharged by performance is to look at the actual terms of the contract – what did the parties agree to do? It is not normally enough for the parties *nearly* to fulfil their obligations; in general, in order to discharge a contract by performance, both parties must do everything that they have promised to do. This has been called the 'entire obligations rule'. Potentially, it may have a harsh effect where one party does not have *any* obligations until the other party has performed his obligations; it is said that the first obligation is a 'condition precedent' to the second obligation. (A 'condition precedent' can be contrasted with interdependent, or concurrent obligations. For instance, under the Sale of Goods Act 1979 s 28 there is an implied term in contracts for sale that the seller be ready and willing to deliver, and the buyer be ready and willing to pay, at the same time.)

Cutter v Powell (1796) 6 Term Reports 320

Panel: Lord Kenyon CJ, Ashurst, Grose and Lawrence JJ

Facts: Powell was in charge of the vessel, *Governor Parry*, and agreed to pay Cutter 'thirty guineas, provided he proceeds, continues and does his duty as second mate from hence to the port of Liverpool.' The agreement was signed at Kingston, Jamaica, on 31 July 1793. Cutter 'proceeded, continued and did his duty as second mate from Kingston until his death' which happened before the vessel reached Liverpool. Cutter's estate sued Powell for the wages.

LORD KENYON CJ

The defendant expressly promised to pay the intestate thirty guineas, provided he proceeded, continued and did his duty as second mate in the ship from Jamaica to Liverpool; and the accompanying circumstances disclosed in the case are that the common rate of wages is four pounds per month, when the party is paid in proportion to the time he serves: and that this voyage is generally performed in two months. Therefore if there had been no contract between these parties, all that the intestate could have recovered on a quantum meruit for the voyage would have been eight pounds; whereas here the defendant contracted to pay thirty guineas provided the mate continued to do his duty as mate during the whole voyage, in which case the latter would have received nearly four times as much as if he were paid for the number of months he served. He stipulated to receive the larger sum if the whole duty were performed, and nothing unless the whole of that duty were performed: it was a kind of insurance. ...

MR JUSTICE GROSE

I have also inquired into the practice of the merchants in the city, and have been informed that these contracts are not considered as divisible, and that the seaman must perform the voyage, otherwise he is not entitled to his wages; though I must add that the result of my inquiries has not been perfectly satisfactory, and therefore I do not rely upon it. ... However in this case the agreement is conclusive[.]... [W]hen we recollect how large a price was to be given in the event of the mate continuing on board during the whole voyage instead of the small sum which is usually given per month, it may fairly be considered that the parties themselves understood that if the whole duty were performed, the mate was to receive the whole sum, and that he was not to receive any thing unless he did continue on board during the whole voyage. That seems to me to be the situation in which the mate chose to put himself; and as the condition was not complied with, his representative cannot now recover anything [sic]. ...

Cutter's estate was therefore not entitled to recover anything – Powell's obligation to pay had never arisen, and therefore Powell was not in breach of contract for non-payment.

Cutter's estate had argued that Cutter should at least be paid a fair price for the work he had done (a '*quantum meruit*') but the court was very clear that the contract expressly provided for payment only on completion of the whole voyage, and there was no reason to imply a term to save Cutter from the deal he had made. In return for being paid a premium (30 guineas not 8 guineas) Cutter *took the risk* that he would not complete the voyage.

Link
See chapter on Implied Terms

There are two ways to protect the contract breaker from the harshness of the entire obligations rule. First, the courts may conclude that a new contact can be *imputed* (ie assumed) under which the innocent party will pay a *quantum meruit* to the contract breaker in return for taking the benefit of the contract breaker's 'partial performance' (see *Sumpter v Hedges* 119 ER 647). Second, the courts may conclude that, looking at the contract as a whole, the parties intended that 'substantial performance' by one party would be enough to trigger the other party's obligation to pay (see *Hoenig v Isaacs* [1952] 2 All ER 176 and *Bolton v Mahadeva* [1972] 1 WLR 1009).

Sumpter v Hedges [1898] 1 QB 673

Panel: AL Smith, Chitty and Collins LJJ

Facts: Sumpter had agreed to build two houses with stables on Hedges' land, in return for 565l. After completing work worth around 333l, Sumpter told Hedges that he did not have enough money to finish the job, so Hedges did it for himself. At first instance, Bruce J had concluded that no contract could be implied *just* because Hedges had finished building work on his own land – something more was needed.

LORD JUSTICE CHITTY

The position therefore was that the defendant found his land with unfinished buildings upon it, and he thereupon completed the work. That is no evidence from which the inference can be drawn that he entered into a fresh contract to pay for the work done by the plaintiff. If we held that the plaintiff could recover, we should in my opinion be overruling *Cutter v. Powell*... In the case of a building erected upon land the mere fact that the defendant remains in possession of his land is no evidence upon which an inference of a new contract can be founded... [In *Pattinson v. Luckley*, Bramwell B stated:] 'In the case of goods sold and delivered, it is easy to shew a contract from the retention of the goods; but that is not so where work is done on real property.' I think the learned judge was quite right in holding that in this case there was no evidence from which a fresh contract to pay for the work done could be inferred. ...

LORD JUSTICE COLLINS

> Where, as in the case of work done on land, the circumstances are such as to give the defendant no option whether he will take the benefit of the work or not, then one must look to other facts than the mere taking the benefit of the work in order to ground the inference of a new contract. In this case I see no other facts on which such an inference can be founded. The mere fact that a defendant is in possession of what he cannot help keeping, or even has done work upon it, affords no ground for such an inference....

 Alert

The circumstances in which a contract will be implied must be rare as, in practice, the innocent party will often be unable to take the benefit of the contract breaker's work without some kind of express agreement that they will accept partial performance. However, the courts are clearly willing to prevent the innocent party from unfairly taking advantage of the contract breaker by *choosing* to profit from his work despite not paying.

The element of choice is important – in *Cutter v Powell,* Powell had no choice about accepting the value of Cutter's work because its value was entirely in the past. In *Sumpter v Hedges*, the building work was carried out on Hedges' land, and Hedges had no real choice about finishing the work, otherwise his land would be useless. Consequently, he could not *voluntarily* accept partial performance.

The second way in which the contract breaker can be protected from the potential harshness of the entire obligations rule is the doctrine of substantial performance, whereby the courts take the view that, on construction of the parties' agreement, substantial performance of the contract is enough.

Hoenig v Isaacs [1952] 2 All ER 176

Panel: Somervell, Denning and Romer LJJ

Facts: Hoenig agreed to redecorate completely and refurnish Isaacs' one bedroom flat in an 'ornate' style. Hoenig finished the work, but the job had some defects which would require further attention. The wardrobe he fitted needed a new door, and the built in bookcase was slightly too short for the space. A built in desk was too large and looked 'unsightly' when cut down to size. The total value of the work was around £750 and the repairs would cost around £55. The contract provided for payment by instalments with the balance on 'completion'.

Hoenig sued Isaacs for the balance (about £350) but admitted that Isaacs was entitled to reduce the balance to reflect the cost of repairs. Isaacs said that entire performance was a condition precedent to any payment, and therefore, following *Sumpter v Hedges,* he only had to pay a *quantum meruit* (in return for taking the benefit of the work). A *quantum meruit* would have been a good deal for Isaacs, because he had overpaid for the contract in the first place.

LORD JUSTICE SOMERVELL

The question here is whether in a contract for work and labour for a lump sum payable on completion the defendant can repudiate liability under the contract on the ground that the work though 'finished' or 'done' is in some respects not in accordance with the contract...

LORD JUSTICE DENNING

When a contract provides for a specific sum to be paid on completion of specified work, the Courts lean against a construction of the contract which would deprive the contractor of any payment at all simply because there are some defects or omissions. The promise to complete the work is therefore construed as a term of the contract, but not as a condition. It is not every breach of that term which absolves the employer from his promise to pay the price, but only a breach which goes to the root of the contract, such as an abandonment of the work when it is only half done. Unless the breach does go to the root of the matter, the employer cannot resist payment of the price. He must pay it and bring a cross-claim for the defects and omissions...The measure is the amount which the work is worth less by reason of the defects and omissions, and is usually calculated by the cost of making them good.

 Alert

It is, of course, always open to the parties by express words to make entire performance a condition precedent... [but] I think this contract should be regarded as an ordinary lump sum contract. It was substantially performed. The contractor is entitled therefore to the contract price, less a deduction for the defects...

 Alert

Contracting parties are therefore still free to state expressly that payment will only be made where one party has performed their obligations in their entirety – but normally the substantial performance by one party of their obligations is sufficient. As Somervell LJ noted, the work was 'finished', but it was also defective in some minor aspects. The court took the view that only serious defects will prevent the condition precedent to payment being fulfilled. In this case, the defects were not serious; the contract had been substantially performed. Thus, Hoenig was entitled to the contract price less the cost of remedying the defects.

Lord Justice Denning used the standard of 'breaches that go to the root of the contract', echoing the test for a repudiatory breach whereby the innocent party may treat the contract as repudiated if the term breached goes to the root of the contract. Similarly, the innocent party cannot escape paying the contract price, unless (i) the parties made clear that only complete performance would do (as had been the case in *Cutter v Powell*), or (ii) the contract breaker's failure to perform is sufficiently serious.

 Link
See chapter on Terms I

The meaning of substantial performance was further considered by the Court of Appeal in *Bolton v Mahadeva* [1972] 1 WLR 1009.

Bolton v Mahadeva [1972] 1 WLR 1009

Panel: Sachs, Buckley and Cairns LJJ

Facts: Bolton agreed to install a central heating system at Mahadeva's house for £560, but he did so defectively. Not only did the system not heat effectively, but it also gave out fumes. The judge at first instance held that Bolton had substantially performed the contract, but because of deficiencies in the performance of the work, Mahadeva was entitled to deduct £174.50, leaving a balance of £385.50. Mahadeva appealed.

LORD JUSTICE CAIRNS

The main question in the case is whether the defects in workmanship found by the judge to be such as to cost £174 to repair — that is, between one third and one quarter of the contract price — were of such a character and amount that the plaintiff could not be said to have substantially performed his contract. That is, in my view, clearly the legal principle which has to be applied to cases of this kind. ...

In considering whether there was substantial performance I am of [the] opinion that it is relevant to take into account both the nature of the defects and the proportion between the cost of rectifying them and the contract price. It would be wrong to say that the contractor is only entitled to payment if the defects are so trifling as to be covered by the de minimis rule.

For my part, I find it impossible to say that the judge was right in reaching the conclusion that in those circumstances the contract had been substantially performed. The contract was a contract to install a central heating system. If a central heating system when installed is such that it does not heat the house adequately and is such, further, that fumes are given out, so as to make living rooms uncomfortable, and if the putting right of those defects is not something which can be done by some slight amendment of the system, then I think that the contract is not substantially performed.

Taking those matters into account and the other matters making up the total of £174, I have reached the conclusion that the judge was wrong in saying that this contract had been substantially completed, and, on my view of the law, it follows that the plaintiff was not entitled to recover under that contract. ...

The Court of Appeal held that Bolton was not entitled to recover any money at all since he had not substantially performed the contract. Lord Justice Cairns made it clear that all the circumstances must be taken into account in determining whether the contract has been substantially performed, not just the cost of curing any defects as a proportion of the contract price. The court must look both at the contract's purpose, as well as the details of the agreement. The purpose of a central heating system is to heat a house – the system installed by Bolton failed properly to heat the house, and fixing it would require major work. In the circumstances, Bolton had failed substantially to perform the contract, and therefore was not entitled to the contract price.

16.2   Discharge by Agreement

The first way that the parties can discharge their contract by agreement is by the formation of a new contract. If both parties have obligations which are unperformed, they may promise to *waive* (ie give up) their right to performance in exchange for a similar promise from the other party; this is known as 'mutual waiver'. After mutual waiver, the original contract is discharged and, since both parties have received what they bargained for under the new contract, there is no question of damages. The mutuality of the promises is important because a gratuitous promise is not binding in contract – a promise is only binding where it is given in return for consideration.

Discharge by agreement is more difficult when one party has already fully performed their obligations under the contract – the other party has no rights that they can waive, and so something else must be given as consideration for the agreement to discharge the existing contract. The consideration can be anything of value, but does not have to be adequate: a peppercorn would be sufficient (see *Chappell & Co Ltd v Nestle Co Ltd* [1960] AC 87). It is said that 'accord' (agreement) (see *D & C Builders v Rees*) and 'satisfaction' (consideration) are necessary for the new contract to be binding.

It is clear, therefore, that consideration, in the context of discharging a contract by agreement, can be provided by (i) a promise to waive existing rights, or (ii) by the provision of something new.

The second way that parties can agree to discharge a contract is by putting their agreement in a deed. Consideration is not needed to give legal effect to a deed, although the parties must fulfill other formality requirements instead. Again, both parties have received what they bargained for so there is no question of damages.

Third, where one party's conduct leads the other to believe that the contract will not be enforced, the party whose conduct induced that belief may be 'estopped' from relying on their rights. This is very similar to promissory estoppel.

Link
See chapter on Promissory Estoppel

Finally, the contract itself might state that it will be discharged in certain circumstances, normally contained in a 'termination clause'. Discharge following such an event is not a breach of contract, but rather the mutually agreed end of the contract, and so there is no injured party who is entitled to damages. For example, commercial contracts commonly include a *force majeure* clause. A *force majeure* clause might state that if further performance of the contract is prevented by extreme circumstances, outside the control of the parties, then neither party is to blame and the contract is discharged without further liability. The parties, therefore, share the risk that an event triggering the activation of the termination clause will occur. Alternatively the parties might agree that the occurrence of a breach of contract of a specified severity (often termed a material breach in commercial contracts) will give rise to the right to terminate and discharge the contract. Again discharge on this basis will not give rise to a claim in damages for loss of performance of a whole (as with a repudiatory breach) because the discharge takes place pursuant to a mutually agreed discharge event (see study notes).

16.3 Discharge by Breach

The usual award for breach of contract is damages to compensate the innocent party for loss suffered.

Link
See chapter on Remedies

In *Photo Production Ltd v Securicor Transport Ltd* [1980] AC 827, Lord Diplock described the obligations agreed by the parties as 'primary obligations' (eg to deliver goods, to perform services, to pay for those goods or services, etc). The obligations to pay monetary compensation to compensate the injured party for loss sustained *as a result of a breach* of these primary obligations are known as 'secondary obligations'. If the breach is not 'repudiatory', Lord Diplock states that 'the primary obligations of both parties so far as they have not yet been fully performed remain unchanged'. However, where the breach is 'repudiatory' (ie breach of a condition or a sufficiently serious breach of an innominate term) this gives the innocent party the additional right to treat the contract as repudiated; in other words they can 'elect' to terminate the contract or, in certain circumstances, affirm the contract. Lord Diplock makes it clear that termination of a contract for breach is not automatic – in order to terminate the contract the innocent party must 'elect' to accept the contract breaker's repudiation. Such election will put an end to all further primary obligations and the contract is said to be discharged.

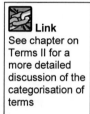

Link
See chapter on Terms II for a more detailed discussion of the categorisation of terms

16.3.1 The Innocent Party's Election

The innocent party must clearly and unequivocally elect to treat the contract as repudiated – otherwise the contract will continue in force. As Lord Justice Asquith memorably said in *Howard v Pickford Tool Co. Ltd* [1951] 1 KB 417 at 422: 'An unaccepted repudiation is a thing writ in water and of no value to anybody: it confers no legal rights of any sort or kind.'

The alternative to an election to terminate is an election to affirm, whereby the innocent party decides to continue the contract, despite the breach; the limits on the availability of affirmation are considered below. Affirmation is achieved either (i) by conduct, where the innocent party continues to perform the contract, or (ii) by clear communication by the innocent party. Sometimes the innocent party is *deemed* to have affirmed by their conduct, for example in a contract for the sale of goods, if the seller breaches a condition of the contract by delivering non-conforming goods, the buyer is normally deemed to have affirmed the contract by accepting delivery (Sale of Goods Act 1979 s 11(4)).

Until the innocent party elects to accept the contract breaker's repudiation, the innocent party must still perform their obligations under the contract. This means that, if the innocent party fails to perform, they will now be in breach (see *Fercometal Sarl v MSC Mediterranean Shipping Co SA (The Simona)* [1989] AC 788 below).

16.3.2 Anticipatory Breach

Sometimes it will become clear *before the time for performance* that the contract is going to be breached. This is known as 'anticipatory breach'. In these circumstances, the innocent party is *not* required to wait for the time of performance – they are entitled to accept the repudiation straight away.

Hochster v de la Tour (1852) 2 Ellis and Blackburn 678

Panel: Lord Campbell CJ

Facts: Edgar Frederick de la Tour agreed to employ Albert Hochster as a courier from 1 June 1852. In that capacity, Hochster would travel with de la Tour for three months in France and act as an assistant. On 11 May 1852, de la Tour wrote to Hochster and told him that his services were no longer required.

LORD CAMPBELL CJ

[I]t cannot be laid down as a universal rule that, where by agreement an act is to be done on a future day, no action can be brought for a breach of the agreement till the day for doing the act has arrived.

If a man promises to marry a woman on a future day, and before that day marries another woman, he is instantly liable to an action for breach of promise of marriage; *Short v. Stone* (8 Q. B. 358). If a man contracts to execute a lease on and from a future day for a certain term, and, before that day, executes a lease to another for the same term, he may be immediately sued for breaking the contract; *Ford* v. *Tiley* (6 B. & C. 325). So, if a man contracts to sell and deliver specific goods on a future day, and before the day he sells and delivers them to another, he is immediately liable to an action at the suit of the person with whom he first contracted to sell and deliver them; *Bowdell* v. *Parsons* (10 East, 359).

One reason alleged in support of such an action is, that the defendant has, before the day, rendered it impossible for him to perform the contract at the day: but this does not necessarily follow; for, prior to the day fixed for doing the act, the first wife may have died, a surrender of the lease executed might be obtained, and the defendant might have repurchased the goods so as to be in a situation to sell and deliver them to the plaintiff...

The declaration in the present case, in alleging a breach, states a great deal more than a passing intention on the part of the defendant which he may repent of... If the plaintiff has no remedy for breach of the contract unless he treats the contract as in force, and acts upon it down to the 1st June 1852, it follows that, till then, he must enter into no employment which will interfere with his promise 'to start with the defendant on such travels on the day and year,'...

But it is surely much more rational, and more for the benefit of both parties, that, after the renunciation of the agreement by the defendant, the plaintiff should be at liberty to consider himself absolved from any future performance of it, retaining his right to sue for any damage he has suffered from the breach of it. Thus, instead of remaining idle and laying out money in preparations which must be useless, he is at liberty to seek service under another employer, which would go in mitigation of the damages to which he would otherwise be entitled for a breach of the contract.

It seems strange that the defendant, after renouncing the contract, and absolutely declaring that he will never act under it, should be permitted to object that faith is given to his assertion, and that an opportunity is not left to him of changing his mind. …

Lord Campbell CJ explains that it would be inefficient for the law to require the innocent party to wait until the time of performance before allowing him to accept the contract breaker's repudiation. Once it is clear that the contract will not be performed, either because (i) the innocent party has clearly expressed that this is his intention, by words or unambiguous conduct, or (ii) because the party in default has rendered performance impossible, the innocent party is entitled to accept this anticipatory repudiation immediately.

16.3.3 Limitations on the Availability of Affirmation for Repudiatory Breach

There are two limitations on the ability of the innocent party to affirm in the case of a repudiatory breach:

(i)   it must be possible for the affirming party to perform the contract without the co-operation of the other party, and

(ii)   the affirming party must have a legitimate interest in performing the contract rather than claiming damages.

White and Carter (Councils) Ltd v McGregor [1962] AC 413

Panel: Lord Reid, Lord Morton of Henryton, Lord Tucker, Lord Keith of Avonholm and Lord Hodson

Facts: White and Carter were advertising contractors who supplied rubbish bins to town councils, and were entitled to print adverts on the side of the bins. William McGregor, a garage owner, contracted with White and Carter for three years of adverts, with payments to be made in regular installments. McGregor changed his mind and purported to cancel the contract. McGregor made clear that he had no intention of performing his part of the contract (ie paying the installments), and therefore put himself in repudiatory breach. Instead of accepting this breach and terminating the contract, White and Carter purported to affirm the contract and performed their obligations under it; they then claimed the contract price.

White and Carter were able to perform their obligations under the contract without the co-operation of McGregor, because the contract gave White and Carter the power to design adverts for McGregor. White and Carter argued that, because they had fulfilled the condition precedent to McGregor's obligation to pay (ie they made and displayed the adverts), he became liable for the contract price. The House of Lords found in favour of White and Carter (Lord Morton and Lord Keith dissenting).

LORD REID

If one party to a contract repudiates it in the sense of making it clear to the other party that he refuses or will refuse to carry out his part of the contract, the other party, the innocent party, has an option. He may accept that repudiation and sue for damages for breach of contract, whether or not the time for performance has come; or he may if he chooses disregard or refuse to accept it and then the contract remains in full effect. ...

Developing this argument, the respondent points out that in most cases the innocent party cannot complete the contract himself without the other party doing, allowing or accepting something, and that it is purely fortuitous that the appellants can do so in this case. In most cases by refusing co-operation the party in breach can compel the innocent party to restrict his claim to damages. Then it was said that, even where the innocent party can complete the contract without such co-operation, it is against the public interest that he should be allowed to do so.

 Alert

An example was developed in argument. A company might engage an expert to go abroad and prepare an elaborate report and then repudiate the contract before anything was done. To allow such an expert then to waste thousands of pounds in preparing the report cannot be right if a much smaller sum of damages would give him full compensation for his loss. It would merely enable the expert to extort a settlement giving him far more than reasonable compensation. ...

It might be, but it never has been, the law that a person is only entitled to enforce his contractual rights in a reasonable way, and that a court will not support an attempt to enforce them in an unreasonable way. One reason why that is not the law is, no doubt, because it was thought that it would create too much uncertainty to require the court to decide whether it is reasonable or equitable to allow a party to enforce his full rights under a contract. ...

It may well be that, if it can be shown that a person has no legitimate interest, financial or otherwise, in performing the contract rather than claiming damages, he ought not to be allowed to saddle the other party with an additional burden with no benefit to himself. If a party has no interest to enforce a stipulation, he cannot in general enforce it: so it might be said that, if a party has no interest to insist on a particular remedy, he ought not to be allowed to insist on it. And, just as a party is not allowed to enforce a penalty, so he ought not to be allowed to penalise the other party by taking one course when another is equally advantageous to him. ...

 Alert

If I may revert to the example which I gave of a company engaging an expert to prepare an elaborate report and then repudiating before anything was done, it might be that the company could show that the expert had no substantial or legitimate interest in carrying out the work rather than accepting damages: I would think that the de minimis principle would apply in determining whether his interest was substantial, and that he might have a legitimate interest other than an immediate financial interest. But if the expert had no such interest then that might be regarded as a proper case for the exercise of the general equitable jurisdiction of the court.

But that is not this case. Here the respondent did not set out to prove that the appellants had no legitimate interest in completing the contract and claiming the contract price rather than claiming damages; there is nothing in the findings of fact to support such a case, and it seems improbable that any such case could have been proved. It is, in my judgment, impossible to say that the appellants should be deprived of their right to claim the contract price merely because the benefit to them, as against claiming damages and re-letting their advertising space, might be small in comparison with the loss to the respondent: that is the most that could be said in favour of the respondent. Parliament has on many occasions relieved parties from certain kinds of improvident or oppressive contracts, but the common law can only do that in very limited circumstances. ...

LORD HODSON

It may be unfortunate that the appellants have saddled themselves with an unwanted contract causing an apparent waste of time and money. No doubt this aspect impressed the [lower court] but there is no equity which can assist the respondent. It is trite that equity will not rewrite an improvident contract where there is no disability on either side. There is no duty laid upon a party to a subsisting contract to vary it at the behest of the other party so as to deprive himself of the benefit given to him by the contract. To hold otherwise would be to introduce a novel equitable doctrine that a party was not to be held to his contract unless the court in a given instance thought it reasonable so to do. ...

Two limits on the right of affirmation were developed. First, the contract breaker will not be forced to co-operate with the innocent party, and so if further co-operation is required, there is no right to affirm the contract. (This aspect is considered further in *Hounslow London Borough Council v Twickenham Garden Developments Ltd* [1970] 3 WLR 538 below.) Second, Lord Reid stated that the innocent party must have a 'legitimate interest, financial or otherwise' in performing the contract rather than terminating and claiming damages. On the facts, his Lordship did not consider it necessary to define what would amount to a legitimate interest, except to state that he thought it 'improbable' that McGregor could show that White and Carter's interest was not legitimate.

The meaning of 'legitimate interest' was not particularly clear from *White and Carter* although it has been confirmed as good law by several later cases in the Court of Appeal. These cases show that the test allows the courts to take some account of the risk that performance is much more inefficient than just claiming damages (see *Clea Shipping Corp v Bulk Oil International (The Alaskan Trader) (No.2)* [1984] 1 All ER 129 below).

LORD MORTON dissenting

My Lords, I think that this is a case of great importance, although the claim is for a comparatively small sum. If the appellants are right, strange consequences follow in any case in which, under a repudiated contract, services are to be performed by the party who has not repudiated it, so long as he is able to perform these services without the co-operation of the repudiating party. Many examples of such contracts could be given. One, given in the course of the argument and already mentioned by my noble and learned friend, Lord Reid, is the engagement of an expert to go abroad and write a report on some subject for a substantial fee plus his expenses. If the appellants succeed in the present case, it must follow that the expert is entitled to incur the expense of going abroad, to write his unwanted report, and then to recover the fee and expenses, even if the other party has plainly repudiated the contract before any expense has been incurred.

It is well established that repudiation by one party does not put an end to a contract. The other party can say 'I hold you to your contract, which still remains in force.' What then is his remedy if the repudiating party persists in his repudiation and refuses to carry out his part of the contract? The contract has been broken. The innocent party is entitled to be compensated by damages for any loss which he has suffered by reason of the breach, and in a limited class of cases the court will decree specific implement. The law of Scotland provides no other remedy for a breach of contract and there is no reported case which decides that the innocent party may act as the appellants have acted. The present case is one in which specific implement could not be decreed, since the only obligation of the respondent under the contract was to pay a sum of money for services to be rendered by the appellants. Yet the appellants are claiming a kind of inverted specific implement of the contract. They first insist on performing their part of the contract, against the will of the other party, and then claim that he must perform his part and of pay the contract price for unwanted services. In my opinion, my Lords, the appellants' only remedy was damages, and they were bound to take steps to minimise their loss, according to a well-established rule of law. Far from doing this, having incurred no expense at the date of the repudiation, they made no attempt to procure another advertiser, but deliberately went on to incur expense and perform unwanted services with the intention of creating a money debt which did not exist at the date of the repudiation. ...

The innocent party's right of affirmation has been criticised – as Lord Morton says in dissent, it allows the innocent party to provide performance that the contract breaker no longer wants, and this might be thought to be inefficient. If it was not for the innocent party's right to affirm, then White and Carter would have had a duty to mitigate their loss by finding someone else to advertise on the bins.

The majority took the view that, although performance might not be what the contract breaker *now* wants, it is what he bargained for. They noted that there is no rule of contract law, whether at common law or equity, that the parties must exercise their rights in a reasonable way, and therefore, if the innocent party is able to perform without the co-operation of the contract breaker, then the law will not stop him from doing so.

Link
Damages, Mitigation

Clea Shipping Corp v Bulk Oil International (The Alaskan Trader) (No.2) [1984] 1 All ER 129

Panel: Lloyd J

Facts: *The Alaskan Trader* was owned by Clea Shipping and hired ('time chartered') to Bulk Oil. Soon after the hire began, the vessel broke down and was repaired by Clea Shipping. Bulk Oil was excused from paying hire while the repairs were undertaken, but when the repairs were finished, they refused to take the vessel back – this was a repudiatory breach of the charter.

Clea Shipping purported to affirm the contract. They kept the vessel with a full crew and with the engine ready for over seven months, waiting for orders which they well knew would never come. They claimed they were entitled to be paid hire even though the vessel was not used.

Bulk Oil's defence was that Clea Shipping had no right to affirm the contract and so ought to have accepted their conduct as repudiatory and claimed damages (which would be much less than hire). The dispute was arbitrated, and the arbitrator concluded that Clea Shipping had no legitimate interest in affirming the contract rather than claiming damages.

MR JUSTICE LLOYD

[Clea Shipping (the owners)] argued that they were entitled to retain the hire, since they had kept the vessel at the disposal of the charterers throughout the period. They relied on the decision of the House of Lords in *White and Carter (Councils) Ltd. v. McGregor*, [1962] 2 A.C. 413, and the decision of Mr. Justice Kerr in *The Odenfeld*, [1978] 2 Lloyd's Rep. 357... [Bulk Oil (the charterers)] on the other hand argued that the owners ought, in all reason, to have accepted the charterers' conduct as a repudiation of the charter, and claimed damages. Even if no alternative employment could be found for the vessel, it would have been a great deal cheaper to lay the vessel up, rather than maintain her with a full crew on board...

In relation to Lord Reid's requirement of a 'legitimate interest', [counsel for Clea Shipping] submitted that Lord Reid was, quite simply, wrong. It seems to me that it would be difficult for me to take that view... Whether one takes Lord Reid's language, which was adopted by Lords Justices Orr and Browne in

The Puerto Buitrago, or Lord Denning, M.R.'s language in that case ('in all reason'), or Mr. Justice Kerr's language in *The Odenfeld* ('wholly unreasonable, quite unrealistic, unreasonable and untenable'), there comes a point at which the Court will cease, on general equitable principles, to allow the innocent party to enforce his contract according to its strict legal terms. How one defines that point is obviously a matter of some difficulty; for it involves drawing a line between conduct which is merely unreasonable ... and conduct which is wholly unreasonable... But however difficult it may be to define the point, that there is such a point seems to me to have been accepted both by the Court of Appeal in The Puerto Buitrago and by Mr. Justice Kerr in The Odenfeld.

 Alert

I appreciate that the House of Lords has recently re-emphasized the importance of certainty in commercial contracts... I appreciate, too, that the importance of certainty was one of the main reasons urged by Lord Hodson in *White and Carter v. McGregor* in upholding the innocent party's unfettered right to elect. But for reasons already mentioned, it seems to me that this Court is bound to hold that there is some fetter, if only in extreme cases; and for want of a better way of describing that fetter, it is safest for this Court to use the language of Lord Reid. ...

In the present case ... the arbitrator has found, and found clearly, that the owners had *no* legitimate interest in pursuing their claim for hire. In my view that finding is conclusive of this appeal. ...

The *Alaskan Trader* confirmed that Lord Reid's 'legitimate interest' test is good law, although it did little to help explain what amounts to a legitimate interest.

The most recent case as to what constitutes a legitimate interest is *Ocean Marine Navigation Limited v Koch Carbon Inc. (the Dynamic)* [2003] EWHC 1936 (Comm), [2003] 2 Lloyd's Rep. 693. In this case, after consideration of the other authorities relating to legitimate interest, Simon J stated that the fetter on the right to affirm only applies in extreme circumstances. He explained the position as follows.

SIMON J

23. These cases establish the following exception to the general rule that the innocent party has an option whether or not to accept a repudiation: (i) The burden is on the contract-breaker to show that the innocent party has no legitimate interest in performing the contract rather than claiming damages. (ii) This burden is not discharged merely by showing that the benefit to the other party is small in comparison to the loss to the contract breaker. (iii) The exception to the general rule applies only in extreme cases: where damages would be an adequate remedy and where an election to keep the contract alive would be unreasonable.

Hounslow London Borough Council v Twickenham Garden Developments Ltd [1970] 3 WLR 538

Panel: Megarry J

Facts: Hounslow Council employed Twickenham Garden Developments ('the developers') to build 1,000 dwelling units on a 27 acre site called Ivybridge in Middlesex. Several labour disputes and an eight-month strike caused significant delays and the Council purported to cancel the contract. Two issues arose for decision.

The first was whether the Council were entitled to remove the developers from their land *irrespective* of whether there had been a breach of contract. In the course of deciding this point, Megarry J considered the developers' argument that they were entitled to refuse to leave the land because, even if the Council were entitled to terminate, the developers could affirm the contract by applying *White and Carter*.

The second issue for decision was whether the Council were entitled to terminate the contract on the facts. Mr Justice Megarry decided this point in favour of the Council.

MR JUSTICE MEGARRY

A number of examples were discussed in argument in addition to the example given by Lord Keith in his dissent [in *White and Carter (Councils) Ltd. v. McGregor*] at p. 442, and mentioned by Lord Reid and Lord Morton at pp. 428 and 432.

Lord Keith took the case of a contract by a man to go to Hong Kong and produce a report for a fee of £10,000. Before he goes, the other party repudiates the contract. Nevertheless, on the majority view the man is entitled to go to Hong Kong, produce the unwanted report and claim the £10,000.

The examples discussed in argument before me applied the doctrine to cases concerning land. A contract to erect buildings on land is let; a few days later the landowner unexpectedly learns that he can obtain a far more advantageous planning permission for developing the land, and he thereupon repudiates the contract; but the contractor insists on performing it, even though the landowner must then either abandon the more valuable development and accept the far less profitable buildings or else pull those buildings down when they have been completed and then carry out the more fruitful scheme.

Another landowner lets a contract to erect an extravagant building which his wealth can afford; before much work has been done his fortune collapses, and he can pay for the building only by using all that is left to him; yet the contractor insists on performing the contract.

A third landowner contracts with an artist to paint extensive frescoes in a new building over a period of two years; the landowner then receives a handsome offer for the unadorned building, provided vacant possession is delivered forthwith; yet the artist insists on painting on for the rest of the two years.

Examples such as these suggest that there may well be limits to the doctrine... It seems to me that the decision is one which I should be slow to apply to any category of case not fairly within the contemplation of their Lordships. The case before me is patently one in which the contractor cannot perform the contract without any co-operation by the borough. The whole machinery of the contract is geared to acts by the architect and quantity surveyor, and it is a contract that is to be performed on the borough's land. True, the contractor already has de facto possession or control of the land; there is no question of the borough being required to do the act of admitting the contractor into possession, and so in that respect the contractor can perform the contract without any 'co-operation' by the borough. But I do not think that the point can be brushed aside so simply.

Quite apart from questions of active co-operation, cases where one party is lawfully in possession of property of the other seem to me to raise issues not before the House of Lords in *White and Carter (Councils) Ltd. v. McGregor* [1962] AC 413. Suppose that A, who owns a large and valuable painting, contracts with B, a picture restorer, to restore it over a period of three months. Before the work is begun, A receives a handsome offer from C to purchase the picture, subject to immediate delivery of the picture in its unrestored state, C having grave suspicions of B's competence.

If the work of restoration is to be done in A's house, he can effectually exclude B by refusing to admit him to the house: without A's 'co-operation' to this extent B cannot perform his contract. But what if the picture stands in A's locked barn, the key of which he has lent to B so that he may come and go freely, or if the picture has been removed to B's premises? In these cases can B insist on performing his contract, even though this makes it impossible for A to accept C's offer? In the case of the barn, A's co-operation may perhaps be said to be requisite to the extent of not barring B's path to the barn or putting another lock on the door: but if the picture is on B's premises, no active co-operation by A is needed. Nevertheless, the picture is A's property, and I find it difficult to believe that Lord Reid intended to restrict the concept of 'co-operation' to active co-operation.

In *White and Carter (Councils) Ltd. v. McGregor* no co-operation by the proprietor, either active or passive, was required: the contract could be performed by the agents wholly without reference to the proprietor or his property. The case was far removed from that of a property owner being forced to stand impotently aside while a perhaps ill-advised contract is executed on property of his which he has delivered into the possession of the other party, and is powerless to retrieve.

Accordingly, I do not think that *White and Carter (Councils) Ltd. v. McGregor* has any application to the case before me. I say this, first, because a considerable degree of active co-operation under the contract by the borough is requisite, and second, because the work is being done to property of the borough. I doubt very much whether the *White* case can have been intended to apply where the contract is to be performed by doing acts to property owned by the party seeking to determine it. …

Mr Justice Megarry was faced with the problem of how to apply *White and Carter* to facts involving the contract breaker's land or property. His Lordship doubted that the innocent party could affirm in such cases, because the innocent party would need the contract breaker's co-operation, albeit in the form of acquiescence in their use of the property – in other words their 'passive' co-operation.

In the case of *Reichman and Dunn v Beveridge and Gauntlett* the court dealt with the two limitations on affirmation in the context of a lease.

Reichman and Dunn v Beveridge and Gauntlett [2006] EWCA Civ 1659

Panel: Auld, Rix, Lloyd LJJJ

Facts: Tenant solicitors left the leased premises 3 years into a 5 year lease. The landlord sued for rent arrears. The tenants argued that the landlord was under a duty to mitigate loss for non- payment of rent for the remaining 2 years of the lease by: finding a replacement tenant, marketing the premises and not rejecting offers from prospective tenants.

Held: there was no duty to mitigate loss in an action for debt, the debt being the action for arrears of rent. So, in landlord and tenant cases, where the tenant defaults, the landlord does have a legitimate interest in affirming. This is because any future tenancy agreements which they would otherwise have entered into in order to mitigate, may be for a lower market rent. The landlord would then have no way of recovering the future losses since there is no authority in English law which allows a landlord to recover loss of future rent from a former tenant.

16.3.4 Risks of Electing to Affirm

As has already been made clear, the innocent party must elect to accept a contract breaker's repudiation, otherwise the contract remains on foot. Affirmation may be beneficial for the innocent party since they avoid the sometimes onerous requirement to mitigate; they can simply perform and claim the contract price as a debt. With an anticipatory breach, the innocent party might prefer to wait until the time of performance (when the anticipatory breach becomes an actual breach) before terminating, thereby removing the risk of wrongly treating the other party as being in repudiatory breach. The problem with this approach is that the innocent party runs the risk that the contract breaker may gain an excuse for non-performance, whether because a supervening event frustrates the contract (*Avery v Bowden* 119 ER 647), or because the *innocent party* breaches the contract (*Fercometal Sarl v MSC Mediterranean Shipping Co SA (The Simona)* [1989] AC 788).

 Link
See chapter on Frustration (Discharge II)

For example, in *Avery v Bowden*, George Avery, the owner of *The Lebanon*, agreed that it should carry a cargo of tallow (animal fat) from the Black Sea for Samuel Boden. When the vessels arrived at Odessa, Mr Boden's representative clearly stated that there was no tallow available to ship and that the contract would not be performed. This was a repudiatory breach, but Mr Avery decided to affirm the contract by waiting to see if tallow would become available.

The Crimean War later broke out, frustrating the contract. The court concluded that, because Avery had affirmed the contract, he had lost the right to treat the contract as repudiated by Bowden, and therefore was not entitled to damages.

Fercometal Sarl v MSC Mediterranean Shipping Co SA (The Simona) [1989] AC 788

Panel: Lord Bridge of Harwich, Lord Templeman, Lord Ackner, Lord Oliver of Aylmerton and Lord Jauncey of Tullichettle

Facts: The owners of *The Simona* hired ('voyage chartered') her out to Fercometal SARL for the carriage of steel from Durban to Bilbao. The contract gave Fercometal the right to cancel the charter if the vessel failed to be ready to load on 9 July 1982.

On 8 July, Fercometal told the owners that they no longer wanted the ship – this was a clear repudiatory breach of the contract and would have allowed the owners to terminate. However, the owners did not elect to accept this repudiation.

The owners failed to be ready to load the next day, on 9 July, giving Fercometal the right to terminate. Fercometal purported to exercise this right, allowing them to walk away from the contract without paying any damages.

The owners claimed that Fercometal lost the right to cancel by committing a repudiatory breach on 8 July.

LORD ACKNER

The way in which a 'supervening circumstance' may turn out to be to the advantage of the party in default, thus relieving him from liability is illustrated by *Avery v. Bowden*, 5 E. & B. 714, where the outbreak of the Crimean War between England and Russia made performance of the charterparty no longer legally possible. The defendant, who prior to the outbreak of the war had in breach of contract refused to load, was provided with a good defence to an action for breach of contract, since his repudiation had been ignored. ... [I]n *Heyman v. Darwins* Ltd. [1942] A.C. 356 ... Viscount Simon L.C. said, at p. 361:

'The first head of claim in the writ appears to be advanced on the view that an agreement is automatically terminated if one party 'repudiates' it. That is not so. 'I have never been able to understand,' said Scrutton L.J. in *Golding v. London & Edinburgh Insurance Co Ltd* (1932) 43 LIL Rep 487, 488, 'what effect the repudiation of one party has unless the other party accepts the repudiation.' If one party so acts or so expresses himself, as to show that he does not mean to accept and discharge the obligations of a contract any further, the other party has an option to the attitude he may take up.

He may, notwithstanding the so-called repudiation, insist on holding his co-contractor to the bargain and continue to tender due performance on his part. In that event, the co-contractor has the opportunity of withdrawing from his false position, and even if he does not, may escape ultimate liability because of some supervening event not due to his own fault which excuses or puts an end to further performance.' ...

If an unaccepted repudiation has no legal effect ('a thing writ in water and of no value to anybody' - per Asquith L.J. in *Howard v. Pickford Tool Co. Ltd.* [1951] 1 K.B. 417, 421) how can the unaccepted acts of repudiation by [Fercometal] in this case provide the owners with any cause of action? ...

When A wrongfully repudiates his contractual obligations in anticipation of the time for their performance, he presents the innocent party B with two choices. He may either affirm the contract by treating it as still in force or he may treat it as finally and conclusively discharged. There is no third choice, as a sort of via media, to affirm the contract and yet to be absolved from tendering further performance unless and until A gives reasonable notice that he is once again able and willing to perform. Such a choice would negate the contract being kept alive for the benefit of *both* parties and would deny the party who unsuccessfully sought to rescind, the right to take advantage of any supervening circumstance which would justify him in declining to complete.

In other words, the owners' failure to accept Fercometal's repudiation meant that the contract continued in existence – the owners were still bound to perform all of their primary obligations. Their failure to have the ship ready to load on a specified date gave Fercometal the right to terminate, bringing the contract to an end.

Further Reading

Dockray, M., 2001. Cutter v Powell: *a trip outside the text*. LQR 117 Oct. pp.664–682

Macfarlane, B & Stevens, R., 2002. 'In defence of Sumpter v. Hedges'. LQR 118 (Oct) pp. 569–599

Peel, E., *The Law of Contract*. 13th ed. Treitel. Ch.17 & 18

Sheppard, A. M., 2007. 'Demystifying the right of election in contract law'. JBL (Jun) pp.442–470

McKendrick, E., *Contract Law* (2017) 12th ed. Ch.19 and 20

17

Discharge II: Frustration

Topic List

Introduction

This chapter describes the ways in which a contract can be discharged by events outside the control of the contracting parties; this is known as frustration of contract. Frustration can be contrasted with the methods for discharge considered in the previous chapter that all depended on the actions and choices of the parties.

There has been much debate as to the theoretical underpinnings of the doctrine of frustration. Historically, the court implied a term to allocate a risk that the parties had failed to allocate expressly. For example, in *Taylor v Caldwell* 122 ER 309, where the music hall which had been hired out, burned down, it was held to be an implied term of the contract that the parties should be excused from performance in the event that the music hall perished. In other words, this is what the parties *would have agreed* at the time of contracting, had they considered the issue. This theory has, however, been criticised due to its artificiality. For example, in *Davis Contractors Ltd. v Fareham Urban District Council* [1956] AC 696 Lord Reid relied on the following example to illustrate the difficulties with the implied term theory:

> I may be allowed to note an example of the artificiality of the theory of an implied term given by Lord Sands in *James Scott & Sons Ltd v Del* Sel 59: 'A tiger has escaped from a travelling menagerie. The milkgirl fails to deliver the milk. Possibly the milkman may be exonerated from any breach of contract; but, even so, it would seem hardly reasonable to base that exoneration on the ground that 'tiger days excepted' must be held as if written into the milk contract.'

Lord Reid's criticism is that it is artificial to suppose that the parties would have implied such a term. Consequently, the construction theory based on 'radical difference' is now more widely accepted. The classical statement of the modern law is that of Lord Radcliffe in *Davis Contractors Ltd v Fareham*:

> ... Frustration occurs whenever the law recognises that without default of either party a contractual obligation has become incapable of being performed because the circumstances in which performance is called for would render it a thing radically different from that which was undertaken by the contract. *Non haec in foedera veni*. It was not this that I promised to do. ...

As Lord Reid observed in the same case:

> ... There is no need to consider what the parties thought or how they or reasonable men in their shoes would have dealt with the new situation if they had foreseen it. The question is whether the contract which they did make is, on its true construction, wide enough to apply to the new situation: if it is not, then it is at an end. ...

Lord Justice Bingham restated the modern law of frustration in *Lauritzen AS v Wijsmuller BV (The 'Super Servant Two')* [1990] 1 Lloyd's Rep 1. He stated the following propositions, which he described as being established by the 'highest authority'. Although not quoted in full here, each proposition was supported by House of Lords or Privy Council authority.

1. The doctrine of frustration was evolved... to give effect to the demands of justice, to achieve a just and reasonable result, to do what is reasonable and fair, as an expedient to escape from injustice where such would result from enforcement of a contract in its literal terms after a significant change in circumstances. ...

2. Since the effect of frustration is to kill the contract and discharge the parties from further liability under it, the doctrine is not to be lightly invoked, must be kept within very narrow limits and ought not to be extended. ...

3. Frustration brings the contract to an end forthwith, without more and automatically. ...

4. The essence of frustration is that it should not be due to the act or election of the party seeking to rely on it. ... A frustrating event must be some outside event or extraneous change of situation. ...

5. A frustrating event must take place without blame or fault on the side of the party seeking to rely on it. ...

Lord Justice Bingham is clear that the first stage of any enquiry into the possible frustration of a contract is to ask whether the risk of the event that occurred was allocated to either party by the contract. Of course, the parties are free to plan for radical changes of circumstance – contracts can include terms dealing with what will happen in such circumstances. These terms are often called *force majeure* clauses. Where a particular risk has been allocated, the doctrine of frustration has no role and the contract still applies. It is only where the risk has not been allocated, that frustration may operate.

The second stage is to ask whether the events that occurred were sufficient to make performance of the contract radically different from the performance that was promised under the contract. This is a high standard and will be difficult to satisfy – particularly for modern commercial parties who often make sophisticated plans to deal with all eventualities.

In the first section, this chapter will consider the cases that illustrate the changes in circumstances that are sufficiently radical to amount to frustration.

It is important not to oversimplify these cases – in each judgment the court sets out the whole range of factors taken into account, and they must be assessed fully to understand properly this area of the law. In *Edwinton Commercial Corporation and Another v Tsavliris Russ (worldwide Salvage & Towage) Ltd (The 'Sea Angel')* [2007] 2 Lloyd's Rep 517, Rix L J said:

[110] In the course of the parties' submissions we heard much to the effect that such and such a factor 'excluded' or 'precluded' the doctrine of frustration,

or made it 'inapplicable'; or, on the other side, that such and such a factor was critical or at least amounted to a prima facie rule. I am not much attracted by that approach, for I do not believe that it is supported by a fair reading of the authorities as a whole.

Of course, the doctrine needs an overall test such as that provided by Lord Radcliffe [in *Davis Contractors v. Fareham*] if it is not to descend into a morass of quasi-discretionary decisions. Moreover, in any particular case, it may be possible to detect one, or perhaps more, particular factors which have driven the result there. However, the cases demonstrate to my mind that their circumstances can be so various as to defy rule making.

[111] In my judgment, the application of the doctrine of frustration requires a multi-factorial approach. Among the factors which have to be considered are the terms of the contract itself, its matrix or context, the parties' knowledge, expectations, assumptions and contemplations, in particular as to risk, as at the time of contract, at any rate so far as these can be ascribed mutually and objectively, and then the nature of the supervening event, and the parties' reasonable and objectively ascertainable calculations as to the possibilities of future performance in the new circumstances.

 Alert

Since the subject matter of the doctrine of frustration is contract, and contracts are about the allocation of risk, and since the allocation and assumption of risk is not simply a matter of express or implied provision but may also depend on less easily defined matters such as 'the contemplation of the parties', the application of the doctrine can often be a difficult one. In such circumstances, the test of 'radically different' is important: it tells us that the doctrine is not to be lightly invoked; that mere incidence of expense or delay or onerousness is not sufficient; and that there has to be as it were a break in identity between the contract as provided for and contemplated and its performance in the new circumstances.

The second section will illustrate the limitations on the application of the doctrine of frustration. The third section will consider the rights and liabilities of the contracting parties after a frustrating event, as determined by the Law Reform (Frustrated Contracts) Act 1943.

17.1 Illustrations of the Requirements of a 'Radical Change in Circumstances'

Bearing in mind Rix LJ's warning that all the circumstances - the 'matrix or context' - must always be taken into account, in broad terms, a radical change of circumstances can occur in at least three ways.

First, performance might become impossible, for example, because the subject matter of the contract is destroyed. Second, performance might become illegal or government intervention might prevent performance. Third, the shared purpose of the contract might be frustrated.

17.1.1 Performance is Impossible

The modern doctrine of frustration can be traced to *Taylor v Caldwell* 122 ER 309 although the court did not explain its decision in terms of frustration.

Taylor v Caldwell (1863) 3 B & S 826, 122 ER 309

Panel: Blackburn J

Facts: Caldwell granted to Taylor the right to use the Surrey Gardens and Music Hall in Newington, Surrey 'for the purpose of giving a series of four grand concerts and day and night fêtes at the said Gardens and Hall' on four days in June and August 1861. Caldwell would provide the Hall, and Taylor would provide all necessary 'artistes'. The contract was entered into on 27 May 1861, but before the day of the first concert, the Hall was destroyed by fire. No provision was made for this risk in the contract.

MR JUSTICE BLACKBURN

The effect of the [agreement] is to shew that the existence of the Music Hall in the Surrey Gardens in a state fit for a concert was essential for the fulfilment of the contract,—such entertainments as the parties contemplated in their agreement could not be given without it.

After the making of the agreement, and before the first day on which a concert was to be given, the Hall was destroyed by fire. This destruction, we must take it on the evidence, was without the fault of either party, and was so complete that in consequence the concerts could not be given as intended. And the question we have to decide is whether, under these circumstances, the loss which the plaintiffs have sustained is to fall upon the defendants.

The parties when framing their agreement evidently had not present to their minds the possibility of such a disaster, and have made no express stipulation with reference to it, so that the answer to the question must depend upon the general rules of law applicable to such a contract. ...

After reviewing the authorities Blackburn J continued:

Where, from the nature of the contract, it appears that the parties must from the beginning have known that it could not be fulfilled unless when the time for the fulfilment of the contract arrived some particular specified thing continued to exist, so that, when entering into the contract, they must have contemplated such continuing existence as the foundation of what was to be done; there, in the absence of any express or implied warranty that the thing shall exist, the contract is not to be construed as a positive contract, but as subject to an implied condition that the parties shall be excused in case, before breach, performance becomes impossible from the perishing of the thing without default of the contractor.

Decipher
Note the application of the implied term theory.

There seems little doubt that this implication tends to further the great object of making the legal construction such as to fulfil the intention of those who entered into the contract. For in the course of affairs men in making such contracts in general would, if it were brought to their minds, say that there should be such a condition. ...

In the present case, looking at the whole contract, we find that the parties contracted on the basis of the continued existence of the Music Hall at the time when the concerts were to be given; that being essential to their performance.

We think, therefore, that the Music Hall having ceased to exist, without fault of either party, both parties are excused, the plaintiffs from taking the gardens and paying the money, the defendants from performing their promise to give the use of the Hall and Gardens and other things. Consequently the rule must be absolute to enter the verdict for the defendants.

Although no explicit reference was made to frustration (which had not yet been recognised), the hallmarks of the modern doctrine are present.

Mr Justice Blackburn began by noting that the risk of fire was not allocated by the contract. His Lordship continued by noting that performance of the contract depended on the existence of the Hall – once the Hall had been destroyed by fire, it was impossible for Caldwell to provide the Hall for Taylor's use. Performing the impossible must be 'radically different' to performing the possible, and therefore in modern language, the contract was frustrated. *Both* parties are excused from further performance, and neither party is liable for the other party's loss – because there has been no breach of contract.

Impossibility of performance does not have to be permanent, provided that at the end of the temporary impossibility, performance is radically different from the performance agreed under the contract (see *Water Board v Dick, Kerr and Company* [1918] AC 119 below for an example of this).

17.1.2 Supervening Illegality or Government Intervention

A contract may become frustrated due to supervening illegality or government intervention.

17.1.2.1 Supervening Illegality

Fibrosa Spolka v Fairbairn [1943] AC 32

Panel: Viscount Simon LC, Lord Atkin, Lord Russell of Killowen, Lord Macmillan, Lord Wright, Lord Roche and Lord Porter

Facts: On 12 July 1939, Fairbairn, an English Company, agreed to sell and deliver 'flax hackling' machines to Gdynia, a port in Poland. Fibrosa Spolka planned to use the machines at their factory at Vilna, Poland. On 1 September 1939, Germany invaded Poland and on 7 September, Fairbairn wrote to Fibrosa Spolka stating that 'Owing to the outbreak of hostilities, it is now quite evident that the delivery of the hackling machines on order for

Poland cannot take place.' Performance of this contract would have amounted to trading with the enemy.

VISCOUNT SIMON LC

The principle is that where supervening events, not due to the default of either party, render the performance of a contract indefinitely impossible, and there is no undertaking to be bound in any event, frustration ensues, even though the parties may have expressly provided for the case of a limited interruption. ...

The situation arising from the outbreak of the present war, so far as this country, Germany and Poland are concerned, makes applicable Lush J.'s well-known observation in *Geipel v. Smith*: 'A state of war' (in that case the Franco-German war of 1870) 'must be presumed to be likely to continue so long and so to disturb the commerce of merchants as to defeat and destroy the object of a commercial adventure like this.'

There is a further reason for saying that this subsidiary contention of the appellants must fail, namely, that, while this country is at war with Germany and Germany is occupying Gdynia, a British subject such as the respondents could not lawfully make arrangements to deliver [to] Gdynia, and, therefore, the contract could not be further performed because of supervening illegality. A provision providing for a reasonable extension of time if dispatch is delayed by war cannot have any application when the circumstances of the war make dispatch illegal.

 Alert

Viscount Simon LC's speech records two reasons why the contract was frustrated. First, Poland was at war, and so delivery of the goods would be impossible. Second, the German occupation of Gdynia meant that it would be illegal to deliver goods there – and because of the legal presumption that a war will last long enough 'to defeat and destroy the object of [the] commercial adventure', the illegality would also last long enough to defeat the commercial adventure.

17.1.2.2 Government Intervention

Metropolitan Water Board v Dick, Kerr and Company **[1918] AC 119**

Panel: Lord Finlay LC, Lord Dunedin, Lord Atkinson and Lord Parmoor

Facts: Dick, Kerr and Company was employed under a contract to build, within six years, a reservoir for the Water Board. The contract included Condition 32 which allowed Dick, Kerr and Company to delay completion in some circumstances.

The Ministry of Munitions ordered Dick, Kerr and Company to stop work in February 1916, but the Water Board claimed that the contract was still on foot.

LORD FINLAY LC

It is admitted that the prosecution of the works became illegal in consequence of the action of the Minister of Munitions. It became illegal on February 21, 1916, and remains illegal at the present time. This is not a case of a short and temporary stoppage, but of a prohibition in consequence of war, which has already been in force for the greater part of two years, and will, according to all appearances, last as long as the war itself, as it was the result of the necessity of preventing the diversion to civil purposes of labour and material required for purposes immediately connected with the war.

Condition 32 provides for cases in which the contractor has, in the opinion of the engineer, been unduly delayed or impeded in the completion of his contract by any of the causes therein enumerated or by any other causes, so that an extension of time was reasonable. Condition 32 does not cover the case in which the interruption is of such a character and duration that it vitally and fundamentally changes the conditions of the contract, and could not possibly have been in the contemplation of the parties to the contract when it was made.

It was not disputed, as I understand the argument for the [Water Board] that in the case of a commercial contract, as for the sale of goods or agency, such a prohibition would have brought it to an end. It was sought to distinguish the present case on the ground that the contract was for the construction of works of a permanent character, which would last for a very long time, and that a delay, even of years, might be disregarded. This contention ignores the fact that, though the works when constructed may last for centuries, the process of construction was to last for six years only. It is obvious that the whole character of such a contract for construction may be revolutionized by indefinite delay, such as that which has occurred in the present case, in consequence of the prohibition.

In other words, although Condition 32 allocated the risk of temporary delays, it did not apply to more radical delays, such as the one created by the Ministry of Munitions' order. The risk that eventuated was not allocated by the contract.

LORD DUNEDIN

To make what I may call a clean case of illegality the illegality must be permanent. The appellants here say that the illegality of working on the reservoir is only temporary, and will some day be withdrawn. …

I should like first to point out that I think the appellants rather mistake the effect of the force of legislation in the present case. The order pronounced under the Defence of the Realm Act not only debarred the respondents from proceeding with the contract, but also compulsorily dispersed and sold the plant. It is admitted that an interruption may be so long as to destroy the identity of the work or service, when resumed, with the work or service when

Alert

interrupted. But quite apart from mere delay it seems to me that the action as to the plant prevents this contract ever being the same as it was.

Express the effect by a clause. If the Water Board had, when the contract was being settled, proposed a clause which allowed them at any time during the contract to take and sell off the whole plant, to interrupt the work for a period no longer than that for which the work has actually been interrupted, and then bound the contractor to furnish himself with new plant and recommence the work, does any one suppose that Dick, Kerr & Co. or any other contractor would have accepted such a clause? And the reason why they would not have accepted it would have been that the contract when resumed would be a contract under different conditions from those which existed when the contract was begun.

Lord Dunedin's speech makes clear that the impact of legal regulation must still be assessed in the context of the wider facts. In *Fibrosa Spolka v Fairbairn*, it was clear that Germany would remain in occupation of Poland during the possible time for performance of the contract, and therefore the illegality on its own would be enough to frustrate the contract.

In *Metropolitan Water Board v Dick, Kerr and Company*, the contract provided that the reservoir be completed within six years – unless the illegality lasted six years, this would not be enough *on its own* to frustrate the contract. It was therefore necessary to consider the impact of the *delay* caused by the illegality. On this second basis, it was clear that the effect of the government regulation was that, when performance became possible again, it would be radically different to the performance anticipated by the contract. The contract was therefore frustrated.

17.1.3 Frustration of Common Purpose

If it is no longer possible to achieve the parties' common purpose due to a supervening event, then the contract will be frustrated. By definition, a common purpose must be shared between the parties – it is not enough that one party's purpose is defeated.

Krell v Henry [1903] 2 KB 740

Panel: Vaughan Williams, Romer and Stirling LJJ

Facts: Krell owned a flat on Pall Mall that would have excellent views of the Coronation of the future King Edward VII, due to take place on 26 and 27 June 1902, and he advertised the flat on this basis. In response to this advert, on 20 June, Henry contracted with Krell for a licence to use the rooms during the daytime to watch the Coronation. The future King became gravely ill with appendicitis and the Coronation was delayed. Henry refused to pay for use of the rooms. (The Coronation eventually went ahead on 9 August.)

LORD JUSTICE VAUGHAN WILLIAMS

I do not think that the principle of [frustration] is limited to cases in which the event causing the impossibility of performance is the destruction or non-existence of some thing which is the subject-matter of the contract or of some condition or state of things expressly specified as a condition of it. I think that you first have to ascertain, not necessarily from the terms of the contract, but, if required, from necessary inferences, drawn from surrounding circumstances recognised by both contracting parties, what is the substance of the contract, and then to ask the question whether that substantial contract needs for its foundation the assumption of the existence of a particular state of things. If it does, this will limit the operation of the general words, and in such case, if the contract becomes impossible of performance by reason of the non-existence of the state of things assumed by both contracting parties as the foundation of the contract, there will be no breach of the contract thus limited.

Now what are the facts of the present case? The contract is contained in two letters[.] .... These letters do not mention the coronation, but speak merely of the taking of Mr. Krell's chambers, or, rather, of the use of them, in the daytime of June 26 and 27, for the sum of 75l., 25l. Then paid, balance 50l. To be paid on the 24th. But the affidavits, which by agreement between the parties are to be taken as stating the facts of the case, shew that the plaintiff exhibited on his premises, third floor, 56A, Pall Mall, an announcement to the effect that windows to view the Royal coronation procession were to be let, and that the defendant was induced by that announcement to apply to the housekeeper on the premises, who said that the owner was willing to let the suite of rooms for the purpose of seeing the Royal procession for both days, but not nights, of June 26 and 27. In my judgment the use of the rooms was let and taken for the purpose of seeing the Royal procession. It was not a demise of the rooms, or even an agreement to let and take the rooms. It is a licence to use rooms for a particular purpose and none other. And in my judgment the taking place of those processions on the days proclaimed along the proclaimed route, which passed 56A, Pall Mall, was regarded by both contracting parties as the foundation of the contract; and I think that it cannot reasonably be supposed to have been in the contemplation of the contracting parties, when the contract was made, that the coronation would not be held on the proclaimed days.

 Alert

It was suggested in the course of the argument that [if the contract is discharged in these circumstances] it would follow that if a cabman was engaged to take some one to Epsom on Derby Day at a suitable enhanced price for such a journey, say 10l., both parties to the contract would be discharged in the contingency of the race at Epsom for some reason becoming impossible; but I do not think this follows, for I do not think that in the cab case the happening of the race would be the foundation of the contract. No doubt the purpose of the engager would be to go to see the Derby, and the price would be proportionately high; but the cab had no special qualifications for the purpose which led to the selection of the cab for this particular occasion. Any other cab would have done as well.

Moreover, I think that, under the cab contract, the hirer, even if the race went off, could have said, 'Drive me to Epsom; I will pay you the agreed sum; you have nothing to do with the purpose for which I hired the cab,' and that if the cabman refused he would have been guilty of a breach of contract, there being nothing to qualify his promise to drive the hirer to Epsom on a particular day.

Whereas in the case of the coronation, there is not merely the purpose of the hirer to see the coronation procession, but it is the coronation procession and the relative position of the rooms which is the basis of the contract as much for the lessor as the hirer; and I think that if the King, before the coronation day and after the contract, had died, the hirer could not have insisted on having the rooms on the days named. It could not in the cab case be reasonably said that seeing the Derby race was the foundation of the contract, as it was of the licence in this case. Whereas in the present case, where the rooms were offered and taken, by reason of their peculiar suitability from the position of the rooms for a view of the coronation procession, surely the view of the coronation procession was the foundation of the contract, which is a very different thing from the purpose of the man who engaged the cab – namely, to see the race – being held to be the foundation of the contract.

 Alert

The common purpose of *both* parties of the licence for the rooms was to view the procession. This was clear due to (i) the particular suitability of the rooms for this purpose, and Krell's advert which advertised the rooms for this purpose, and (ii) the fact that the rooms were hired to be used during the daytime only, when the procession would be happening, but not during the evening.

Lord Justice Vaughan Williams' reasoning is an important reminder that the automatic effect of frustration means that *neither* party is able to insist on performance of the contract; ie neither Krell nor Henry could sue for breach. By contrast, in the example of the cab hired to take the hirer to Epsom on Derby Day, one would expect that *either* party could insist on performance by the other, even if the race did not take place. In other words, considering the position from the perspective of both parties to the contract may be a useful way of determining whether the frustrated purpose was genuinely shared.

Herne Bay Steamboat v Hutton [1903] 2 KB 683

Panel: Vaughan Williams, Romer and Stirling LJJ

Facts: Edward VII's Coronation was also due to include a 'Royal Naval Review' on 28 June 1902. Mr Hutton contracted with Herne Bay Steamboat to use their steamship, *The Cynthia*. The contract stated that the hire was 'for the purpose of viewing the Naval review and for a day's cruising round the fleet'. Mr Hutton refused to take the vessel or pay hire after the announcement of the future King's illness.

LORD JUSTICE ROMER

I may point out that this case is not one in which the subject-matter of the contract is a mere licence to the defendant to use a ship for the purpose of seeing the naval review and going round the fleet. In my opinion, as my Lord has said, it is a contract for the hiring of a ship by the defendant for a certain voyage, though having, no doubt, a special object, namely, to see the naval review and the fleet; but it appears to me that the object was a matter with which the defendant, as hirer of the ship, was alone concerned, and not the plaintiffs, the owners of the ship. ...

The view I have expressed with regard to the general effect of the contract before us is borne out by the following considerations. The ship (as a ship) had nothing particular to do with the review or the fleet except as a convenient carrier of passengers to see it: any other ship suitable for carrying passengers would have done equally as well. Just as in the case of the hire of a cab or other vehicle, although the object of the hirer might be stated, that statement would not make the object any the less a matter for the hirer alone, and would not directly affect the person who was letting out the vehicle for hire. ...

LORD JUSTICE STIRLING

The plaintiffs are owners of a steam vessel for carrying passengers from Herne Bay to Gravesend and other places on the Thames. The defendant is a gentleman who seems to have formed the idea of making a profit by the conveyance of passengers on June 28 and 29 from Southampton to see the naval review, and afterwards for a cruise round the fleet. From the correspondence it appears to me to be clear that this venture was the venture of the defendant alone, and that although the plaintiffs assisted him by selling tickets and posting notices of what was proposed to be done, yet the risk was entirely that of the defendant. …

It seems to me that the reference in the contract to the naval review is easily explained; it was inserted in order to define more exactly the nature of the voyage, and I am unable to treat it as being such a reference as to constitute the naval review the foundation of the contract so as to entitle either party to the benefit of the doctrine in *Taylor v. Caldwell*.

I come to this conclusion the more readily because the object of the voyage is not limited to the naval review, but also extends to a cruise round the fleet. The fleet was there, and passengers might have been found willing to go round it. It is true that in the event which happened the object of the voyage became limited, but, in my opinion, that was the risk of the defendant whose venture the taking the passengers was.

Their Lordships make it clear that viewing the Naval review was not the common purpose of this contract since there was nothing about the steamship which made it particularly suitable to see this review; any other ship would have been just as suitable.

Lord Justice Romer argues that Hutton's special purpose was unique to him, by noting that Hutton wished to use of the ship for a particular voyage, much like the man who hires a cab to take him to Epson. He could still bring ten people on board the vessel and they could still take the voyage. As Stirling LJ notes, some of the fleet was still in place and could still be viewed. This can be contrasted with the terms (the 'licence') on which Henry hired Krell's room in *Krell v Henry* – Henry was only entitled to use the room for the purposes of viewing the Coronation, and no other purpose.

It is often said that it is rare that a contract will be frustrated by the failure of the parties' *shared* purpose – comparing *Krell v Henry* with *Herne Bay Steamboat v Hutton* might suggest why. Normally, the purpose of a contract is of interest to one party, but not the other. A taxi driver (or steamboat operator) is not concerned with the passenger's purpose in taking a journey – even when the taxi driver can charge a premium for the journey. From the taxi driver's perspective, he is performing the same service whatever the purpose. It follows that such a purpose is at one party's risk.

A further, and important reason, why Stirling LJ, was able to find that the common purpose of the contract was not frustrated, was that there were in fact two purposes: to see the Naval review *and* to cruise around the fleet. It would still have been possible to cruise around the fleet. Consequently, it could not be said that the entire purpose of the contract had been frustrated.

17.2 Limitations on the Doctrine of Frustration

17.2.1 Insufficient that Performance has become more Difficult or Expensive

A contract is only frustrated by a radical change in circumstances – it is not enough that the contract has become more or unexpectedly onerous or expensive for one party.

Davis Contractors v Fareham Urban District Council [1956] AC 696

Panel: Viscount Simonds, Lord Morton of Henryton, Lord Reid, Lord Radcliffe and Lord Somervell of Harrow

Facts: Davis Contractors agreed to build 78 houses within eight months for Fareham Council. The work started in June 1946 but, for various reasons, the work took 22 months. The delay was caused by: a lack of skilled labour, occasional stoppages due to a shortage of materials including bricks, timber and plumbers' goods, and an exceptionally long frost followed by excessively muddy conditions. Davis Contractors incurred an additional cost of £17,600 in this time, on top of the £92,400 contract price, and they sought to claim this additional cost from Fareham – as the law stood at that time, if the contract had been frustrated, they would have been entitled to do so.

VISCOUNT SIMONDS

The contract was for completion of certain work in eight months: the contractors made their tender in the expectation that they would be able to do the work in the time and made a price accordingly. It may then be said that they made the contract on the 'basis' or on the 'footing' that their expectations would be fulfilled. Nor presumably were the expectations, or at least the hopes, of the respondents in any way different. Let it be said, then, of them, too, that they contracted upon the same basis or footing. But it by no means follows that disappointed expectations lead to frustrated contracts.

I do not propose to revive the controversy about the juridical basis of the doctrine of frustration. If it rests on an implied term of the contract to the effect that the parties will not be bound if a certain event happens or does not happen, I can see no ground for saying that such a term must be implied in this contract. If it is permissible to judge by the event, it is clear that the parties would not have agreed on any such term.

I pause to observe that it is not enough to say that in the event of something unexpected happening some term must be implied: it must be clear also what that term should be. In such a case as this I can see no reason for supposing that the parties would have agreed either at what moment the frustrating event was to be deemed to happen, or what was to be the position when it in fact happened.

Equally, if, as is held by some, the true doctrine rests, not on an implied term of the contract between the parties, but on the impact of the law on a situation in which an unexpected event would make it unjust to hold parties to their bargain, I would emphasize that in this aspect the doctrine has been, and must be, kept within very narrow limits. No case has been cited in which it has been applied to circumstances in any way comparable to those of the present case.

[It is not enough to say] 'A twenty-two month project is not an eight month project,' or less formidably, 'An expenditure of £111,000 is not an expenditure of £94,000, therefore the original contract must be regarded as frustrated...' My Lords, I say it with all respect to the arguments of counsel, but it appears to me that that is to make nonsense of a doctrine which, used within its proper limits, serves a valuable purpose. ...

[W]here, without the default of either party, there has been an unexpected turn of events, which renders the contract more onerous than the parties had contemplated, that is [not] by itself a ground for relieving a party of the obligation he has undertaken. ...

Alert

LORD REID

In a contract of this kind the contractor undertakes to do the work for a definite sum and he takes the risk of the cost being greater or less than he expected. If delays occur through no one's fault that may be in the contemplation of the contract, and there may be provision for extra time being given: to that extent the other party takes the risk of delay. But he does not take the risk of the cost being increased by such delay. It may be that delay could be of a character so different from anything contemplated that the contract was at an end, but in this case, in my opinion, the most that could be said is that the delay was greater in degree than was to be expected. It was not caused by any new and unforeseeable factor or event: the job proved to be more onerous but it never became a job of a different kind from that contemplated in the contract. ...

17.2.2 Self-Induced Frustration

Frustration cannot be caused by the 'default' of one of the parties, or to put it another way, frustration must arise without blame or fault on the side of the party seeking to rely on it.

The difficulty lies in determining what amounts to 'fault'. This was considered by the House of Lords in *Joseph Constantine v Imperial Smelting Corporation* [1942] AC 154. Lord Russell of Killowen said, at 179:

My Lords, I desire to add a word in relation to the phrase 'self-induced frustration.' No question arises on this appeal as to the kind or degree of fault or default on the part of the contractor which will debar him from relying on the frustration. The possible varieties are infinite, and can range from the criminality of the scuttler who opens the sea-cocks and sinks his ship, to the thoughtlessness of the prima-donna who sits in a draught and loses her voice. I wish to guard against the supposition that every destruction of corpus for which a contractor can be said, to some extent or in some sense, to be responsible, necessarily involves that the resultant frustration is self-induced within the meaning of the phrase. ...

This issue has been revisited by the detailed judgment of the Court of Appeal in *Lauritzen AS v Wijsmuller BV (The 'Super Servant II')* [1990] 1 Lloyd's Rep 1.

Lauritzen AS v Wijsmuller BV (The Super Servant II) [1990] 1 Lloyd's Rep 1

Panel: Dillon and Bingham LJJ

Facts: On 7 July 1980, Wijmuller BV agreed to carry Lauritzen AS' drilling rig (*The Dan King*) from the Hitachi Shipyard in Japan to the Netherlands for arrival in the summer of 1981. The rig was contracted to be carried on either *The Super Servant I* or *The Super Servant II*. On 29 January 1981, *The Super Servant II* sank. Wijmuller had already contracted with third parties for the use of *The Super Servant I* during the relevant period and, on 16 February 1981, Wijmuller informed Lauritzen that they would not perform the contract.

LORD JUSTICE BINGHAM

[Wijsmuller argued that they] could not perform all their contracts once *Super Servant Two* was lost; they acted reasonably (as we must assume) in treating the Dan King contract as one they could not perform; so the sinking had the direct result of making that contract impossible to perform.

[Lauritzen argued] that since the contract provided for the carriage to be performed by one or other vessel the loss of one did not render performance radically different, still less impossible. That apart, Wijsmuller's argument fell foul of [the rules on frustration] since (among other things) the frustration they sought to establish did not bring the contract to an end forthwith, without more and automatically and was not independent of the act or election of Wijsmuller. ...

Alert

Had the Dan King contract provided for carriage by *Super Servant Two* with no alternative, and that vessel had been lost before the time for performance, then assuming no negligence by Wijsmuller... I feel sure the contract would have been frustrated. The doctrine must avail a party who contracts to perform a contract of carriage with a vessel which, through no fault of his, no longer exists.

But that is not this case. The Dan King contract did provide an alternative[.] ... Wijsmuller have not alleged that when the Dan King contract was made either vessel was earmarked for its performance. That, no doubt, is why an option was contracted for. Had it been foreseen when the Dan King contract was made that Super Servant Two would be unavailable for performance, whether because she had been deliberately sold or accidentally sunk, Lauritzen at least would have thought it no matter since the carriage could be performed with the other.

The first justification for the Court of Appeal's decision therefore depended on the terms of the contract. Wijsmuller contracted to carry *The Dan King* on one of two ships – the loss of one ship did not make any difference to the availability of the other ship. Rather, it was Wijsmuller's prior *choice* to contract to use the *Super Servant I* elsewhere which prevented them from being able to perform *The Dan King* contract. Had this been a contract just for the use of *The Super Servant II* then it may have been frustrated when it sank, but the whole point of contracting for the use of one of two ships was that, were one ship to become unavailable, the second could still be used.

Lord Justice Bingham continued by saying that the contract had not been frustrated for two additional reasons.

If, as was argued, the contract was frustrated when Wijsmuller made or communicated their decision on Feb. 16, it deprives language of all meaning to describe the contract as coming to an end automatically. It was, indeed, because the contract did not come to an end automatically on Jan. 29, that Wijsmuller needed a fortnight to review their schedules and their commercial options.

I cannot, furthermore, reconcile Wijsmuller's argument with the reasoning or the decision in *Maritime National Fish Ltd* [*v. Ocean Trawlers Ltd* [1935] AC 524, Privy Council]. In that case the Privy Council declined to speculate why the charterers selected three of the five vessels to be licensed but, as I understand the case, regarded the interposition of human choice after the allegedly frustrating event as fatal to the plea of frustration. If Wijsmuller are entitled to succeed here, I cannot see why the charterers lost there.

[I]t is in my view inconsistent with the doctrine of frustration as previously understood on high authority that its application should depend on any decision, however reasonable and commercial, of the party seeking to rely on it.

Alert

In *Maritime National Fish v. Ocean Trawlers Ltd* [1935] AC 524, the defendants planned to operate five vessels as otter trawlers. They hired one of the five boats, the *St Cuthbert,* from the claimants. They applied to the Minister of Fisheries for five licences to operate the five otter trawlers but were only granted three. The defendants chose to which of the vessels to allocate the three licences but excluded the *St Cuthbert*. When they were sued for the hire charge, the defendants claimed that the contract of hire had been frustrated. The defendants' argument was unsuccessful as the Privy Council found that the frustration was self-induced. It was the defendants' choice not to allocate a licence to the *St Cuthbert*.

17.2.3 Foreseeability

It should be remembered that prior to any question of frustration, one must consider whether the risk that occurred was allocated by the parties. Where a risk was foreseeable, but not allocated, the court is likely to conclude that the risk should lie where it falls.

Walton Harvey v Walker and Homfrays Limited [1931] 1 Ch 274

Panel: Lord Hanworth MR, Romer LJ, and Eve J

Facts: A hotel owner contracted with an advertising agency to allow the latter to put adverts on the roof of their hotel. The hotel was then compulsorily purchased by the Local Authority and demolished. The advertising agency sued for breach of contract and the hotel argued the contract had become frustrated.

LORD HANWORTH MR

[His Lordship quoted from Lord Dunedin's speech in *Metropolitan Water Board v. Dick, Kerr & Co* that] 'When people enter into a contract which is dependent for the possibility of its performance on the continued availability of a specific thing, and that availability comes to an end by reason of circumstances beyond the control of the parties, the contract is prima facie regarded as dissolved. The contingency which has arisen is treated, in the absence of a contrary intention made plain, as being one about which no bargain at all was made.'

Now is it possible to apply that principle to the present case? As I have said, and the learned judge has found [at first instance] it would appear that the defendants were aware of the fact that their premises might be taken under the statutory powers[.] ... The plaintiffs had no such knowledge, nor can knowledge be imputed to them.

But there seems to be a difficulty in saying that the parties impliedly agreed that there should be a continued existence of the St. Peter's Hotel as the basis of their contract, for the defendants must have known that while they had a sure and certain continuance of their rights until October 31, 1925 (that is for at least some ten months beyond the date when the agreement was made), there was some risk after that date. They could have provided against that risk, but they did not[.] ... The parties must, if they desire to be safeguarded against subsequent contingencies, provide for them in their agreement. If they do not do so, but have entered into a contract in terms which are absolute, those terms must be carried out unless in the somewhat rare cases where it can be found that there was an implied understanding on both sides that the basis of the contract was the continued existence of an essential matter to the contract.

Having regard to the knowledge on the part of the defendants, the terms of the contract and the fact that the defendants were sure of their possessory rights for a certain time only, it does not seem to the Court to be possible to apply [the doctrine of frustration].

It would therefore seem that the learned judge was right in saying that there must be judgment for the plaintiffs.

It is important to note that events do not have to be completely unforeseeable to frustrate the contract. The more unforeseeable an event, the more likely it is to frustrate the contract. In *The Sea Angel* (above) Rix LJ said at para 127:

In a sense, most events are to a greater or lesser degree foreseeable. That does not mean that they cannot lead to frustration. Even events which are not merely foreseen but made the subject of express contractual provision may lead to frustration: as occurs when an event such as a strike, or a restraint of princes, lasts for so long as to go beyond the risk assumed under the contract and to render performance radically different from that contracted for. However, as Treitel shows through his analysis of the cases, and as Chitty summarises, the less that an event, in its type and its impact, is foreseeable, the more likely it is to be a factor which, depending on other factors in the case, may lead on to frustration.

17.2.4 Frustration of Leases

The issue as to whether a lease can be frustrated has troubled the court for many years. It used to be thought that a lease could not be frustrated because a lease creates an interest in land which is unaffected by frustrating events.

However, since the case of *National Carriers v Panalpina (Northern) Ltd* [1981] AC 675, it is clear that in principle, a lease can be frustrated, although due to the special features of a lease it will rarely happen in practice. In particular (i) the risk of damage to the property is normally on the lessee, subject to narrow exceptions, (ii) leases generally have a long life, and (iii) property is generally resilient to irreparable damage (e.g. land is close to indestructible, and a building can be rebuilt). To date, there are no reported cases in which a lease has been frustrated.

National Carriers v Panalpina (Northern) Ltd [1981] AC 675

Panel: Lord Hailsham of St Marylebone LC, Lord Wilberforce, Lord Simon of Glaisdale, Lord Russell of Killowen and Lord Roskill

Facts: National Carriers owned a warehouse on English Street in Kingston-upon-Hull. On 12 July 1974, they leased it to Panalpina for ten years, who used it for commercial storage. Access to the warehouse was via a loading bay and large doors on Kingston Street.

Opposite the warehouse leased to Panalpina, lay 'a derelict and ruinous Victorian warehouse which at some time has become, under the laws for the conservation of our national heritage, a 'listed building''. This meant that the Secretary of State for the Environment's permission was required to demolish the building, and local conservationists were entitled to object to the demolition, and the matter would be decided by an enquiry.

In 1978, the Victorian warehouse became dangerous as well as derelict, and Kingston-upon-Hull City Council closed Kingston Street and erected a barrier across it, making it impossible to access the street and rendering the warehouse leased to Panalpina 'totally useless for the one purpose, that of a commercial warehouse, for which alone it is fitted, and for which alone, by the terms of the contract between the parties, it may be lawfully used.'

Local conservationists objected to the demolition of the Victorian warehouse and an enquiry was started – until it was complete, Kingston Street would remain closed. The lease was due to run until July 1984.

LORD HAILSHAM LC

This discussion brings me to the central point at issue in this case which, in my view, is whether or not there is anything in the nature of an executed lease which prevents the doctrine of frustration, however formulated, applying to the subsisting relationship between the parties. That the point is open in this House is clear from the difference of opinion expressed in *Cricklewood Property and Investment Trust Ltd. V. Leighton's Investment Trust Ltd.* [1945] A.C. 221 between the second Lord Russell of Killowen and Lord Goddard on the one hand, who answered the question affirmatively, and Viscount Simon L.C. and Lord Wright on the other, who answered it negatively, with Lord

Porter reserving his opinion until the point arose definitively for consideration. The point, though one of principle, is a narrow one. It is the difference immortalized in HMS Pinafore between 'never' and 'hardly ever,' since both Viscount Simon and Lord Wright clearly conceded that, though they thought the doctrine applicable in principle to leases, the cases in which it could properly be applied must be extremely rare.

With the view of Viscount Simon and Lord Wright I respectfully agree. ...

LORD WILBERFORCE

So the position is that the parties to the lease contemplated, when Kingston Street was first closed, that the closure would probably last for a year or a little longer. In fact it seems likely to have lasted for just over 18 months. Assuming that the street is reopened in January 1981, the lease will have three more years to run.

My Lords, no doubt, even with this limited interruption the appellant's business will have been severely dislocated. It will have had to move goods from the warehouse before the closure and to acquire alternative accommodation. After reopening the reverse process must take place. But this does not approach the gravity of a frustrating event. Out of 10 years it will have lost under two years of use: there will be nearly three years left after the interruption has ceased.

This is a case, similar to others, where the likely continuance of the term after the interruption makes it impossible for the lessee to contend that the lease has been brought to an end. The obligation to pay rent under the lease is unconditional, with a sole exception for the case of fire, as to which the lease provides for a suspension of the obligation. No provision is made for suspension in any other case: the obligation remains. I am of opinion therefore that the lessee has no defence to the action for rent, that leave to defend should not be given and that the appeal must be dismissed.

LORD ROSKILL

One submission in favour of preserving the old rule [the frustration does not apply to leases] was that to hold that the doctrine is applicable to leases would encourage unmeritorious litigation by lessees denying liability for rent which was plainly due. This is the not unfamiliar 'floodgates' argument invariably advanced whenever it is suggested that the law might be changed.

My Lords, such an argument should have little appeal. If a defence of frustration be plainly unarguable, it will always be open to the master or judge in chambers so to hold and to give summary judgment for the lessors on the ground that the lessees have failed to show any arguable defence. I respectfully agree with Viscount Simon L.C. and Lord Wright in the *Cricklewood* case that the cases in which the doctrine will be able to be successfully invoked are likely to be rare, most frequently though not necessarily exclusively where the alleged frustrating event is of a catastrophic character. If that be so the 'floodgates' argument ceases to have any weight.

The House of Lords concluded that, although a lease could be frustrated in certain circumstances, the circumstances in which a lease would be frustrated would be rare. Lord Hailsham LC went as far as to say:

> I am struck by the fact that there appears to be no reported English case where a lease has ever been held to have been frustrated. I hope this fact will act as a suitable deterrent to the litigious, eager to make legal history by being first in this field. …

Loss of use of a commercial property for less than two out of ten years in this case was not sufficient to frustrate the lease.

It is important to read this case together with Rix LJ in *The Sea Angel* at para 111, that the entire factual matrix must be considered. Although the loss of use or delay will first be compared against the time remaining under the contract or lease, other factors (e.g. the underlying risk allocation in the contract, the ability of the parties to insure against or prevent risks etc) will often be relevant.

17.3   Remedies for Frustration

At common law, frustration discharges the contract automatically irrespective of the parties' wishes.

All obligations which arise after the frustrating event are discharged as a matter of common law as frustration automatically discharges the contract.

All obligations which arose prior to the frustrating event are usually dealt with by the *Law Reform (Frustrated Contracts) Act 1943* ('the Act'), although there are some exceptions set out in s 2(5) where the Act does not apply. The Act does not apply if the parties have made express provision for what should happen if a frustrating event occurs (see s 2(3)).

The parties are not entitled to any remedies except those contained in the Act – so, in contrast to discharge for breach, the parties are not entitled to damages for any loss caused by the frustration.

Link
See Discharge I: Breach

17.3.1 Section 1(2)

Under section 1(2), money paid or payable under the contract prior to frustration must be returned to the payer or ceases to be payable. Expenses incurred by the payee can be retained or claimed from the money paid or payable if the court considers it 'just' in 'all the circumstances'. It is for the payee to prove his expenses.

The expenses that the payee can retain or claim are capped (i) at the amount paid or payable prior to the frustrating event, and (ii) at the amount of expenses actually incurred. Within these limits, it is for the court to decide what sum would be just in all the circumstances for the payee to retain. The method by which the court should make this decision was considered in *Gamerco SA v ICM/Fair Warning (Agency)* [1995] 1 WLR 1226.

Gamerco SA v ICM/Fair Warning (Agency) [1995] 1 WLR 1226

Panel: Garland J

Statute: Law Reform (Frustrated Contracts) Act 1943 s 1(2)

Facts: The plaintiffs, Gamerco, were Spanish pop concert promoters who agreed to promote the Madrid leg of a Guns N' Roses tour; ICM were Guns N' Roses' agents for the purposes of organising the tour. In essence, Gamerco were to organise the concert in Madrid, and sell the tickets. The concert was due to take place at the Vicente Calderon Stadium, but that become impossible due to safety concerns that led to both Madrid City Council and the national government banning use of the venue for the concert.

When the contract was frustrated, Gamerco had already paid over US$412,000 to ICM 'on account'; they claimed return of this money under s 1(2). Prior to frustration, Gamerco had incurred $450,000 in expenses, and ICM had incurred around $50,000 expenses. Gamerco was entitled, under s1(2), to recover the $412,000 already paid. The question arose as to how the court should exercise its discretion in determining what portion, if any, of the $412,000, ICM should be able to retain to account for its expenses of $50,000.

MR JUSTICE GARLAND

Various views have been advanced as to how the court should exercise its discretion and these can be categorised as follows.

1. *Total retention*. This view was advanced by the Law Revision Committee in 1939 (Cmd. 6009) on the questionable ground 'that it is reasonable to assume that in stipulating for prepayment the payee intended to protect himself from loss under the contract.' ...

    In *B.P. Exploration Co. (Libya) Ltd. V. Hunt (No. 2)* Robert Goff J. Considered the principle of recovery under subsections (2) and (3). He said, at pp. 799–800:

    'The Act is not designed to do certain things: (i) It is not designed to apportion the loss between the parties. There is no general power under either section 1(2) or section 1(3) to make any allowance for expenses incurred by the plaintiff (except, under the proviso to section 1(2), to enable him to enforce pro tanto payment of a sum payable but unpaid before frustration); and expenses incurred by the defendant are only relevant in so far as they go to reduce the net benefit obtained by him and thereby limit any award to the plaintiff. (ii) It is not concerned to put the parties in the position in which they would have been if the contract had been performed. (iii) It is not concerned to restore the parties to the position they were in before the contract was made. A remedy designed to prevent unjust enrichment may not achieve that result; for expenditure may be incurred by either party under the contract which confers no benefit on the other, and in respect of which no remedy is available under the Act.'

He then turned to section 1(2) and said:

'There is no discretion in the court in respect of a claim under section 1(2), except in respect of the allowance for expenses; subject to such an allowance … the plaintiff is entitled to repayment of the money he has paid. The allowance for expenses is probably best rationalised as a statutory recognition of the defence of change of position. True, the expenses need not have been incurred by reason of the plaintiff's payments; but they must have been incurred in, or for the purpose of, the performance of the contract under which the plaintiff's payment has been made, and for that reason it is just that they should be brought into account.'

I do not derive any specific assistance from the *B.P Exploration Co.* case. There was no question of any change of position as a result of the plaintiffs' advance payment.

2. *Equal division*. This was discussed by Professor Treitel in Frustration and Force Majeure, pp. 555–556, paras. 15–059 and 15–060. There is some attraction in splitting the loss, but what if the losses are very unequal? Professor Treitel considers statutory provisions in Canada and Australia but makes the point that unequal division is unnecessarily rigid and was rejected by the Law Revision Committee in the 1939 report to which reference has already been made. … It may well be that one party's expenses are entirely thrown away while the other is left with some realisable or otherwise usable benefit or advantage. Their losses may, as in the present case, be very unequal. Professor Treitel therefore favours the third view.

3. Broad discretion. It is self-evident that any rigid rule is liable to produce injustice. The words, 'if it considers it just to do so having regard to all the circumstances of the case,' clearly confer a very broad discretion. Obviously the court must not take into account anything which is not 'a circumstance of the case' or fail to take into account anything that is and then exercise its discretion rationally. I see no indication in the Act, the authorities or the relevant literature that the court is obliged to incline towards either total retention or equal division. Its task is to do justice in a situation which the parties had neither contemplated nor provided for, and to mitigate the possible harshness of allowing all loss to lie where it has fallen.

 Alert

I have not found my task easy. … In all the circumstances, and having particular regard to the plaintiffs' loss, I consider that justice is done by making no deduction under the proviso. …

The court had a 'broad discretion' as to the 'just' amount of the prepayment which it would allow ICM to retain to cover ICM's expenses. (Bear in mind that the discretion is limited by the caps mentioned above). Mr Justice Garland decided that, in all the circumstances, ICM should not be allowed to retain any of the money to cover their expenses given the considerable expenses which Gamerco had also incurred.

17.3.2 Section 1(3)

Under section 1(3), if a party to a frustrated contract obtained a (non-money) benefit under the contract prior to frustration, the party receiving that benefit must pay to the other party such 'just' sum (if any) as is determined by the court. The sum awarded may not exceed the benefit received.

In determining a 'just' amount, the court must take account of all the circumstances including (i) any expenses incurred by the benefitted party and (ii) the effect of the frustration on the benefit received.

In *B.P. Exploration Co (Libya) Ltd v Hunt (No 2)* [1982] 2 WLR 253, Robert Goff J set out a two stage test in applying s 1(3). The first stage is to identify and value the benefit conferred on the other party, by calculating the value of the 'end product' of the services. The second stage is to assess a 'just' sum to be deducted from this value.

B.P. Exploration Co (Libya) Ltd v Hunt (No 2) [1979] 1 WLR. 783

Panel: Robert Goff J

Statute: Law Reform (Frustrated Contracts) Act 1943 s 1(3)

Facts: Hunt owned the right to oil from a Libyan oil field. He could not afford to develop the oil field on his own, so he entered an agreement with BP whereby they would pay the development costs in return for (i) a half stake in the oil field,   and (ii) reimbursement of some of the costs out of Hunt's half, once the oil started pumping. In other words, Hunt would not have to contribute to the high costs of finding and extracting the oil in the field.

Large sums were spent by BP and they found and extracted some oil. Libya expropriated BP's half of the concession after Gaddafi's 1969 revolution – at this point, they had only received about one third of the money they had invested. The Libyan government allowed Hunt to take oil for about two more years before his half was also expropriated.

BP brought a claim against Hunt on the basis that their agreement had been frustrated, and therefore they were entitled to a just sum to reflect the non-money benefits accrued to Hunt, for example the oil he received, but also the benefit of BP's expertise in finding and extracting the oil for him.

MR JUSTICE ROBERT GOFF

(a) ... First, it has to be shown that the defendant has, by reason of something done by the plaintiff in, or for the purpose of, the performance of the contract, obtained a valuable benefit (other than a payment of money) before the time of discharge. That benefit has to be identified, and valued, and such value forms the upper limit of the award.

Secondly, the court may award to the plaintiff such sum, not greater than the value of such benefit, as it considers just having regard to all the circumstances of the case, including in particular the matters specified in section 1(3)(a) and (b) [of Law Reform (Frustrated Contracts) Act 1943].

In the case of an award under section 1(3) there are, therefore, two distinct stages — the identification and valuation of the benefit, and the award of the just sum.

The amount to be awarded is the just sum, unless the defendant's benefit is less, in which event the award will be limited to the amount of that benefit. The distinction between the identification and valuation of the defendant's benefit, and the assessment of the just sum, is the most controversial part of the Act. It represents the solution adopted by the legislature of the problem of restitution in cases where the benefit does not consist of a payment of money, but the solution so adopted has been criticised by some commentators as productive of injustice[.] ...

 Decipher
Note that the just sum is capped at the amount of the valuable benefit.

(b) *Identification of the defendant's benefit*. In the course of the argument before me, there was much dispute whether, in the case of services, the benefit should be identified as the services themselves, or as the end product of the services. One example canvassed (because it bore some relationship to the facts of the present case) was the example of prospecting for minerals. If minerals are discovered, should the benefit be regarded ... as the services of prospecting, or ... as the minerals themselves being the end product of the successful exercise? Now, I am satisfied that it was the intention of the legislature, to be derived from section 1(3) as a matter of construction, that the benefit should in an appropriate case be identified as the end product of the services. This appears, in my judgment, not only from the fact that section 1(3) distinguishes between the plaintiff's performance and the defendant's benefit, but also from section 1(3)(b) which clearly relates to the product of the plaintiff's performance.

Alert

Let me take the example of a building contract. Suppose that a contract for work on a building is frustrated by a fire which destroys the building and which, therefore, also destroys a substantial amount of work already done by the plaintiff. Although it might be thought just to award the plaintiff a sum assessed on a *quantum meruit* basis, probably a rateable part of the contract price, in respect of the work he has done, the effect of section 1(3)(b) will be to reduce the award to nil, because of the effect, in relation to the defendant's benefit, of the circumstances giving rise to the frustration of the contract.

It is quite plain that, in section 1(3)(b), the word 'benefit' is intended to refer, in the example I have given, to the actual improvement to the building, because that is what will be affected by the frustrating event; the subsection therefore contemplates that, in such a case, the benefit is the end product of the plaintiff's services, not the services themselves.

This will not be so in every case, since in some cases the services will have no end product; for example, where the services consist of doing such work as surveying, or transporting goods. In each case, it is necessary to ask the question: what benefit has the defendant obtained by reason of the plaintiff's contractual performance? But it must not be forgotten that in section 1(3) the relevance of the value of the benefit is to fix a ceiling to the award. If, for example, in a building contract, the building is only partially completed, the value of the partially completed building (i.e. the product of the services) will fix a ceiling for the award; the stage of the work may be such that the uncompleted building may be worth less than the value of the work and materials that have gone into it, particularly as completion by another builder may cost more than completion by the original builder would have cost.

 Alert

In other cases, however, the actual benefit to the defendant may be considerably more than the appropriate or just sum to be awarded to the plaintiff, in which event the value of the benefit will not in fact determine the quantum of the award.

I should add, however, that, in a case of prospecting, it would usually be wrong to identify the discovered mineral as the benefit. In such a case there is always (whether the prospecting is successful or not) the benefit of the prospecting itself, i.e. of knowing whether or not the land contains any deposit of the relevant minerals; if the prospecting is successful, the benefit may include also the enhanced value of the land by reason of the discovery; if the prospector's contractual task goes beyond discovery and includes development and production, the benefit will include the further enhancement of the land by reason of the installation of the facilities, and also the benefit of in part transforming a valuable mineral deposit into a marketable commodity.

Mr Justice Robert Goff was therefore clear that, in principle, BP was not entitled to a fair price for their exploration and development work. Rather, s 1(3) capped the just sum according to the end product of BP's work. If the frustrating event destroys some of the value of the end product (i.e. on the facts, the developed oil field was significantly devalued by the Libyan expropriation) then this limits the sum that can be recovered under s 1(3).

His Lordship continued by noting that s 1(3) could have been designed differently, and that some commentators had taken the view that it would have been fairer if s 1(3) allowed the claimant to recover for the fair value of the work requested by the defendant.

I add by way of footnote that all these difficulties would have been avoided if the legislature had thought it right to treat the services themselves as the benefit. In the opinion of many commentators, it would be more just to do so; after all, the services in question have been requested by the defendant, who normally takes the risk that they may prove worthless, from whatever cause.

In the example I have given of the building destroyed by fire, there is much to be said for the view that the builder should be paid for the work he has done, unless he has (for example by agreeing to insure the works) taken upon himself the risk of destruction by fire. But my task is to construe the Act as it stands. On the true construction of the Act, it is in my judgment clear that the defendant's benefit must, in an appropriate case, be identified as the end product of the plaintiff's services, despite the difficulties which this construction creates, difficulties which are met again when one comes to value the benefit.

Having reached his conclusion as to what should be identified as the defendant's benefit, his Lordship continued by considering how that benefit should be valued – should this be based on the objective value of the work (ie the amount that would have been paid for it on the market), or should it be calculated subjectively according to the value of the benefit *to the defendant*.

(d) *Valuing the benefit*. Since the benefit may be identified with the product of the plaintiff's performance, great problems arise in the valuation of the benefit. First, how does one solve the problem which arises from the fact that a small service may confer an enormous benefit, and conversely, a very substantial service may confer only a very small benefit? The answer presumably is that at the stage of valuation of the benefit (as opposed to assessment of the just sum) the task of the court is simply to assess the value of the benefit to the defendant. For example, if a prospector after some very simple prospecting discovers a large and unexpected deposit of a valuable mineral, the benefit to the defendant (namely, the enhancement in the value of the land) may be enormous; it must be valued as such, always bearing in mind that the assessment of a just sum may very well lead to a much smaller amount being awarded to the plaintiff.

But conversely, the plaintiff may have undertaken building work for a substantial sum which is, objectively speaking, of little or no value — for example, he may commence the redecoration, to the defendant's execrable taste, of rooms which are in good decorative order. If the contract is frustrated before the work is complete, and the work is unaffected by the frustrating event, it can be argued that the defendant has obtained no benefit, because the defendant's property has been reduced in value by the plaintiff's work; but the partial work must be treated as a benefit to the defendant, since he requested it, and valued as such.

Secondly, at what point in time is the benefit to be valued? ... Section 1(3)(b) makes it plain that the plaintiff is to take the risk of depreciation or destruction by the frustrating event. If the effect of the frustrating event upon the value of the benefit is to be measured, it must surely be measured upon the benefit as at the date of frustration.

For example, let it be supposed that a builder does work which doubles in value by the date of frustration. And is then so severely damaged by fire that the contract is frustrated; the valuation of the residue must surely be made on the basis of the value as at the date of frustration. ... [*sic*]

Mr Justice Robert Goff made it clear that it is the 'end product' rather than the 'services rendered' which represents the benefit. If the end product has been destroyed by the frustrating event, then there will be no valuable benefit and the party providing the service (eg the builders) will be entitled to nothing.

Further Reading

Burrows, A., (1991). *Frustration, Restitution and Loss Apportionment, Essays on the Law of Restitution*. pp. 147

Pawlowski, M., (2007). Mistake, frustration and implied conditions in leases, *L & T Review* 11(5). pp.158

Peel, E., *The Law of Contract*. 13th ed. Treitel. Ch.19

McKendrick, E., *Contract Law* (2017) 12th ed. Ch.14

18

Remedies I

Topic List

Contract Law

Introduction

When one party to a contract fails to perform his obligations, the other party may be entitled to a remedy. In some circumstances, the aggrieved party is entitled to specific performance of the contract, giving him exactly what he bargained for. More commonly, the aggrieved party is entitled to damages to compensate him for the losses caused by the breach. The aim of damages in contract law is to compensate the innocent party for the losses caused by the breach. The aim is not to punish the party in breach.

This chapter considers the different methods of measuring contractual damages. The next chapter considers the limiting factors which render some losses suffered irrecoverable (for example, because they are too remote).

18.1 Agreed (Liquidated) Damages Clauses

Contracts arise from the agreement of the parties, and so it is unsurprising that the parties can agree what the consequences of a breach of contract will be. For example, they can use exemption clauses to restrict the recoverable losses.

Link
See also Chapters 11 & 12 on Exemption Clauses

Alternatively, they could agree that a certain sum will be payable on breach. Such a clause will either be regarded as a penalty clause (and be struck out by the court) or enforceable as a valid liquidated damages clause. The courts explored what could constitute a penalty in the following Supreme Court decisions.

Cavendish Square Holdings BV v Talal El Makdessi [2015] UKSC 67; 2015 WL 6655167

The Supreme Court has effectively overruled the old test of "genuine pre-estimate of loss" set out in Dunlop. In *Cavendish Square Holdings BV v Talal El Makdessi* the Lordships held that the test for a penalty clause now depends on whether the clause is a secondary obligation which imposes a detriment which is out of all proportion to the legitimate interest of the innocent party. If the clause satisfies this test it is a penalty clause and unenforceable. This decision acknowledges that a party can sometimes have a legitimate interest in enforcing performance which goes beyond simply being compensated for losses.

Panel: Lord Neuberger, Lord Mance, Lord Clarke, Lord Sumption, Lord Carnwath, Lord Toulson, Lord Hodge

Facts: Mr Makdessi agreed to sell Cavendish a stake in his advertising group. Mr Makdessi retained a 20% shareholding in the company. The purchase price was payable in instalments. The contract contained a restrictive covenant which prevented Makdessi competing with the business following completion of the sale. If Makdessi breached the covenant, the agreement provided that he would not be entitled to receive the final two instalments of the price paid by Cavendish (clause 5.1). Further, Makdessi could be required

384

to sell his remaining shares to Cavendish, at a price that excluded the value of the goodwill of the business (clause 5.6), the goodwill being the most valuable part of the business.

Makdessi breached the covenants but argued that clauses 5.1 and 5.6 were unenforceable penalty clauses.

The Court of Appeal held the provisions were unenforceable penalty clauses; they also considered whether there was a commercial justification for the clauses.

In the Supreme Court all the Lordships agreed that clauses 5.1 and 5.6 were not penalties. However, they had different justifications for their decisions.

[LORD NEUBERGER AND LORD SUMPTION

32....... The true test is whether the impugned provision is a secondary obligation which imposes a detriment on the contract-breaker out of all proportion to any legitimate interest of the innocent party in the enforcement of the primary obligation. The innocent party can have no proper interest in simply punishing the defaulter. His interest is in performance or in some appropriate alternative to performance. In the case of a straightforward damages clause, that interest will rarely extend beyond compensation for the breach, and we therefore expect that Lord Dunedin's four tests would usually be perfectly adequate to determine its validity. But compensation is not necessarily the only legitimate interest that the innocent party may have in the performance of the defaulter's primary obligations. This was recognised in the early days of the penalty rule, when it was still the creature of equity, and is reflected in Lord Macclesfield's observation in Peachy (quoted in para 5 above) about the application of the penalty rule to provisions which were "never intended by way of compensation", for which equity would not relieve. It was reflected in the result in Dunlop. And it is recognised in the more recent decisions about commercial justification. And, as Lord Hodge shows, it is the principle underlying the Scottish authorities.

33. The penalty rule is an interference with freedom of contract. It undermines the certainty which parties are entitled to expect of the law. Diplock LJ was neither the first nor the last to observe that "The court should not be astute to descry a 'penalty clause'": Robophone at p 1447. As Lord Woolf said, speaking for the Privy Council in Philips Hong Kong Ltd v Attorney General of Hong Kong (1993) 61 BLR 41, 59, "the court has to be careful not to set too stringent a standard and bear in mind that what the parties have agreed should normally be upheld", not least because "[a]ny other approach will lead to undesirable uncertainty especially in commercial contracts".

[LORD HODGE

255. .... the correct test for a penalty is whether the sum or remedy stipulated as a consequence of a breach of contract is exorbitant or unconscionable when regard is had to the innocent party's interest in the performance of the contract. Where the test is to be applied to a clause fixing the level of damages to be paid on breach, an extravagant disproportion between the stipulated sum and the highest level of damages that could possibly arise from the breach would amount to a penalty and thus be unenforceable. In other circumstances the contractual provision that applies on breach is measured against the interest of the innocent party which is protected by the contract and the court asks whether the remedy is exorbitant or unconscionable.

270. There is clearly a strong argument, which Lord Neuberger and Lord Sumption favour, that in substance clause 5.1 is a primary obligation which made payment of the interim and final payments conditional upon the seller's performance of his clause 11.2 obligations. But even if it were correct to analyse clause 5.1 as a secondary provision operating on breach of the seller's primary obligation, I am satisfied that it is not an unenforceable penalty clause for the following six reasons.

271. First, it is important to consider the nature of the obligations of the sellers which could trigger the withholding of the instalments under clause 5.1. Clause 11.2 imposed restrictive covenants on the sellers, prohibiting them from competing with the company. Having sold substantial blocks of shares in the company for a price which attributed a high value to its goodwill, the sellers were prohibited from derogating from what they had sold.

272. Secondly, the factual matrix in the uncontested evidence of Mr Andrew Scott, WPP's director of corporate development, and Mr Ghossoub and recorded in the agreed statement of facts and issues showed the importance of personal relationships in the marketing sector and particularly in the Middle East. The statement of facts and issues recorded (at para 5) that the success of the Group's business depended on the personal relationships which Mr Ghossoub and Mr El Makdessi had built up with their key clients and in para 33, which Lord Neuberger and Lord Sumption quote at para 66 of their judgment, it explained that the agreement was structured to protect the goodwill of the Group. The continued loyalty of the sellers was critically important to preserving the value of the Group's goodwill.

273. Thirdly, that evidence and the agreement itself showed that a large proportion of the agreed purchase price was attributable to that goodwill. Extrapolating from the maximum consideration which the sellers could have received for the shares which they sold, the company had a maximum value of $300m which compares with its certified NAV (without goodwill) of $69.7m.

274. Cavendish therefore needed to be assured of the sellers' loyalty. It had a very substantial and legitimate interest in protecting the value of the company's goodwill. It did so by giving the sellers a strong financial incentive

to remain loyal to the company by complying with the restrictions set out in clause 11.2. The sellers, who, like Cavendish, had access to expert legal advice and negotiated the contract over several months, agreed to peril their entitlement to the deferred consideration on their continued loyalty.

275. Fourthly, I am not persuaded by Mr Bloch's argument that clause 5.1 was exorbitant because it could be triggered by a minor breach of clause 11.2, such as an unsuccessful solicitation of a senior employee. That appears to me to be unrealistic. Clause 5.1 was not addressing the loss which Cavendish might suffer from breach of the restrictive covenant, whether an isolated and minor breach or repeated and fundamental breaches. It was addressing the disloyalty of a seller who was prepared in any way to attack the company's goodwill. No question therefore arises of a presumption of a penalty where the same sum is payable on the occurrence of several events which may cause serious or trifling damages as in Lord Dunedin's proposition 4(c) in Dunlop. In any event, that presumption would not apply because the losses arising from any breach of clause 11.2 were generically the same – see Lord Parker of Waddington in Dunlop at p 98. As Lord Neuberger and Lord Sumption have said (para 75), loyalty is indivisible.

276. Fifthly, Mr Bloch submitted that clause 5.1 might operate perversely as far as Mr El Makdessi was concerned because a minor breach of clause 11.2, which did not harm the company's goodwill, would result in his losing more by the loss of the interim and final payments than a major breach which diminished the profits of the

277. Finally, I am not persuaded that the company's entitlement to seek a disgorgement of Mr El Makdessi's profits arising from his breach of fiduciary duty and the possibility that Cavendish itself might have a claim in damages if Mr El Makdessi breached clause 11.2 after he ceased to be a director make the operation of clause 5.1 exorbitant or unconscionable. The former is res inter alios acta as each of Cavendish and the company have separate legal personality. Any award of damages to Cavendish would be designed to place it in the same position financially as if the contract had been performed. If an award of damages together with the price reduction which clause 5.1 effects involved double counting, I would expect the price reduction to be credited against the claim for damages.

278. In summary, I am persuaded that in the circumstances of this share purchase, Cavendish had a very substantial legitimate interest to protect by making the deferred consideration depend upon the continued loyalty of the sellers through their compliance with the prohibitions in clause 11.2. I do not construe clause 5.1 as a stipulation for punishment for breach; it is neither exorbitant nor unconscionable but is commensurate with Cavendish's legitimate interests. It may therefore be enforced.

LORD CLARKE

291. I agree that the appeal in Cavendish should be allowed .....and that we should make the declarations proposed by Lord Neuberger and Lord Sumption. In reaching those conclusions I agree with the reasoning of Lord Neuberger and Lord Sumption, Lord Mance and Lord Hodge, save that on the question whether clauses 5.1 and 5.6 are capable of constituting penalties, I agree with Lord Hodge in having an open mind about clause 5.1, and in concluding that clause 5.6 is a secondary obligation – see paras 270 and 280 respectively. As to the relationship between penalties and forfeiture, my present inclination is to agree with Lord Hodge (in para 227) and with Lord Mance (in paras160 and 161) that in an appropriate case the court should ask first whether, as a matter of construction, the clause is a penalty and, if it answers that question in the negative, it should ask (where relevant) whether relief against forfeiture should be granted in equity having regard to the position of each of the parties after the breach.]

Each of their Lordships described the new test with slightly different nuances as to the right approach. As such it has proved slightly challenging for academics and practitioners to determine a settled version of the new test. However, in the recent case of *Vivienne Westwood Limited v Conduit Street Development Limited* [2017] EWHC 350 (CH) the Court described the test as follows:

1. Is the clause a Primary or Secondary obligation? If primary, it will not engage the penalty rule.

    a. A clause will be primary if it is part of the primary obligations in the commercial context of the contract i.e. furthers the commercial objective of the contract.

    b. A clause will be secondary if it is an obligation triggered by breach of contract to compensate the innocent party.

2. If secondary, the clause will be a penalty if it imposes a detriment out of all proportion to any legitimate interest of the innocent party in the performance of the primary obligation.

The Lordships confirmed that the burden of proof is on the person alleging that the clause is a penalty to provide that the test has been met. Furthermore they made it clear that the law on penalties is a clear interference with freedom of contract so will not be invoked lightly by the Court to strike down a clause in contract freely negotiated between parties of equal bargaining power. In determining the proportionality of the detriment to the legitimate interest the traditional concepts of characterising the disparity as "extravagant" or "unconscionable" may still be of assistance.

ParkingEye Limited v Beavis [2015] UKSC 67

The appeal for ParkingEye was heard at the same time as the Makdessi decision.

Panel: Lord Neuberger, Lord Mance, Lord Clarke, Lord Sumption, Lord Carnwath, Lord Toulson, Lord Hodge

Facts: ParkingEye managed a car park for the owners of a Riverside Retail Park. ParkingEye displayed numerous signs at the entrance to the carpark and at frequent intervals throughout it. The notices stated that a failure to comply with a two hour time limit would result in a parking charge of £85. Mr Beavis parked his car at the car park; he exceeded the two hour limit. ParkingEye demanded payment of the £85 charge. Beavis refused to pay on the basis the £85 charge was unenforceable as a penalty.

Held: The Lordships concluded that the penalty rule applied to the facts but that the £85 charge was not a penalty. The Lordships agreed that ParkingEye had a legitimate interest in charging motorists for any period they occupied the car park beyond the 2 hours. Although the amount of the charge exceeded any likely loss, Parking Eye had a responsibility to manage the car parks effectively and it was legitimate to use the charges as a means of influencing the conduct of motorists in order to ensure they did not overstay. In this context the £85 charge was proportionate to that interest.

[LORD TOULSON

293. On the essential nature of a penalty clause, I would highlight and endorse Lord Hodge's succinct statement at para 255 that "the correct test for a penalty is whether the sum or remedy stipulated as a consequence of a breach of contract is exorbitant or unconscionable when regard is had to the innocent party's interest I the performance of the contract". Parties and courts should focus on that test, bearing in mind a) that it is impossible to lay down abstract rules about what may or may not be "extravagant or unconscionable", because it depends on the particular facts

and circumstances established in the individual case (as Lord Halsbury said in the Clydebank case, [1905] AC 6, 10, and Lord Parmoor said in the Dunlop case, [1915] AC 79, 101), and b) *that "exorbitant or unconscionable" are strong words. I agree with Lord Mance (para 152) that the word "unconscionable" in this context means much the same as "extravagant"*]

18.2 The Expectation Interest

When there is no liquidated damages clause, it is up to the court to decide the level of damages which should be awarded in order to compensate the innocent party. In other words, the court will quantify the 'unliquidated' damages to be awarded. There are three different methods of measuring the unliquidated damages to be awarded: (i) the expectation interest, (ii) the reliance interest and (iii) the restitution interest.

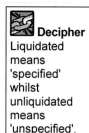 **Decipher**
Liquidated means 'specified' whilst unliquidated means 'unspecified'.

The aim of the expectation interest is set out in the classic definition given by Parke B in *Robinson v Harman* (1848) 1 Ex 850 at p. 855.

'The rule of the common law is that where a party sustains a loss by reason of a breach of contract, he is, so far as money can do it, to be placed in the same situation, with respect to damages, as if the contract had been performed.'

The House of Lords recently confirmed this was the "fundamental principle governing the quantum of damages for breach of contract" (see *Golden Strait Corporation v Nippon Yusen Kubishika Kaisha, 'The Golden Victory'* [2007] UKHL 12 at para. 12 per Lord Scott).

18.2.1 Calculating the expectation interest

In order to calculate the expectation interest, it is usually sufficient to ask how much money must the innocent party be awarded in order to put them in the position they would have been in had the contract been properly performed. This can be worked out by calculating the difference between the position they would have been in and the position they are actually in.

However, there are certain circumstances, for instance, the construction of a building which does not meet a particular specification, when the situation is a little more complicated. This is because there may be a difference between the amount of money which it would cost to put the defect right and the diminution in value of the building (see *Ruxley Electronics and Construction Ltd. v Forsyth* [1996] AC 344 for a good example of this situation). In such circumstances, you will need to consider the three alternative methods of calculating the expectation measure set out below.

18.2.2 Cost of cure, diminution in value and loss of amenity

There are three alternative methods of calculating the expectation interest:

(i) the cost of cure – the sum required to remedy the defect in performance.

(ii) the diminution in value – the difference in value between the performance received and the performance promised.

(iii) the loss of amenity – this compensates the claimant for a loss of a personal preference or pleasurable amenity.

The normal measure of damages for breach of a contract involving defective works (eg if a building was defectively built) is the cost of cure (*Birse Construction Ltd. v Eastern Telegraph Co. Ltd* [2004] EWHC 2512). However, this will not be awarded when such an award would be unreasonable. This is clearly illustrated by *Ruxley Electronics v Forsyth*.

Ruxley Electronics and Construction Ltd. v Forsyth [1996] AC 344

Panel: Lord Keith of Kinkel, Lord Bridge of Harwich, Lord Jauncey of Tullichettle, Lord Mustill and Lord Lloyd of Bewick

Facts: Mr Forsyth employed Ruxley Electronics to build a swimming pool in his garden at a cost of £17,797.40. The contract provided that the pool should be 7 feet 6 inches deep, but in fact it was built only to a depth of 6 feet. The pool was still perfectly safe for diving, and there was no diminution of value as a result of the breach of contract. Mr Forsyth claimed that he was entitled to the 'cost of cure' (or 'cost of reinstatement'), that is damages to allow him to rebuild the pool to the contract depth – this would mean completely demolishing the existing pool and starting again, at a cost of £21,560. The judge at first instance made an award of £2,500 in order to compensate Mr Forsyth for his loss of amenity. The Court of Appeal allowed Mr Forsyth's appeal and granted the cost of cure. Ruxley Electronics appealed to the House of Lords.

LORD MUSTILL

... There are not two alternative measures of damage ['cost of cure' and 'diminution in value'], at opposite poles, but only one; namely, the loss truly suffered by the promisee. In some cases the loss cannot be fairly measured except by reference to the full cost of repairing the deficiency in performance. In others, and in particular those where the contract is designed to fulfil a purely commercial purpose, the loss will very often consist only of the monetary detriment brought about by the breach of contract. But these remedies are not exhaustive, for the law must cater for those occasions where the value of the promise to the promisee exceeds the financial enhancement of his position which full performance will secure. This excess, often referred to in the literature as the 'consumer surplus' (see for example the valuable discussion by Harris, Ogus and Philips (1979) 95 L.Q.R. 581) is usually incapable of precise valuation in terms of money, exactly because it represents a personal, subjective and non-monetary gain. Nevertheless where it exists the law should recognise it and compensate the promisee if the misperformance takes it away. The lurid bathroom tiles, or the grotesque folly instanced in argument by my noble and learned friend, Lord Keith of Kinkel, may be so discordant with general taste that in purely economic terms the builder may be said to do the employer a favour by failing to install them. But this is too narrow and materialistic a view of the transaction. Neither the contractor nor the court has the right to substitute for the employer's individual expectation of performance a criterion derived from what ordinary people would regard as sensible. As my Lords have shown, the test of reasonableness plays a central part in determining the basis of recovery, and will indeed be decisive in a case such as the present when the cost of reinstatement would be wholly disproportionate to the non-monetary loss suffered by the employer. But it would be equally unreasonable to deny all recovery for such a loss. The amount may be small, and since it cannot be quantified directly there may be room for difference of opinion about what it should be. But in several fields the judges are well accustomed to putting figures to intangibles, and I see no reason why the imprecision of the exercise should be a barrier, if that is what fairness demands.

My Lords, once this is recognised the puzzling and paradoxical feature of this case, that it seems to involve a contest of absurdities, simply falls away. There is no need to remedy the injustice of awarding too little, by unjustly awarding far too much. The judgment of the trial judge acknowledges that the employer has suffered a true loss and expresses it in terms of money. Since there is no longer any issue about the amount of the award, as distinct from the principle, I would simply restore his judgment by allowing the appeal.

LORD LLOYD OF BEWICK

Reasonableness

... If reinstatement is not the reasonable way of dealing with the situation, then diminution in value, if any, is the true measure of the plaintiff's loss. If there is no diminution in value, the plaintiff has suffered no loss. His damages will be nominal.

... If the court takes the view that it would be unreasonable for the plaintiff to insist on reinstatement, as where, for example, the expense of the work involved would be out of all proportion to the benefit to be obtained, then the plaintiff will be confined to the difference in value. If the judge had assessed the difference in value in the present case at, say, £5,000, I have little doubt that the Court of Appeal would have taken that figure rather than £21,560. The difficulty arises because the judge has, in the light of the expert evidence, assessed the difference in value as nil. But that cannot make reasonable what he has found to be unreasonable.

...

Intention

I fully accept that the courts are not normally concerned with what a plaintiff does with his damages. But it does not follow that intention is not relevant to reasonableness, at least in those cases where the plaintiff does not intend to reinstate. ...

... [I]f, as the judge found, Mr. Forsyth had no intention of rebuilding the pool, he has lost nothing except the difference in value, if any.

The relevance of intention to the issue of reasonableness is expressly recognised by the respondent in his case. In paragraph 37, Mr. Jacob says:

'The respondent accepts that the genuineness of the parties' indicated predilections can be a factor which the court must consider when deciding between alternative measures of damage. Where a plaintiff is contending for a high as opposed to a low cost measure of damages the court must decide whether in the circumstances of the particular case such high cost measure is reasonable. One of the factors that may be relevant is the genuineness of the plaintiff's desire to pursue the course which involves the higher cost. Absence of such desire (indicated by untruths about intention) may undermine the reasonableness of the higher cost measure.'

I can only say that I find myself in complete agreement with that approach... .

...

Loss of amenity

I turn last to the head of damages under which the judge awarded £2,500. ...

Addis v. Gramophone Co. Ltd. established the general rule that in claims for breach of contract, the plaintiff cannot recover damages for his injured feelings. But the rule, like most rules, is subject to exceptions. One of the well established exceptions is when the object of the contract is to afford pleasure, as, for example, where the plaintiff has booked a holiday with a tour operator. If the tour operator is in breach of contract by failing to provide what the contract called for, the plaintiff may recover damages for his disappointment: see *Jarvis v. Swans Tours Ltd.* [1973] Q.B. 233 and *Jackson v. Horizon Holidays Ltd.* [1975] 1 W.L.R. 1468.

This was, as I understand it, the principle which Judge Diamond applied in the present case. He took the view that the contract was one 'for the provision of a pleasurable amenity.' ... This was a view which the judge was entitled to take. If it involves a further inroad on the rule in *Addis v. Gramophone Co. Ltd.* [1909] A.C. 488, then so be it. But I prefer to regard it as a logical application or adaptation of the existing exception to a new situation.

The court recognised that there will be instances in which the innocent party should be compensated for their loss of enjoyment. Since an award for the cost of cure was unreasonable and there was no diminution in value, Mr Forsyth was awarded £2,500 to compensate him for his loss of a pleasurable amenity.

18.3   The Reliance Interest

The aim of the reliance interest is to put the innocent party in the position which they would have been in had they not entered into the contract in the first place. In other words, it compensates the innocent party for their pre-breach expenditure.

Generally speaking, the innocent party has an unfettered choice as to whether to claim their expectation interest or their reliance interest (*Anglia*

Television Ltd v Reed [1972] 1 QB 60). However, there are two exceptions to this:

(i) The innocent party cannot claim their expectation interest if it is too speculative.

(ii) The innocent party cannot claim their reliance interest in order to escape from a bad bargain.

18.3.1 Expectation interest too speculative

If the calculation of the expectation interest is too speculative, the innocent party will be forced to claim their reliance interest instead. This is illustrated by *Anglia Television Ltd v Reed* and *McRae v Commonwealth Disposals Commission* (1951) 84 CLR 377.

Anglia Television Ltd v Reed [1972] 1 QB 60

Panel: Lord Denning MR, Phillimore and Megaw LJJ

Facts: Anglia Television contracted with Robert Reed, a famous American actor, to appear in their film, 'The Man in the Wood'. They choose Mr Reed because they needed a strong actor to hold the production together. Mr Reed's agents double booked him for the relevant dates, and Mr Reed repudiated the contract.

LORD DENNING MR

Anglia Television do not claim their profit. They cannot say what their profit would have been on this contract if Mr. Reed had come here and performed it. So, instead of claiming for loss of profits, they claim for the wasted expenditure. They had incurred the director's fees, the designer's fees, the stage manager's and assistant manager's fees, and so on. It comes in all to £2,750. Anglia Television say that all that money was wasted because Mr. Reed did not perform his contract. ...

It seems to me that a plaintiff in such a case as this has an election: he can either claim for loss of profits; or for his wasted expenditure. But he must elect between them. He cannot claim both. If he has not suffered any loss of profits - or if he cannot prove what his profits would have been - he can claim in the alternative the expenditure which has been thrown away, that is, wasted, by reason of the breach. ...

Alert

If the plaintiff claims the wasted expenditure, he is not limited to the expenditure incurred after the contract was concluded. He can claim also the expenditure incurred before the contract, provided that it was such as would reasonably be in the contemplation of the parties as likely to be wasted if the contract was broken.

Applying that principle here, it is plain that, when Mr. Reed entered into this contract, he must have known perfectly well that much expenditure had already been incurred on director's fees and the like. He must have contemplated - or, at any rate, it is reasonably to be imputed to him - that if he broke his contract, all that expenditure would be wasted, whether or not it was incurred before or after the contract. He must pay damages for all the expenditure so wasted and thrown away.

Anglia Television Ltd v Reed clearly establishes the principle in English law that the aggrieved party is entitled to elect between claiming his expectation interest and his reliance interest. However, if his expectation interest is too speculative, he must choose to claim his reliance interest. The point is further illustrated by an older case under Australian law.

McRae v Commonwealth Disposals Commission (1951) 84 CLR 377

Panel: Dixon, McTiernan and Fullagar JJ

Facts: During World War II, a number of ships had become wrecked in the waters adjacent to New Guinea. After the war, the Commonwealth Disposal Commission ('CDC') had the function of disposing of these as it thought fit. The CDC sold these shipwrecks to interested parties. A purchaser might, but would not necessarily, make a large profit by salvaging and selling the vessel, her hull, equipment or cargo – but only after spending considerable money.

McRae purchased a shipwrecked 'oil tanker lying on Jourmand Reef, which is approximately 100 miles north of Samarai.' Jourmand Reef does not exist, and no tanker could be found. CDC were found to be in breach of contract, and the issue for decision was the proper measure of damages.

JUSTICES DIXON AND FULLAGAR

22. The question of damages, which is the remaining question, again presents serious difficulties. It is necessary first to arrive at the appropriate measure of damages. The contract was a contract for the sale of goods, and the measure of damages for non-delivery of goods by a seller is defined in very general terms by s. 55(2) of the Goods Act 1928 as being 'the estimated loss directly and naturally resulting in the ordinary course of events from the seller's breach of contract'. This states, in substance, the general prima-facie rule of the common law as to the measure of damages for breach of contract, [but it] is quite impossible to place any value on what the Commission purported to sell. ...

23. It was strongly argued for the plaintiffs that mere difficulty in estimating damages did not relieve a tribunal from the responsibility of assessing them as best it could. This is undoubtedly true. In the well-known case of *Chaplin v. Hicks* (1911) 2 KB 786, at p 792 Vaughan Williams L.J. said:- 'The fact that damages cannot be assessed with certainty does not relieve the wrongdoer of the necessity of paying damages for his breach of contract'. ...

24. There is, however, more in this case than that, and the truth is that to regard this case as a simple case of breach of contract by non-delivery

of goods would be to take an unreal and misleading view of it. The practical substance of the case lies in these three factors - (1) the Commission promised that there was a tanker at or near to the specified place; (2) in reliance on that promise the plaintiffs expended considerable sums of money; (3) there was in fact no tanker at or anywhere near to the specified place. In the waste of their considerable expenditure seems to lie the real and understandable grievance of the plaintiffs, and the ultimate question in the case (apart from any question of quantum) is whether the plaintiffs can recover the amount of this wasted expenditure or any part of it as damages for breach of the Commission's contract that there was a tanker in existence. ...

...The fact is that the impossibility of assessing damages on the basis of a comparison between what was promised and what was delivered arises not because what was promised was valueless but because it is impossible to value a non-existent thing. It is the breach of contract itself which makes it impossible even to undertake an assessment on that basis. It is not impossible, however, to undertake an assessment on another basis... .

 Alert

27. For these reasons we are of opinion that the plaintiffs were entitled to recover damages in this case for breach of contract, and that their damages are to be measured by reference to expenditure incurred and wasted in reliance on the Commission's promise that a tanker existed at the place specified.

This case provided a further clear example of when the innocent party will not be able to claim his expectation interest but would instead be limited to claiming his reliance interest. It was not possible to value the expectation interest, because no one knew how much profit would be made on a particular salvage mission. Consequently, McRae was forced to claim the reliance interest.

18.3.2 Reliance interest claimed in order to escape a bad bargain

The innocent party cannot claim its reliance interest in order to escape a bad bargain. This means that the innocent party will not be able to claim its expenses if it would not have made back those expenses had the contract been properly performed. In other words, you cannot claim your reliance interest if you would not have broken even had the contract been properly performed.

C & P Haulage v Middleton [1983] 1 WLR 1461

Panel: Ackner and Fox LJJ

Facts: C & P Haulage contracted to allow Mr Middleton to use their premises for a vehicle repair business. Under the terms of the agreement (i) Mr Middleton's licence was renewable every six months, and could be cancelled with one month's notice, and (ii) any fixtures put into the premises by Mr Middleton were to be left on the premises. Mr Middleton carried out substantial work on the premises to make them suitable for use as a garage. The parties fell out and, on 5 October 1979, Mr Middleton was ejected from the premises and had to carry on his business from the garage at his house. Mr Middleton claimed £1,767.51 damages, to cover the money spent on putting the premises in a fit state to use as a garage.

It was accepted by Mr Middleton that, under the contract, he was not entitled to take out any of the fixtures he had installed, and that he would not have been entitled to payment for the work he had done in relation to the premises. He also accepted that the agreement could have been lawfully terminated ten weeks after it was actually ended.

The judge at first instance concluded that C & P Haulage were in breach of contract, but that because during the 'ten weeks' the defendant had been able to return to his own garage and pay no rent, he had suffered no loss. Mr Middleton appealed.

LORD JUSTICE ACKNER

[Mr Middleton] is not claiming for the loss of his bargain, which would involve being put in the position that he would have been in if the contract had been performed. He is not asking to be put in that position. He is asking to be put in the position he would have been in if the contract had never been made at all. If the contract had never been made at all, then he would not have incurred these expenses, and that is the essential approach he adopts in mounting this claim; because if the right approach is that he should be put in the position in which he would have been had the contract been performed, then it follows that he suffered no damage. He lost his entitlement to a further ten weeks of occupation after October 5, and during that period he involved himself in no loss of profit because he found other accommodation, and in no increased expense — in fact the contrary — because he returned immediately to his own garage, thereby saving whatever would have been the agreed figure which he would have to have paid the plaintiffs.

... The case which I have found of assistance — and I am grateful to counsel for their research — is a case in the British Columbia Supreme Court: *Bowlay Logging Ltd. v. Domtar Ltd.* [1978] 4 W.W.R. 105 . Berger J., in a very careful and detailed judgment, goes through various English and American authorities and refers to the leading textbook writers, and I will only quote a small part of his judgment. ... Berger J. said, at p. 117:

> 'The law of contract compensates a plaintiff for damages resulting from the defendant's breach; it does not compensate a plaintiff for damages resulting from his making a bad bargain. Where it can be seen that the plaintiff would have incurred a loss on the contract as a whole, the expenses he has incurred are losses flowing from entering into the contract, not losses flowing from the

Alert

defendant's breach. In these circumstances, the true consequence of the defendant's breach is that the plaintiff is released from his obligation to complete the contract — or in other words, he is saved from incurring further losses. If the law of contract were to move from compensating for the consequences of breach to compensating for the consequences of entering into contracts, the law would run contrary to the normal expectations of the world of commerce. The burden of risk would be shifted from the plaintiff to the defendant. The defendant would become the insurer of the plaintiff's enterprise. Moreover, the amount of the damages would increase not in relation to the gravity or consequences of the breach but in relation to the inefficiency with which the plaintiff carried out the contract. The greater his expenses owing to inefficiency, the greater the damages. The fundamental principle upon which damages are measured under the law of contract is restitutio in integrum. The principle contended for here by the plaintiff would entail the award of damages not to compensate the plaintiff but to punish the defendant.'

... In my judgment, the approach of Berger J. is the correct one. It is not the function of the courts where there is a breach of contract knowingly, as this would be the case, to put a plaintiff in a better financial position than if the contract had been properly performed. ...

LORD JUSTICE FOX

I agree. ... The present case seems to me to be quite different both from *Anglia Television Ltd. v. Reed* [1972] 1 Q.B. 60 and from *Lloyd v. Stanbury* [1971] 1 W.L.R. 535 in that while it is true that the expenditure could in a sense be said to be wasted in consequence of the breach of contract, it was equally likely to be wasted if there had been no breach, because the plaintiffs wanted to get the defendant out and could terminate the licence at quite short notice. A high risk of waste was from the very first inherent in the nature of the contract itself, breach or no breach. The reality of the matter is that the waste resulted from what was, on the defendant's side, a very unsatisfactory and dangerous bargain.

 Alert

Lord Justice Ackner's judgment clearly establishes the principle that an aggrieved party cannot recover for expenses that would have been wasted whether or not the breach of contract occurred. The losses must flow from the breach, not from making a bad bargain. As Fox LJ explains, Mr Middleton had made a bad deal – he spent a great deal of money improving premises that he had only a limited right to occupy. Mr Middleton was only entitled to stay for six months at a time, and had no right under the contract for compensation for the money he spent improving the premises as, under the contract, all fixtures and fittings were to be left on the premises. Mr Middleton's loss therefore came from making a bad bargain, not from the breach.

The High Court recently established that the defendant has the burden of proving the claimant would not have recouped the expenditure had the contract been performed. In *Omak Maritime Ltd v Mamola Challenger Shipping Co Ltd* [2010] EWHC 2026 (Comm), the claimant claimed reliance interest. Even when calculating reliance interest, the principle from *Robinson v Harman* is still relevant because no award of damages can put the claimant in a better position than he would have been in had the contract been performed. Teare J followed *C&P Haulage v Middleton*, finding the claimant's expenditure should only be recoverable where the likely gross profit would at least cover that expenditure. The burden was on the defendant to show that the likely profits would not at least equal the claimant's expenditure.

18.4 The Restitution Interest

In narrow circumstances, contract damages will be measured on a restitutionary basis. This means that the contract breaker will be required to account for the profit which he has made as a result of the breach.

Attorney General v Blake (Jonathan Cape Ltd Third Party) [2001] 1 AC 268

Panel: Lord Nicholls of Birkenhead, Lord Goff of Chieveley, Lord Browne-Wilkinson, Lord Steyn and Lord Hobhouse of Woodborough

Facts: Mr Blake was employed by the British intelligence services from 1944 to 1961. His contract included a term which stated: '...I undertake not to divulge any official information gained by me as a result of my employment, either in the press or in book form. I also understand that these provisions apply not only during the period of service but also after employment has ceased.'

In 1951, he became an agent for the Soviet Union and disclosed valuable British intelligence to the Soviet Union gained through his employment. He was convicted and imprisoned for treason but managed to escape to Moscow. In Moscow, he wrote an autobiography which, in breach of the term of his contract with the British intelligence services, disclosed official information.

The Attorney General sued Mr Blake for breach of contract in an attempt to prevent him from receiving royalties from the publication of the book.

LORD NICHOLLS OF BIRKENHEAD

So I turn to established, basic principles. I shall first set the scene by noting how the court approaches the question of financial recompense for interference with rights of property... Damages are measured by the plaintiff's loss, not the defendant's gain. But the common law, pragmatic as ever, has long recognised that there are many commonplace situations where a strict application of this principle would not do justice between the parties. Then compensation for the wrong done to the plaintiff is measured by a different yardstick. A trespasser who enters another's land may cause the landowner

 Alert

no financial loss. In such a case damages are measured by the benefit received by the trespasser, namely, by his use of the land.

For social and economic reasons the court refused [in *Wrotham Park Estate Co Ltd v Parkside Homes Ltd* [1974] 1 WLR 798] to make a mandatory order for the demolition of houses built on land burdened with a restrictive covenant. Instead, Brightman J made an award of damages under the jurisdiction which originated with Lord Cairns's Act. The existence of the new houses did not diminish the value of the benefited land by one farthing. The judge considered that if the plaintiffs were given a nominal sum, or no sum, justice would manifestly not have been done. He assessed the damages at 5% of the developer's anticipated profit, this being the amount of money which could reasonably have been demanded for a relaxation of the covenant. ...

In reaching his conclusion the judge applied by analogy the cases mentioned above concerning the assessment of damages when a defendant has invaded another's property rights but without diminishing the value of the property. I consider he was right to do so. Property rights are superior to contractual rights in that, unlike contractual rights, property rights may survive against an indefinite class of persons. However, it is not easy to see why, as between the parties to a contract, a violation of a party's contractual rights should attract a lesser degree of remedy than a violation of his property rights. As Lionel D Smith has pointed out... it is not clear why it should be any more permissible to expropriate personal rights than it is permissible to expropriate property rights. ...

The Wrotham Park case, therefore, still shines, rather as a solitary beacon, showing that in contract as well as tort damages are not always narrowly confined to recoupment of financial loss. In a suitable case damages for breach of contract may be measured by the benefit gained by the wrongdoer from the breach. The defendant must make a reasonable payment in respect of the benefit he has gained. In the present case the Crown seeks to go further. The claim is for all the profits of Blake's book which the publisher has not yet paid him.

My conclusion is that there seems to be no reason, in principle, why the court must in all circumstances rule out an account of profits as a remedy for breach of contract. I prefer to avoid the unhappy expression 'restitutionary damages'. Remedies are the law's response to a wrong (or, more precisely, to a cause of action).

When, exceptionally, a just response to a breach of contract so requires, the court should be able to grant the discretionary remedy of requiring a defendant to account to the plaintiff for the benefits he has received from his breach of contract. In the same way as a plaintiff's interest in performance of a contract may render it just and equitable for the court to make an order for specific performance or grant an injunction, so the plaintiff's interest in performance may make it just and equitable that the defendant should retain no benefit from his breach of contract.

Alert

The state of the authorities encourages me to reach this conclusion, rather than the reverse. The law recognises that damages are not always a sufficient remedy for breach of contract. This is the foundation of the court's jurisdiction to grant the remedies of specific performance and injunction. Even when awarding damages, the law does not adhere slavishly to the concept of compensation for financially measurable loss. When the circumstances require, damages are measured by reference to the benefit obtained by the wrongdoer.

Having established that, in principle, damages for breach of contract might be measured according to the contract breaker's gain, his Lordship considered the circumstances in which, in practice, damages will be measured in this way.

Normally the remedies of damages, specific performance and injunction, coupled with the characterisation of some contractual obligations as fiduciary, will provide an adequate response to a breach of contract. It will be only in exceptional cases, where those remedies are inadequate, that any question of accounting for profits will arise. No fixed rules can be prescribed. The court will have regard to all the circumstances, including the subject matter of the contract, the purpose of the contractual provision which has been breached, the circumstances in which the breach occurred, the consequences of the breach and the circumstances in which relief is being sought. A useful general guide, although not exhaustive, is whether the plaintiff had a legitimate interest in preventing the defendant's profit-making activity and, hence, in depriving him of his profit. ...

Lord Woolf MR [in the Court of Appeal] suggested three facts which should not be a sufficient ground for departing from the normal basis on which damages are awarded: the fact that the breach was cynical and deliberate; the fact that the breach enabled the defendant to enter into a more profitable contract elsewhere; and the fact that by entering into a new and more profitable contract the defendant put it out of his power to perform his contract with the plaintiff. I agree that none of these facts would be, by itself, a good reason for ordering an account of profits.

LORD STEYN

If the information was still confidential, Blake would in my view have been liable as a fiduciary. That would be so despite the fact that he left the intelligence services many years ago. The distinctive feature of this case is, however, that Blake gave an undertaking not to divulge any information, confidential or otherwise, obtained by him during his work in the intelligence services. This obligation still applies to Blake. He was, therefore in regard to all information obtained by him in the intelligence services, confidential or not, in a very similar position to a fiduciary. The reason of the rule applying to fiduciaries applies to him. Secondly, I bear in mind that the enduring strength of the common law is that it has been developed on a case-by-case basis by judges for whom the attainment of practical justice was a major objective of their work. It is still one of the major moulding forces of judicial decision-making. These observations are almost banal: the public would be astonished if it was thought that judges did not conceive it as their prime duty to do practical justice whenever possible. ...

For my part practical justice strongly militates in favour of granting an order for disgorgement of profits against Blake. ... Our law is also mature enough to provide a remedy in such a case but does so by the route of the exceptional recognition of a claim for disgorgement of profits against the contract breaker. In my view therefore there is a valid claim vesting in the Attorney General against Blake for disgorgement of his gain.

LORD HOBHOUSE OF WOODBOROUGH (dissenting)

Your Lordships have concluded that this claim should be allowed.

I cannot join your Lordships in that conclusion. I have two primary difficulties. The first is the facts of the present case. The speech of my noble and learned friend explores what is the 'just response' to the defendant's conduct. The 'just response' visualised in the present case is, however it is formulated, that Blake should be punished and deprived of any fruits of conduct connected with his former criminal and reprehensible conduct. The Crown have made no secret of this. It is not a commercial claim in support of any commercial interest. It is a claim relating to past criminal conduct. The way it was put by the Court of Appeal [1998] Ch 439 , 464 was:

> 'The ordinary member of the public would be shocked if the position was that the courts were powerless to prevent [Blake] profiting from his criminal conduct.'

The answer given by my noble and learned friend does not reflect the essentially punitive nature of the claim and seeks to apply principles of law which are only appropriate where commercial or proprietary interests are involved. Blake has made a financial gain but he has not done so at the expense of the Crown or making use of any property of or commercial interest of the Crown either in law or equity.

My second difficulty is that the reasoning of my noble and learned friend depends upon the conclusion that there is some gap in the existing state of the law which requires to be filled by a new remedy. He accepts that the term 'restitutionary damages' is unsatisfactory but, with respect, does not fully examine why this is so, drawing the necessary conclusions.

Lord Nicholls (with whom Lord Browne-Wilkinson and Lord Goff agreed) set out two key features that would identify circumstances where a profit-based measure of damages would be appropriate:

- normal contractual remedies must be 'inadequate'

- the contract breaker must have a legitimate interest in preventing the defendant's profit-making activity and, hence, in depriving him of his profit.

Turning to the facts, Lord Nicholls was in no doubt that these were appropriate circumstances to grant damages measured on a restitutionary basis.

A similar test is seen in the judgment of Lord Steyn, who also emphasised the needs of 'practical justice'. His Lordship continued by noting (as Lord Nicholls had done) that if the information in the book had been confidential, Blake's 'fiduciary duty' to protect the confidentiality of the information would have entitled the Crown to damages measured according to Blake's profit.

The circumstances in *Attorney General v Blake* were quite unusual, although it is important to consider the more recent cases (not covered by this book) that have further developed the law.

18.5 Other 'Heads of Damage'

The law has been cautious about recognising other 'heads of damage', such as mental distress, loss of reputation, or loss of a chance to profit from the acts of a third party – often because it is difficult to put a pecuniary value on these losses.

18.5.1 Damages for mental distress and inconvenience

Jarvis v Swan Tours Ltd. [1973] QB 233

Panel: Lord Denning MR, Edmund Davies and Stephenson LJJ

Facts: James Jarvis was a solicitor for a local authority in Barking. He only took one holiday each year, and preferred it to be in the winter. After consulting Swan Tours' brochure, he booked a skiing holiday in Switzerland with Swan Tours. The brochure promised, amongst other things, a friendly welcome from Herr and Frau Weibel. It also stated:

'Swans House Party in Morlialp. All these House Party arrangements are included in the price of your holiday. Welcome party on arrival. Afternoon tea and cake for 7 days. Swiss dinner by candlelight. Fondue party. Yodeler evening. Chali farewell party in the 'Alphütte Bar'. Service of representative.'

The total charge for the holiday was £63.45. The trial judge awarded £31.72 in damages. Mr Jarvis appealed.

LORD DENNING MR

The plaintiff went on the holiday, but he was very disappointed. He was a man of about 35 and he expected to be one of a house party of some 30 or so people. Instead, he found there were only 13 during the first week. In the second week there was no house party at all. He was the only person there. Mr. Weibel could not speak English. So there was Mr. Jarvis, in the second week, in this hotel with no house party at all, and no one could speak English, except himself. He was very disappointed, too, with the ski-ing. ... So his ski-ing holiday, from his point of view, was pretty well ruined.

There were many other matters, too. They appear trivial when they are set down in writing, but I have no doubt they loomed large in Mr. Jarvis's mind, when coupled with the other disappointments. He did not have the nice Swiss cakes which he was hoping for. The only cakes for tea were potato crisps and little dry nut cakes. The yodeller evening consisted of one man from the locality who came in his working clothes for a little while, and sang four or five songs very quickly. The 'Alphütte Bar' was an unoccupied annexe which was only open one evening. There was a representative, Mrs. Storr, there during the first week, but she was not there during the second week.

The matter was summed up by the judge:

> 'During the first week he got a holiday in Switzerland which was to some extent inferior ... and, as to the second week, he got a holiday which was very largely inferior'

to what he was led to expect. ...

In a proper case damages for mental distress can be recovered in contract, just as damages for shock can be recovered in tort. One such case is a contract for a holiday, or any other contract to provide entertainment and enjoyment. If the contracting party breaks his contract, damages can be given for the disappointment, the distress, the upset and frustration caused by the breach. I know that it is difficult to assess in terms of money, but it is no more difficult than the assessment which the courts have to make every day in personal injury cases for loss of amenities. Take the present case. Mr. Jarvis has only a fortnight's holiday in the year. He books it far ahead, and looks forward to it all that time. He ought to be compensated for the loss of it. ...

 Alert

A good illustration was given by Edmund Davies L.J. in the course of the argument. He put the case of a man who has taken a ticket for Glyndbourne. It is the only night on which he can get there. He hires a car to take him. The car does not turn up. His damages are not limited to the mere cost of the ticket. He is entitled to general damages for the disappointment he has suffered and the loss of the entertainment which he should have had. Here, Mr. Jarvis's fortnight's winter holiday has been a grave disappointment. It is true that he was conveyed to Switzerland and back and had meals and bed in the hotel. But that is not what he went for. He went to enjoy himself with all the facilities which the defendants said he would have. He is entitled to damages for the lack of those facilities, and for his loss of enjoyment.

...

I think the judge was in error in taking the sum paid for the holiday £63.45 and halving it. The right measure of damages is to compensate him for the loss of entertainment and enjoyment which he was promised, and which he did not get.

Looking at the matter quite broadly, I think the damages in this case should be the sum of £125. I would allow the appeal, accordingly.

This case establishes an exception to the general rule that damages cannot be recovered for mental distress in English contract law. Mr Jarvis received damages to compensate him for his mental distress as the very object of the contract was to provide pleasure, relaxation and peace of mind. *Farley v Skinner* [2002] 2 AC 732 extends the situations in which such damages may be awarded to cases in which 'a major or important object of the contract is to give pleasure, relaxation or peace of mind'.

Farley v Skinner [2002] 2 AC 732

Panel: Lord Steyn, Lord Browne-Wilkinson, Lord Clyde, Lord Hutton and Lord Scott of Foscote

Facts: Graham Farley employed Michael Skinner to carry out a survey on 'Riverside House', a property in the countryside that Mr Farley was considering buying and moving to in his retirement. As Lord Steyn noted 'The property is in the heart of the countryside. There is a stream running through the middle of it. The property has a croquet lawn, tennis court, orchard, paddock and swimming pool... [but] for the plaintiff a property offering peace and tranquillity was the raison d'être of the proposed purchase. He wanted to be reasonably sure that the property was not seriously affected by aircraft noise.' Mr Farley employed Mr Skinner to carry out the normal surveys required by house-buyers, and specifically asked him to investigate whether the property would be affected by aircraft noise.

Mr Skinner negligently failed to notice that the property was close to a navigation beacon. In the morning, early evening and weekends, aircraft waiting to land at Gatwick would spiral around the beacon. Mr Farley did not discover this until after he had spent a considerable amount of money renovating the property. He decided to remain in the house, and brought this claim against Mr Skinner.

LORD STEYN

... In the words of Bingham LJ in *Watts v Morrow* [1991] 1 WLR 1421, 1443 as a matter of legal policy 'a contract-breaker is not in general liable for any distress, frustration, anxiety, displeasure, vexation, tension or aggravation which his breach of contract may cause to the innocent party' (my emphasis). There are, however, limited exceptions to this rule. One such exception is damages for pain, suffering and loss of amenities caused to an individual by a breach of contract. ... It is not material in the present case. But the two exceptions mentioned by Bingham LJ, namely where the very object of the contract is to provide pleasure (proposition (2)) and recovery for physical inconvenience caused by the breach (proposition (3)), are pertinent. The scope of these exceptions is in issue in the present case....

David Capper, 'Damages for Distress and Disappointment The Limits of *Watts v Morrow*' (2000) 116 LQR 553, 556 has persuasively argued:

> 'A ruling that intangible interests only qualify for legal protection where they are the 'very object of the contract' is tantamount to a ruling that contracts where these interests are merely important, but not the central object of the contract, are in part unenforceable. It is very difficult to see what policy objection there can be to parties to a contract agreeing that these interests are to be protected via contracts where the central object is something else. If the defendant is unwilling to accept this responsibility he or she can say so and either no contract will be made or one will be made but including a disclaimer.'

There is no reason in principle or policy why the scope of recovery in the exceptional category should depend on the object of the contract as ascertained from all its constituent parts. It is sufficient if a major or important object of the contract is to give pleasure, relaxation or peace of mind.

 Alert

LORD CLYDE

It is suggested that because this point was wrapped up together with a number of other matters in the instructions given by the plaintiff it cannot be regarded as constituting the 'very object' of the contract. But that approach seems to me simply to be playing with words. ...

The present case is not an 'ordinary surveyor's contract'. The request for the report on aircraft noise was additional to the usual matters expected of a surveyor in the survey of a property and could properly have attracted a extra fee if he had spent extra time researching that issue. It is the specific provision relating to the peacefulness of the property in respect of aircraft noise which makes the present case out of the ordinary. The criterion is not some general characteristic of the contract, as, for example, that it is or is not a 'commercial' contract. The critical factor is the object of the particular agreement.

LORD HUTTON

Whilst *Ruxley Electronics and Construction Ltd v Forsyth* [1996] AC 344 was concerned with the proper measure of damages for breach of a construction contract, I consider that the principle stated in it can be of more general application and that, as Lord Mustill stated, at p 360, there are some occasions 'where the value of the promise to the promisee exceeds the financial enhancement of his position which full performance will secure' and for which the law must provide a remedy. In my opinion the present case falls within the ambit of this principle as the defendant in breach of contract failed to alert the plaintiff to the presence of aircraft noise with the result that the plaintiff bought a house which he would not have bought if he had been made aware of the true position. ...

Whilst I do not accept the submission advanced on behalf of the defendant that, where there is no pecuniary loss, damages can only be recovered where the claim is for breach of an obligation which is the very object of the contract, I think that (other than in building contract cases where the principle stated by Lord Mustill in *Ruxley Electronics and Construction Ltd v Forsyth*, at p 360, gives direct guidance) there is a need for a test which the courts can apply in practice in order to preserve the fundamental principle that general damages are not recoverable for anxiety and aggravation and similar states of mind caused by a breach of contract and to prevent the exception expanding to swallow up, or to diminish unjustifiably, the principle itself.

It will be for the courts, in the differing circumstances of individual cases, to apply the principles stated in your Lordships' speeches in this case, and the matter is not one where any precise test or verbal formula can be applied, but, adopting the helpful submissions of counsel for the plaintiff, I consider that as a general approach it would be appropriate to treat as cases falling within the exception and calling for an award of damages those where:

 Alert

1. the matter in respect of which the individual claimant seeks damages is of importance to him, and

2. the individual claimant has made clear to the other party that the matter is of importance to him, and

3. the action to be taken in relation to the matter is made a specific term of the contract.

If these three conditions are satisfied, as they are in the present case, then I consider that the claim for damages should not be rejected on the ground that the fulfilment of that obligation is not the principal object of the contract or on the ground that the other party does not receive special and specific remuneration in respect of the performance of that obligation.

Their Lordships were broadly agreed that although damages for loss of amenity were not generally available for breach of contract, they would be available where an important object of the contract is to give pleasure, relaxation or peace of mind. This was clearly satisfied on the facts.

Lord Hutton set out a more extensive test, which emphasises the importance of the particular purpose to the (claimant) contracting party. This provides a clear link to the discussion of the individual preferences and 'consumer preferences' of the contracting parties, also discussed in the quotations from *Ruxley Electronics and Construction Ltd. v Forsyth* [1996] AC 344.

18.5.2 Damages for loss of reputation

Malik v Bank of Credit and Commerce International S.A. (In Compulsory Liquidation) [1997] 3 WLR 95

Panel: Lord Goff of Chieveley, Lord Mackay of Clashfern, Lord Mustill, Lord Nicholls of Birkenhead and Lord Steyn

Facts: Qaiser Malik was employed by BCCI for twelve years. In the summer of 1991, the bank collapsed leading thousands of people around the world to suffer loss, and Mr Malik to be made redundant. Mr Malik brought a claim against BCCI claiming 'stigma' damages. He said that (and it was assumed for the purposes of the hearing) the bank operated in a corrupt and dishonest manner, and that his future employability was handicapped by his former employment by the bank even though he was innocent of any wrongdoing and that he had suffered financial loss as a result.

The breach of contract alleged by Mr Malik was a breach of the employer's implied obligation not to carry on a dishonest or corrupt business, which Mr Malik said was an example of the widely accepted implied term of mutual trust and confidence found in every employment contract. After confirming the existence of this implied term, their Lordships continued by considering the loss suffered by Mr Malik.

LORD STEYN

The availability of the remedy of damages

In considering the availability of the remedy of damages it is important to bear in mind that the applicants claim damages for financial loss. That is the issue. It will be recalled that the Court of Appeal decided the case against the applicants on the basis that there is a positive rule debarring the recovery of damages in contract for injury to an existing reputation, and that in truth the two applicants were claiming damages for injury to their previously existing reputations. ...

The true ratio decidendi of the House of Lords' decision in *Addis v. Gramophone Co. Ltd.* has long been debated. ... A company had dismissed an overseas manager in a harsh and oppressive manner. The House of Lords held that the employee was entitled to recover his direct pecuniary loss, such as loss of salary and commission. But the jury had been allowed to take into account the manner in which the employee had been dismissed and to reflect this in their award. The House of Lords, with Lord Collins dissenting, held that this was wrong.

The headnote to the case states that in a case of wrongful dismissal the award of damages may not include compensation for the manner of his dismissal, for his injured feelings, or for the loss he may suffer from the fact that the dismissal of itself makes it more difficult to obtain fresh employment.

... Lord Loreburn L.C. and the other Law Lords in the majority apparently thought they were applying a special rule applicable to awards of damages for wrongful dismissal. It is, however, far from clear how far the ratio of *Addis's* case extends. It certainly enunciated the principle that an employee cannot recover exemplary or aggravated damages for wrongful dismissal. That is still sound law. The actual decision is only concerned with wrongful dismissal. It is therefore arguable that as a matter of precedent the ratio is so restricted. But it seems to me unrealistic not to acknowledge that *Addis's* case is authority for a wider principle. There is a common proposition in the speeches of the majority. That proposition is that damages for breach of contract may only be awarded for breach of contract, and not for loss caused by the manner of the breach. No Law Lord said that an employee may not recover financial loss for damage to his employment prospects caused by a breach of contract, and no Law Lord said that in breach of contract cases compensation for loss of reputation can never be awarded, or that it can only be awarded in cases falling in certain defined categories. *Addis's* case simply decided that the loss of reputation in that particular case could not be compensated because it was not caused by a breach of contract: Nelson Enonchong, 'Contract Damages for Injury to Reputation' (1996) 59 M.L.R. 592, 593. So analysed *Addis's* case does not bar the claims put forward in the present case.

...

The principled position is as follows. Provided that a relevant breach of contract can be established, and the requirements of causation, remoteness and mitigation can be satisfied, there is no good reason why in the field of employment law recovery of financial loss in respect of damage to reputation caused by breach of contract is necessarily excluded....

The effect of my conclusions

Earlier, I drew attention to the fact that the implied mutual obligation of trust and confidence applies only where there is 'no reasonable and proper cause' for the employers conduct, and then only if the conduct is calculated to destroy or seriously damage the relationship of trust and confidence. That circumscribes the potential reach and scope of the implied obligation. Moreover, even if the employee can establish a breach of this obligation, it does not follow that he will be able to recover damages for injury to his employment prospects. The Law Commission has pointed out that loss of reputation is inherently difficult to prove: Consultation Paper No. 132 on Aggravated, Exemplary and Restitutionary Damages, p. 22, para 2.15. It is, therefore, improbable that many employees would be able to prove 'stigma compensation.' The limiting principles of causation, remoteness and mitigation present formidable practical obstacles to such claims succeeding.

But difficulties of proof cannot alter the legal principles which permit, in appropriate cases, such claims for financial loss caused by breach of contract being put forward for consideration.

The case establishes that damages for loss of reputation may be awarded but *only* when such damage to reputation leads to financial loss e.g. when employment prospects are handicapped.

18.5.3 Damages for loss of a chance

There are times when the aggrieved party is unable to say what would have happened, on the balance of probabilities, had a breach of the contract not occurred. Under the normal rules for damages, this would suggest that the aggrieved party is unable to prove any loss. An exception exists when the innocent party has lost a real or substantial chance to profit.

***Chaplin v Hicks* [1911] 2 KB 786**

Panel: Vaughan Williams, Fletcher Moulton and Farwell LJJ

Facts: Mr Hicks organised a competition in which ladies, for an entry fee, were to send in photographs of themselves. These photographs would then be published in a local newspaper and the public would vote for the prettiest lady thus narrowing the applicants down to 50. Mr Hicks would interview the 50 ladies and select 12 to whom he would award the prize of theatrical employment for a salary.

Six thousand applications were submitted and Ms Chaplin made it into the final 50 as a result of the public vote. However, in breach of contract, Mr Hicks provided her with insufficient notice of the time for her interview. Consequently, she was not selected. The jury found that Mr Hicks was in breach of contract and they awarded Ms Chaplin £100 for her loss of a chance of winning the competition. The issue on appeal was whether damages were available.

LORD JUSTICE FLETCHER MOULTON

[Counsel] says that the damages are difficult to assess, because it is impossible to say that the plaintiff would have obtained any prize. This is the only point of importance left for our consideration. Is expulsion from a limited class of competitors an injury? To my mind there can be only one answer to that question; it is an injury and may be a very substantial one.

Therefore the plaintiff starts with an unchallengeable case of injury, and the damages given in respect of it should be equivalent to the loss. But it is said that the damages cannot be arrived at because it is impossible to estimate the quantum of the reasonable probability of the plaintiff's being a prize-winner. I think that, where it is clear that there has been actual loss resulting from the breach of contract, which it is difficult to estimate in money, it is for the jury to do their best to estimate; it is not necessary that there should be an absolute measure of damages in each case.

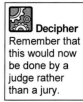
Decipher
Remember that this would now be done by a judge rather than a jury.

There are no doubt well-settled rules as to the measure of damages in certain cases, but such accepted rules are only applicable where the breach is one that frequently occurs. In such cases the Court weighs the pros and cons and gives advice, and I may almost say directions, to the jury as regards the measure of damages. This is especially the case in actions relating to the sale of goods of a class for which there is an active and ready market. But in most cases it may be said that there is no recognized measure of damages, and that the jury must give what they think to be an adequate solatium under all the circumstances of the case. Is there any such rule as that, where the result of a contract depends on the volition of an independent party, the law shuts its eyes to the wrong and says that there are no damages? Such a rule, if it existed, would work great wrong. Let us take the case of a man under a contract of service to serve as a second-class clerk for five years at a salary of 200l. a year, which expressly provides that, at the end of that period, out of every five second-class clerks two first-class clerks will be chosen at a salary of 500l. a year. If such a clause is embodied in the contract, it is clear that a person thinking of applying for the position would reckon that he would have the advantage of being one of five persons from whom the two first-class clerks must be chosen, and that that might be a very substantial portion of the consideration for his appointment. If, after he has taken the post and worked under the contract of service, the employers repudiate the obligation, is he to have no remedy? He has sustained a very real loss, and there can be no possible reason why the law should not leave it to the jury to estimate the value of that of which he has been deprived. Where by contract a man has a right to belong to a limited class of competitors, he is possessed of something of value, and it is the duty of the jury to estimate the pecuniary value of that advantage if it is taken from him. The present case is a typical one. From a body of six thousand, who sent in their photographs, a smaller body of fifty was formed, of which the plaintiff was one, and among that smaller body twelve prizes were allotted for distribution; by reason of the defendant's breach of contract she has lost all the advantage of being in the limited competition, and she is entitled to have her loss estimated. I cannot lay down any rule as to the measure of damages in such a case; this must be left to the good sense of the jury. They must of course give effect to the consideration that the plaintiff's chance is only one out of four and that they cannot tell whether she would have ultimately proved to be the winner. But having considered all this they may well think that it is of considerable pecuniary value to have got into so small a class, and they must assess the damages accordingly.

Ms Chaplin was able to recover damages for her loss of a chance to win as her chance was real or substantial. This can be distinguished from *McRae v Commonwealth* (discussed above) since in *McRae* the chance of profiting was purely speculative. You will recall that since the expectation measure was too speculative, McRae was limited to claiming his reliance interest.

Further Reading

Burrows, 'Limitations on Compensation' in *Commercial Remedies* (eds Burrows and Peel, 2003) pp 27-43

Coote, 'Contract Damages, Ruxley and the Performance Interest' [1997] CLJ 537

Chen-Wishart, Restitutionary Damages for Breach of Contract, (1998) 114 LQR 363

Friedmann, 'The Performance Interest in Contract Damages' (1995) 111 LQR 628

Enonchong, 'Contract Damages for Injury to Reputation' (1996) 59 MLR 592

Harris, Ogus and Philips 'Contract Remedies and the Consumer Surplus' (1979) 95 LQR 581

Fuller and Perdue, 'The Reliance Interest in Contract Damages' (1936) 46 Yale LJ 52, 373

McKendrick, 'Breach of Contract, Restitution for Wrongs and Punishment' in *Commercial Remedies* (eds Burrows and Peel, 2003) pp 93-123

McKendrick, E., *Contract Law* (2017) 12th ed. Ch.21 and 22

19

Remedies II (Limiting Factors)

Topic List

Introduction

Remedies I considered the definition of loss in contract law and how that loss can be measured. Underlying the cases in the previous chapter was the principle that contractual promises should be kept, and when not kept, the aggrieved party should be compensated for the loss caused by the contract breaker's failure to perform properly.

However, there are a number of factors which may limit the innocent party's ability to recover damages for loss suffered ie causation, remoteness, mitigation and contributory negligence. These limiting factors will be considered in this chapter.

19.1   Causation

Basic logic requires that the aggrieved party can only recover for losses caused by the breach of contract – losses that were not caused by the breach are of no concern to the contract breaker.

Galoo Ltd (in liquidation) v Bright Grahame Murray (a firm) **[1994] 1 WLR 1360**

Panel: Glidewell, Evans and Waite LJJ

Facts: Galoo Ltd was a company that formerly traded in animal health products, but had been put into liquidation after it was discovered that, as a result of fraud (presumably by the directors), significant liabilities had been incurred by the company. The current claim was brought by its liquidators, on behalf of the company, against the company's accountants, Bright Grahame Murray ('BGM'). The claim was that, in breach of contract, the accountants had been negligent when auditing Galoo. The hearing was to determine the losses caused by the breach.

LORD JUSTICE GLIDEWELL

The second head of damage claimed by Galoo and Gamine is that they incurred trading losses as a result of relying on the negligent auditing by B.G.M. and thus continued to trade when they would otherwise not have done. The claim under this head is for damages for trading losses of approximately £25m. incurred in and between 1986 and 1990 and for making a dividend payment of £500,000 in 1988, as set out in the particulars to which I have referred. This claim requires more detailed consideration.

It can be expressed as follows: (a) if they had not acted in breach of their duty in contract or tort, B.G.M. would have detected the fraud during their audit of the 1985 accounts; (b) in that case, Galoo and Gamine would have been put into liquidation in mid-1986 and thus ceased to trade at that date; (c) if the companies had ceased to trade, they would neither have incurred any further trading losses nor paid the dividend in 1988; (d) therefore the trading losses and the loss caused by the dividend payment were caused by the breach of duty by B.G.M.

This argument depends upon the nature of the causation necessary to establish liability for breach of duty, whether in contract or in tort. There is no doubt that this is one of the most difficult areas of the law. ...

Mr. Hunter, for the defendants, submits that the plaintiff's case depends upon the adoption of the 'but for' test of causation which, at least in contract, is not the proper test in English law. This is causation of the kind which has sometimes been referred to as a 'causa sine qua non.'

In Chitty on Contracts , 26th ed. (1989), vol. 2, pp. 1128–1129, para. 1785, the editors say:

'The important issue in remoteness of damage in the law of contract is whether a particular loss was within the reasonable contemplation of the parties, but causation must also be proved: there must be a causal connection between the defendant's breach of contract and the plaintiff's loss. The courts have avoided laying down any formal tests for causation: they have relied on common sense to guide decisions as to whether a breach of contract is a sufficiently substantial cause of the plaintiff's loss. (It need not be the sole cause).'

...

In *Quinn v. Burch Bros. (Builders) Ltd.* [1966] 2 Q.B. 370 the defendants were main contractors on a building project. The plaintiff was an independent subcontractor carrying out plastering and similar work. Under the contract between them, the defendants were to supply any equipment reasonably necessary for the plaintiff's work. On the day in question, the plaintiff required a step-ladder in order to carry out work to ceilings, but despite his request the defendants did not supply one. The plaintiff found a folded trestle, which he propped against the wall and used as if it were a ladder to allow him to reach the ceiling. While he was standing on the trestle the foot of it slipped and he fell and broke his heel. He claimed that his injuries and resultant loss were the result of the defendants' breach of contract.

Paull J. held that the defendants were in breach of contract in failing to supply a step-ladder, but that the breach did not cause the plaintiff's accident. The Court of Appeal unanimously dismissed the plaintiff's appeal. Danckwerts L.J., in a short judgment, expressed his reasoning, at p. 391, in four propositions, of which the third and fourth were:

'(3) The cause of the plaintiff's accident was the choice by the plaintiff to use the unsuitable equipment. (4) The failure of the defendants to provide the equipment required may have been the occasion of the accident but was not the cause of the accident.'

Salmon L.J said, at pp. 394–395:

'the defendants realised that, if there were a breach of contract on their part to supply the step-ladder, that breach would afford the plaintiff the opportunity of acting negligently, and that he might take it and thereby suffer injury. But it seems to me quite impossible to say that in reality the plaintiff's injury was caused by the breach of contract. The breach of contract merely gave the plaintiff the opportunity to injure himself and was the occasion of the injury. There is always a temptation to fall into the fallacy of post hoc ergo propter hoc; and that is no less a fallacy even if what happens afterwards could have been foreseen before it occurred.'

[Lord Justice Glidewell then turned to a number of Australian cases, before continuing] The passages which I have cited from the speeches in Monarch Steamship Co. Ltd. v. Karlshamns Oljefabriker A/B [1949] A.C. 196 make it clear that if a breach of contract by a defendant is to be held to entitle the plaintiff to claim damages, it must first be held to have been an 'effective' or 'dominant' cause of his loss. The test in Quinn v. Burch Bros. (Builders) Ltd. [1966] 2 Q.B. 370 that it is necessary to distinguish between a breach of contract which causes a loss to the plaintiff and one which merely gives the opportunity for him to sustain the loss, is helpful but still leaves the question to be answered 'How does the court decide whether the breach of duty was the cause of the loss or merely the occasion for the loss?'

Alert

The answer in my judgment is supplied by the Australian decisions to which I have referred, which I hold to represent the law of England as well as of Australia, in relation to a breach of a duty imposed on a defendant whether by contract or in tort in a situation analogous to breach of contract. The answer in the end is 'By the application of the court's common sense.'

Alert

Doing my best to apply this test, I have no doubt that the deputy judge arrived at a correct conclusion on this issue. The breach of duty by the defendants gave the opportunity to Galoo and Gamine to incur and to continue to incur trading losses; it did not cause those trading losses, in the sense in which the word 'cause' is used in law.

[Lord Justice Glidewell quoted a useful illustration provided by Mahoney J.A in the Australian case of *Alexander v. Cambridge Credit Corporation Ltd.* (1987) 9 N.S.W.L.R. 310 at pp. 333–335]

'If a defendant promises to direct me where I should go and, at a cross-roads, directs me to the left road rather than the right road, what happens to me on the left road is, in a sense, the result of what the defendant has done. If I slip on that road, if it collapses under me, or if, because I am there, a car driving down that road and not down the right road strikes me, my loss is, in a sense, the result of the fact that I have been directed to the left road and not the right road. But, in my opinion, it is not everything which is a result in this broad sense which is accepted as a result for this purpose in the law. Thus, if, being on the left road, I slip and fall, the fact alone that it was the defendant's direction, in breach of contract, which put me there will not, without more, make the defendant liable for my broken leg. I say 'without more:' if there be added to the breach the fact that, for example, the left road was known to be dangerous in that respect I may, of course, be liable. But, in relation to losses of that kind, the fact that the breach has initiated one train of events rather than another is not, or at least may not, be sufficient in itself. It is necessary, to determine whether there is a causal relationship, to look more closely at the breach and what (to use a neutral term) flowed from it.'

Lord Justice Glidewell emphasised three issues. First, the appropriate test for causation in contract law is not the 'but for' test. Second, it is not sufficient that the breach provided the opportunity to sustain loss – the breach must have caused the loss. This is determined by the application of common sense. (Although his Lordship accepted elsewhere in the judgment that this test provides little guidance and that different judges can take quite different views on what constitutes common sense.) Third, the breach of contract must be an 'effective' or 'dominant' cause of the loss.

19.2 Remoteness

It would be unfair for a contract breaker to be held responsible for all losses caused by a breach of contract regardless of how unpredictable or unusual those losses may be. Consequently, the courts have developed the principle of remoteness. The innocent party will not be able to recover for losses which are too remote.

Hadley v Baxendale (1854) 156 ER 145

Panel: Alderson B

Facts: Hadley were the owners of a flour mill in Gloucester. Hadley contracted with Baxendale to take a broken mill shaft to some manufacturers in Greenwich who would use the shaft as a template to produce a new shaft. In breach of contract, the delivery to the manufacturers was delayed, causing Hadley to lose profits for the additional time it was unable to operate the mill. The issue for decision was whether these lost profits were recoverable by Hadley.

BARON ALDERSON

Now we think the proper rule in such a case as the present is this:—Where two parties have made a contract which one of them has broken, the damages which the other party ought to receive in respect of such breach of contract should be such as may fairly and reasonably be considered either arising naturally, i.e., according to the usual course of things, from such breach of contract itself, or such as may reasonably be supposed to have been in the contemplation of both parties, at the time they made the contract, as the probable result of the breach of it.

 Alert

Now, if the special circumstances under which the contract was actually made were communicated by the plaintiffs to the defendants, and thus known to both parties, the damages resulting from the breach of such a contract, which they would reasonably contemplate, would be the amount of injury which would ordinarily follow from a breach of contract under these special circumstances so known and communicated.

But, on the other hand, if these special circumstances were wholly unknown to the party breaking the contract, he, at the most, could only be supposed to have had in his contemplation the amount of injury which would arise generally, and in the great multitude of cases not affected by any special circumstances, from such a breach of contract. For, had the special circumstances been known, the parties might have specially provided for the breach of contract by special terms as to the damages in that case; and of this advantage it would be very unjust to deprive them. Now the above principles are those by which we think the jury ought to be guided in estimating the damages arising out of any breach of contract. ...

But it is obvious that, in the great multitude of cases of millers sending off broken shafts to third persons by a carrier under ordinary circumstances, [lost profits] would not, in all probability, have occurred; and these special circumstances were here never communicated by the plaintiffs to the defendants. It follows, therefore, that the loss of profits here cannot reasonably be considered such a consequence of the breach of contract as could have been fairly and reasonably contemplated by both the parties when they made this contract. For such loss would neither have flowed naturally from the breach of this contract in the great multitude of such cases occurring under ordinary circumstances, nor were the special circumstances, which, perhaps, would have made it a reasonable and natural consequence of such breach of contract, communicated to or known by the defendants.

The Judge ought, therefore, to have told the jury, that, upon the facts then before them, they ought not to take the loss of profits into consideration at all in estimating the damages. There must therefore be a new trial in this case.

Baron Alderson set out a two limb test. Losses will not be too remote if they fall under *either* of the two limbs.

The first limb: Losses will be recoverable if they 'arise naturally, i.e., according to the usual course of things, from such breach of contract itself.' This limb relates to imputed knowledge. In other words, losses will be recoverable if they are the type of normal loss which one would expect to result from the breach.

The second limb: Losses will be recoverable if they may 'reasonably be supposed to have been in the contemplation of both parties, at the time they made the contract, as the probable result of the breach of it.' This limb relates to actual knowledge at the time of contracting of special circumstances giving rise to unusual types of loss. In other words, if the type of loss is unusual, the loss will nonetheless be recoverable if the parties had actual knowledge of the special circumstances giving rise to it.

The loss of profit in *Hadley* was too remote as it did not fall under limb one or limb two. It did not fall under the first limb because it was unusual for a mill not to have a spare mill shaft. Consequently, the loss of profit was not a normal loss. It did not fall under the second limb as Hadley did not tell Baxendale that they only had one shaft and would consequently suffer a loss of profit if there was a delay in delivery.

Victoria Laundry (Windsor) v Newman Industries [1949] 2 KB 528 is a good example of the two limbs in action.

Victoria Laundry (Windsor) v Newman Industries [1949] 2 KB 528

Panel: Tucker, Asquith and Singleton LJJ

Facts: Victoria Laundry operated a business washing and dyeing clothes. To expand their business, they bought a new boiler with a larger capacity from Newman Industries. Newman knew that the boiler was to be used immediately in Victoria Laundry's business. What Newman did not know was that Victoria Laundry was going to enter into particularly lucrative dyeing contracts with the government. In breach of contract, Newman delivered the boiler about twenty weeks late. Victoria Laundry claimed for their ordinary loss of profits as a result of not having a larger boiler and also the lost profit from the particularly lucrative deals with the government. The judge at first instance refused to award any damages for loss of profit. Victoria Laundry appealed to the Court of Appeal.

LORD JUSTICE ASQUITH

[Delivering the judgment of the court]

What propositions applicable to the present case emerge from the authorities as a whole, including those analysed above? We think they include the following:-

1. It is well settled that the governing purpose of damages is to put the party whose rights have been violated in the same position, so far as money can do so, as if his rights had been observed: (*Sally Wertheim v. Chicoutimi Pulp Company* [1911] A.C. 301.). This purpose, if relentlessly pursued, would provide him with a complete indemnity for all loss de facto resulting from a particular breach, however improbable, however unpredictable. This, in contract at least, is recognized as too harsh a rule. Hence,

2. In cases of breach of contract the aggrieved party is only entitled to recover such part of the loss actually resulting as was at the time of the contract reasonably forseeable as liable to result from the breach.

3. What was at that time reasonably so foreseeable depends on the knowledge then possessed by the parties or, at all events, by the party who later commits the breach.

Alert

4. For this purpose, knowledge 'possessed' is of two kinds; one imputed, the other actual. Everyone, as a reasonable person, is taken to know the 'ordinary course of things' and consequently what loss is liable to result from a breach of contract in that ordinary course. This is the subject matter of the 'first rule' in Hadley v. Baxendale 9 Exch. 341. But to this knowledge, which a contract-breaker is assumed to possess whether he actually possesses it or not, there may have to be added in a particular case knowledge which he actually possesses, of special circumstances outside the 'ordinary course of things,' of such a kind that a breach in those special circumstances would be liable to cause more loss. Such a case attracts the operation of the 'second rule' so as to make additional loss also recoverable.

5. In order to make the contract-breaker liable under either rule it is not necessary that he should actually have asked himself what loss is liable to result from a breach. As has often been pointed out, parties at the time of contracting contemplate not the breach of the contract, but its performance. It suffices that, if he had considered the question, he would as a reasonable man have concluded that the loss in question was liable to result (see certain observations of Lord du Parcq in the recent case of *A/B Karlshamns Oljefabriker v. Monarch Steamship Company Limited* [1949] A.C. 196.)

6. Nor, finally, to make a particular loss recoverable, need it be proved that upon a given state of knowledge the defendant could, as a reasonable man, foresee that a breach must necessarily result in that loss. It is enough if he could foresee it was likely so to result. It is indeed enough, to borrow from the language of Lord du Parcq in the same case, at page 158, if the loss (or some factor without which it would not have occurred) is a 'serious possibility' or a 'real danger.' For short, we have used the word 'liable' to result. Possibly the colloquialism 'on the cards' indicates the shade of meaning with some approach to accuracy.

...

[Lord Justice Asquith commented, as follows, on the judgment delivered at first instance]. First, that the learned judge appears to infer that because certain 'special circumstances' were, in his view, not 'drawn to the notice of' the defendants and therefore, in his view, the operation of the 'second rule' was excluded, ergo nothing in respect of loss of business can be recovered under the 'first rule.' This inference is, in our view, no more justified in the present case than it was in the case of *Cory v. Thames Ironworks Company* L.R. 3 Q.B. 181. Secondly, that while it is not wholly clear what were the 'special circumstances' on the non-communication of which the learned judge relied, it would seem that they were, or included, the following:- (a) the 'circumstance' that delay in delivering the boiler was going to lead 'necessarily' to loss of profits. But the true criterion is surely not what was bound 'necessarily' to result, but what was likely or liable to do so, and we think that it was amply conveyed to the defendants by what was communicated to them (plus what was patent without express communication) that delay in delivery was likely to lead to 'loss of business'; (b) the 'circumstance' that the plaintiffs needed the boiler 'to extend their business.' It was surely not necessary for the defendants to be specifically informed of this, as a precondition of being liable for loss of business. Reasonable, persons in the shoes of the defendants must be taken to foresee without any express intimation, that a laundry which, at a time when there was a famine of laundry facilities, was paying 2,000l. odd for plant and intended at such a time to put such plant 'into use' immediately, would be likely to suffer in pocket from five months' delay in delivery of the plant in question, whether they intended by means of it to extend their business, or merely to maintain it, or to reduce a loss; (c) the 'circumstance' that the plaintiffs had the assured expectation of special contracts, which they could only fulfil by securing punctual delivery of the boiler. Here, no doubt, the learned judge had in mind the particularly lucrative dyeing contracts to which the plaintiffs looked forward and which they mention in para. 10 of the statement of claim. We agree that in order that the plaintiffs should recover specifically and as such the profits expected on these contracts, the defendants would have had to know, at the time of their agreement with the plaintiffs, of the prospect and terms of such contracts. We also agree that they did not in fact know these things. It does not, however, follow that the plaintiffs are precluded from recovering some general (and perhaps conjectural) sum for loss of business in respect of dyeing contracts to be reasonably expected, any more than in respect of laundering contracts to be reasonably expected.

The court seems to have been of the view that the loss of ordinary profit which resulted from late delivery of the boiler, was not too remote as it fell under the first limb.

However, the losses flowing from the particularly lucrative dyeing contracts were too remote. These losses did not fall under the first limb as they were unusual – no knowledge of such lucrative deals could be imputed to Newman. The losses did not fall under the second limb as Victoria Laundry had not informed Newman about these particularly lucrative deals at the time of contracting - Newman had no actual knowledge of this particularly lucrative deal.

The outcome in *Victoria Laundry v Newman* was orthodox, however, some of Asquith LJ's language has been criticised. In particular, he states that the test for remoteness is whether the loss was '*reasonably foreseeable* as liable to result from the breach'. This is the same language as for the test for remoteness in tort. For some time, there was speculation that the test for remotenesss in contract and tort were the same. This idea was laid to rest by the case of *Koufos v C. Czarnikow Ltd. (The Heron II)* [1969] 1 AC 350.

Koufos v C. Czarnikow Ltd. (The Heron II) **[1969] 1 AC 350**

Panel: Lord Reid, Lord Morris of Borth-y-Gest, Lord Hodson, Lord Pearce and Lord Upjohn

Facts: Koufos owned a vessel, The Heron II. Czarnikow ('the charterers') voyage chartered The Heron II to carry sugar from Constanza to Basrah. The charterers planned to sell the sugar in Basrah. Koufos did not know this but he knew that there was a market for sugar in Basrah. In breach of contract, the vessel took an indirect route, and so arrived nine days late. The market price for sugar dropped during those nine days and, consequently, the sugar was worth less than it would have been had it been delivered on time.

LORD REID

[The shipowners] did not know what the charterers intended to do with the sugar. But he knew there was a market in sugar at Basrah, and it appears to me that, if he had thought about the matter, he must have realised that at least it was not unlikely that the sugar would be sold in the market at market price on arrival, and he must be held to have known that in any ordinary market prices are apt to fluctuate from day to day: but he had no reason to suppose it more probable that during the relevant period such fluctuation would be downwards rather than upwards - it was an even chance that the fluctuation would be downwards.

So the question for decision is whether a plaintiff can recover as damages for breach of contract a loss of a kind which the defendant, when he made the contract, ought to have realised was not unlikely to result from a breach of contract causing delay in delivery. I use the words 'not unlikely' as denoting a degree of probability considerably less than an even chance but nevertheless not very unusual and easily foreseeable. ...

In cases like Hadley v. Baxendale or the present case it is not enough that in fact the plaintiff's loss was directly caused by the defendant's breach of contract. It clearly was so caused in both. The crucial question is whether, on the information available to the defendant when the contract was made, he should, or the reasonable man in his position would, have realised that such loss was sufficiently likely to result from the breach of contract to make it proper to hold that the loss flowed naturally from the breach or that loss of that kind should have been within his contemplation.

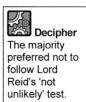

Decipher The majority preferred not to follow Lord Reid's 'not unlikely' test.

The modern rule of tort is quite different and it imposes a much wider liability. The defendant will be liable for any type of damage which is reasonably foreseeable as liable to happen even in the most unusual case, unless the risk is so small that a reasonable man would in the whole circumstances feel justified in neglecting it, and there is good reason for the difference. In contract, if one party wishes to protect himself against a risk which to the other party would appear unusual, he can direct the other party's attention to it before the contract is made, and I need not stop to consider in what circumstances the other party will then be held to have accepted responsibility

Alert

in that event. But in tort there is no opportunity for the injured party to protect himself in that way, and the tortfeasor cannot reasonably complain if he has to pay for some very unusual but nevertheless foreseeable damage which results from his wrongdoing. I have no doubt that today a tortfeasor would be held liable for a type of damage as unlikely as was the stoppage of Hadley's Mill for lack of a crankshaft: to anyone with the knowledge the carrier had that may have seemed unlikely but the chance of it happening would have been seen to be far from negligible. But it does not at all follow that *Hadley v. Baxendale* would today be differently decided.

[Lord Reid then considered the *Victoria Laundry* case and disapproved of it in so far as what Asquith LJ had said went beyond previous authorities.]

To bring in reasonable foreseeability appears to me to be confusing measure of damages in contract with measure of damages in tort. A great many extremely unlikely results are reasonably foreseeable: it is true that Lord Asquith (sic) may have meant foreseeable as a likely result, and if that is all he meant I would not object further than to say that I think that the phrase is liable to be misunderstood. For the same reason I would take exception to the phrase 'liable to result' in paragraph (5). Liable is a very vague word but I think that one would usually say that when a person foresees a very improbable result he foresees that it is liable to happen. ...

Alert

I agree with the first half of paragraph (6). For the best part of a century it has not been required that the defendant could have foreseen that a breach of contract must necessarily result in the loss which has occurred. But I cannot agree with the second half of that paragraph. It has never been held to be sufficient in contract that the loss was foreseeable as 'a serious possibility' or 'a real danger' or as being 'on the cards.' It is on the cards that one can win £100,000 or more for a stake of a few pence - several people have done that. And anyone who backs a hundred to one chance regards a win as a serious possibility - many people have won on such a chance. And the *Wagon Mound (No. 2)* could not have been decided as it was unless the extremely unlikely fire should have been foreseen by the ship's officer as a real danger. It appears to me that in the ordinary use of language there is wide gulf between saying that some event is not unlikely or quite likely to happen and saying merely that it is a serious possibility, a real danger, or on the cards. Suppose one takes a well-shuffled pack of cards, it is quite likely or not unlikely that the top card will prove to be a diamond: the odds are only 3 to 1 against. But most people would not say that it is quite likely to be the nine of diamonds for the odds are then 51 to 1 against. On the other hand I think that most people would say that there is a serious possibility or a real danger of its being turned up first and of course it is on the cards.

If the tests of 'real danger' or 'serious possibility' are in future to be authoritative then the *Victoria Laundry* case would indeed be a landmark because it would mean that *Hadley v Baxendale* would be differently decided today. I certainly could not understand any court deciding that, on the information available to the carrier in that case, the stoppage of the mill was neither a serious possibility nor a real danger. If those tests are to prevail in future then let us cease to pay lip service to the rule in *Hadley v Baxendale*. But in my judgment to adopt these tests would extend liability for breach of contract beyond what is reasonable or desirable. From the limited knowledge which I have of commercial affairs I would not expect such an extension to be welcomed by the business community and from the legal point of view I can find little or nothing to recommend it.

LORD HODSON

A close study of the rule was made by the Court of Appeal in the case of the *Victoria Laundry (Windsor) Ltd. v. Newman Industries Ltd*. The judgment of the court, consisting of Tucker, Asquith and Singleton L.JJ., was delivered by Asquith L.J., who referred to the *Monarch Steamship* case and suggested the phrase 'liable to result' as appropriate to describe the degree of probability required. This may be a colourless expression but I do not find it possible to improve on it. If the word 'likelihood' is used it may convey the impression that the chances are all in favour of the thing happening, an idea which I would reject.

LORD PEARCE

Accordingly in my opinion the expressions used in the *Victoria Laundry* case were right. I do not however accept the colloquialism 'on the cards' as being a useful test because I am not sure just what nuance it has either in my own personal vocabulary or in that of others. I suspect that it owes its attraction, like many other colloquialisms, to the fact that one may utter it without having the trouble of really thinking out with precision what one means oneself or what others will understand by it, a spurious attraction which in general makes colloquialism unsuitable for definition, though it is often useful as shorthand for a collection of definable ideas. It was in this latter convenient sense that the judgment uses the ambiguous words 'liable to result.' They were not intended as a further or different test from 'serious possibility' or 'real danger.'

LORD UPJOHN

Asquith L.J. in *Victoria Laundry* used the words 'likely to result' and he treated that as synonymous with a serious possibility or a real danger. He went on to equate that with the expression 'on the cards' but like all your Lordships I deprecate the use of that phrase which is far too imprecise and to my mind is capable of denoting a most improbable and unlikely event, such as winning a prize on a premium bond on any given drawing. ...

It is clear that on the one hand the test of foreseeability as laid down in the case of tort is not the test for breach of contract; nor on the other hand must the loser establish that the loss was a near certainty or an odds-on probability. I am content to adopt as the test a 'real danger' or a 'serious possibility.' There may be a shade of difference between these two phrases but the assessment of damages is not an exact science and what to one judge or jury will appear a real danger may appear to another judge or jury to be a serious possibility. I do not think that the application of that test would have led to a different result in *Hadley v. Baxendale*. I cannot see why [the contract breaker] in the absence of express mention should have contemplated as a real danger or serious possibility that work at the factory would be brought to a halt while the shaft was away.

In *The Heron II*, the majority approved the expressions 'real danger' and 'serious possibility' of the loss (Lord Morris of Borth-y-Gest, Lord Pearce and Lord Upjohn). Lord Hodson preferred the expression 'liable to result'.

On the other hand, Lord Reid disapproved of the expressions 'a serious possibility', 'a real danger' and 'on the cards', preferring the 'not unlikely' and 'sufficiently likely to result' tests, set out above.

To an extent, these differences must be a matter of linguistic taste, and the underlying principle is reasonably clear. Chitty on Contract Law, the main text used by practitioners summarises (at 26-054):

'The principles laid down in *Hadley v Baxendale*, ... have been interpreted and restated by the Court of Appeal in 1949 in *Victoria Laundry (Windsor) Ltd v Newman Industries Ltd* and by the House of Lords in 1967, in *Koufos v C. Czarnikow Ltd (The Heron II)*. The combined effect of these cases may be summarised as follows: A type or kind of loss is not too remote a consequence of a breach of contract if, at the time of contracting (and on the assumption that the parties actually foresaw the breach in question), it was within their reasonable contemplation as a not unlikely result of that breach.'

The test for remoteness must be read in light of the recent House of Lords decision of *Transfield Shipping Inc v Mercator Shipping Inc (The Achilleas)* [2009] 1 AC 61. Unfortunately, the ratio of this case is not clear. Chitty on Contracts interprets the case as follows (26-051):

'However, following the very recent decision of the House of Lords in *Transfield Shipping Inc v Mercator Shipping Inc (The Achilleas)* it now seems that a defendant is not necessarily liable for losses, whether they were usual or unusual, merely because he knew or should have known that they were not unlikely to occur. There is an additional limitation, namely that a defendant will not be liable if he cannot reasonably be regarded as assuming responsibility for losses of the particular kind suffered. Thus the test of liability is no longer applied in a standardised fashion, depending on the principally factual questions of the likelihood or knowledge of the loss. There now appear to be two tests, the remoteness test and, in addition, whether in the particular circumstances it can be said that the defendant was implicitly undertaking responsibility.'

19.3 Mitigation

It is said that the innocent party has a duty to take reasonable steps to limit his losses. This is known as mitigation. This means that, if the innocent party does not mitigate, he will be unable to claim for any losses which occur as a result of his failure to mitigate.

British Westinghouse Electric and Manufacturing Company v Underground Electric Railways Company of London [1912] AC 673

Panel: Viscount Haldane LC, Lord Ashbourne, Lord MacNaghten and Lord Atkinson

Facts: Underground Electric Railways Company of London bought steam turbines from British Westinghouse Electric to power the Metropolitan line in London. The turbines were defective, as a result of which they were inefficient and used more fuel than they would have done if they had been within the contract specification. Underground Electric eventually decided to replace the turbines, and bought 'Parsons' machines which were much more efficient than the original machines would have been even if they had satisfied the contract specifications.

VISCOUNT HALDANE LC

The arbitrator appears to me to have found clearly that the effect of the superiority of the Parsons machines and of their efficiency in reducing working expenses was in point of fact such that all loss was extinguished, and that actually the respondents made a profit by the course they took. They were doubtless not bound to purchase machines of a greater kilowatt power than those originally contracted for, but they in fact took the wise course in the circumstances of doing so, with pecuniary advantage to themselves. They had, moreover, used the appellants' machines for several years, and had recovered compensation for the loss incurred by reason of these machines not being during these years up to the standard required by the contract. After that period the arbitrator found that it was reasonable and prudent to take the course they actually did in purchasing the more powerful machines, and that all the remaining loss and damages was thereby wiped out. ...

Subject to these observations I think that there are certain broad principles which are quite well settled. The first is that, as far as possible, he who has proved a breach of a bargain to supply what he contracted to get is to be placed, as far as money can do it, in as good a situation as if the contract had been performed.

The fundamental basis is thus compensation for pecuniary loss naturally flowing from the breach; but this first principle is qualified by a second, which imposes on a plaintiff the duty of taking all reasonable steps to mitigate the loss consequent on the breach, and debars him from claiming any part of the damage which is due to his neglect to take such steps.

 Alert

In the words of James L.J. in *Dunkirk Colliery Co. v. Lever*, 'The person who has broken the contract is not to be exposed to additional cost by reason of the plaintiffs not doing what they ought to have done as reasonable men, and the plaintiffs not being under any obligation to do anything otherwise than in the ordinary course of business.'

As James L.J. indicates, this second principle does not impose on the plaintiff an obligation to take any step which a reasonable and prudent man would not ordinarily take in the course of his business. But when in the course of his business he has taken action arising out of the transaction, which action has diminished his loss, the effect in actual diminution of the loss he has suffered may be taken into account even though there was no duty on him to act.

... provided the course taken to protect himself by the plaintiff in such an action was one which a reasonable and prudent person might in the ordinary conduct of business properly have taken, and in fact did take whether bound to or not, a jury or an arbitrator may property look at the whole of the facts and ascertain the result in estimating the quantum of damage.

I think the principle which applies here is that which makes it right for the jury or arbitrator to look at what actually happened, and to balance loss and gain. The transaction was not res inter alios acta, but one in which the person whose contract was broken took a reasonable and prudent course quite naturally arising out of the circumstances in which he was placed by the breach. Apart from the breach of contract, the lapse of time had rendered the appellants' machines obsolete, and men of business would be doing the only thing they could properly do in replacing them with new and up-to-date machines.

There are two important points to note from the *British Westinghouse* case. First, an aggrieved party can only claim for the loss he would have suffered had he taken all reasonable steps to mitigate his loss.

Second, if the innocent party has successfully reduced his losses by taking steps to mitigate, this will normally be taken into account when damages are assessed. For instance, if losses are reduced to nil as a result of mitigation, the innocent party will not receive any damages. This is because he has not suffered any loss.

Payzu v Saunders [1918] 2 KB 581

Panel: Banks, Scrutton LJJ and Eve J

Facts: Saunders was a fabric merchant, who contracted to sell 200 pieces of crêpe de chine to Payzu. The first delivery was made in November 1917, and Payzu sent payment by cheque, which was not received. In January 1918, Saunders telephoned Payzu to chase payment, but due to delays obtaining signatures the cheque was not received until 16 January 1918. On that day, Payzu requested a further delivery under the contract, but Saunders, worried about payment, demanded cash. Payzu refused, and when Saunders, in breach of contract, continued to refuse to deliver further goods until paid cash, Payzu brought a claim for breach of contract. Payzu claimed the difference between the market price for the goods (which had risen) and the contract price. The question for the court was whether it was reasonable to expect Payzu to mitigate by entering into a new contract with Saunders on a cash payment basis. Mr Justice McCardie found that, by failing to contract with Saunders on these new terms, Payzu had failed to mitigate.

LORD JUSTICE BANKS

It is plain that the question what is reasonable for a person to do in mitigation of his damages cannot be a question of law but must be one of fact in the circumstances of each particular case. There may be cases where as matter of fact it would be unreasonable to expect a plaintiff to consider any offer made [by the defendant] in view of the treatment he has received from the defendant. If he had been rendering personal services and had been dismissed after being accused in presence of others of being a thief, and if after that his employer had offered to take him back into his service, most persons would think he was justified in refusing the offer, and that it would be unreasonable to ask him in this way to mitigate the damages in an action of wrongful dismissal. But that is not to state a principle of law, but a conclusion of fact to be arrived at on a consideration of all the circumstances of the case. [Counsel for Payzu] complained that [Saunders] had treated his clients so badly that it would be unreasonable to expect them to listen to any proposition she might make. I do not agree. In my view each party was ready to accuse the other of conduct unworthy of a high commercial reputation, and there was nothing to justify the appellants in refusing to consider the respondent's offer. I think the learned judge came to a proper conclusion on the facts, and that the appeal must be dismissed.

These judgments establish that the duty to mitigate extends to accepting offers to renegotiate from the contract breaker. In a rising market, this means that the aggrieved party must accept a demand to pay more for the goods (provided it is still a better offer than the aggrieved party can get elsewhere) although he will be able to claim the difference as damages for breach of contract.

This may place the aggrieved party in a difficult position, because he either pays more and takes the risk that he is unable to recover the difference, or refuses to pay more but accepts that his claim in damages will be limited by his failure to mitigate.

Banco de Portugal v Waterlow and Sons, Limited [1932] AC 452

Panel: Viscount Sankey LC, Lord Warrington of Clyffe, Lord Atkin, Lord Russell of Killowen and Lord Macmillan

Facts: Waterlow were employed by the Portuguese national bank to print Vasco da Gama 500 escudo notes. After delivering 600,000 notes, which were put into circulation in Portugal, Waterlow were conned into delivering a further 580,000 notes ('the forged notes') to a gangster named Marang van Ysselvere. After Marang had put the notes into circulation, Banco de Portugal discovered the fraud. On 7 December, they decided to withdraw all 500 escudo notes (ie both the real notes and the fraudulent ones), and pay their holders their value using other notes. Waterlow argued that this action was unreasonable and that they should only be liable for the cost of printing new notes, not the cost of paying the note holders.

VISCOUNT SANKEY LC

In England the law is that a person is not obliged to minimize damages on behalf of another who has broken a contract if by doing so he would have injured his commercial reputation by getting a bad name in the trade: James Finlay & Co. v. N. V. Kwik Hoo Tong Handel Maatschappij 1929 1 K.B. 400. The evidence is that the Bank - remembering always that they were the issuing Bank of the paper currency - had to protect before anything else the confidence which such currency inspired in the Portuguese public. 'What confidence,' they asked, 'would all the other notes of the Bank of Portugal merit if the Bank did not adopt such a policy?' 'It is one,' they say, 'always adopted and similar to that adopted as a rule by banks of issue, even when they can allege the forgery is manifest and that the public has not taken the precautions necessary in receiving false notes.' I have come to the conclusion that the Bank would have been failing in their duty to their shareholders, their customers and their country if they had not taken the step they did.

Alert

In my opinion these findings are correct, and the Bank had no alternative on December 7 but to do what they in fact did. They were in a position of extreme difficulty and extreme danger, caused, as I think, by the unfortunate and unwitting breach of contract on the part of Messrs. Waterlow.

LORD MACMILLAN

I confess I am not disposed to regard with much sympathy the criticism which Messrs. Waterlow have directed at the Bank's action. Where the sufferer from a breach of contract finds himself in consequence of that breach placed in a position of embarrassment the measures which he may be driven to adopt in order to extricate himself ought not to be weighed in nice scales at the instance of the party whose breach of contract has occasioned the difficulty. It is often easy after an emergency has passed to criticize the steps which have been taken to meet it, but such criticism does not come well from those who have themselves created the emergency. The law is satisfied if the party placed in a difficult situation by reason of the breach of a duty owed to him has acted reasonably in the adoption of remedial measures, and he will not be held disentitled to recover the cost of such measures merely because the party in breach can suggest that other measures less burdensome to him might have been taken. On this part of the case I find myself in agreement with the reasoning of Scrutton L.J. In my opinion the action of the Bank in honouring all notes of the type in question, genuine and spurious alike, between December 7 and December 26, 1925, was reasonable and justifiable in the

Alert

circumstances, and Messrs. Waterlow ought to be held responsible for whatever loss was occasioned to the Bank by the adoption of that policy.

Viscount Sankey LC's speech indicates an important limit inherent to the duty to mitigate. The aggrieved party must take 'all reasonable steps' to mitigate its loss, but this does not extend to steps that would injure the aggrieved party's commercial reputation. Further, as Lord Macmillan makes clear, the aggrieved party is entitled to some latitude in determining the appropriate course of action, and will not be criticised on the basis that, with hindsight, a different approach might have been preferable.

19.4　Contributory Negligence

Normally, if the claimant is negligent, it is not possible for the contract breaker to rely on the claimant's contributory negligence to reduce the damages payable.

The only exception to this rule is where the contract breaker has breached a concurrent obligation in both contract and tort. Where the contract breaker is under concurrent duties in contract and tort and the claimant was negligent, damages will be apportioned under the Law Reform (Contributory Negligence) Act 1945 s 1 according to the fault of the contract breaker and the aggrieved party.

Forsikringsaktieselskapet Vesta v Butcher and Aquacultural Insurance Services Ltd. Bain Dawes Ltd [1989] AC 852

Panel: O'Connor and Neill LJJ and Sir Roger Ormrod

Statute: Law Reform (Contributory Negligence) Act 1945 s 1

Facts: The facts of this case are complex, involving contracts of insurance and re-insurance, and the case was appealed to the House of Lords on several points, one of which related to the Law Reform (Contributory Negligence) Act 1945.

LORD JUSTICE O'CONNOR

The important issue of law is whether on the facts of this case there is power to apportion under the Law Reform (Contributory Negligence) Act 1945 and thus reduce the damages recoverable by Vesta.

I start by pointing out that Vesta pleaded its claim against the brokers in contract and tort. This is but a recognition of what I regard as a clearly established principle that where under the general law a person owes a duty to another to exercise reasonable care and skill in some activity, a breach of that duty gives rise to a claim in tort notwithstanding the fact that the activity is the subject matter of a contract between them. In such a case the breach of duty will also be a breach of contract. The classic example of this situation is the relationship between doctor and patient. Since the decision of the House of Lords in *Hedley Byrne & Co. Ltd. v. Heller & Partners Ltd.* [1964] A.C. 465 the relationship between the brokers and Vesta is another example. ...

[Lord Justice O'Connor quoted Hobhouse J, the judge at first instance, who said]

'The question whether the 1945 Act applies to claims brought in contract can arise in a number of classes of case. Three categories can conveniently be identified. (1) Where the defendant's liability arises from some contractual provision which does not depend on negligence on the part of the defendant. (2) Where the defendant's liability arises from a contractual obligation which is expressed in terms of taking care (or its equivalent) but does not correspond to a common law duty to take care which would exist in the given case independently of contract. (3) Where the defendant's liability in contract is the same as his liability in the tort of negligence independently of the existence of any contract.'

The present case fell fairly and squarely within the judge's category (3). He said...

'The category (3) question has arisen in very many different types of case and the answer is treated as so obvious that it passes without any comment. It is commonplace that actions are brought by persons who have suffered personal injuries as the result of the negligence of the person sued and that there is a contractual as well as tortious relationship. In such cases apportionment of blame is invariably adopted by the court notwithstanding that the plaintiff could sue in contract as well as in tort.

I will return to [the authorities] but first I will consider the true construction of the Act of 1945. Section 1(1) reads:

'Where any person suffers damage as the result partly of his own fault and partly of the fault of any other person or persons, a claim in respect of that damage shall not be defeated by reason of the fault of the person suffering the damage, but the damages recoverable in respect thereof shall be reduced to such extent as the court thinks just and equitable having regard to the claimant's share in the responsibility for the damage: Provided that - (a) this subsection shall not operate to defeat any defence arising under a contract; (b) where any contract or enactment providing for the limitation of liability is applicable to the claim, the amount of damages recoverable by the claimant by virtue of this subsection shall not exceed the maximum limit so applicable.'

By section 4, 'fault' is defined:

''fault' means negligence, breach of statutory duty or other act or omission which gives rise to a liability in tort or would, apart from this Act, give rise to the defence of contributory negligence.'

The opening words of section 1(1) are very wide: 'Where any person suffers damage as the result partly of his own fault and partly of the fault of any other person or persons ...' When considering the 'fault of any other person or persons' it is the first part of the definition in section 4 that applies: 'negligence, breach of statutory duty or other act or omission which gives rise to a liability in tort.' In my judgment the phrase 'which gives rise to a liability in tort' defines the kind or type of negligence etc. which is to rank as 'fault' when considering 'the fault of any other person or persons.'

When considering the fault of the person who suffers damage both parts of the definition apply. The second part is necessary because, whereas the defendant cannot be at fault unless in breach of duty owed to the plaintiff, the plaintiff's contributory negligence may or may not involve a breach of duty owed to the defendant. Thus the drivers of two motor cars which collide at crossroads because both failed to keep a good look out are both within the first part of the definition, regardless of which is plaintiff and which defendant. In contrast, the injured front seat passenger not wearing a seat belt is at fault only within the second part of the definition (at all events vis-à-vis the driver of the car in which he was not a passenger; I say that lest it be suggested that he owed a duty to his own driver not to damage the windscreen).

I appreciate that, when considering the fault of the plaintiff, if the fault is within the first part of the definition it will also be within the second part.

Once damage caused partly by categories of the faults defined in section 4 is proved then a claim in respect of that damage:

'shall not be defeated by reason of the fault of the person suffering the damage, but the damages recoverable in respect thereof shall be reduced to such extent as the court thinks just and equitable having regard to the claimant's share in the responsibility for the damage.'

I think it is important to remember that the Act of 1945 not only abolished the rule that contributory negligence defeated the whole claim but also made a very wide extension of the power to apportion liability so as to permit recovery of a proportion of the damage sustained. Before the Act the only power to apportion was in respect of property damage at sea: see section 1 of the Maritime Conventions Act 1911. In cases of shared responsibility for damage it is as unjust that the person suffering the damage should recover 100 per cent. as it is that he should recover nothing.

[Applying this to the facts, there was power to apportion liability; fault had been assessed by Hobhouse J at 75 per cent. to Vesta and 25 per cent. to Aquacultural Insurance.]

The simple way of thinking of the Law Reform (Contributory Negligence) Act 1945 is that it gave the court the power to apportion damages only in circumstances where the defendant is liable in tort to the claimant *and* the claimant is at fault, although the claimant's fault does not have to be tortious. So in O'Connor LJ's example, in circumstances where the driver of a second car has a duty of care towards passengers in the first car, but passengers in the first car have no duty of care to the driver of the second car, damages will be apportioned to reflect the fault of a passenger who does not wear a seat belt. In the absence of words in the statute indicating otherwise, this power to apportion arises irrespective of whether the defendant is also liable in contract.

The Law Reform (Contributory Negligence) Act 1945 did not give the court any power to apportion damages in other circumstances however (i.e. the first two classes of cases indentified by Hobhouse J and quoted by O'Connor LJ). As such, the Act only applies where the contract breaker is under concurrent liability arising from 'negligence, breach of statutory duty, or other act or omission which gives rise to a liability in tort'. In circumstances where the Act does not apply, the default position remains that damages for breach of contract do not depend on the fault of the parties, but only their promises.

Further Reading

Kramer, 'The new test of remoteness in contract' (2009) 125 LQR 408

Law Commission No.114 (1990) 'Contributory Negligence as a Defence in Contract'

Peel, 'Remoteness Revisited' (2009) 125 LQR 6

McKendrick, E., *Contract Law* (2017) 12th ed. Ch.21 and 22